The Border

The Border

The Border

Policy and Politics in Europe and the United States

MARTIN A. SCHAIN

OXFORD
UNIVERSITY PRESS

OXFORD
UNIVERSITY PRESS

Oxford University Press is a department of the University of Oxford. It furthers
the University's objective of excellence in research, scholarship, and education
by publishing worldwide. Oxford is a registered trade mark of Oxford University
Press in the UK and certain other countries.

Published in the United States of America by Oxford University Press
198 Madison Avenue, New York, NY 10016, United States of America.

CIP data is on file at the Library of Congress
ISBN 978–0–19–993869–8 (pbk.)
ISBN 978–0–19–993867–4 (hbk.)

1 3 5 7 9 8 6 4 2

Paperback printed by Marquis, Canada
Hardback printed by Bridgeport National Bindery, Inc., United States of America

For Sophie Body-Gendrot, my friend and colleague, a Eurostar for whom borders have been bridges, and my grandchildren—Lilah, Aidan, and Oliver—who will have a lifetime of borders to cross.

CONTENTS

FIGURES AND TABLES

Figures

Tables

ACKNOWLEDGMENTS

I first encountered the importance of borders in Europe when I was a summer-school student in Leiden, the Netherlands, in 1961. I decided to spend a weekend in Berlin, which meant traveling by train from the Netherlands, through the Federal Republic of Germany, and then across the German Democratic Republic into Berlin. I discovered, only after I arrived, that the Soviets had decided to close the border between East and West Berlin, and then begin the construction of a wall to separate the two parts of the city that very weekend. Since then, borders have sometimes strangely meandered in and out of my scholarly and personal life, as if to emphasize that they are still there. A decade ago I was invited to speak on immigration at York University, Toronto. When I arrived at the airport with my wife, we were detained, without explanation, in an unmarked room, along with more than a hundred other people seeking entry. Only many hours later did I learn that the passport control officer was mistaken in thinking that I needed a work permit to give a university lecture. We then passed through the border, into Canada.

I have dedicated this book to Sophie Body-Gendrot, a scholar and a friend with whom I worked and collaborated for more than thirty years. We co-authored only one article together, but our scholarly and personal lives overlapped frequently on both sides of the Atlantic. I have also dedicated this book to my grandchildren—Lilah, Aidan and Oliver—who are already frequent flyers and Eurostars. The ease with which they have crossed borders during their young lives gives us hope that the alarming spread of walls, fences and barriers, documented in this study, may become a passing phenomenon.

This book was researched and written in New York, Washington, Paris, London and Brussels. I am grateful to the many friends and colleagues who welcomed us into their homes, particularly to Jen and Chloe in Washington, to Rebecca, Elisabeth and Michel in Paris, and to Ivor and Bette in London. I am also indebted to the Jean Monnet Center, and its director Joseph Weiler, at the

School of Law at New York University; and to the Centre d'Études de la Vie Politique Française (CEVIPOF), and its director, Pascal Perrineau at SciencesPo in Paris, for providing me with a rich intellectual environment, where I was able to work and engage with a remarkable group of colleagues.

I am also thankful to the many people who are responsible for border policy and border control that spent time with me, answered my many questions, and provided me with invaluable information and direction. In London, the Asylum Policy team, Immigration and Border Directorate, of the UK Home Office was particularly generous over several months; in France, representatives of the Secrétariat Général à l'immigration et à l'intégration at the French Ministry of the Interior met with me numerous times; and in Brussels, three members of DG Home Affairs in the European Commission agreed to extended interviews with follow-up communications. Charles Clarke, UK Home Secretary between 2004 and 2006, took time out of his busy schedule to spend a long afternoon with me, and Jean-Claude Piris, who served as the Legal Counsel of the Council of the EU, spent many hours at NYU discussing parts of this book. I am also grateful to the staff at the Tinsley House Immigration Removal Center at Gatwick Airport in the UK, who took time to show me the facility, and answer questions about its operation. The French border police (DCPAF) were unusually generous in meeting with me, and explaining the operations of the Zone d'Attente des Personnes (ZAP) at Charles de Gaulle Airport in Paris.

I am privileged to have had colleagues with whom I have been able share ideas and analyses over several years. Randall Hansen and Mabel Berezin read the entire manuscript, and their comments and criticism improved the final manuscript in important ways. James Hollifield, Simon Reich, Joseph Weiler, Ariane Chebel d'Appollonia, Daniel Kelemen, Giovanna Dell'Orto, Vicki L. Birchfield, Virginie Guiraudon, Marc Rosenblum, Catherine de Wenden and Paul Linden-Retek commented on papers and presentations that I gave at various stages of researching and writing this book. I am grateful for their comments as well. I am thankful to David McBride, my editor at Oxford, for his comments and encouragement over a long period of time. Writing a book is a process, and he has been very much a part of this process.

Finally, I am most grateful for the support of my family, above all my wife, Wendy. Wendy has been a part of this project in many important ways. She has been my most challenging critic, and has taken the time to be my best editor. She has made this a better book.

Of course, the usual disclaimers apply. Although friends and scholars I have acknowledged have improved this book, only I am responsible for what I have written.

1

The Problem of the Border

"Drawbridges Up"

Great walls built to repel the "other" have recently become part of the
global conversation, sparked by politics and popular culture.[1]

This book is about how and why border policy has become increasingly important, politicized, and divisive. It focuses on how border governance has emerged
as an important focus of policy in itself, rather than merely contingent on trade
and, above all, on immigration policy. I argue that for the United States and
Europe in the twenty-first century, there has been a growing movement toward
the reassertion of borders and border control.

Both for Europe and the United States the border that delineates the frontier
between national space (for Europe, the space of the European Union) and the
rest of the world appears to have become increasingly important as a focus of
politics during the past decade. In *The Wall Around the West*, Peter Andreas and
Timothy Snyder argued almost two decades ago that far from disappearing or
even growing softer,

> Borders in North America and Europe are being reasserted through
> ambitious and innovative state efforts to regulate the transnational
> movement of people. . . . As the military and economic functions of
> borders lose some of their significance, the traditional police function
> of borders has been reasserted in both Europe and North America.[2]

Today, the trends outlined in this book appear to have accelerated. In August
2016 *The Economist* reported on a new political fault line: "not between right
and left, but between open and closed." During an unusually event-filled political summer of 2016, voters in the United Kingdom chose to leave the European
Union (EU) and re-establish the hard border between Britain and the continent;
at the same time, across the channel, workers in eight countries in Eastern and

Central Europe were rapidly constructing walls and fixed fences to prevent the movement across their territory of asylum seekers from wars in the Near East.

The new president of the United States elected in 2016, Donald Trump, pledged as a candidate to build a wall between the United States and Mexico and impose stronger restrictions of entry against these same asylum seekers from Syria, and more generally against Muslims. "Americanism, not globalism, will be our credo," Trump thundered in his acceptance speech. Moreover, walls against trade, as well as migrants, were also on the political agendas of both major political parties in the United States, as well as the resurgent parties of the extreme right in Europe.[3] More generally, data gathered by a group of Canadian scholars indicated a massive increase of walls and barriers between countries after 2001. They counted twenty in 2001 and sixty-three in 2016.[4] Clearly, in our more globalized world, borders are back with a vengeance.

However, at the same time that more controls have been established, the flow of people and the growth of trade have continued at an impressive rate. The claims by scholars and political actors of an emerging "Fortress Europe," and "Fortress America" have clearly been exaggerated. They express goals and intentions, rather than outcomes.

I argue here that this gap cannot be understood simply as a failure of commitment or capabilities, but should be seen as a result of the complex politics of the border and border control. Although there has been consistent support for harder border control on both sides of the Atlantic, there has also been important, if more focused, support for more open borders and more permissive border control.[5] If public opinion provides context and may provide constraints for policy, political elites depend primarily on their ability to mobilize voters in elections and gain the support of different publics in the policymaking process. If electoral politics often favor border restriction, the politics of policymaking can be more advantageous for groups that favor access. These are separate political tracks, I maintain, but they are always in dynamic interaction.

Matthew Gibney and Randall Hansen have noted that there has been a growing tension between the demands of treaty-based rights of access and demands of democratic majorities. They summarize this tension in what they have called "the liberal democratic paradox."[6] The emergence of a transnational human rights regime since the Second World War, through treaties signed by all countries in Europe as well as the United States, has attributed rights (asylum, due process, appeal, and limits on deportation) to those who are able to reach and penetrate the border. This establishes a continuing tension at the border around the questions of entry and exit, especially deportation.[7]

Gibney and Hansen contend that the limits imposed on expulsion create greater democratic pressures for harsher exclusionary policies that would prevent potential immigrants from entering or even approaching the border in the first place. Thus, more liberal rules of entry for asylum seekers have been driving more exclusionary policies for immigrant entry. Because these rules apply to the border itself, I would argue, they have driven the transformation of questions of migration, identity, and sometimes trade into questions of border governance and control. Each element of this tension can be seen as a dynamic of politics, each generating and mobilizing a different set of political forces.

This tension has been accentuated by the contradiction between policies designed to expand international trade, interchange, and communication, on the one hand, and policies designed to limit and control the movement of people, on the other. If the first set of policies implies the easing of border controls, even to the point of free movement, the second implies the reinforcement of controls, even to the point of creating an impenetrable border.

These tensions help us to understand the contradictions in border policy, as well as changes. A great deal has been written about border policies in Europe and the United States, but very little about how and why policies change, both over time and across space.

After all, in the United States, even during the most severe period of immigration restriction, borders were a minor focus of attention, and the northern and southern borders remained relatively open and only lightly patrolled. In Europe, even after the dismantling of the internal borders when the Schengen Agreement was implemented after 1995, the external borders still remained the responsibility of the member states, with relatively little coordination at the EU level. The increasingly harsh policies of immigrant entry imposed by member states were not coordinated with stronger policies of border governance.

But the walls around the West are only one part of the story. Until relatively recently, and especially since the fall of the Iron Curtain, researchers and journalists focused attention on the progressive opening of previously closed frontiers, and the forces of globalization and commerce that seemed to support movement in this direction.[8] Previously closed frontiers between East and West, but also within the West, were now more open and penetrable. Even as barriers—legal, administrative, and physical—have been erected, vast numbers of people have continued to cross, emphasizing that borders are zones not just of restriction, but also of flows of population and trade.

At the same time, frontier policy—how, and with what means the border should be governed—was a problem that was "puzzled" more than "powered," in the words of Hugh Heclo.[9] The pressures of power were certainly not absent in the development of more restrictive border policy, but it is important to keep in mind that at least until recently, those pressures were toward more open policies that led to more open internal borders in Europe (Schengen), and relatively open borders between Canada and Mexico and the United States.

Moreover, more open border policies were relatively uncontested, and not sharply politicized until the 1990s. At least until the mid-1980s, the United States spent only modest amounts of money on border enforcement. Spending increased slowly after 1985, and then more rapidly in the 1990s.[10] In Europe, the dismantling of the internal borders was related primarily to trade, and the benefit to the free movement of people was considered a plus. However, by 2016, border control had become a major issue in American politics. In Europe it had become a core issue in numerous European countries, including those that had most benefited from free movement.

In a world in which analysts have argued that the dynamics of globalization make borders increasingly difficult to maintain, the question of open and closed borders has become more complicated. Border policy is generally neither fixed (closed/open borders) nor arbitrary, but variable and related to patterns of politics that can be understood and analyzed. Like other policy arenas, border policy is a process that is puzzled and learned when it is not strongly contested; when contested, it is the product of a process that begins with agenda formation that develops from interest and party conflict, and is then implemented by state action. First let us examine the question of the importance of borders.

1.1 A World Without Borders: Are Borders Still Important in the West?

From the perspective of 2018, it seems astonishing that there is vast literature that argues that borders may no longer be important, and that closed borders may be impossible to maintain. It would appear from the increase in resources that are being devoted to border control on both sides of the Atlantic that a reinforced border must be important. However, this is not clear from the scholarly debate.

Borders and the Decline of the State: The Liberal Problem

In 2009 Peter Andreas summarized one problem of border politics for both the United States and Europe. In support of expanded trade, state controls of the border have been rolled back. At the same time, however, more open borders for trade have made border control for migration more problematic.[11] As economic interdependence in North America and Europe has grown, there has been considerable pressure to ease border crossing, and scholars have focused on what had been an old idea in international relations (and in politics), that greater economic interdependence generates more harmonious cross border relations and more interstate cooperation around the border.

Former UK Home Secretary Charles Clarke, for example, explained the public policy problem for the United Kingdom and the EU in the following terms in 2013:

> The development of a Single European Market for goods and services, not only requires freedom of movement of capital and labour but requires common manufacturing standards for everything from cars to pharmaceuticals, common trade agreements with other counties, common consumer standards, common health and safety requirements, common environmental safeguards and approaches, common approaches to the regulation of business, including competition policy, common agricultural and fisheries policies and a whole range of other common approaches.[12]

Thus, the idea of the growing irrelevance of borders tends to reflect the growing importance of trade, but also the tendency of trade priorities to bleed into other areas. Richard Rosencrance developed the notion that "territory is passé"; that trade, rather than territory, would determine power in the twenty-first century; that control over territory remains a "fetish" of poor countries; and that "the virtual state—a state that has downsized its territorially based production capability—is the logical consequence of this emancipation from the land."[13] Kenichi Ohmae provocatively wrote of *The Borderless World* and *The End of the Nation-State* in a similar way, arguing that the importance of borders was being diminished by the dynamics of regional and global trade, although the argument in each book is far more nuanced than the title.[14] Ohmae's focus is on loss of control, and the declining ability of states to impose their frontiers.

But is there really a loss of control? Do states still have the capability to impose effective controls at the border, and have they exercised it? The penetrability of borders is a theme that goes well beyond those who focus on the powerful forces of international trade. Saskia Sassen directly challenged the continuing importance of state sovereignty in her book *Losing Control: Sovereignty in an Age of Globalization*. Borders, she argues, have largely given way to the regulation of goods and services through the transnationalization of economic space, and the regulation of the movement of people through human rights regimes. Nevertheless, she hedges her bets in the third of three chapters, "Immigration Tests the New Order," in which she explores the renationalizing of politics and the reassertion of sovereign control over borders.[15]

On both sides of the Atlantic, there has been growing pressure for a large and continuing expansion of border policing and a greater securitization of the border.[16] "In order to maintain a competitive advantage, governments must keep their economies and societies open to trade, investment, and migration. But unlike goods, capital, and services, the movement of people involves greater political risks."[17]

Scholars who have written on the impact of immigration, particularly James Hollifield, have tended to focus on the difficulty of strengthening border controls. They have cited two consequences of the new wave of immigration in the West since the 1960s. The first is the capabilities—even the will—of liberal Western democracies to limit and control the movement of migrants across their frontiers. The second, on a more positive note, is the new borderless world within the Schengen area, the external border of the EU. This is a world that transcends almost all of the old divisions of Europe, that in many ways looks and feels like an emerging United States of Europe, a world that was unthinkable until after 1989. In this world, the fluid movement of students, businessmen, and middle-class travelers (referred to as "Eurostars") across open borders testifies that "A European Union is being built. . . . A European society seems to be in the making."[18]

Control over frontiers—that essential aspect of sovereignty, it has been argued—is subject to legal and judicial controls. Thus, what has been referred to as "embedded liberalism" in the legal and political systems—values that protect individual and collective rights—makes it difficult to pass legislation that restricts access, and makes it even more difficult to enforce legislation that has actually been passed.[19] Indeed, this is at the root of the argument that legislated policies may be less important than they appear to be, while administration and court decisions may loom more important.

Attempts to define and establish controls over entry, over who has a right to cross national frontiers and settle in the space within those frontiers, has often evoked impassioned debate and conflicting politics. Such issues raise basic questions about the nation-state: control over the frontiers of the state and the identity of the nation. The core question is whether and how the capability of the state in liberal democracies to control entry has been eroded by a combination of international agreements and the increased role of courts in establishing individual and collective rights.

Nevertheless, I will argue in chapters 4 through 7 that states on both sides of the Atlantic have hardened both borders and border controls. What Hollifield has called embedded liberalism can be seen more simply as a political and legal resource, among others, that has determined the effectiveness of legislative control over the movement of people. In this sense, Christian Joppke argues that scholarly diagnoses of international constraints on the state's ability to control immigration highly overrate changes that have taken place, either because they are based on erroneous assumptions of strong enforcement of sovereignty that never was, or because the limits on frontier controls are more obviously those of domestic politics than limits imposed by international law or courts.

In a collection edited by Christian Joppke, Saskia Sassen expands on what she had concluded a few years earlier, and largely confirms Joppke's critique.[20] She revisits her argument in *Losing Control*, and argues that policymaking on immigrant entry has been made more complex by international agreements and judicial development of human rights and by ethnic lobbies, but that both in Europe and the United States there has been a reaction of "renationalizing" immigration policymaking. Moreover, if there is an ascendance of "agencies linked to furthering globalization and a decline of those linked to domestic equity questions," their impact on the immigration agenda and their effectiveness may be very limited, in part because the enforcement of immigrant rights supported by transnational human rights regimes is closely tied to support by agencies that deal with domestic equity questions.[21]

Then there is the question of whether anything substantial has changed, whether liberal-democratic regimes are less capable of maintaining a more restricted frontier than were less liberal-democratic regimes in the past. Gary Freeman claims that only by analyzing domestic politics—and the domestic forces of powerful economic interests, ethnic lobbies, and civil libertarians—can we understand the changing political constraints on policymakers, either for or against stronger entry controls. Why, for example, is the more or less consistent opposition of host populations to immigration frequently ignored by governments? For domestic political actors, the legal system and international accords are means and resources in the domestic political process.[22]

Finally, there is the question of whether the unification of Europe has diminished the ability of states within the EU to control their frontiers with regard to immigration. Within Europe the issue of sovereignty has become increasingly complex, especially with the incorporation of the Schengen Convention into the Amsterdam Agreement in 1999. Member states have made strides in cooperation on transferring sovereignty to the Union for the migration of EU nationals, but they have made lesser strides in the development of common policies with regard to non-EU immigrants (third-country nationals, or TCNs).[23] The Lisbon Treaty (2009) provides for the EU to "frame a common policy on asylum, immigration and external border control," which includes "conditions of entry and residence" (Articles 67(2) and 79(2)); at the same time, Article 79(5) stipulates that member states retain control over the volume of admissions.[24] Within these tight restrictions, the EU has begun to develop a framework that regulates conditions of entry, expulsion, and integration, and this framework has been supported and interpreted by the EU Court of Justice.[25]

Rey Koslowski maintains that such agreements on harmonization effectively cede sovereignty.[26] Citing this argument, the French Constitutional Council overturned some elements of the Schengen accords in 1993 and the government was forced to amend the constitution to make the accords consistent with national law. Of course, since the beginning of the refugee surge in 2010, there has been a revival of national control over internal frontiers in all major EU countries. In addition, the resistance of UK voters to even free movement within the EU led to a vote in 2016 in favor of UK withdrawal.

The key question for Europe, however, is whether it can control its external border. On balance, Schengen border control (the external border) has become embedded in a network of European and global institutions and rules that are as dynamic as they are constraining. They are not fixed in place, and can be used by domestic political actors to alter the domestic *rapports de force*. Thus, there is an abundance of new tools and institutions that are emerging, but these are not the same as capabilities.

Notions of state sovereignty have been linked to control over frontiers since the sixteenth century, but effective control of borders through military and administrative mechanisms barely goes back to the late nineteenth century.[27] Ever since state capabilities began to catch up with theories of sovereignty, the struggle to maintain the frontier has been a balance between what the state is capable of doing, and contradictory interests that support a more open or closed border.[28] Gibney and Hansen argue that the capacity to exercise border control (over immigration, but presumably over trade, as well as the establishment of citizenship rights) is "fundamental to liberal democracy," first, because the construction of liberal democracy is essentially linked to the sovereignty of the state, and second, because in some way, the policies of a democratic state must reflect "the aggregated preferences of its citizens."[29]

I find this argument more compelling for understanding the evolving politics of the border in both Europe and the United States than the previous arguments that focus on the limitations on the state imposed by trade and rights regimes. In chapters 4 through 7 I will examine various aspects of how these dynamics have played out. One question that this raises, however, is the relationship between democratic process and the pressure for strong borders. In general, it is true that "nowhere does a majority of the citizenry support open borders." It is also true, however, that the democratic process is more complicated than simple expressions of public opinion, and that support for who should enter, and for which purpose, varies considerably among different minorities capable of forming political coalitions. Moreover, it raises interesting questions about the role that public opinion plays in the democratic political process, from elections to lobbying to legislative voting.[30]

Fortress Europe and Protected America: Borders Are Exclusion

Some scholars have argued that Europe is rapidly moving toward a model of fortress Europe, toward a securitization of the external Schengen border, and the development of increasingly sophisticated border controls to keep out TCNs.[31] A growing literature emphasizes what Karolina Follis has called "the antidemocratic, ethically dubious and socially unjust elements of state and policing practices, often relating them to the historical trend of contemporary states to withdraw from responsibility for human welfare, broadly associated with the ideology of neo-liberalism."[32]

The trends in Western liberal democracies toward erecting walls and "rebordering" began long before the events of 9/11, and are only partially related to threats of terrorism. Certainly, this is true in Europe. The United States has been moving in the same direction along the border with Mexico. Peter Andreas notes that while the US–Mexican border is the most heavily traveled land crossing in the world, it is also one of the most heavily fortified.[33]

The reinforcement of the external European border is directly related to the implementation of the Schengen Agreement after 1990. The implementation has created pressure on Italy, Spain, and Greece to do what they would not otherwise do in terms of controlling immigration through their external frontiers. In this way, Schengen may be important in itself for the assertion of influence by some member states over others, a process that goes beyond the states that are within the Schengen area. There is now considerable evidence that although the United Kingdom is not within the Schengen zone, it has successfully forced Schengen countries—the French in particular—to strengthen their Channel border, and to prevent the crossing of asylum seekers and undocumented migrants.

The analyses of fortress Europe are dealing with very different populations than those of Eurostars cited above. Fortress Europe deals with TCNs and more so with undocumented immigrants and asylum seekers who attempt to cross the external frontiers of Europe and the United States without authorization. Zygmunt Bauman has stated that the new dividing line in the world is between those who are able to live globally and those who are increasingly anchored to their localities, "between freedom to move for some and the incapacity to enjoy it and the fate of being trapped in the local for the others."[34] Perhaps nowhere has this contrast been more evident than in the painful episode of the Red Cross-run Sangatte camp near Calais, opened in 1999 and closed by the French government first in 2002, and again in 2016. Just half a mile from the entrance to the Eurotunnel, the camp (which has endured) became the take-off point for asylum seekers and undocumented immigrants who attempted to cross into the United Kingdom by using the undercarriages of the Eurostar rail cars within which were travelers (the "Eurostars" mentioned earlier) whose travel-time between Paris and London had been cut by more than half.

And yet as Didier Bigo and Elspeth Guild have responded, Bauman —and Adrian Favell—may be too optimistic if they actually believe that the securitization implied by the construction of fortress Europe has no impact on the fate and freedom of Eurostars. Bigo and Guild, however, may be too pessimistic about the ability of states to constrain the movement of the less privileged TCNs who will move nevertheless.[35]

This brings us back to the question of state capability to maintain frontiers and exclude those whom they do not want to admit. What do we know about the effectiveness of the growing means that states now possess to control the frontier? We know that the imposition of greater controls in Europe along the Mediterranean, and between the California coast across to Texas in the United States, has made it more difficult and more dangerous for migrants to cross. One result of increased controls has been that access has become more expensive, and that in both cases has moved farther and farther east, into the more difficult-to-patrol Chihuahuan Desert in the case of the United States and toward the Greek–Turkish border in the case of Europe. People have continued to penetrate the frontier, albeit with greater difficulty.

A world without borders remains an elusive objective that applies far more to goods and services than to most people. Indeed, the reinforcement of borders, and the renewed proliferation of fences and walls, is directed against the movement of people. Although enhanced controls are often presented as a reaction to a surge of unauthorized movement of migrants and asylum seekers, it began well before the surge in Europe and is far more complicated in the United States. It is, I will argue, driven by a politically instrumentalized response fed by developing fears of strangers and loss of identity.

However, in part because of the liberal-democratic paradox, fortress Europe and America remain elusive as well. Trade issues, and the movement toward free trade in both Europe and the United States, have driven policies for more open borders. Within Europe, the Single European Act, combined with the European treaties, has virtually eliminated internal European border controls for trade and people as well. Even with the suspension of the Schengen agreements that became more widespread after 2016, people continue to cross intra-European borders more or less unimpeded.

Across the Mexican border trade moves freely under the NAFTA regulations, but people move as well, back and forth, in huge numbers each day. Thus there is a persistent policy tension on both sides of the Atlantic between fortress and free-movement policies, or as one political theorist has argued: "Those who promise free trade and a border secure from illicit crossing promise more than can be delivered."[36]

On the other hand, Elia Zureik and Mark Salter have drawn an important an-alytical distinction between the policing of the frontier and the policing of the border of a state, "where border functions are increasingly distant from territorial frontiers." To the extent that this is valid, the process of controlling the movement of people can become separated from the process of controlling trade. Another way of understanding this, they argue, is that "as the policing function of the border is undermined or interrupted, a more general policing of the population must take place."[37] "Must" may be an overstatement, but this adds a causal dynamic to Susan Martin's differentiation between external (border) enforcement and internal enforcement of immigration controls.[38]

1.2 Where Is the Border, and Which Authorities Control the Border?

The question of control raises questions of where the border is enforced. The Italian island of Lampedusa is a part of the external border of Europe but is controlled by Italian authorities, and entry through this border is governed mostly by a national—Italian—legal framework. On the other hand, should those who are rescued at sea choose to move from Italy to another member state, their movement is governed by a European legal framework that deals with TCNs. Similarly, Spain and Greece control major ports of entry for the rest of Europe.

In the American case, the Rio Grande is part of the federal external border, patrolled by federal border police who act in accordance with federal law. The right to asylum is claimed under federal law and is decided by federal authorities, which more or less override state jurisdictions, although the young asylum seekers who surrendered to US border authorities between 2012 and 2015 were also subject to laws of the state where they finally moved.[39] The external border of Europe is in Italy; in the United States, the external border is the federal frontier, which coincides with the border of Texas, but over which Texas does not have control.

The Localized Border

The Mediterranean sea border of Europe is about as long as the US land border with Mexico from San Diego, California, to Brownsville, Texas—each about 1,200 miles. Although in each case the border is long, controls along the border vary considerably and have changed over time. The US border has become increasingly militarized in many places. By comparison, the Mediterranean border of Europe has been relatively lightly patrolled, except for the area around Italy.

The entry of undocumented migrants, for example, has been mostly localized. European Frontex statistics indicate few crossings over the years along the long French coast, and the rising number of undocumented entries has been concentrated in the relatively remote ports of Lampedusa, Malta, and some ports in Southern Spain. (There had been a shift between 2009 and 2014 from the Eastern Mediterranean, around Greece, Bulgaria, and Cyprus, to the Central Mediterranean around Italy and Malta.)[40]

Similarly, US Border Patrol statistics indicate that apprehensions have been concentrated overwhelmingly along sectors of the southwest border. Apprehensions are now less than half the levels of the 1990s, but they have moved gradually east, from heavily patrolled San Diego and El Paso to Tucson and the Rio Grande Valley. The spike of Unaccompanied Alien Children movement in 2014 was entirely in the Rio Grande Valley.[41]

The change of locality is related to two variables. The first, particularly for the United States, is relative ease of access. The concentration of border forces in the San Diego and El Paso sectors forced networks of guides to move to more remote desert crossings. The second, for both the United States and Europe, has been the variation of origin and purpose of those seeking to cross, and the routes that they have taken to approach the border. Consider those seeking asylum in both the United States and Europe.

The mostly unaccompanied children crossing the narrow Rio Grande in 2014 and 2015 in Texas were seeking, not avoiding, the uniformed Border Patrol agents. They then claimed asylum under trafficking legislation meant to protect women and children from what was understood as a new form of slavery.

> Border Patrol agents in olive uniforms stood in broad daylight on the banks of the Rio Grande, while on the Mexican side smugglers pulled up in vans and unloaded illegal migrants. The agents were clearly visible on that recent afternoon, but the migrants were undeterred. Mainly women and children, 45 in all, they crossed the narrow river on the smugglers' rafts, scrambled up the bluff and turned themselves in.[42]

The Syrian and Eritrean asylum seekers, fleeing from Africa and the Middle East, connected through networks in Egypt and North Africa to Italy, while those fleeing Afghanistan arrived through Turkish networks, either by land or sea, often via Greece. The networks of smugglers took them through several countries before the migrants arrived at the boats that would finally take them across the Mediterranean, where access was more difficult. Even after they arrived in

Italy or Greece, however, the objective of most was to claim asylum further north, in Austria, Germany, or Sweden. In each case the initial impact of the surge of entries was local, but the political impact quickly became European or national, in the case of the United States.

1.3 Territory and Controlling the Border

Borders are generally about exclusion, but the meaning of exclusion varies with enforcement. Of course the ongoing discussions about movement across borders and the effectiveness of border controls presume some understanding of what the border is and how it is controlled. Borders have been identified and defined in a variety of ways, from those that define the borderlands of identity and culture, to those that focus on variable soft borders to negotiate terms of social cooperation, to those that focus on hard borders of territory and control over space. None of these definitions is mutually exclusive, but as Mabel Berezin has written, "territory is inescapable," primarily because politics and authoritative political decision-making is tied to physically bounded space. "Territories and borders are coterminous," she argues, and "the consolidation of power always requires the closing of frontiers."[43] But which frontiers?

Scholars have usefully differentiated among territorial, organizational, and conceptual borders. Territorial borders define the limits within which the state asserts its authority—those lines on the map, but sometimes extraterritorial areas such as embassies and physical space in other countries, or military bases temporarily ceded by treaty. Of course there are ambiguities. At passport control at Heathrow Airport in London, there is a large blue sign on which is inscribed "UK Border." This implies that before you pass that point you are not in the territory of the United Kingdom, which works for some purposes but not for others, since there is no other jurisdiction between the airplanes on which you have just arrived and the sign.[44]

Organizational borders that differentiate access to the labor market, welfare, and citizenship rights distinguish among residents within the territorial borders based on various functions. Conceptual borders separate populations on the basis of class, identity, and claims to entitlements, also within the territorial boundaries.[45] Finally, although borders are generally understood in terms of exclusion—those who are included and excluded—Julie Mostov has analyzed the variable range of harder and softer borders that may be possible, to the extent that states give priority to inclusion, equal standing, democratic accountability, and effectiveness of meeting needs.[46] Our focus in this study will be on territorial borders, but, as we shall see, for an understanding of the politics of borders, considerations of organizational and conceptual borders may be important as well.

A Harder, More Militarized Territorial Border

A dimension common to most understandings of the border is the ease or difficulty of penetrating the territorial border. In general, it has become more difficult for most people on both sides of the Atlantic. In part as a result of the widespread acceptance of the security frame (to be discussed), resources for border controls have been vastly increased in Europe and the United States. The external borders of Europe and the United States appear to be better patrolled compared to a decade ago, and the growth of emerging European and US border institutions is being driven by policy priorities that are related to the border focus. Policy cooperation at the European level appears to have grown, and the federal institutional border structure in the United States has grown as well. Moreover, the content of border policy has expanded. Entry requirements for most European countries have never been easy, although they have been generally related to family unification or need for labor. They have now become "thicker" and more demanding, and criteria for cultural integration are becoming the European norm for entry.

The most striking change in US policy since the 1980s has not been more restrictive requirements for entry. Indeed, the possibilities for legal entry have been expanded. What has changed is enhanced enforcement mostly on the southern border, but on the norther border as well. Easy access back and forth across the Mexican border that provided cheap labor to agribusiness has been gradually formalized and restricted. Far more quietly, informal access across the Canadian border has been restricted as well. The number of Border Patrol agents there has increased to 2,200 since 2001, compared with almost 20,000 on the border with Mexico (up from a mere 340 before 2001). In addition, sophisticated surveillance detectors have been added, and greater cooperation with Canadian border police has been set in place.[47]

In Europe, as border controls were eliminated within the Schengen area, frontier police, sometimes related to Frontex (The European Agency for the Management of Operational Cooperation at the External Borders of Member States of the European Union) operations, patrolled the ports of entry and beyond. At the same time, hundreds of detention camps were built and extended, legally separate from national territory in terms of human rights requirements.[48] The network of detention camps has also grown in the United States, along with a more militarized approach to border enforcement. As in Europe, armed paramilitary police are supported by expensive and complex equipment.

The intention of changes in European border policies was to make entry into the Schengen area more difficult, and strengthen the ability of the police to track those who enter. The most striking change was embodied in the Dublin Convention of 1997, which effectively transferred major responsibilities for determining the entry of asylum seekers to countries on the external European border.[49] In fact, provisions of Dublin externalize these responsibilities beyond the European frontier by establishing a cordon sanitaire of "safe countries of origin/safe third countries" around Europe's borders, from which applications for asylum should not be considered.

The most obvious difference between the allocations of resources in the United States compared with Europe is that the United States has vastly increased its resources directly on the physical frontier, the southern border in particular. Although Europe has given greater attention to the physical frontier in recent years (in the United Kingdom in particular), allocation of resources has been far more ad hoc and crisis-driven. Nevertheless, when we look at collective resources devoted to border control, the total amount has been impressive.[50]

The focus on the border calls our attention to the hazards endured by those who seek to cross. The increasing number of deaths among refugees attempting to cross the Mediterranean in rickety boats, the places for which are purchased at a high price from unscrupulous middlemen and guides, is a well-worn story in the United States, where annual deaths along the southern border gradually increased along with enforcement.[51] What is often less appreciated is that the Mediterranean border of Europe has become the deadliest border in the world, far more deadly than the US–Mexican border.

Yet the reinforcement of the border does not necessarily indicate more effective border control. The terrorist attacks in Paris and Brussels in 2015–2016 laid bare the weak controls in major European airports, as well as the lack of coordination of systems of security, including the Schengen Information System, across Europe.[52] Similar criticism has been made of the United States, particularly after the attacks of 9/11.[53]

1.4 Democracy and the Politics of the Border

This book is a comparative study, in which an analysis of the politics of the border in Europe and the United States offers a way of understanding similarities and differences of policy on either side of the Atlantic. Nevertheless, policy that deals with movement across the dividing frontier from either side is almost never a result of within-country decision-making alone; it is also the result of decisions made in other countries, as well as actions and events both on the border and at a distance from the border. The Mariella boat-lift in 1980, the Communist victory in South Vietnam in 1975, a drought in Africa, or a famine in Ireland have all had a dramatic impact on policy made in the United States. The decisions of the United States to massively limit immigration in 1924, failed states in North Africa, and the breakup of the Soviet Union have all been events not decided in Europe, but have framed immigration policy there. Moreover, border policy is sometimes developed through international bargains that result in an agreement or treaty, such as the agreement between the EU and Turkey in 2016, as well as the numerous readmission agreements between EU countries and countries sending immigrants.[54]

Nevertheless, while international interaction may frame decision-making policy and even account for the initiation of policy, the decisions on policy are ultimately national, decided through national preference formation, and "policies preferences are always developed through national political systems."[55] But how and when does national policy formation develop, and how does the democratic process define border control?

One approach to understanding this has been formulated by Theodore Lowi as an arena of power, within which public actors contend in a limited political process and policy is made with intended consequences. By understanding the choice and the structure of this arena we can understand how border policies are made. In this sense, how an issue is framed is related to the arena in which decision-making takes place, which provides one key to the policy outcomes.[56] This is similar to the approach taken by Ruben Zaiotti in his study of policy development and evolution. For Zaiotti, the interactions among political actors are dynamic, and change policy through their interactions. Within the policy domain of border control, shifts in policy are due less to what have been called "technocratic policy exercises involving carefully crafted compromises among rational policymakers" than to the fundamental transformations that border control *practices* have undergone in recent years, practices that have affected the location of border controls, as well as intergovernmental relations.[57]

Finally, the literature on policy networks and communities has been described as a broad (but limited) coalition of political forces—a network of bureaucracies, interest groups, and experts—that constitute a policy network or a (tighter) policy community.[58] Actors share common interests, as well as a more or less common understanding of the problem that the policy is meant to address. As with arenas of power and policy domains, the process is less one of conflict than of problem-solving. Moreover, it is a process that is less politically visible, and while the consequences may be important, it is less politically important in terms of electoral consequences and political mobilization. Although political conflict is not absent from this process, it is constrained by a more or less common assumption about the policy paradigm (similar to Zaiotti's concept of culture).[59]

John Peterson has argued that:

> Decision rules and dominant actors vary significantly between policy
> sectors.... One consequence is that EU policy networks tend to be dis-
> crete, distinct, and largely disconnected from one another, even when
> they preside over policies that are clearly connected, such as agriculture
> and environmental protection.... EU policy-making is underpinned by
> an extraordinarily complex labyrinth of committees that shape policy
> options before policies are "set" by overtly political decision-makers.[60]

Looking at policy networks gives us some indication of why there is a gap
between policy intentions or outputs and policy outcomes. The problem is indicated by the literature that deals with control over administrative agents (principal agents), as well as scholarship that deals with the relationship between
bureaucratic agents and the interests of those they administer (representative
bureaucracy).[61] Each analysis makes the case that enforcement agents, though
constrained by hierarchy and law, maintain a considerable degree of discretion,
in part because of their relationship with the subjects of enforcement. Therefore,
there is often a gap between policy objectives and the outcomes of control.

Each of these approaches, however, indicates a relatively stable, nonconflictual
process of policymaking, in which key understandings about the framing of the
problem and the interests involved have already been resolved. Border policy,
on the other hand, has become far more conflictual as common understandings
break down. The framing of the issue has become part of the struggle; policy
decisions have been driven by political party and institutional conflict both in
Europe and the United States. Conflict has been about every aspect of border
policy, from whether and how the border is important to what should be done
and how.

Framing the Issue: The Shift to the Border

But for each of these approaches to the decision-making process, there is a prior
question of issue definition that holds the arena together. Policy choices are part
of a struggle over how events should be framed, and framing is related to the
arena within which political decision-making takes place. E. E. Schattschneider
associated the initial struggle about policy to the prior question of the way that
policy issues are portrayed through the arguments and strategies of political
leaders. How issues are defined in policy debates, he argued, is driven by strategic calculations among conflicting political actors about the mobilization of
what Schattschneider calls "the audience" at which they are aiming. From this

point of view, political leaders skilled in formulating issues to their own advantage strongly influence how, as well as who, in "the audience"—voters, militants,
and groups—becomes involved. The motor-force behind policy portrayal or
framing is issue-driven conflict among political elites, and different formulations
of issues can mobilize different coalitions of supporters in different arenas of
power, each of which has its policy bias.

Consider for a moment some of the different ways the problem of the border
has been framed, even when there is agreement that the border is a problem. At
least until recently, the open borders enshrined in the Schengen Agreement in
Europe were positively defined in terms of free trade and ease of movement of
people around the European area. At the same time, free movement, particularly
from East European countries, increasingly became an issue framed in terms of
identity and welfare burden in UK politics, driving the support for withdrawal
from the EU in 2015–2016. Then, as the routes of TCNs seeking asylum shifted
from Italy and Greece to central and Eastern Europe, the same countries that
had benefited the most from free movement within the EU framed their own
problems of border control in terms of invasion and identity. For the United
States, enforcement of the Mexican border has become a question of law enforcement against the illegal entry of people and drugs.[62] In each case pressures
generated by democratic politics focused on border issues generated in part by
rights secured by treaties, laws, and court decisions.

The framing of immigration as an entry/border issue is also related to what
has been seen as the "securitization" of immigration issues. At least for the last
decade, Western governments have linked immigration policy to issues of internal (criminality) and external security. By focusing on immigrants as a challenge to internal security and identity, and as a danger to the general security of
the state, more mundane socioeconomic problems and conflicts can be merged
with existential threats. Although this has been developed into an analytic framework,[63] the link between immigrants and security is not new either in Europe or
in the United States.[64]

Nevertheless, undocumented immigrants have become the new "dangerous
class," and, as Ariane Chebel d'Appollonia has noted, terrorist attacks in the
United States and Europe, both before and after the attacks on September 11,
2001, have intensified this immigration-security nexus. The links between immigration and integration issues and insecurity are now deeply ingrained in public
discourse and policy on both sides of the Atlantic, and are now firmly related to
the politics of border control.[65]

But perhaps the policy content of how the issue is framed is less important
than what the policy implies about the government and state. Peter Andreas has
added the dimension of political effectiveness. He has argued that border policies
are essentially "image management and image-creating," a way of creating the

appearance of effectiveness while the level of undocumented immigration was growing and lincreasing amounts of drugs continued to arrive across the border.

> The unprecedented expansion of border policing . . . has ultimately been less about achieving the stated instrumental goal of deterring illegal border crossers and more about politically recrafting the image of the border and symbolically reaffirming the state's territorial authority. Although the escalation of policing has largely failed as a deterrent and has generated perverse and counterproductive consequences that reinforce calls for escalation, it has been strikingly successful in projecting the appearance of a more secure and orderly border.[66]

Indeed, consistent with the liberal-democratic paradox outlined by Gibney and Hansen, the increased flow of undocumented immigrants in the United States and the surge of asylum seekers in the United States and Europe has been framed by policymakers as a failure of border policy in each case. I will explain in chapter 7 how the buildup at the Mexican border has created an image of failure rather than success, and has generated a political dynamic in favor of committing even more resources to turning the problem around. Fundamentally borders are for exclusion, for keeping people out, and sometimes in. They create a fixed defense for the state to maintain. Inevitably, then, every undocumented crossing becomes a sign of failure.

Similarly, the European focus on asylum seekers and undocumented immigrants, while politically potent, has also created an image of failure and the inability of Schengen to control its external frontier. This perception of failure has also contributed to a federal dynamic that empowers territorial actors (see chapter 6). The strengthening of border structures and the process of decision-making have been cited as evidence for a developing fortress Europe. However, at moments of crisis, such as the terrorist attacks in Paris and Brussels and the refugee crisis after 2010, the weakness of the European border control system becomes more apparent.

Political Drivers

The construction of this issue, I would argue, is driven primarily by electoral considerations of political parties and leaders. They may be related to pressures of public opinion, to pluralist pressures of organized interests, to initiatives within administrations, or to all three. The point is that issues do not generally just emerge. They are constructed within specific institutional arenas in specific ways for specific purposes linked to political conflict.[67] Thus, border issues may be constructed around questions of security, nationalism, history, or immigration. Each of these has a rationale and understanding about the importance of the border, but they share the border as a focus of their interest and help to define the border as an arena of power. Indeed, the persistent question of whether political authorities are capable of defending the border increasingly appears to be a preoccupation of Western electoral politics, and has become the focus of immigration politics in both the United States and Europe.

However, in the two crises noted previously, framing the crisis was not so clear, and the struggle over how to frame it was at the very heart of the question of how to respond. Like the surge into Lampedusa, the surge of children across the Mexican border raised complicated issues, fueled by claims for asylum. If those trying to penetrate the gates of Europe and the United States were undocumented and therefore illegal immigrants, they could be turned back by sea or land, and prevented from entering. If, on the other hand, they were in need of rescue or were victims of trafficking, or were viable cases for asylum, they would come under different rules.

On the ground (or in the sea), this meant the difference between the approach of Mare Nostrum (the priority of rescue) by the Italian Navy, or Operation Triton (the priority of prevention of entry) initiated by Frontex (see chapter 5). The tension between these two approaches continued to reverberate, even during the months after the Italians appeared to concede the operations at sea to Frontex.[68] When more than 300 asylum seekers were lost at sea at the beginning of February 2015, despite the efforts of the Italian Coast Guard, human rights groups blamed Triton, the mission of which was limited to rescues only thirty miles from the coast. "The Triton operation does not have saving human lives as its principle mandate, and therefore cannot be a response to urgent need. . . . Whoever thought that closing Mare Nostrum might have a deterring effect was clearly wrong."[69]

Similarly, the use of border police in Texas to turn back and expel 60,000 children and women, or the application of the 2008 legislation on trafficking also presented two different ways of understanding the problem. The problem was that once migrants were simply turned back at the border, or boats were turned back at sea, it was more difficult to make a legal determination. However, a political determination about framing the problem one way or the other could make a legal inquiry impossible.

Political and Federal Dynamics: The Salience of Territory

Political drivers, and the way that the democratic process works, are biased by the territorial organization of power. The story of both cases indicates a second driver of policy, a federal dynamic, and an exercise in the politics of territorial relations—more than for most issues—in both Europe and the United States. Both the EU and the United States are federally organized territorial units (member states and states), within which organizational boundaries are some- what different and conceptual borders form differential bases of interest organi- zation. Territorial divisions, and the interactions of territorially bounded space, matter because of what Grant McConnell once referred to as "the constituency problem," or the relationship between territorial interaction and the distribution of political power among interests within these constituencies. There tends to be a bias against two kinds of interests, he argues: minorities distributed evenly among the constituent territorial units (ethnic minorities, or groups without ef- fective representation); and interests with diffuse support—where support is not central for any major group (he gives the example of "the public interest"). On the other hand, territorial politics may accentuate the political power of more dominant constituency interests (ethno-territorial groups and farmers). Borders, then, are important because they define the question of power within their units of organization.

In the American federal system, the most important border is the national frontier; although "internal," state frontiers have only gradually diminished in importance over time, and for some purposes remain important. However, fed- eral control over the "external" frontier (including ports of entry) goes back barely more than a century, and tension for control between the states and the federal authorities has been a continuing element of the politics of the border.

In the complex system of European borders there is also a common fron- tier, but without a comparable system of government control over the external border. Moreover, some countries within the EU remain outside of the Schengen frontier (the UK and Ireland), while a few countries in Europe but outside of the EU have been integrated into the Schengen system (Iceland, Norway, and Switzerland). The internal borders of Europe also remain important for some purposes. However, as we will see, it is of overriding importance that the member states remain in control of the external border. Once again, this leaves us with the question of where the frontier of Europe is, and what its importance is, and also the question of which territorial unit controls the frontier, and how.

In this way, for both Europe and the United States, the politics of the border are very much related to territorial relations. The arena of power for border pol- itics, I would argue, is a variation of what Samuel Beer has defined as the "in- tergovernmental lobby" in the United States, and what Andrew Moravcsik has defined as "liberal intergovernmentalism" in Europe.

Beer has analyzed two kinds of vertical bureaucratic networks that have be- come a main feature of American federalism, a feature that can explain a large range of policies that have evolved in the United States. In key areas of public policy, people in government service—the "technocracy"—tend to initiate policy, and form alliances with their functional counterparts in state and local government and associational interest groups across state lines. Their territorial check and counterpart has been the intergovernmental lobby of governors, mayors, and other local office-holders—elected officials within states who exercise general territorial responsibilities in state and local governments. If the interests of the technocracy vary by the function of government for which they work, the intergovernmental lobby focuses on how policy needs, costs, and benefits are distributed among territorial units.

From the perspective of federalism, this evolution has been both centralizing, because it has created a national network for local elected officials with territorial interests, and decentralizing, because it has enhanced the ability of state local officials to defend their local interests at and from the national level.[70] It has also developed as an arena with limited access for interests without connections with state and local officials.

In this way it is similar to the liberal intergovernmentalist system in Europe defined by Andrew Moravcsik, essentially an interstate regime that expresses policy preferences that have been developed through a process of national (member state) preference formation. He referred to this approach as a "sequential analysis" of national preference formation and intergovernmental strategic action. In addition, he recognized that the intensity of transactions within the system create "international policy externalities" that have an impact on groups outside of each national jurisdiction, and that domestic goals are therefore influenced by policies of foreign governments. He also noted that within the EU federal system national governments used EU institutions to overcome domestic opposition more successfully.[71] Compared to the federal system in the United States, Moravcsik implies that in Europe the intergovernmental network has become highly developed, but that the technocratic network remains weak, and mostly contained within each national system.

The federal systems of both the United States and Europe can also be understood from the perspectives of the relationship between space and political power. In the United States, Grant McConnell argued that the smaller, relatively protected space of state and local government tends to favor the defense of local private interests, while the national federal arena tends to dilute that power.[72]

However, scholars have turned this analysis on its head with regard to the EU. Within the EU, the arena of policy development of strengthened border control has been the relatively protected space of the central administration, space chosen by ministries of the interior and justice of member states to avoid many national constraints that had become evident by the 1980s. During the 1980s, ministries of justice and interior were increasingly constrained by domestic forces from carrying out policies of immigration restriction. Court decisions prevented

wholesale restriction of family unification, and made expulsions far more difficult to implement. They also faced conflicts with bureaucracies charged with the
integration of immigrants already in the country. As Guiraudon explains:

> The incentive to seek new policy venues sheltered from national legal
> constraints and conflicting policy goals thus dates from the turn of the
> 1980s. . . . It thus accounts for the timing of transgovernmental coop-
> eration on migration but also for its character: an emphasis on non-
> binding decisions or soft law and secretive and flexible arrangements.
> The idea is not to create an "international regime," i.e. a constraining set
> of rules with monitoring mechanisms but rather to avoid domestic legal
> constraints and scrutiny.[73]

On high-salience immigration issues, studies have argued that harmonization at
the EU level has tended to reinforce the capacities of states to control member
state frontiers and exclude immigrants, leaving more expansive immigration
policies to the member states themselves.[74]

Pro-immigrant NGOs that have battled for access to the decision-making
framework of the EU have been forced to seek a different decision-making arena
at the EU level—the rights-oriented framework of "social exclusion." This framework may very well benefit migrants already in the EU, but will have little impact
on the entry of immigrants into the EU. Their strongest support at the EU level
comes from within the equivalent of the technocracy.[75] In the case of Europe this
is a technocracy without significant executive leadership capacity.

However, it is important not to exaggerate the opposition to fortress Europe
policies at the member state level. Antje Ellermann's work effectively refutes the
easy assumption that more open immigration and immigrant rights are better
protected in the domestic political arena. She has demonstrated that domestic
politics in Germany and the United States have not impeded, and in many ways
have supported, the development of tools for deportation.[76] She argues that "socially coercive capacity" has grown both in legislative capability and in terms of
executive capacity for enforcement, although the strength of this capacity has
varied with the effectiveness of the intergovernmental lobbies (lobbies that support territorial interests) in the federal systems of each country.

Nevertheless, the emphasis on exclusion and restriction—the "securitization" of immigration policy at the EU level—is no accident. It has been shaped
by the federal system of decision-making, and directly reflects the biases of territorial organization of power. Although the US and EU territorial organization
of decision-making may favor biases of different kinds on border and immigration policy, in both systems preferences are influenced by competing territorial interests that must be reconciled through negotiation and the exchange of

resources and ideas. In today's systems of cooperative and interdependent federalism, John Peterson has argued that structured but informal policy networks
are the logical arenas within which such negotiations take place.[77] They are indeed the arenas chosen by key political actors to minimize constraints and conflict on the harmonization and development of immigrant integration policy,
and to maximize the possibility of agreement.[78]

Therefore, on both sides of the Atlantic there appear to be two kinds of
border networks, which are not mutually exclusive. There are border networks
that focus on governing entry and exclusion, which may involve transborder
cooperation, usually among national government and administrative agencies
seeking to enhance border control. There are also transborder networks that are
organized both by national authorities as well as by regional and local authorities
in frontier regions, for particular purposes—to enhance public services, for economic development, and for specific cooperative projects. Indeed, focusing on
border regions gives us specific insights into the cooperative relations among
both peoples and governing authorities in areas that are frequently termed "nat-
ural borders" or divisions.[79] These kinds of transborder networks have existed for
many years, and were at the core of the development of the EU and NAFTA.[80]

In the chapters that follow, I will examine the variability of borders, border
policy and its implementation, and how border politics work. First, in chapter 2
we look at the primary question of what and where the border is. I will first examine general questions as they have been presented in the considerable literature on this question, and then focus on some empirical questions about the
border in Europe and the United States. In the subsequent chapters, we will analyze first how border policies have evolved in Europe and the United States, and
then how they have been enforced. In the final two chapters, I will examine the
politics of border policy: how the problem has been framed, and how it has been
driven by interest group, party, and federal competition.

Where Are the Gates?

The Variable Border and Border Control

A country's borders should not be confused with those familiar dotted lines drawn on some musty old map of nation-states.[1]

It generally seems accepted that the border is a line on the map, often agreed to by treaty, sometimes imposed by force. However, the border, as it is experienced by those who cross and as it is governed by state authorities, is more complicated. The border is frequently controlled at places other than the line on the map, and is always enforced unevenly and with variable commitment across space and over time. Moreover, it is enforced differently for different types of crossings, differently for goods and people, and differently for different kinds of goods, and different types of people.

In this chapter I will examine the question of the variable border in Europe and the United States. If we look at where entry is actually regulated by state authorities, it becomes apparent that the border is not a uniform area of control, but an area that is controlled at different points in different ways. Some points of control may indeed be somewhere on the lines of the map, while others may be deep within the territory of the state. Others, moreover, are far from the state itself, in the territory of other states.

In the first part of this chapter I will look at how border control varies and defines different aspects of the frontier itself. In the second part I will explore how the border varies between the regulation of people and trade. How is it possible to regulate movement of people across the border, in the face of economic forces that push for greater openness, while security concerns and powerful political forces push toward greater closure? I will examine what has been termed "the liberal paradox" of the conflict between control over the movement of people and impediments to trade, and will then look at whether the hardening of border control for people necessarily obstructs the growth of free trade.

2.1 The Variable Border: Where Are the Gates?

One way that the border varies for people is where they arrive and where the border is controlled. Most studies (national statistics gathered by Eurostat and Frontex) indicate that a majority of people crossing the external European border—either for long-term stays or short-term tourism—do so at airports. Despite the drama of Lampedusa and the movement across the Balkans from Turkey, fewer than 10 percent of people normally enter Europe by sea for long-term stays; estimates of land entry prior to the current crisis were about 20 percent to 30 percent of the entries into Europe.[2] Not surprisingly, border controls have been generally enforced most strongly, with the most commitment of resources, at airports, and far less strongly at seaports and land entry points. Indeed, the current crisis of migration in Europe is in part due to a low allocation of resources at land and sea borders. Airports are internal to each of the member states of the EU, but the external land and sea borders are governed by only a few of the member states (see chapter 5). In the United States, however, nonresident arrivals have been almost as high at land ports as they have at airports, mostly from Canada and Mexico.[3]

However, the key decisions about entry for people may not be made at the point of entry, regardless of where that might be. An applicant can be accepted or refused at three different "gates": in his or her home country; at the border of the country of entry in Europe or the external border of the United States (preclearance) from Mexico, Canada, or Ireland; or after entry, when the applicant attempts to validate a long-term visa within the country of arrival. Each of these gates is somewhat different, and each plays a different role.

The Gates Are Somewhere Else: The Externalized Border

To determine acceptable from unacceptable migrants, most countries have established two ways to externalize border controls. The first is to establish border enforcement in countries of origin and in other "third" countries as well (neither the country of origin or of destination). The second is to establish enforcement areas at ports of entry that are set aside as special zones.

Procedures abroad may include far more than processing visa applications by embassy personnel.[4] Border agents of the United States and European countries check passports and visas in a multitude of foreign countries, not just at their own ports of entry. They also run background checks, examine security evaluations that have been made in the home country, and, increasingly, evaluate how well the applicant may integrate into the destination country in Europe.[5] What Aristide Zolberg called "remote control" entry regulation was imposed well before the current period of immigration, and has effectively extended the legal border outward for the points of entry for immigrants. The United States was one of the first countries to extend its border controls beyond its physical frontiers. As far back as 1924, the United States required all foreign nationals wishing to enter to produce an entry visa before boarding a US-bound vessel (a procedure similar to what takes place at virtually all airports today). As a result, all of the screening that had formerly taken place at Ellis Island now took place abroad, and embassies now included all of the personnel necessary for screening applicants.[6] Prior to that, the 1902 Passenger Act made carriers responsible for transporting passengers who were not admitted to the United States back to their ports of embarkation.

A procedure similar to the Passenger Act was integrated into the Schengen Agreement in 1990, and fines were added in 1994 (see chapter 5).[7] Thus, a "remote control" procedure for entry regulation was harmonized well before the current period of immigration, and has effectively extended the legal frontier of Europe to the points of exit for some visitors and for almost all long-term immigrants. In addition, as more restrictions have been imposed for family unification, many of the long-term migrants are required to demonstrate their ability to integrate in their home countries.[8]

Visas issued in countries outside of the country of destination will get applicants through the first gate. However, aside from tourist visas, those for long-terms stays and work permits are granted as "Schengen visas" by European (EU) consulates in the country of departure, which are valid for a short period (generally three months), and must then be revalidated by the receiving country in Europe for long-term stay. Therefore, although general procedures, and even forms and stamps, are harmonized, decisions on entry and residence are made by member states themselves under their own procedures.[9] Entry for asylum is more complicated and more variable.

Both the United States and Europe have made different kinds of efforts to externalize the processing of refugees and asylum seekers, and to prevent asylum from becoming an alternative to immigration. This has taken the form of a growing restructuring of the border within a country itself through the establishment of what Gerald Neuman has called "anomalous zones," extraterritorial areas within which normal national law does not apply, or applies in a different way.[10] Typically, these are centers of detention in or near airports or other ports, the number and capacity of which has fluctuated with the number of asylum seekers.

The Gates Are Here: Movement Through Different Gates

If we examine entries and rejections from Europe and the United States, it seems clear that any notion of fortress Europe is an exaggeration at best. Immigration into the European area for a period of a year or more is higher (as a proportion of

the total population) than long-term immigration into the United States over the
past decade. It is marginally higher even if we consider only the TCNs (migrants
from outside of the European area) entering into the European area, which
would be the rough equivalent of the US entries. As we can see in Table 2.1, the
annual flow of long-term immigrants into the EU has been around 2 million,
about half of whom are nowTCNs (up from less than 20% before 2000). During
the past decade, this movement peaked in 2007 (about the same time as in the
United States), then declined with the onset of the economic crisis, and then
began to increase slightly once again in 2011. These entries include the impact
of the refugee crisis after 2010, and include those approved for entry (i.e., those
that are "recognized").

However, four countries—Germany, Spain, Italy, and the United Kingdom—
in the European area have accounted for most of the recent entries of TCNs
into Europe, almost 60 percent of the total each year. Spain and Italy provide
interesting case studies, where, at least until the onset of the economic crisis,
there was a massive increase of entries after 2000. The change was most striking
because until the last decade of the twentieth century these two countries had
been the largest exporters of migrants to the rest of Europe. In Spain entries grew
from about 360,000 in 2000 to a peak of almost a million in 2007; they then
dropped back to about 360,000 by 2010, no doubt a reaction to the grave economic crisis in Spain. Less dramatically, Italy's grew from 225,000 to 560,000,
and then dropped by a third by 2011.

The United Kingdom was an exception to the pattern of declining entries
after 2007. The number of both TCNs and internal migrants actually increased
during these years of crisis.[11] While the flow into Spain and Italy decreased by a
third to half after 2007, the annual flow into the United Kingdom grew by 55 percent during the past decade. Similarly, although the flow of EU internal migrants
(under free movement) into other major receiving countries has declined, it has
remained stable in the United Kingdom, despite the fact that the country is not
part of the Schengen area.

The flow of entries appears to be more sensitive to economic conditions in
Europe than in the United States, and remains variable (both up and down)
among countries in Europe. Although the flow of legal entries, overwhelmingly
tied to family unification, does not appear to be related to variations in US economic conditions, undocumented entries into the United States do. Thus, an important study released by the Pew Research Center in 2013 in the United States
notes that for the first time since the 1930s, more undocumented migrants had
returned to Mexico than had arrived.[12]

Actual control over the border varies considerably with how territorial
jurisdictions are organized, and how the policies related to these jurisdictions
are enforced. Italy, Germany, Denmark, Malta, and Cyprus have most of the

Table 2.1 Inflows of Long-Stay Immigrants into EU Countries and the United States

	1995–1999	2007	2008	2010	2012	2015
EU: TCNs	1,865,000*	1,400,200	1,328,400	1,194,800	933,600	1,093,500
Free movement within EU	373,000*	1,215,700	899,900	739,300	1,006,900	1,243,200
TOTAL	2,238,000*	2,615,900	2,228,300	1,934,100	1,940,500	2,336,700
EU immigration inflow/1,000 population	6.0*	5.2	4.4	3.8	3.9	4.6
TCNs alone	5.0*	2.8	2.7	2.4	2.0	2.1
US: foreign nationals inflow	747,400*	1,052,400	1,107,100	1,041,900	1,061,400	1,051,000
US immigration inflow/1,000 population	2.8*	3.5	3.6	3.4	3.4	3.3

Sources: Data from *International Migration Outlook, 2013* (OECD Publications: 2013), Table 1.1, p. 20; *Trends in International Migration, Annual Report 2003* (Paris: Organization for Economic Cooperation and Development Publications: 2003), p. 323; David Thorogood and Karin Winqvist, "Women and Men Migrating to and from the European Union," *Statistics in Focus, Population and Social Conditions*, Theme 3, 2003 (Eurostat, European Communities, 2003), p. 2.

*An average per year for the five years indicated for EU; 1992 for US.

sea-access points in Europe, mostly small ports that are difficult to control. In the United States only a minority of states have international ports, and access by sea is limited by long distances, compared to Europe. The 256 land border crossings in Europe are primarily in Eastern Europe, and normally are only lightly used by TCNs who enter. Most migrants enter through 665 air borders, primarily in France and Germany.

The differences among territorial units result in an asymmetric pattern of entry, as well as interdependence among member states on both sides of the Atlantic. In the case of Europe:

> The EU is one open area of free movement, which means that some countries control sections of the EU's external border on behalf of others. For example, the number of border crossings at the air borders of the Netherlands were 27.7 million in 2008, while 2.5 million in Hungary; at the land borders 23.4 million in Poland while obviously 0 in the 15 member states /associated countries . . . without an external land border; at the sea borders 5.8 million in Greece while 110,000 in Sweden. In terms of migratory pressure at the sea borders Spain registered 16,000, Malta 2,000, Italy 35,000, and Greece 32,000 illegal border crossings, while figures for the other Member States were negligible.[13]

In Europe, decisions about and control of entry, made by individual member states, affect many other states in the EU. So, decisions made by Italy about the rescue of asylum seekers from North Africa, and how they deal with these migrants under the Dublin rules, have an impact on other states of the EU because of the relatively easy access by these asylum seekers to other member states (under the Schengen accords). In this way, the administration of Dublin rules about the processing and admission of asylum seekers creates problems for the internal open borders under the Schengen rules (see chapter 4).

In the same way, decisions made about the entry by land into the United States in Washington have a substantial impact on border states in the Southwest in which entrants tend to concentrate. As we shall see, however, the political implications are quite different. In Europe, the potential conflict is among different member states; in the United States, it is between the states and the federal government.

The United Kingdom has been in the EU, but has remained outside of the Schengen area of open interstate borders. Therefore the border between the United Kingdom and the rest of the Schengen area (France in particular, because of the Channel Tunnel) remains a hard and patrolled border. Nevertheless, the United Kingdom is heavily dependent on the cooperation of other EU countries to maintain this independent stance. EU citizens traveling to and from the United Kingdom are still required to go through border controls through the external border of the Schengen area, although both "countries" (the UK and Schengen) have signed agreements (in 2000 and 2002) for cooperation in police, judicial, and criminal matters.[14] Since 2000 the United Kingdom has signed 130 agreements that enhance cooperation with Schengen in maintaining and developing the compensatory measures that strengthen the external border of Europe, but that also ease movement across the internal border between Schengen and the United Kingdom. These are among the many agreements that will have to be modified or renegotiated with Brexit.

The Borders Within Borders, and Control Within

Although the external gates are important from the perspective of entry, borders are also controlled within Europe and the United States. There are two ways that we can understand internal controls. The first are the complex controls that result from the European and American federal systems. The second involves the question of where the federal state chooses to impose controls, either at the border or within the country. I will discuss the problem here, and then in chapter 5 elaborate more on questions of how controls are enforced.

Both Europe and the United States can be understood as federal systems of territorial control with widely dispersed centers of power, albeit with important differences in territorial relations and controls over the external frontier. The governance of the internal borders in Europe and the United States is related to the federal structure in each case, but also to the complex development of what Andrew Geddes called "conceptual boundaries" that define different groups of peoples.[15]

Although the external border of Europe has become the primary entry point for non-EU TCN immigration, large numbers of EU citizens pass through the internal borders to establish residence in another EU country. As Table 2.1 indicates, roughly half of the total inflow into EU countries each year is from other EU countries. As a result of this steady inflow, seven of the ten highest citizenships of foreigners residing in the twenty-seven EU countries in 2011 were other EU citizens. There were 2.3 million Romanians, about the same as the number of Turks, and almost 2 million Moroccans; but there were also 1.6 million Poles, 1.4 million Italians, 1.2 million UK citizens, a million Portuguese, and 800,000 Germans. Of the 33 million foreigners living in the EU in 2011, almost 40 percent were from another EU country,[16] and internal migrants are now staying for longer periods of time. Between 2007 and 2011, the number of EU nationals returning to their country of origin declined by 20 percent.[17] This is a considerable tribute to the success of free movement, but also the root of a growing political problem within the EU. There has been much discussion about the large movement of Romanians and Poles, but far less has been said about the Italian, Portuguese, British, and German citizens, who are also among the top ten.

This movement has been facilitated by the development of EU law, and by the implementation of the Schengen Agreement. Citizens of the EU (independently of Schengen) have an established right to move freely for employment under Article 45 of the Treaty on the Functioning of the European Union (TFEU), a right confirmed by the European Court of Justice in 1991 and elaborated in a series of EU regulations and directives (see chapter 4).[18] For those countries that are party to the Schengen Agreement, their citizens also have the right to cross the internal borders for any purpose, and to remain for up to three months. For all practical purposes, these borders are also open to the citizens of any country who have already penetrated the external border, although TCNs do not formally have the same privilege, and their right to remain stops at the border of the country into which they have been admitted.

Primarily for political reasons, even after the accession of twelve new member states to the EU in 2007, the free-movement principle for these new accession countries was not universally applied by each of the original EU fifteen countries. These restrictions were lifted in 2014, but there remain serious shortcomings on the ground. Therefore, within the EU, there are different rights to cross (internal) borders for those who are tourists (no problem within the Schengen area); those who wish to remain under free-movement provisions of the TEU (EU citizens and their families, after three months, must have sufficient resources and health insurance); those who wish to work, and have found work (no problem for most EU citizens); those who wish to settle (EU citizens, after five years of permanent residence); as well as those who wish to exercise fuller rights of citizenship (depends on member state citizenship laws).[19] For TCNs who have crossed the external border, the internal borders, in theory, still remain barriers to free movement and settlement.[20]

The internal borders of the Schengen area are still under the control of the member states, but despite the complexity of the variable arrangements, are no longer the barriers that they were barely a generation ago. Once admitted to the Schengen area, it is possible to go to any country within the area, without once again passing through border controls, much as if you are going from New York to California. Although all of the major countries in the Schengen area have imposed temporary border controls since 2006 (in February 2018, controls were still being imposed by six countries, primarily to resist the movement of asylum seekers) this freedom of movement has been the result of a long and continuing process of "rebordering" over the past twenty-five years.[21]

This does not at all mean that the issue of open internal borders in Europe has finally been settled. Although the guarantees by treaties and law seem reasonably clear, their application is subject to decisions by national (member state) authorities. In individual cases, for example, France rejected (on average) 6.2 percent of visa applications of TCNs from other EU member states. In addition, the Republic of Cyprus has restricted rights of entry of both EU nationals, and TCNs under a "doctrine of necessity."[22] Finally, as we shall see in chapter 6, various EU states have threatened to reduce free rights of movement across their borders to citizens of other member states, and others, members of the Schengen area, have threatened to close, or have closed, their frontiers for periods of time.

This complex arrangement of the internal borders of Europe is further complicated by differences among EU countries that are party to the Schengen accords, and those countries that have opted out. The four non-EU members of Schengen (Switzerland, Norway, Iceland, and Liechtenstein) can move freely across internal boundaries, but do not benefit from the same EU rights of settlement: Swiss rights of free movement are based on a more limited (1999) bilateral treaty with the EU, while the remaining EEA countries adhere to the relevant EU directives. Finally, even after the accession of twelve new member states to the EU, the free-movement-for-labor principle was not universally applied by each of the original fifteen EU countries.[23]

Although we usually think of the internal borders of the United States as free of frontier controls, and that US state borders are no longer barriers to human movement, they retained some aspects of barriers to goods, services, police, and people well into the twentieth century. The removal of these barriers has also been a process that has involved legislation, interstate agreements, and judicial decisions over a long period of time, and the tensions of federalism are still present.

The issue of free movement of people was not finally established legally until 1941, when the US Supreme Court overturned a California depression-era law that made it a misdemeanor to bring into California "any indigent person, who is not a resident of the State, knowing him to be an indigent person."[24] Even after 1941, eligibility for welfare benefits for residents of other states who had recently moved from one state to another continued to be a political issue, because of differences in levels of benefits. This same issue has also been raised by member states in Europe, particularly after the accession of poorer EU states, such as Bulgaria and Romania.[25]

At the same time, however, individual US states have moved in other ways to control their own space both for commerce and for people. Attempts by the states to restrict interstate commerce through taxation and regulation have been generally restricted by the United States Supreme Court under the doctrine of the Dormant Commerce Clause, which holds that the states are prohibited from passing legislation that creates burdens or discriminates against the movement of interstate commerce. On the other hand, court decisions have also authorized Congress to pass legislation that would permit the states "to engage in conduct that would otherwise violate the Dormant Commerce Clause." Indeed, among many examples, Congress has authorized states to restrict the importation of al-cohol from other states, to protect in-state insurance companies, and to protect in-state banks from out-of-state competitors and acquisition.[26]

Similarly, states have attempted to restrict the movement and settlement of immigrants crossing their borders, both from other countries and from other states. State and local restrictions often did not differentiate citizens from aliens in their notion of immigrants. Although the United States Supreme Court, in principle, established the pre-eminent right of the federal government to control entry into the United States, as the right to regulate "human commerce," in 1875, it was only during the last decade of the nineteenth century that the government actually established that control.[27] Although the right of the states to control mi-gration across their borders was severely limited by a Supreme Court decision in 1941, free movement has continued to be the subject of court decisions; each time, the Supreme Court has reaffirmed this right.[28]

In addition, the *sole* right of the federal government to control movement of people and goods across the frontier was still being contested by state governments in 2015. For example, in 2015, at one land port of entry in Arizona federal and state authorities share the responsibility for trucks from Mexico en-tering the United States. The Arizona transportation authorities have been in conflict with federal authorities on safety standards rather than illegal entry of people, and have attempted to ease the entry of goods from Mexico essential to Arizona economic interests.[29]

The crisis on the US–Mexican border in 2014–2015 of the entry of unac-companied children and women who had come from Central America, and who claimed that they were seeking asylum from extreme violence, presented the American government with a problem of differentiated access that had not been anticipated. Under the Trafficking Victims Protection Reauthorization Act (2000 and 2013), the children (and women) could not be sent back, either to Mexico or to their home countries, if they could demonstrate their claims. Indeed, the United States was obliged to find the resources to house and feed them, and reunite them with family members in the United States. On the other hand, many of those who accompanied them across the border did not benefit from the exemptions provided by the act; nor, in principle, did they benefit from resources provided for the children.[30]

Finally, the border is also within Europe and the United States in the sense that each has tended to enforce the border in different ways. Susan Martin has compared the Anglo-Saxon "island model" of enforcement with the interior model of most EU countries.

> With regard to enforcement, countries tend to fall into two camps: those that follow the "island" model, focusing their activities on the border; and those that follow an interior model, focusing their enforcement on activities inside their countries. The island model is generally characteristic of the Anglophone countries (whether they are islands or have contiguous neighbors) that tend to eschew national identity documents, sweeps of immigrant neighborhoods, buses and subways, or businesses that employ immigrants. The emphasis is on keeping irregular migrants out, not on finding them after they have entered. By contrast, continental European countries tend to focus more heavily on interior enforcement, with greater willingness to ask foreign looking residents for identity documents and stronger systems for enforcing sanctions against employers who hire irregular workers. These two systems are, of course, pure types, with most countries practicing elements of both types of enforcement.[31]

Both of these patterns have proven to be durable, if somewhat variable over time, and apply not simply to keeping unauthorized immigrants out, but also to defining how the line is drawn.

The internal controls over migrants in Europe rely largely on the use of identity papers and labor market inspections within countries. Both of these depend on sufficient numbers of police dedicated to immigrant and labor market control, as well as the ability of these police to operate beyond ports of entry. In Germany, Italy, and France, subdivisions of the border police operate on the railway system, and, in some cases in cities and towns.

In the United States, the internal border force, Immigration and Customs Enforcement (ICE) is separate from the far larger number of customs and border police. Although ICE is one of the largest police forces in the federal government, it often depends on the cooperation of sometimes resistant local police, and is less than 15 percent of the total number of border forces.

As we shall see in chapter 5, each pattern also has different implications for the allocation of resources for border control. Compared to most countries of the EU, the United States has devoted relatively meager resources to internal enforcement. On the other hand, the border control activities of EU countries responsible for the external frontier have varied considerably, and have generally responded in an ad hoc manner to the rolling series of refugee crises since 2010.

It is also useful to point out that at least until recently, the kind of militarized "firewall" border that has been built by the United States along the Mexican border would have been considered an anathema in Europe, where memories of the Cold War Iron Curtain are still strong. On the other hand, until recently, the range of internal checks and policing that have become commonplace in Europe would have been seen as "an offensive and unwarranted invasion of privacy" in the United States.[32]

2.2 The Border for Trade and People: Examining the Liberal Paradox

Much of the discussion of the public policy and politics comes back to "the liberal paradox" elaborated by James Hollifield: "the economic logic of liberalism is one of openness, but the political and legal logic is one of closure," argues Hollifield. At the same time that the movement of trade policy has been toward more open borders for the movement of goods and services, there have been increasing political pressures that have led to stronger and even militarized border controls for the movement of people. "Unlike trade in goods or international financial flows, migration can change the ethnic composition of societies and disrupt what Rey Koslowski has aptly described as the 'demographic maintenance regime.'"[33] If more open borders for asylum and trade imply a retreat of the state from the border, stronger and more militarized borders, as a reaction to asylum and unauthorized crossing, imply a stronger and even a more arbitrary state. The problem, then, is the tension between the more open borders required by rights of asylum and of the trading state and security demanded by the politics of the migration state.[34]

But are higher levels of free trade and investment intimately linked to higher levels of international migration—are they are part of the same process? Of course, as I have noted in chapter 1, numerous scholars have recognized that the border for people is related to the border for commerce, but it has never been simple. Borders for people have always been filters, barriers, but also processes, to provide variable entry for some, and variable exclusion for others. Although states in the West have become both more open to goods and services and more closed to certain kinds of people, the scholarship on entry has tended to focus on state mechanisms and processes for the exclusion of people.

Still, looking at the relationship between trade policy and immigration policy, Margaret E. Peters has argued the opposite. She has shown that there has frequently been an inverse relationship between open trade and more open immigration. She links high tariffs (and periods of high tariffs) to the development of more labor-intensive industries, with greater need for labor, and business pressure for more open immigration. More open trade, on the other hand, she relates to greater international competition and the development of capital intensive industries, with less dependence on, and therefore less business pressure for, more open immigration. Although other interests have certainly influenced immigration policy, over time business interests, and the needs of business, have tended to be dominant.[35]

If we assume that people and goods cross at more or less the same points, however, the potential impact of immigration restriction on the flow of trade cannot be avoided. As Peter Andreas has written:

> As in the United States, German law enforcement officials also face the growing challenge of trying to deter illegal border crossings which at the same time encourages the rising volume of legal crossings. . . . As the number of legal crossings has skyrocketed, so too has the number of arrests for illegal entry. . . . Since only a small percentage of trucks are inspected, an increasingly popular method of migrant smuggling has been to hide migrants within commercial cargo being trucked across the border (a method that also become more common along the U.S.-Mexican border).[36]

In practical terms, it has been argued that to make the border impenetrable, it would be necessary to impede not simply the rickety boats moving toward Lampedusa and the Greek islands, or convoys of people moving across the Mexican wilderness, but also the trucks and trains that move across Europe, and the vast commerce that freely moves under NAFTA among the United States, Mexico, and Canada. After the 2011 refugee crisis began, the rules for entry of TCNs into the Schengen area, as well as movement across external Schengen border, were effectively hardened, and there is some evidence that the economic consequences have been serious. The European Commission estimated that, because of the imposition of temporary border controls by Austria, Belgium, Denmark, France, Germany, Norway, and Sweden after 2011, the economic costs of border controls would be as much as 18 billion to 19 billion euros a year due to lost trade, as well as a reduction of cross-border labor and commerce.[37]

In the same spirit, Stephen Castles and Mark Miller have argued that "the amount of control and surveillance needed to make borders impenetrable is inconsistent with the trend toward increased interchange and communication."[38] The United States and Canada are each other's largest trading partners.

> Yet while the United States sees the border through the lens of security, Canada thinks of bilateral trade worth $2 billion a day. Businesses of all kinds moan that stringent procedures depress activity. Costs rise when lorries have to queue for hours to be inspected several times over.[39]

Indeed, although there are other factors involved, *The Economist* argued, Canada's share of trade in the United States has declined, and then leveled off, since the imposition of greater security restrictions since 2001.

The logic that argues that there is a strong relationship between exclusionary immigration policy and strong border controls, on the one hand, and impediments to trade on the other, appears to be very strong. Despite this, there is growing evidence of a trend toward exclusionary policies for people together with more open trade. Even within exclusionary entry policies, there are nuances of openness. Studies that emphasize policy patterns of exclusion tend to see the strengthening of fortress Europe and exclusionary America.[40] Nevertheless, scholars who focus on legal entry and internal European migration are usually struck by the relative openness of American borders, and the permeability of European borders.[41] Although both analyses are correct, in the sense that both patterns are empirically verifiable, what frequently gets lost in scholarship is that the larger forces that account for both legal and undocumented entry are similar, but the details of entry may vary. As Susan Martin has argued:

> Generally, irregular migration for employment purposes is fueled by the same forces that propel people to move through legal channels: a ready supply of people seeking greater economic opportunities, particularly from developing countries; a demand for usually inexpensive labor in destination countries; and networks that are able to match workers to employers. In contrast to legal immigration, however, irregular migration is the resort of those who are unable to enter under the often strict requirements imposed by governments on their temporary or permanent foreign work programs. These requirements may be numerical— rigid limits on the number of visas issued each year—or they may be qualitative—educational, occupational or skill requirements. Often, they are imposed on employers, rather than workers—requirements regarding wages, working conditions, or benefits in addition to what may be costly administrative procedures to obtain permission to hire legal foreign workers.[42]

On balance, by at least two kinds of measures, entry criteria have become more demanding in most countries in Europe, and at least some of this regulation has been generalized throughout the EU through harmonization. Ongoing studies indicate that the number and variety of measures regulating entry have increased and become more complex. Regulations have also become generally more restrictive. Although restrictiveness has varied considerably among regulatory categories, and among countries, the complexity of regulations has grown in almost every country. This would imply much more demanding border control and regulation.[43]

Restrictions on family unification have been a particular target for immigration restriction in Europe. This is the *"immigration subie"* (suffered or uncontrolled immigration) against which French President Nicolas Sarkozy famously railed. Although such immigration has been protected (primarily) by judicial decisions, this has not prevented restrictions and controls from being imposed. These include age requirements, maintenance bonds, integration, and naturalization tests and contracts, as well as limits on welfare benefits available to migrant families. These restrictions have been widespread among European countries—in particular Austria, Belgium, Denmark, Germany, France, the Netherlands, Sweden, and Britain. As they have been imposed, the proportion of migrants arriving on family unification visas has fallen, often dramatically, but without comparable increases in work visas.[44]

Compared to Europe, regulatory criteria for entrance into the United States appear to be generally less complex and less restrictive, with the exception of asylum regulation. The United States, by law, provides a set of visas under which applicants for entry can qualify. Two-thirds of the roughly 750,000 annual visas are allocated for residency for family preferences. However, the absolute ceiling is generally much higher, because there is no limit on visas for *immediate* family members of United States citizens or legal permanent residents.[45] Therefore, as we can see in Table 2.1, the actual number of entries per year is generally around a million. It is also important to note that included in this number are a total of 55,000 "diversity visas," which are distributed randomly (that is, by lottery) to applicants from countries that have sent fewer than 55,000 immigrants over the previous five years. Therefore, US law provides positive incentives for family immigration as well as diversity.

Perhaps the greatest disincentive for legal entry into the United States, however, has been the wait: the growing gap in time between applications for permanent entry visas and actually receiving the visa. Visas for immediate relatives of US citizens (IR1-5 visas), for which there are no limits (except for the per-country limit), are processed relatively quickly, in about six months, depending on the country from which the application originates. About 200,000 of these visas are granted each year, and they constitute about 20 percent of total entries.

The waiting times for other family-based visas, for which there are limited numbers, can be so long, however, that they are unlikely to be granted during the life of some applicants from some countries. The US Department of State issues a monthly visa bulletin that indicates the waiting times for each type of visa, broken down by country of application.[46] For January 2016, the waiting time for the highest priority visa (F1, for close relatives of American citizens) was about eight years, but longer for some countries; for married sons and daughters of American citizens (F3), the delay was twelve years.

In 2015, the State Department reported that 4.5 million visa applicants were in the queue, and a quarter of these were from Mexico, with most of the others from the Philippines, India, Vietnam, and China. These long waits can be accounted for, in part, by the 7 percent rule that limits entry from any country to a maximum of 7 percent of the total entries in any given year. On the other hand, there was no waiting time indicated for most employment-based visas, unless they were no longer available in January 2016. So, unlike Europe, the formal US rules on family unification are relatively open and generous, but the actual acceptance rate is effectively a small proportion of the actual demand.

But how is this related to the actual movement of people across borders, and how is restriction related to patterns of trade? There is evidence that although access regulations for people in both Europe and the United States have become more demanding over time, movement of people and merchandise appears to have varied more with changes in the economy than with changes in immigration control policies. The annual flow of immigrants into Europe slowed with the onset of the economic crisis in 2008–2009, and then slowly increased as the economic crisis began to ease in 2011 and the inflow of asylum seekers began to grow. Indeed, the flow of TCNs into Europe is about as high as the annual immigrant flows into the United States, where immigration policies have been relatively open (see Table 2.1). In the United States, the impact of the economic crisis on legal immigration has not been significant. In Europe, the total annual nonresident arrivals more than doubled between 1990 and 2014.[47]

Arrivals of nonresidents from North America into the United States for short-tem visits have increased over time, both from the north and from the south. In 2010, even after the militarization of the Mexican border and the imposition of far stronger controls on the Canadian border and at international airports, over 50 million foreign visitors arrived, over 11 million from Mexico and 17 million from Canada.[48] We can compare this level of entry to the 16 million foreign visitors who arrived in 1975, 2 million of whom were from Mexico and 10 million from Canada.

At the same time, what has been the impact of new restrictions at the border on the flow of trade in the United States and Europe? What is most evident is that trade has grown impressively, in fact far more rapidly than the flow of people. Trade between the United States and its NAFTA partners may have declined a year after the September 11, 2001, attacks, but it recovered rapidly after 2002. Trade then declined once again during the Great Recession, but has rebounded again since 2010. While control and surveillance may have inhibited even greater growth in NAFTA trade, by 2012 the value of imports and exports of merchandise with Canada had grown more than 50 percent compared with

2000; the growth in trade with Mexico was even greater, despite the imposition of massive controls over the movement of people (see Figure 2.1).

For the United States, trade with Canada, and especially Mexico, has boomed at the same time as the border has been increasingly reinforced and militarized. The value of trade with NAFTA partners almost doubled, from a total value of less than $600 billion in 2001 to over $1,100 billion by 2015.[49] However, the best indicator of whether the border has inhibited trade is the value of goods that moved by truck in and out of the United States, the mode of transportation most sensitive to reinforced border control. As Table 2.2 indicates, trade by truck almost doubled, between 2001 and 2015, and remained at about 60 to 65 percent of the value of all trade between the United States and its NAFTA partners. The value of trade by modes of transportation less subject to the controls imposed on the movement of people has certainly grown (with the exception of rail), but it remains far below that of trade by truck.

The evolution of trade between the EU and the rest of the world has continued to progress, even as the external border of the EU has been subject to

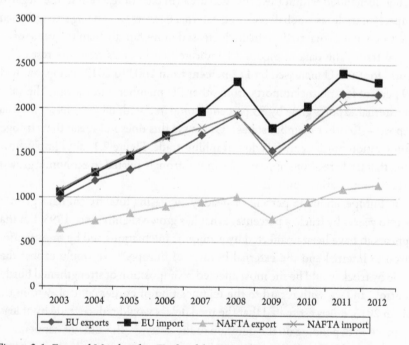

Figure 2.1 External Merchandise Trade of the EU and Intercountry Trade among the NAFTA Countries (in Billions of US Dollars 2003–2012).
Because our focus is on trade that could be inhibited by migration control, I have presented trade that crossed the external border of the EU, and trade among the three countries that compose NAFTA. Source: World Trade Organization statistics, https://www.wto.org/english/res_e/statis_e/stat_appendix_e.htm, Table A3, 2013.

Table 2.2 **Value of US Trade with Mexico and Canada, by Mode of Transport
(in Billions of Current US Dollars)**

	2001	2005	2013	2015
Truck	395	491	684	711
Rail	93	116	111	107
Air	37	33	44	43
Ship	29	58	104	73
Truck transport as a percentage of total trade	68%	65%	60%	64%

Source: United States Department of Transportation, Bureau of Transportation Statistics, *2015 North American Freight Numbers*, Washington, DC, 2015, http://www.bts.gov.

greater surveillance and scrutiny. The value of EU trade has remained generally higher than NAFTA trade. During a period when internal border controls were being dismantled within the Schengen area (in part in reaction to the negative impact on trade, as we shall see), and external barriers were being strengthened, the value of external trade actually increased more rapidly than the value of internal trade. The data in Figure 2.1 indicate that imports from the rest of the world for the EU increased by 117 percent from 2003 to 2012 (compared with 69 percent for internal imports, from other EU member states), while the value of external exports grew by 83 percent (compared with 68 percent for internal exports—to other member states). Of course this does not mean that stronger immigration border controls do not inhibit trade. Figure 2.1, does imply, however, that trade relations appear to be more strongly related to economic growth than to immigration control.

In Europe, about 45 percent of steadily increasing total freight haulage from year to year is by truck, a percentage that has grown slightly since 1995, but that appears to have been unaffected by economic fluctuations and by the attention given to internal and the external borders of Europe.[50] We would expect that trade by truck would be the most affected by imposition of strengthened border controls. In fact, with regard to the reimposition of border controls within the EU in 2015, it was estimated that the road delays would reduce trade by at least 10 percent, depending on the duration of the delays.[51] This did not happen.

Schengen border closings have not been unusual. Indeed, one estimate of the reintroduction of internal border controls between1995 and 2011 elaborates a total of seventy suspensions of the agreement by seventeen countries. Half of these were initiated by France (eighteen), Spain (twelve), and Finland (five), but with a few notable exceptions, they lasted only a day or two. The suspensions since 2011 have been more serious and lengthier, although they have only involved seven of the Schengen member states.[52]

During the earlier period border closings seemed to have had little impact on cross-border trade. Freight transport by truck grew faster in terms of volume than by any other mode of transport after 1995, and did not diminish until the onset of the financial crisis (see Figure 2.2). International haulage by road increased by 49 percent from 1995 to 2007, and after that declined slightly. The imposition of border controls during the current refugee crisis may have a more serious impact on international trade within Europe, primarily because the border closings have endured for longer periods of time, but also because the closings have become more politicized, and the counties involved are important trading partners, with large numbers of transborder commuters (Germany, France, and Italy; Germany and Austria; Sweden and Denmark).

The imposition of stronger controls on the immigration of TCNs in Europe over the last ten years also appears to have had little impact on the growth of external trade.[53] Exports from Europe have risen 50 percent since 2000, with no decline due to the economic crisis. Imports increased more than 25 percent, and then declined to a 10 percent increase after 2008.[54]

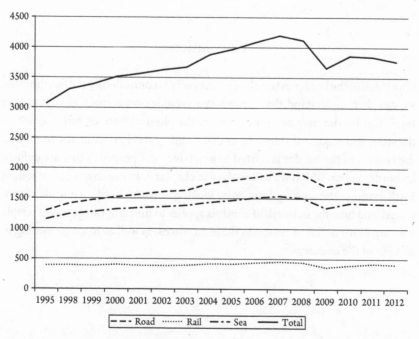

Figure 2.2 Total EU Trade (Goods) by Mode of Transport (in Billion Ton-Kilometers Each Year). Source: *EU Transport in Figures, Statistical Pocketbook 2014* (Brussels: European Commission, 2014), p. 36, http://europa.eui.

Perhaps one reason that the imposition of stronger controls on entry appears to have had little impact on long-term trade patterns is that many of the controls on people have been externalized away from the territorial frontier, and internalized within the country itself. In this way, the sites of controlling the international movement of people have been separated from the sites of dealing with the international movement of trade, which is overwhelmingly through land ports in both Europe and the United States.

Europe has not always succeeded in separating entry and exit of people from that of trade. Indeed, the continuing struggle at the entry to the Eurotunnel in Calais is a good illustration of this continuing struggle to manage (in this case) exit (see chapter 5).

The United States has done better. After trial pilot programs of joint inspection with Canada and Mexico, preinspection programs on Mexican and Canadian territory for imports into the United States were officially launched in 2015.[55] Because the visa procedures have been moved away from the border, at least until people finally arrive at the actual physical frontier, there is little conflict in entry approval for the movement of people and the movement of goods either in Europe or in the United States. Indeed, the United States has moved toward inspection and approval for the movement of goods, as well as people, away from the physical frontier.

Conclusion

If we think of the border as the place where entry is controlled by state authorities, we can then understand that control as a variable across space as well as over time. This border may be at the limits of the physical frontier, but also within the state, and at some distance from that frontier, in other countries. Moreover, the control of the border is related to objectives and processes that are defined by border policy, which we will analyze in chapter 4. In the chapters that follow, I will examine the moving frontier by looking at where border controls are enforced, and how the network of controls applies to different categories of people who arrive for different reason in different places, as well as to cargo moving in and out of the country.

Border Policies

Open and Closed Gates

In theory, there is no difference between theory and practice. But in practice, there is.[1]

In this chapter I will examine how border policies have evolved in Europe and the United States. By focusing on policy, I go beyond law and deal more broadly with what has been termed "output." Public policy is generally understood as the rhetoric framing and actions of public officials, based on law, administration, and the judicial interpretation of law over time. So, for example, French policy on *laïcité* (roughly, secularism) is only partly related to actual law, and is far more related to evolving interpretation and practice.[2] Similarly, American policies that deal with religious practice are based on constitutional guarantees, but have evolved in many important ways, based on court interpretations and the actions of public officials over time.[3] I conclude the chapter by dealing with outcomes, which help us to understand the relevance of policy objectives.

I also consider how policies have varied over time and space. I argue that in both Europe and the United States immigration policy has increasingly become focused on the border, the reinforcement of border controls, and the link between other aspects of immigration to these controls. Thus, the framing of the political problem of immigration—of entry and integration in particular—has been related to border control. Even as levels of immigration have been stable, or even in decline, policy on the border has become more important.

Europe presents a problem in comparison with the United States, since it is not a single state. In this context, it is useful to examine border control co-operation in Europe in terms of an evolving regime of common rules, norms, principles, and decision-making procedures.[4] Clearly, there are strengths and weaknesses in this conceptualization. At least some of the rules governing the movement across the internal frontiers are under EU law and treaties, but the governance of the external EU border is mostly by national law, and under the control of national authorities. While there have been some common agreements on border controls, the organization and effectiveness of border control vary considerably by country.

In addition, it is useful to understand three different entry regimes that involve the migration of people that apply both to both the United States and Europe. Each of these regimes implies a different kind of border with rules, norms, principles, and decision-making procedures different from the others, but often related. Each focuses on entry, but not at the same border, and not under the same rules. There are different ways of understanding border regimes. Thomas Nail, for example, empirically derives from historical analysis four types of border regimes that have organized border control at the US–Mexican border in different ways. Although he understands borders as a social process that is not state-centered, each of the regimes, as it is applied, is state centered and state organized.[5] The border regimes presented in this chapter, however, derive from a way of dealing with what is understood as different categories of human migration.

The first is the immigration system. In the United States, immigrants enter legally under criteria established primarily by the Immigration and Nationality Act and its amendments. The legislation establishes rules for entry, but also priorities and preferences, which are then administered by the United States Department of Homeland Security and the Department of State. Beyond the rules for entry, there is also additional legislation that provides for exclusion and expulsion, as well as for means and financing for carrying this out.

In Europe, the EU initiated efforts to cooperate on immigration policy in the 1980s, and established the goals of a Common Migration and Asylum Policy in 1999. It continued to modify these goals through three 5-year programs, but progress has relied on a high degree of formal and informal cooperation among member states.[6] Although there have been some common agreements on border controls, the organization and effectiveness of border control vary considerably by country. European policy choices on migration are made at the member state level. In both Europe and the United States, points of entry, particularly for long-term immigrants, are defined by visa requirements.

The second regime is the free-movement provisions of the Treaties on European Union, which is primarily governed by European treaties, European regulations and directives, and European courts. Beyond the rules there are also norms and principles, both stated and implied, about the meaning of a European "union," as well as the decision-making institutions of the EU, which have given substance to the commitments made in the treaties. In the run-up to the Brexit referendum in the spring of 2016 the restriction of free movement for work and residence in the EU became an important focus of the "leave" campaign, and indeed, Brexit "was largely, if not entirely, about reducing immigration."[7] What were questioned were not simply the rules, but the norms and principles behind the rules. Nevertheless, opposition to free movement was gaining strength in other EU countries as well, as large numbers of East Europeans began moving west.

The third regime is the admission of asylum seekers and refugees. On both sides of the Atlantic, claims are based on the Convention Relating to the Status of Refugees signed in Geneva in 1951, amended by the Protocol relating to the Status of Refugees of 1967 (see chapter 4). Both refugee and asylum claims must be based on "a well-founded fear of persecution" because of race, religion, nationality, membership in a social group, or political opinion. Gender considerations were added in 2002. Therefore, the guiding principle is that those who qualify should be admitted, and that rules and decision-making should be guided by that principle.

European rules under which asylum is administered are also governed by the European Convention on Human Rights, originally ratified in 1952 by a series of EU directives, the most important of which is the asylum qualification directive of 2004, and by the series of Dublin regulations. The core principle of Dublin is to assign responsibility for decision-making on granting asylum ("recognition") to member states that first receive those seeking asylum.[8] This policy implicitly recognizes that most claims for asylum will be made at the weakest patrolled entry points, sea and land ports on the periphery of Europe. Enforcement of the Dublin Regulation relies on decision-making at the member state level.

The United States is also a signatory to the Geneva Convention and the 1967 Protocol. The United States, however, differentiates between applications, which are processed in consulates outside of the United States ("refugees"), and are subject to the limits imposed by the Immigration and Naturalization Act (but set by the president of the United States each year, normally about 80,000), and applications for asylum within the United States. Migrants, granted refugee status, are then required to apply for lawful permanent resident status. Asylum seekers (20,000 to 25,000 a year) submit requests while in the United States, sometimes at ports of entry, sometimes after being apprehended for undocumented status. Those whose requests are rejected are subject to deportation.

At least until 2014, the number of asylum seekers admitted to Europe was about 45,000 per year (with some variation) before 2006, and then half that between 2006 and 2014. The acceptance rate ("recognition") was about 25 percent of those who had applied. Until 2014, the acceptance rates for asylum tended to decline as the requests increased (see Table 4.5).

3.1 Immigration and Entry Policy in Europe and the United States

Since the end of the Second World War, immigration control policies have varied between policies meant to highly limit access and those meant to encourage at least limited entry. Unlike the United States, where entry is regulated by federal law, there are only a limited number of European, EU, or Schengen entry policies. Entry to Europe is regulated primarily through the policies and administration of member states. What European states have in common has been an array of policies and instruments for limiting entry, with few corresponding policies for attracting desired immigrants.

The diversity of entry criteria, both over time and across European space, is amply demonstrated by the work of Michel Bein and his colleagues (who have developed the IMPALA database). Their work reveals patterns of migration regulation that are diverse over time since the end of the Second World War, and over space, among different countries. These cross-country variations include major differences across nine major Organization for Economic Cooperation and Development (OECD) countries that are important as leaders and examples in the development of international migration policy.[9] Harmonization and regulation of entry policy within the EU has been largely limited to process: the granting of visas, criteria for entry and expulsion. The EU has also developed structures of cooperation for border control and expulsion.

Europe: The Gates Are Open—France, Britain, and Germany

During the first two decades after World War II, major countries in Europe actively sought to attract immigrant workers for postwar construction. This was done with positive policy: the United Kingdom recruited in Poland; France actively recruited immigrant labor from Spain, Italy, Portugal, and Yugoslavia; and Germany recruited in Turkey after 1961. As recruitment shifted from Europe to non-European countries in the 1960s, formal policies were supplemented with informal permissive policies that included amnesties for workers encouraged to move to Europe.

Drawing on a long history of immigrant recruitment dating from the end of the nineteenth century, France maintained a generally open policy of immigration and settlement, supported by majorities in parliament, which was framed in terms of domestic labor requirements. In 1889, after four decades of immigrant growth, France produced its first naturalization legislation. It was intended to consolidate policy, reform law, and practice, and address evident labor shortages—most pointedly in the military.

It tied immigration to settlement by firmly establishing *jus solis*, or (birth-right citizenship), and ensured that successive generations would serve in the military. The legislation emphasized the need for manpower for labor, and to defend a country whose chief rival, Germany (since the French loss of the Franco-Prussian War in 1871), was experiencing rapid population growth.

This framing of immigration as a labor-market issue was consistently challenged over several decades. The alternate perspective, often posed by legislators allied with demographers, stressed the racial challenge posed by immigration to French identity. However, a proposal to institute a quota system failed in both 1926 and 1945. The labor-market focus remained dominant and relatively uncontroversial, primarily as a result of continuing labor shortages.

During the period of strong economic growth between 1956 and 1962 in France and in Europe, the French government encouraged immigrants from other parts of Europe to enter the country without formal entry permits. This effort was often organized by private employers, and then officially recognized by the state. By the 1960s, perhaps 90 percent of immigration was processed in this way.[10] Recruitment from Europe, both for France and for other European countries in need of labor, became more difficult, however, as the economic growth in Western Europe spread to those countries that had been supplying workers until then. Italians were replaced by Spanish, and Spanish by Portuguese, and then, finally, Portuguese by North Africans.

Until 1974, immigration in France remained relatively free of open political conflict, parliamentary debate, or significant legislation. France's frame of policy endured so long because the benefits were regarded as widely distributed, a view reinforced by industry and business representatives. Even trade unions regarded immigrants as potential recruits rather than a challenge to their membership's interests.[11] However, the shifting patterns of migration, combined with a diminishing need for labor, contributed to a historic shift in policy in 1974.

Like France, Britain too had a long history of relatively open entry. However, unlike France, Britain was not primarily a country of immigration. Indeed, until well after the Second World War, the United Kingdom was clearly a country of net emigration with a net population outflow of over 3 million between 1871 and 1931.[12] This pattern, however, began to change, if not reverse, after 1990 as Britain also gradually became a country of immigration.[13]

The composition of the immigrant population in Britain has also been different from that of France (and the United States). Before the 1960s the overwhelming proportion of immigrants into France and the United States was from foreign countries (generally European), while the highest proportion of immigrants into Britain was overwhelmingly from former colonies, even before

World War II. This balance changed since the 1960s, but what has changed most
is the mix of immigrants from former colonies. The proportion of entries from
Ireland (and the "Old Commonwealth" of Canada, Australia, and New Zealand)
declined, while that from the "New Commonwealth" (NCW, meaning primarily India and Pakistan) proportionately increased. As a percentage of foreigners
in the United Kingdom, NCW residents jumped from 14 percent in 1951 to
33 percent in 1966.[14]

The development of British policy between the British Nationality Act of
1948 and the British Nationality Act of 1981 was novel in that it redefined the
border by redefining British citizenship. Most people who had been subjects
of the British Empire (then the Commonwealth) were gradually deprived of
what had been British citizenship. The legislation passed in 1981, essentially
concluded the process by placing them in the general pool of applicants seeking
entry into the UK. Until the 1950s, the question of immigration, first from the
British Empire and then from the British Commonwealth, was considered to be
an internal matter rather than a question of immigration. Throughout the nineteenth century, British subjects had the formal right, established by custom, to
move freely within Britain's dominions. Until 1948, no linkage was made between open immigration from the colonies and Commonwealth (as opposed
to immigration from elsewhere) and the question of British national identity.
Indeed, a bipartisan consensus on freedom of movement dominated party politics, with the only partisanship being over whether entry should be reflected
in open citizenship (expressing the Labour party preference for equality) or
"subjectship" (the Conservative party preference for inequality).[15]

A more complex, informal administrative system of regulation that paralleled
the open formal system made "coloured" British subjects unwelcome until well
into the 1950s, although many evaded the informal administrative restrictions.
By then British labor needs had begun to overwhelm the system of informal
restrictions, and the balance between more acceptable Canadians, Australian
New Zealanders, and even the Irish, and far less acceptable immigrants from the
Indian subcontinent and the Caribbean had begun to shift toward the latter.[16]
This change in the composition of immigration strongly contributed to the shift
in policy, even when British labor needs still remained strong.

German recruitment began in the 1950s, and was related to the growing
success of German economic recovery and pressures on the labor market that
resulted from growing labor shortages. Like the French, the federal government signed bilateral agreements, first with Italy in 1955 and with Spain and
Greece in 1960; then, after the Berlin wall cut off the movement from East to
West Germany, with Turkey in 1961 and Portugal in 1964. In part, the contracts
were an attempt to gain control over what was often termed "wild" immigration: workers from Spain, Italy, Greece, and Turkey arriving at the factory gates

in Germany and signing contracts directly with employers. When it became clear that the flow of workers from these countries was not sufficient, agreements with Tunisia and Morocco (1965) and Yugoslavia (1968) followed.

Compared with France, the recruitment was remarkably well organized.[17] It was coordinated with the trade unions, who were assured that domestic workers would be given priority for all appropriate jobs, and that immigrant workers would be guaranteed wages and social benefits equal to equivalent German workers. It was also coordinated with employers seeking these workers. Official offices were opened in each of these countries by the Federal Employment Office, which then selected applicants, provided them with work and residency permits, and then organized their transportation directly to the employers for whom they would be working. Unlike France, their residency was directly linked to their employment, and, since Germany was not a country of immigration, their status was defined as "guest workers."

Under German law, the Foreigner Law of 1965—before that, laws were from the prewar and even the Nazi period— provided generous protections for guest workers, protections that increased in important ways by administrative rules. Nevertheless, continued residency was contingent on state interests, and return to their home countries was presumed.[18]

Europe: The Gates Are Closed

This presumption was initially confirmed when up to 500,000 of these workers returned home when Germany suffered is first postwar economic recession.[19] Indeed, between 1960 and 1999, 70 percent of guest workers who had remained in Germany more than 90 days did leave; but 30 percent—9 million—stayed. Recruitment ended in November 1973.[20]

It was often noted that Turkish workers comprised the bulk of the guest worker population. In fact, they were never more than a third. When recruitment ended in 1973, the Turkish workers were 23 percent of the foreign workers in the country. Italians and Yugoslavs comprised 33 percent of the foreign population. Nevertheless, governments generally regarded the Turks as the least integratable among the workers still in the country.

However, there was no rule in the bilateral agreements (or the work contracts) that the guest workers return home after some period of time, and they tended to stay longer as their numbers increased. By 1973, the oil crisis and a series of militant strikes among guest workers moved the German government away from continuing the guest worker program, despite the pleas of employers.[21]

Other major immigration countries either ended or suspended immigration about the same time, or, in the case of the United Kingdom, before. Beginning in the 1960s (in the UK), and then more frequently during the economic crisis of the 1970s, countries across Europe either legislatively or administratively began to halt the postwar wave of immigration. In each case, the context and process were quite different. However, as we shall see in chapter 6, there were several common themes that emerged in framing the issue.

In 1974, France formally terminated its traditional immigration policy by suspending immigration through administrative action—not by law—without any parliamentary debate, and without significant dissent. This was not a highly charged political decision, although the issue itself was becoming more politicized.[22] Rather, as we shall see, the framing of the issue shifted the understanding of immigration from a collective labor shortage to a more divisive issue in terms of the willingness of migrants to culturally integrate, reflecting a debate that had begun long before immigration was finally suspended.

The German movement toward exclusionary policy was closer to the French process at the same time. In 1973 the federal government simply halted recruitment, and encouraged repatriation of unemployed foreigners. It also refused to renew work permits, or to issue work permits for spouses or children (although this policy was eventually abandoned). Like the French approach at the time, the government negotiated agreements with Greece and Turkey for the organized return of guest workers with special German financing.[23]

In each case, new rules of entry were put into place with somewhat different objectives. In France and Germany, new rules were gradually elaborated that would restrict (though not eliminate) labor migration, and that would more or less eliminate family and marriage immigration, the kind of immigration which most contributed to the growth of "unassimilable" immigrant communities. The British rules were defined by labor needs, but also by the open Commonwealth rules that were left in place.

The intention and implementation of the changed policies in these three countries was to close the gates to most immigration. As we shall see, however, although the rates of entry slowed, immigration did not end. The reasons for this are complex, but the gap between the reality of continuing immigration and the rhetoric of exclusion created a political impression that immigration was out of control.

The Problem of the Common European Frontier

The Schengen Agreement was negotiated (outside the context of the EU) to facilitate the movement of EU trade, once it became clear that border controls were increasingly costly. Nevertheless, there is some evidence that German Chancellor Herman Kohl was also motivated by a broader project to make the benefits of European integration more obvious for ordinary European citizens in their daily lives.[24] Transportation strikes at the internal borders of Europe, in particular the truckers' strike in the spring of 1984, created an important impetus for action at the European level. Thus the first understandings that resulted · in the Schengen Agreement were reached between Germany and France at Rambouillet in May 1984, with agreement a year later by France, Germany, Belgium, the Netherlands, and Luxembourg in Schengen. The adoption and ultimately the expansion of the Schengen accords to 26 countries was very much related to the considerations of the expansion of the single market in Europe taking place at the same time.[25] Nevertheless, the dismantling of internal border controls greatly facilitated the movement of people as well.

Schengen suspended internal borders controls among member states, but also created a common Schengen border. There was then an increased effort to harmonize important border control standards as they were applied. The EU has issued common consular instructions on how to deal with applications for visas, as well as the Schengen Borders Code and a handbook for Border Guards at the Schengen borders. Under the Schengen borders code, members of the Schengen area have a single set of common regulations that govern external border checks on persons, entry requirements, and duration of stays in the Schengen area. Similarly, through the Schengen Visa Code, EU states have harmonized conditions and procedures for issuing short-stay visas (visas for stays that do not exceed three months).[26] The regulations are overseen by the Unit for Border Management and Return, within the European Commission's Home Directorate. There has also been agreement on minimal standards for detention and expulsion of undocumented immigrants, and of asylum seekers whose applications have been denied.

More substantively, the EU has passed legislation (mostly directives) that have established common (i.e., primarily Schengen) visas for short-time stays and a common visa for highly skilled workers with numerous privileges to attract them to Europe (the Blue Card). For less sought-after workers, a directive in 2011 created a single procedure for issuing work permits that regulates entry, residence, and rights.[27] A second directive aimed to harmonize rights for family unification,[28] and a third to create minimal rights for long-term residents (more than five years).[29] Finally, a directive was passed in 2004 that dealt with the conditions of admission of TCNs for purposes of study.[30] All of these directives reflect agreement on minimal standards of admission, minimal rights for those already resident in Europe, and minimal standards for those being detained or expelled. New common instruments have been created (the Schengen visa and the Blue Card), but actual admission into the EU area remains firmly in the control of the member states. Still, most of the legislation that has been passed reflects both the success and limits in dealing with the common border.

By design, the Schengen system of open internal borders was developed with compensatory measures to make entry through the external border more difficult, and to make it easier to track those who entered. The most important of these measures, agreed to by the Schengen partners on June 19, 1990, is the Schengen Information System (SIS), a vast database (the Council of the EU reports that there are now 32 million entries and growing), nominally under French responsibility and controlled by a committee that has the responsibility to protect the personal data collected.[31] SIS, which now includes the United Kingdom and Ireland under separate agreements, has been expanded (a fingerprint system, Eurodac, was added in 2003) and has become a valuable tool available to police coordination throughout the Schengen area.[32]

More broadly, member state police forces have been given expanded responsibilities for border and immigration control. Malcolm Anderson and his colleagues have argued that quite early in the process, the dismantling of border controls was exploited by national police and security services to deepen their mandate, to increase their budgets, and to increase their resources.[33] In addition, to oversee the effectiveness of the Schengen system, a Schengen evaluation mechanism (SEM) was set up by Council decision in 1999 to monitor the governance of the Schengen/Dublin system (for Dublin, see the following section) and was attributed to a Schengen Evaluation Working Group, then to committees of experts named by member states.

By December 2011, with the emerging refugee crisis testing the effectiveness of the governance of the external border, the European Council (Justice and Home Affairs) recommended "an effective and reliable monitoring and evaluation system . . . which should be EU-based." It would also involve experts from the member states, as well as the Commission and "competent agencies."[34] A year later, the Council adopted two regulations that reinforced the evaluation mechanism in two ways: first by giving the Commission the primary role of investigation; second, by expanding the justification for reimposing border controls if there are "serious and persistent deficiencies" in controls over the external border.[35] The limits of these efforts were most evident in the attempts to regulate asylum: the Common European Asylum system.

The Problem of Free Movement

Within the EU, what has usually been termed "free movement" has become a core policy rooted in the Treaties on European Union, and therefore predates the Schengen system. In addition, free movement applies to all member states, and therefore includes those member states that have elected not to join Schengen (the UK and Ireland), as well as those countries that have not yet been admitted (Cyprus, Croatia, Bulgaria, and Romania); free movement also applies to non-EU countries that are part of the Schengen zone (Iceland, Norway, and Switzerland); and applies with some limitations to the microstate of Lichtenstein as well. It is established by Article 45 of the Treaties on European Union, and in 2002 a European Commission report summarized both the directives for the application of this treaty commitment and the decisions of the European Court of Justice through which this right had been established.

> Free movement of persons is one of the fundamental freedoms guaranteed by Community law and includes the right to live and work in another Member State. Initially, this freedom was essentially directed towards economically active persons and their families. Today the right of free movement within the Community also concerns other categories such as students, pensioners and EU citizens in general. It is perhaps the most important right under Community law for individuals, and an essential element of European citizenship.[36]

Although the right to free movement is broadly linked to employment, it also applies to family members of those employed. Indeed, protection of family members may apply in the member state, even if it does not apply in the state of origin, an issue that came up during the Brexit campaign in the United Kingdom in 2016.[37] Free movement also implies rights to certain benefits and services in the receiving member state. Moreover, once employment has been established, a worker may not be expelled if he or she becomes unemployed (involuntarily). As interpreted by subsequent directives and court decisions, the right to free movement is broadly applied to all family members:

> Children will retain their right of residence even if the migrant worker leaves the host Member State, and a third country national parent will retain his or her right of residence, even if he or she is divorced from the EU migrant worker, in order that the children can continue to enjoy their right to education. The spouse and children of the migrant worker have the right to work in the host Member State and benefit from the provisions on the recognition of qualifications.[38]

Nevertheless, the application of free movement within the EU has varied and the range of its application has been challenged in court.

The United States: Policies Are Closed and Opened

Variable criteria for entry also have a long history in the United States. Until 1921, the borders of the United States were open to all immigrants, except for specific nationalities and people with specific characteristics. Restriction on entry for people from different countries and different races first became established with the passage of the Chinese Exclusion Act in 1882, which was then deepened and made permanent by subsequent legislation. Nevertheless, this restriction was considered exceptional.

The Emergency Quota Act of 1921 and the Johnson–Reed Act of 1924 then established national quotas based on national origins for entry into the United States, which in effect established preferential entry for immigrants from Northern Europe, with far smaller quotas for immigrants from Southern and Eastern Europe. However, the deeper change was that after 1921 the borders of the United States were closed, and those who wished to enter were obliged to demonstrate that they were within the national quotas that had been imposed, as well as not excluded on the basis of more specific criteria of health and literacy.

On the other hand, even after legislation was passed, entry for citizens of the Western Hemisphere continued to be subject only to the narrower restrictions of health and literacy. In fact, under the pressure of Southwest business interests, criteria of literacy were suspended during both world wars.

The most important restriction was that of literacy, under legislation passed in 1917, which necessitated special agreements with the Mexican government to permit the temporary entry of Mexican workers during World War I and World War II. The two systems (the Western Hemisphere and the rest of the world) of immigration were finally merged after the passage of the Hart–Cellar Act of 1965.[39]

Thus, although The United States has been thought of as a nation of immigrants, the gates to entry were mostly closed during the forty-year period after 1924, except in the Western Hemisphere. The requirements of the Johnson–Reed Act were finally implemented in 1929. Although the ceiling on immigration from outside of the Western Hemisphere had been set at 150,000 per year, after 1929, there was no year during which the quotas for that year were actually fulfilled. By the end of the decade, only a third or fewer of the quota places for entry into the United States were filled. In 1938, as Europe moved toward war, fewer than 68,000 immigrants were admitted to the United States, a third of them from the Western Hemisphere.[40] During the decade before the passage of Johnson–Reed, an average of 1,563 immigrants arrived per year.

This pattern began to change after 1946, as increasing numbers of nonquota immigrants (those for whom the quotas established by the Johnson–Reed Act did not apply) were admitted, either through special legislation or under the

Western Hemisphere exemptions. By 1959, less than a third of the immigrants admitted had arrived through the quotas. In fact, by 1963, the United States was admitting more than double the number established by the ceiling set in 1924, but the pattern had changed.

Immigration from Europe per year more than doubled (to about 100,000), compared with those entering before the war, but by 1961 the number of those entering from the Western Hemisphere had grown even more—almost ten times (146,000)—compared to prewar levels. From the mid-1950s on, the persistent growth of immigration can be attributed, above all, to the arrival of nonquota immigrants from the Western Hemisphere, overwhelmingly from Mexico and the Caribbean. Until then, most of the arrivals from the Western Hemisphere were from Canada, and most migrants from Mexico were temporary nonimmigrants.

Therefore, by the time the immigration system was altered by the 1965 Hart–Celler Immigration and Nationality Act (INA), the system had already broken down. The quota legislation had been effectively altered by a series of postwar laws that opened the border to many from Europe and Asia who normally would have been excluded; and a growing number of immigrants were walking through the open door of the Mexican border.

The new law recast the framework for immigration and immigration control. It abolished the national origins quota system, and in place of preferences based on nationality and ethnicity, the law established a system based on family unification and needed job skills. It established a preference system of seven categories, beginning with unmarried adult children of citizens of the United States, then spouses and unmarried children of legal residents. No limit was placed on spouses, parents, and unmarried minor children of US citizens. Preference was also given to married children and adult brothers and sisters of US citizens. Finally, preference was given to gifted intellectuals and skilled workers. For the first time, refugees were also given a preference category. All in all, 74 percent of admissions were given to family immigrants, 20 percent for employment, and 6 percent to refugees. A ceiling was established at 170,000, with a limit of 20,000 per country for the Eastern Hemisphere. The ceilings would increase over the next twenty-five years, and by 1990 the INA also built in a preference for national diversity through a lottery system. Perhaps most important, the new legislation fundamentally changed the message of American immigration law: the frontier was now open—not totally open, but open.

On the other hand, the message was somewhat different for those seeking to enter from the Western Hemisphere. For the first time, a limit of 120,000 was placed on the Western Hemisphere, with no country limit. This total ceiling of 290,000 doubled the existing ceiling, and it would continue to rise over the next twenty-five years. In 1976 and 1978, the system was somewhat modified, and the separate ceilings between the Western Hemispheres and the rest of the world were collapsed into the general ceiling; country limits were also generalized, and imposed on each country in the Western Hemisphere. Because the dynamics of the politics of immigration were vastly different from what they had been before 1965, the general ceiling continued to rise. By adding new visa categories, and increasing the number of visas available in existing categories, Congress increased the limit to 675,000 by 1990, with the proviso that there would be no limitation on immediate family. So, compared with 1963, when about 250,000 legal immigrants entered the United States, there are now about a million who enter each year.

The great debate over Americanization and the assimilability of a diverse population of immigrants, a debate that led up to the closing of the frontier in 1924, appeared to have changed substantially. In the 1970s, although there was some negative reaction to the unanticipated rise in immigration from Latin America and Asia, restrictionists were unable to gain sufficient political support to limit immigration. The best they could do was to place the same per-country ceilings on Western Hemisphere immigration (enacted in 1978) that had been applied to the Eastern Hemisphere.

The United States has expanded the number of categories of admissible immigrants, has increased the legislated annual ceiling on immigration, and has facilitated the entry of migrants from countries that have been underrepresented among existing categories. American policy since 1965 has become far more welcoming and has encouraged immigration of a broad range of people, from families of US citizens and residents to people seeking employment in the United States. At the same time, American border policy has become increasingly restrictive and militarized, particularly the land border between the United States and Mexico. In a way that is different from Europe, the tensions of border policy on the southern border have also challenged some aspects of the federal system.

It would appear that European policy focuses on closing entry borders while American policy has focused on more open borders, but of course it is more complicated than that. European policy has been more open in trying to attract highly skilled immigrants, with only limited success, while American policy has clearly been to restrict access through the Mexican land border, also with only limited success. At a time when all major countries in Europe were debating how, not whether, to reduce immigration, the debate in the United States was focused on how, not whether, to expand legal immigration. As we shall see in Chapter 6, Republican interest in expanding the number of skilled workers for business has merged, somewhat uneasily, with Democratic interest in expanding entry for families of ethnic constituents.

Border policies in Europe and the United States have had the broadly similar objective to strengthen barriers to control the entry of people seeking short- and long-term entry. Immigration control, however, has come to mean different policy orientations in Europe and in the United States. Since the 1970s European policy has focused on the exclusion of TCNs, at the same time that the internal gates have become increasingly open to internal migrants. Europeans have passed legislation meant to discourage immigration even of those whose entry has been sanctioned by court decisions. At the same time, the coordination of European entry policy has proven to be elusive, particularly with the massive growth of asylum seekers. Indeed, the crisis has challenged the institutional foundations of European border policy.

3.2 Asylum Policy

On both sides of the Atlantic, asylum and refugee policies policy provide rules of entry that have little to do with the normal rules and limits on entry that have been developed for immigration. Asylum is different from immigration, although both systems provide means of entry. There is a problem in the contradiction between the rules of immigration and asylum regimes that have confounded the assumptions of each, both in Europe and the United States. Asylum is treaty-based—formed and interpreted by national and European laws and courts—while immigration is based primarily on national legislation.[41] Policy under the rules of asylum tends to be relatively open-ended in terms of the number of asylum seekers permitted to be admitted, assuming that they meet the criteria of "well-founded fear of persecution," but it tends to be restrictive in practice, in terms of actual admission. Policy under immigration regimes tends to be restrictive as defined by law and administration, but is often more open in practice. Therefore, how entry is framed both by the state and by those seeking entry becomes crucial. In addition, special cases, for immigrants, but especially for refugees and asylum seekers, have always distorted policy on both sides of the Atlantic.

Europe: The Dublin System

In many ways the Dublin system, or the Dublin Regulation, represents the basic agreement in Europe on border control.[42] As we shall see in chapter 4 (enforcement), however, the dynamics of the operation of Dublin are frequently in conflict with the operation of the Schengen system of border controls. There are two core pillars to the Dublin system.

The first is that of assignment of responsibility. At the very heart of the Dublin system of regulation has been the commitment of receiving countries to rapidly register and fingerprint asylum seekers in the country where a person first requests asylum: "This Regulation lays down the criteria and mechanisms for determining the Member State responsible for examining an application for asylum lodged in one of the Member States by a third-country national."[43] Although the intent has been to establish a common European asylum system, with uniform criteria and procedures in each country, the EU has never gotten past this means of attributing national responsibility for those who seek asylum.

Part of the problem is that while most immigrants to Europe arrive at airports of member states with visas in hand, issued at consulates outside of Europe, asylum seekers arrive disproportionately at seaports and land entry ports in countries at the periphery of Europe without valid papers. In addition, if most immigrants into Europe arrive in the country in which they intend to settle or work, asylum seekers frequently intend to settle in countries other than those in which they arrive. Once they have crossed the external frontier, they are then more or less free to move about "Schengen-land" even if they have not been registered in the country of arrival. Asylum seekers are not legally bound to claim asylum, although member states can choose to return them to the country where they first entered.

The second pillar is the establishment of what has been termed a *"cordon sanitaire"* around Europe. An application for asylum should or can be rejected if the applicant is arriving from a safe third country (STC) or a safe country of origin (SCO) (see chapter 4). The Dublin Convention, as well as its updates in Dublin II and Dublin III (2013), recognizes that "any member state shall retain the right, pursuant to its national laws, to send an applicant for asylum to a third state, in compliance with the provisions of the Geneva Convention, as amended by the New York Protocol."[44] Because it was understood that for most purposes, countries bordering on the EU were STCs, and that many others were SCOs, these criteria would make asylum more difficult to claim. Of course, these assumptions became more difficult to assert as the number of failed states in Africa began to multiply and as the wars in Syria, Afghanistan, and Iraq endured.

Therefore the Dublin Regulation has set up a procedure under European law for processing applicants for asylum that requires cooperation among member states. It does not, however, establish criteria for acceptance and recognition, or interpretation of the treaties that all member states have signed. In addition, it does not create an administration for processing applicants, nor a commission similar to the SEM to evaluate the behavior of member states.

The clear intention of the Dublin Regulation has been to prevent what is often termed "asylum shopping." All member states are recognized as STCs. Therefore, under the Regulation it is not possible to claim asylum in one EU country to avoid being returned to the member state where an asylum seeker first arrived: "In this respect, and without affecting the responsibility criteria laid down in this Regulation, Member States, all respecting the principle of nonrefoulement, are considered as safe countries for third-country nationals."[45] It is the right of any EU country to return an asylum seeker to a second EU country if that second country was the first country in which the migrant landed.

The United States: A Dual System

The United States has two tracks for asylum: refugee admission and asylum. Refugees are admitted by visa from countries outside of the United States, with ceilings established each year; asylum seekers are only admitted within the borders of the United States, and there are no official ceilings. For each track, the process is different (with different results), but the criteria for admission are essentially the same. As in Europe, applicants for asylum must actually cross the border, and, generally, are undocumented.

Ceilings for refugees by world regions are proposed each year by the president to the judiciary committees of both houses of Congress, and a process has been put in place for the reception of refugees under those ceilings. Although the 1965 Immigration Act had allocated approximately 10,000 refugee visas (actually a percentage of the overall ceiling), these allocations were rapidly overrun and surpassed by a series of presidential paroles and exceptions that began the very day that President Johnson signed the act. The Freedom Flight program for Cubans who fled from the Castro regime, Czech refugees after the Soviet invasion of 1968, special provisions for Soviet Jews, and finally the exceptions made for the refugees after the fall of Vietnam in 1975 all surpassed the numerical ceilings on refugee visas.[46]

Prior to 1980, the priority of admission of refugees was largely given to those fleeing from communist countries. After the passage of the 1980 Refugee Act, the focus shifted to one more consistent with the 1967 protocol, and opened more claims for refugee status from a broader range of countries. It also continued to make it possible for the president to recommend admission for additional refugees either by increasing the legislative limit or by using special parole powers. By law, the highest priority ("Priority 1") is now given to applicants who have been referred by the United Nations High Commissioner for Refugees (UNHCR).

Nevertheless, there were exceptions, the most important of which involved Cuba. As a result of the Cuban Adjustment Act (1966), Cubans who fled to United States would be given legal permanent residence after two years (later modified to one year). After almost thirty years, however, the Clinton administration sought to bring Cuban migration at least partially into the context of US immigration and refugee law.

The compromise Cuban Migration Agreement (CMA) was meant to discourage people from embarking on the dangerous passage across the Florida straits by easing normal immigration to the United States and normal claims to refugee status within Cuba. The agreement also added a special immigration lottery. Finally, the accord added a provision that has become known as "wet foot, dry foot." People fleeing Cuba and interdicted by American naval vessels ("wet foot") would be sent back to Cuba (or a third country); however, if they reached US shores ("dry foot") they would be permitted to remain in the United States, and benefit from an expedited process for legal permanent residency and citizenship.[47]

This exceptional status for Cuban refugees was partially ended in 2017, as President Obama moved toward a normalization of US–Cuban relations. The Department of Homeland Security issued a new regulation simply stipulating that Cuban nationals entering the United States illegally would be subject to removal, unless they qualified for asylum. This appeared to leave in place, however, many of the other special advantages of the CMA.

Applications for asylum in the United States are on a different track than those for refugee status, and that track is most similar to the process in European countries. The most important difference from consideration for refugee status is that applications for asylum can only be made either at the border or within the United States. Affirmative applications are made directly by applicants to an officer of the US Citizens and Immigration Service (USCIS), formerly the Immigration and Naturalization Service (INS), now part of Homeland Security; defensive applications are made during removal proceedings, before an immigration judge of the Executive Office for Immigration Review (EOIR), part of the Department of Justice. Generally half to a third of asylum applications are filed "defensively." Affirmative applicants who are denied asylum, and are then placed in removal proceedings, normally file for defensive asylum. Therefore, the EOIR is the ultimate arbiter for asylum. To apply for asylum in the United States the applicant must be on American soil, but because virtually all of these applicants are undocumented, they are subject to deportation once their application is denied.

As with the 1980 Refugee Act, there were exceptions to the standard asylum procedure. The Trafficking Victims Protection Reauthorization Act was unanimously passed by Congress in 2008 (a prior law was passed in 2000) and signed into law by President George W. Bush. It was understood as a way to deal with cross-border sex trafficking, although it did not apply to asylum seekers from either Mexico or Canada. However, as we shall see in chapter 4, it did apply to unaccompanied children from Central America who surged across the Mexico border between 2011 and 2015.

By law, the Administration for Children and Families (ACF) of the Department of Health and Human Services was required to take custody of all unaccompanied children who file claims to remain in the United States. ACF was also required to place these children in state-licensed shelters ("in the least restrictive setting that is in the best interest of the child") "until ACF can place them with sponsors, usually parents or other relatives."[48] In fact, one objective of the 2008 legislation was to prevent unaccompanied children from being quickly sent back to their native countries, and it required that they have access to counsel, and consult with an advocate. The law also recommended that authorities explore reuniting these children with family members.

The dual system for asylum in the United States was developed in the context of a series of refugee crises, some of which it shared with Europe (the Cold War and the crisis in Southeast Asia), some of which it did not (Cuba and instability in Central and South America). If the former crises were somewhat removed from direct contact with the United States, the latter imposed direct contact on land and sea, and were most similar to patterns of asylum in Europe.

3.3 The Focus on the Border

In both Europe and the United States there has been an increased focus of policy on the border in three ways. The first effort has been the increase in legislative and administrative action on border control. In Europe, we can see this both on both the member state and on the EU levels.

The development of European border policy is best understood by examining the core agreements among EU states about the external border that are contained within the Treaties on European Union.[49] The consolidated treaties contain many references to the internal borders, most specifically to those of the countries that are part of the Schengen system, but also to a common understanding of "an area of freedom, security and justice without internal frontiers, in which the free movement of persons is ensured." However, the trade-off is "in conjunction with appropriate measures with respect to external border controls" (Article 3). Nevertheless, the framework for the governance of internal borders under the Schengen system is far clearer than trade-off of the control of the external frontier, which remains vague.

Article 77 commits member states to develop "an integrated management system for external borders," and member states have agreed to a common borders code, as well as a common visa policy. Each of these agreements carefully frames control of the external border as the responsibility of the member states, with a minimum of harmonized standards. For example, Schengen visas are issued by the consulates of the member states for short-term stays that then permit their holders to move freely within the Schengen area. The Schengen Borders Code commits member states to subject non-EU citizens crossing the external frontier to a thorough check that includes passport control, and verification that no European security alert has been issued. However, control over the common frontier remains firmly in member state hands, and there is no agreed-upon procedure to verify that these minimal standards are being upheld.

After the 1998–2003 spike of asylum seekers to the United Kingdom, governments developed policies of what they called "exporting the border." This was done primarily by putting in place policies of juxtaposed controls in France and Belgium for Eurostar trains and cross-channel ferries.[50] However, these efforts also involved more extensive use of short-term detention.[51]

Since 2002, French governments have also made a concerted effort to focus on the border, to multiply "barriers at the entrance" both at the national level and at the European and international levels: a new procedure to issue visas by consular authorities, increased cooperation with transportation authorities, reinforced collaboration among different police organizations, and a multiplication of what they have termed "airport measures of dissuasion."[52]

Even before the agreement to abolish border controls within the Schengen area, France began to strengthen its controls at its external crossings, particularly at airports. By effectively moving the border to a no-man's land at administrative detention centers, France established a new border (see the following section).[53]

At the European level there has also been a growing focus of policy and policymaking on the common external border of the Schengen area, as well as the management of the internal borders. The focus by the EU has been to coordinate and harmonize member state control of the external border, but also to create new and more robust instruments of border control.

The initial plans for the management of the external border were first developed in 2002 with what is often referred to as the central pillar of external border management, the Schengen borders code that would apply to all TCNs entering into Europe. This was followed by a handbook for border police, and by the *Common Consular Instructions on Visas*, for issuing visas in countries of origin. Most of these regulations are meant to facilitate entry, but some, setting out regulations for biometric passports and entry/exit systems, are meant to strengthen security at the border.

Still other efforts at the EU are attempts to provide more security and muscle for the common border. Security information is contained in the central data bases of the SIS, composed of data on those entering the Schengen area combined with other information—the Visa Information System, for visa data, and Eurodac, a fingerprint database. The most notable example of more muscle was the establishment in 2004 of Frontex. Frontex is a modestly financed organization meant to assist member states in implementing "operational aspects of external border management through joint operations and rapid border interventions, risk analysis, information exchange, relations with third countries and the return of returnees." Frontex was never meant to be a European border force. There has also been an attempt to establish a European border and Coast Guard agency. Although these policy proposals for new structures and institutions have multiplied since 2002, the external border still remains under the control of the member states. There has been considerable cooperation, but it has remained sporadic and limited.

The second effort at policy development was to shift decision-making away from the actual point of entry—that is, to move the border away from the physical land, sea, and air points where migrants actually arrive. By reinforcing visa processing points at consulates in countries of origin and by setting rules that make it difficult for migrants to board aircraft, ships, or international trains in countries of origin without visas, the border is effectively moved away from the frontier. In Europe, requirements for obtaining a visa have grown more demanding and have been more firmly framed in terms of meeting criteria of identity and integration.[54]

The third effort to focus on the border has been to make entry more difficult by allocating more resources to border control. The most obvious difference between the United States and Europe is that the United States has increased more of its resources directly at the physical frontier, the southern border in particular. "Border patrol staffing, technology, and infrastructure have reached historic highs," argues a 2013 report.[55]

Europe has also given greater attention to the physical frontier in recent years (the UK in particular), but allocation of resources has been far more ad hoc and crisis driven. Most frontier resources have been devoted to airport security, where most people arrive, and to land borders with Turkey and Morocco, which had been the sources of undocumented entry. The exceptional commitment made by Italy to sea patrols (Mare Nostrum) is an indication of how otherwise little attention had been given to this part of the physical frontier. Eventually, Frontex Operation Triton was initiated in 2014 as a cooperative effort among twenty-six European countries to control entry of asylum seekers from North Africa. It replaced the Italian operation Mare Nostrum. By 2015, these border control efforts gradually shifted to Operation Sophia, a military operation authorized by the EU Political and Security Committee, responsible for crisis management operations on the international level (see chapter 5).

When we look at collective resources devoted to border control, the collective resources devoted by EU member countries to border control are comparable to those of the United States. More importantly, these resources have been growing, even as internal controls have been more or less removed under the Schengen Agreement (see chapter 5, Table 5.3). Indeed, Rey Koslowski has argued that European forces are larger than their American counterparts.[56] Moreover, the financing for Frontex has gradually increased since 2010, and more resources have been moved to sea and land ports, where the majority of asylum seekers have arrived (see Table 5.4).

On both sides of the Atlantic, entry policy for both immigrants and asylum seekers has become enmeshed in how the border is crossed. This is a particular problem for asylum, which most often must be claimed after illegal crossing. The pressure of asylum seekers in Europe has therefore accentuated the importance of the border itself. For the United States, the pressure of asylum has grown as well, although decisions on the admission of most refugees are made in countries of origin or third countries far from American shores.

3.4 Outcomes

As we have seen, border policies in Europe and the United States have been closely linked to objectives of immigration control. How can we understand the success and failure of these policies? Of course, no policy, particularly no regulatory policy, can totally succeed. Nevertheless, if we examine the basic intentions of a policy, we can analyze whether the outcomes are generally consistent with what was intended. For example, if the intention of the 1924 Johnson–Reed Act was first to reduce the number of immigrants entering the United States, and then to shape immigration to perpetuate the ethnic composition of the country of the early nineteenth century, the outcome was largely successful, at least until the 1950s. For our purposes here, I would include a second set of criteria of success or failure: support and opposition in public opinion. In a democracy, intense public opposition to a policy has electoral implications, depending on the issue priorities of political parties.[57]

Although policies in Europe are generally oriented toward exclusion, entry policies, either by choice or by necessity, have tended to favor certain categories of immigrants. At the EU level, for example, there has been a recognition that Europe needs to attract highly skilled workers with instruments such as the Blue Card, and at the national level, large numbers of work permits have been issued each year for less skilled workers. Somewhat more reluctantly, European countries have permitted relatively high levels of immigration through family unification, primarily due to court decisions, and famously referred to by French President Sarkozy as *immigration subie* or suffered immigration, over which the government had no choice.[58]

Nevertheless, the drumbeat of political rhetoric appears to indicate that the gates of Europe are more or less closed, and that the most desired outcome would be sharply limited access and declining immigration. As the politics of every European country have focused increasingly on identity and integration, these considerations have been built into national controls over entry, as well as EU programs to promote integration.[59]

The United States, by contrast, has maintained a relatively open immigration policy since 1965 that has given strong priority to *immigration subie*, as well as to labor immigration. Although there has been a growing drumbeat of political rhetoric against undocumented immigrants and immigration, support for legal immigration appears to remain strong.[60]

Legal Entries

For Europe, the outcomes of entry policy are close to those intended by policy. However, policies have been a mix of those legislated and those imposed. Those legislated have limited immigration to some categories of labor, and the outcomes appear to be close to those intended. Those imposed by court decisions have resulted in a volume of family unification that has had two un-expected outcomes: first, although entry has largely leveled off, it has done so at higher levels than expected; second, family unification has changed a population of immigrant workers into a set of ethnic family communities that have challenged European identity. The third category of entries has been those of other Europeans, a result of the Treaties on European Union. Here too the outcome has been unexpected, because of the unanticipated volume of movement that has increased in recent years.

Therefore, we might presume that because European policies on legal entry appear to be far more demanding and harsher than the more open policies of the United States, there would be a considerable gap in the flow of legal entries. It is true that the inflow of migrants into EU countries has declined slightly during the past decade, if we use the average number of entries during the last five years of the twentieth century as a baseline. At the same time, entries into the United States have increased. However, immigration flows per thousand population remain slightly higher in Europe compared with the United States. Compared with the period 1995–1999, the structure of migration in the EU has changed considerably.

While the movement of TCNs has steadily declined, particularly per thousand population of the EU, the movement of EU nationals within the union now accounts for 40 percent or more of all migration from year to year (see Table 2.1). Thus in proportion to the population, the United State accepts more

TCNs each year than Europe, and while European foreign immigration has steadily declined, US foreign immigration has steadily increased. Therefore, on both sides of the Atlantic, trends in legal immigration appear to be somewhat related to the policies in place.

For the United States, some outcomes of entry policy had been consistent with the policies, but other outcomes were unanticipated, at least at the beginning. The 1965 legislation was written with an eye toward immigrants from Europe. However, the largest beneficiaries of the new visa categories were from the Western Hemisphere and Asia. Nevertheless, as these outcomes became evident the legislation was not revised, but was expanded to include more diversity, with greater numbers of immigrants.

Increased levels of legal immigration have not provoked a serious political challenge, primarily because the Select Commission on Immigration and Refugee Policy (SCIRP), which issued its final report in 1981, effectively decoupled the questions of legal and illegal immigration.[61] Sixteen years later the Jordan Commission, at a time of reaction to the relatively open immigration legislated in 1965, made recommendations for severe cutbacks in legal immigration. However, by the time that its final report came out in 1997, the reaction to the reaction had begun to emerge.

As a result, general support for continued immigration was affirmed by the Clinton administration, and the more controversial recommendations for reductions in legal immigration—proposals that amounted to a reversal of the trend of immigration policy since 1965—were never implemented. The commission's recommendations on illegal immigration, however, which echoed those of the SCIRP, are still part of the immigration debate in 2018.[62]

At least until early 2018, there had been no serious attempt to recouple legal and undocumented immigration.[63] Then the president and other members of his administration launched an attack on several core elements of the system of legal immigration that had been constructed since 1965, in particular the system of family visas, which account for more than 70 percent of US entries each year. No legislation had been proposed as of March 2018, but at least until now, all attempts to limit legal immigration, as well as the general framework of legal immigration established in 1965, have been unsuccessful.

Policy on undocumented immigration, however, has taken a far harder turn in the United States. By 1990, immigration legislation that dealt with legal immigration had been separated from legislation that dealt both with refugees and with illegal immigration. Daniel Tichenor argues that one important impact of the SCIRP report was to make it far more difficult for restrictionists to use one against the other.[64] Instead, the challenge to entry has centered on undocumented immigrants. What has largely gone unnoticed is that all three failed proposals for immigration reform contained modifications of visa categories for legal immigration that *increased* overall immigration ceilings, including those for family visas.[65] Generally, the inflows of legal migration have been consistent with the objectives of policy on both sides of the Atlantic.

Undocumented Entries

A second, perhaps inevitable outcome of policies on legal entry is the question of undocumented entry. Politically, the most important indicator of the failure of border controls is undocumented immigration and the presence of large numbers of unauthorized migrants within a country. Of course, estimating the number of undocumented migrants in any country is a formidable task, which always comes with political overtones. The task is complicated by a lack of any good way of knowing how many illegal immigrants have left the country. The difficulty is fully elaborated in the comparative report for the European Commission, *Clandestino Project.*[66]

At least until the surge of asylum seekers into Europe after 2011, the estimates of the annual entry of undocumented immigrants into the EU were far lower than comparable entries into the United States. The resources devoted to the policing of the external borders of Europe were relatively less compared with those of the United States, but unauthorized entries were far fewer (see Figure 3.1).

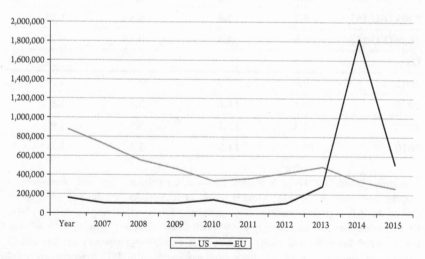

Figure 3.1 Entries of Undocumented Migrants in Europe and the United States. Sources: US Customs and Border Protection, apprehensions, https://www.cbp.gov/newsroom/media-resources/stats; US Department of Homeland Security, Immigration Enforcement, *Annual Flow Reports;* Detections of Illegal Border Crossing, https://www.dhs.gov/immigration-statistics/enforcement-actions; Frontex, *Annual Risk Analysis,* https://frontex.europa.eu/assets/Publications/Risk_Analysis/Annual_Risk_Analysis_2015.pdf.

Both the scholarly and the political estimates for unauthorized migrants resident in Europe are that they are relatively low compared with the United States,
even if we consider variations by country. These estimates vary between 1.9 and
3.8 million for the twenty-seven EU countries in 2008, compared with 11 to
12 million for the United States, relatively close to the more political figures
released by governments during the past decade (see Table 3.1). The estimate
is that undocumented migrants make up at most 0.68 percent of the population
for France (2008), is slightly higher than in Germany (.61% in 2010) and lower
than Britain (approximately 1.4% in 2008), and far lower than that of the United
States (3.8% of the population). Indeed, current estimates from France (2015)
indicate a decline in the unauthorized population. The only country in Europe
that compares with the United States is Greece.[67]

Until recently, the stock of undocumented migrants in Europe appeared
to have been declining (by at least 40%), both at the European level and

Table 3.1 **Estimates of Undocumented Immigrant Populations, 2002–2010**

Year	Population in Millions		As % of Population	
	Minimum	Maximum	Minimum	Maximum
EU				
2002 (EU 15)	3.1	5.3	0.8	1.4
2005 (EU 15)	2.2	4.8	0.58	1.23
2008 (EU 27)	1.9	3.8	0.39	0.77
US				
2002	9.0	9.9	2.9	3.2
2005	10.6	11.6	3.5	3.8
2008	11.1	12.1	3.6	3.9
2010	10.7	11.7	3.5	3.8

Sources: Clandestino Research Project, European Commission, "Size and Development of
Irregular Migration to the EU," October 2009, http://irregular-migration.net/typo3_upload/
groups/31/4.Background_Information/4.2.Policy_Briefs_EN/ComparativePolicyBrief_
SizeOfIrregularMigration_Clandestino_Nov09_2.pdf; Pew Hispanic Center, "Unauthorized
Immigrant Population: National and State Trends, 2010," http://www.pewhispanic.org/2011/02/01/
unauthorized-immigrant-population-brnational-and-state-trends-2010/. For a comprehensive analysis
and explanation of these estimates, see Vesela Kovacheva and Dita Vogel, "The Size of the Irregular
Foreign Resident Population in the European Union in 2002, 2005 and 2008: Aggregated Estimates,"
International Migration 49(5), 2011, pp. 78–96. The estimates presented here are considerably higher
than those given by Eurostat (about 500,000 for the same time period): http://ec.europa.eu/eurostat/
statistics-explained/index.php/File:Non-EU_citizens_apprehended_and_found_to_be_illegally_
present_in_the_five_most_affected_EU_Member_States,_2008-2016_(number)_MI17.png.

among most of the member states. The most notable exception was the United Kingdom, where the clearing of backlogs of asylum seekers resulted in a sharp increase due to a change in status of some people. An increase in the stock of undocumented migrants in Europe, however, has been driven by the spike in entries of asylum seekers, which peaked in 2015 (see chapter 4, Figure 4.1). By 2016, the peak of 1.8 million entries had dropped to just over half a million, far higher than it had been in 2009 (104,000), but dramatically lower than the peak in 2015.

The most important change during the past decade has been the changing balance between unauthorized migrants present because they entered illegally, and those who overstayed their visas. In Europe, both scholars and government officials have argued that the vast majority of illegal migrants entered legally, and then overstayed their visitor or work visas (90%, according to some estimates).[68] More than two-thirds of Frontex detections monitored since 2008 have been for "illegal stay" (and have been detected inland) rather than "detections of illegal border crossing."[69] In the United States, the estimates of the percentage of visa overstayers have been much lower, about 40 percent of the stock of unauthorized migrants. However, as the number of illegal entries declined on both sides of the Atlantic, the relative importance of visa overstayers increased.

In the United States, the undocumented immigrant population peaked around 2007, somewhat diminished, then began to increase slightly in 2012.[70] The increase reflects the steady increase in visa overstayers among the total of unauthorized arrivals each year since the 1990s. Almost 60 percent of the flow of undocumented migrants in the United States in 2013 entered legally through air and sea ports of entry and overstayed the limit of their visas; this was double the percentage of the 1990s. As the number of entries without inspection (EWI), or illegal entries, began to drop dramatically after 2000 (from a peak of 675,000 to an estimated 150,000 in 2013), the number of estimated overstayers also declined, but much more modestly. After 2008, the overstayers entering the ranks of the undocumented exceeded those of the EWIs.[71] As a result of this changing balance of entries, the Pew Hispanic Center estimates that almost 50 percent of those now present in the United States illegally entered legally through various ports of entry. This percentage is continuing to increase, and perhaps was as high as 66 percent in 2014.[72]

Thus, in both cases there are emerging trends: the most vulnerable part of the border is increasingly the internal frontier, where those overstaying short-term visitor or work visas are the typical undocumented migrants. In both Europe and the United States, resources for policing of the border have been increased. However, there remains a substantial difference between Europe and the United States.

Death at the Border

Another, perhaps also inevitable, outcome of entry policy and border control has been death at the border. Even if Europe and the United States are not fortresses, entry policies have meant that their frontiers cannot be freely crossed. One measure of the gap between the push and the pull of entry has been the level of death at the border. Although the land borders of the United States have become far more fortified than those of Europe, the external border of Europe is far more dangerous than that of the United States, as measured by the number of deaths at the border (see Table 3.2). The use of enhanced capabilities to keep people out has inevitably resulted in an increase of deaths among those seeking to enter. European governments have not kept consistent, detailed records of deaths among those seeking to cross into Europe by sea or land, but nongovernmental organizations (NGOs) have made estimates of fatalities based mostly on media reports. By these estimates, there has been a dramatic increase of fatalities toward stunning levels since 2010. Until 2001, the estimates were five hundred or less per year. The number of deaths then began to rise, to around 1,500 to 2,500 by 2011.

The US Border Patrol has reported the recovery of the bodies of at least three hundred or more migrants every year on the US side of the Mexican border since 2000, but these numbers have risen considerably since 2005, and have varied between 350 and over 500, even as apprehensions have declined. The total estimated deaths over a fifteen-year period have been almost four times higher in Europe than they have in the United States. Despite increases of resources at the border (see chapter 5), particularly at the sea borders in the Mediterranean, there have been increasingly high death levels among those attempting to make the crossing into Europe.

Table 3.2 **Estimates of Migrant Border-Related Deaths**

Region	Number of Estimated Deaths	Years	Source
The US–Mexican border	6,029	1998–2013	US Border Patrol
The external borders of Europe	22,394	2000–2014	International Organization for Migration Files

Source: Tara Brian and Frank Laczko, *Fatal Journeys: Tracking Lives Lost during Migration* (Geneva: International Organization for Migration, 2014), p. 24.

Conclusions

Policy on entry into the United States and Europe has differentiated among categories of entry: immigration, free movement (within Europe), and asylum seekers and refugees. Each of these policies has a different basis in law, and a different administration of entry. What they have in common is that the policy trend has been toward increasing restriction.

The joutcomes of these policies have been more consistent with stated objectives than is generally acknowleged. Their success in promoting or preventing change has inevitably varied, in part because the policy choices were sometimes in conflict with market forces. For example, the long US battle to close the border with Mexico was in conflict with the longtime pattern of migratory circulation that was supported on both sides of the border. In the two chapters that follow, I will examine the gap between policies and outcomes, how policies are applied on the ground, and why the politics of policymaking has made the border more, not less important.

4

The Shaping of Policy

A nation without borders is not a nation. There must be a wall across
the southern border.[1]

In chapter 3, I explored the patterns of policies governing border control in
Europe and the United States. Although the heated rhetoric around immigration
has sometimes indicated otherwise, policy objectives in Europe and the United
States have never been simply to exclude migrants. Policies reflect intentions to
control migration patterns across the variable border, and to shape and constrain
how the border actually functions. In this chapter I will examine how the implementation of border controls reshapes policy on the ground.

Donald Trump's assertion during the US presidential campaign of 2016 (see
the chapter epigraph) is the echo of a wide-ranging debate by scholars of international relations. The ability of the state to control the border has often been
seen as a political litmus test of state authority more generally. The question that
James Hollifield asks about immigration, for example, specifically implies control over the border as the essence of sovereignty:

> Given public opposition to immigration and the attempt by states to
> gain greater control over entry of foreign nationals, how can we explain
> the persistence of immigration? . . . from the standpoint of national se-
> curity and international relations, the first and most obvious problem
> is that of sovereignty. The legitimacy of the state would be threatened
> were it unable to exercise control of its borders.[2]

The meaning and usefulness of border policies becomes more evident as I examine patterns of control and enforcement, and how they are related to policies.
Of course it is important to begin with what we might address as the inevitable
gap between policies and enforcement outcomes. The problem is indicated
by the literature on control over administrative agents, and the scholarship on
the relationship between bureaucratic agents and the interests of those they

administer that I analyzed in chapter 1. This literature argues that enforcement agents maintain a considerable degree of discretion because of their relationship with the subjects of enforcement. Therefore, it is not surprising that there is often some gap between policy objectives and the outcomes of border control. Administrative patterns set the priorities of policy that I analyzed in chapter 3. These patterns also indicate ways in which policies are not enforced, and those that are enforced with a limited basis in formal law.[3]

4.1 Pressure on the Border: Where and Who

How open or closed are the frontiers of Europe and the United States? As I argued in chapter 2, patterns of long-term immigration appear to be related more to the economy than to restrictive legislation (see Table 2.1). By most measures, immigration of TCNs into the EU has declined since 2007, while immigration into the United States has remained stable in recent years (see Table 2.1). Although the numbers seem clear, scholars and serious journalists who have written about immigration have disagreed most about the effectiveness of immigration control. The question is whether borders are effectively controlled, whether policy is beneficial, and whether the objectives of policy are being achieved. Paul Scheffer, a Dutch sociologist, and Christopher Caldwell, a journalist, pose deep questions about the unanticipated challenges of immigration and integration, and document the failures of control on both sides of the Atlantic.[4] Other scholars, focusing on securitization of the border, have made a case for a growing "fortress" Europe and America, in effect arguing that enforcement is increasingly oppressive and effective (see chapter 1).[5]

In fact, if we examine where and how immigrants have been accepted and rejected, the picture is more complicated. Our focus in this chapter is not on where migrants are admitted, but where they are refused admission. I use rejection as an indicator of pressure on the border. Refusal rates indicate either unsuccessful attempts by migrants who do not meet the legal criteria to enter, or more intensive enforcement of these criteria by border authorities. In either case, refusal is where the boots of border enforcement meet the ground of the border.

I will argue that control appears to be effective on both sides of the Atlantic, but that nevertheless, a large number of migrants have gained access for long-term residence. Effective controls have shaped migration, but have permitted large numbers of immigrants to enter from year to year. Most decision-making on entry has been externalized to countries of origin, where most people desiring to enter are granted visas. Other decisions are made at (or within) the border, but they are usually made at airports, where controls are most effective. Finally, most rejections are at land and sea ports, in part because these applications for admission are made for asylum, which is governed by more demanding rules and a different process. However, border pressure varies among land and sea ports, both in Europe and the United States.

Where?

The shaping of immigration policy begins with where decisions on entry are made. Rejection is the most active way that a state uses to control its borders, but how many people are actually refused entry to Europe and the United States? Migrants enter Europe and the United States through a series of decision-making gates, each with different patterns of administration, and each in a different space relative to the border. In fact, each gate is a part of the variable border.

Somewhere Else

Both Europe and the United States enforce entry policy first by controlling exit directly from most sending countries through visa distribution, and then by enforcing these visas at ports of entry. In Europe, short-term travel visas valid for ninety days are issued for entry and travel by consulates outside of Europe, and sometimes at the borders of all of the Schengen countries. Visas for long stays ("D" visas), however, are also issued by individual countries at their consulates abroad, according to their own rules for entry and residence.[6] Table 4.1 indicates that rates of rejection for long-term visas in countries of origin are somewhat lower than those for the United States. What is most striking, however, is that the actual number of visa applications and acceptances is almost four times higher for Europe.

Consistent with the "island model" of enforcement, the rates of refusal for immigrant visas for the United States were about 18 percent each year between 2008 and 2010.[7] However, real US refusal rates were somewhat lower, since there are no formal visa limits for immediate family of citizens and legal residents living in the United States, and these entries account for over a third of immigration each year. These numbers are not counted in the figures for Table 4.1 for the United States, but family entries are counted in the figures for EU countries.[8]

With far higher numbers of applicants for Europe, the refusal of long-term "D" visas in countries of origin were about 14 to 15 percent in 2008, and then declined slightly as the economic crisis set in. Because each EU member state issues long-term visas through its own procedures, there has been considerable variation of rejection rates at consulates, with Spain and France on the low end

Table 4.1 **Visa Applications in Consulates (Thousands) and Percent Rejected (Long-Term "D" and Equivalent)**

	EU*	% Reject	US	% Reject
2008	3,197.6	15.5	577.4	18.6
2009	3,241.2	15	575.6	18.6
2010	3,368.3	13.4	585.1	17.6

Source: **US**: US Department of State, Bureau of Consular Affairs, 2008–2014, Report of the Visa Office, Tables I and XX, http://travel.state.gov/content/visas/english/law-and-policy/statistics/annual-reports/report-of-the-visa-office-2010.html. EU: Calculated from data in EMN, *Visa Policy as Migration Channel* (Brussels: European Commission, 2012), pp. 13–14.

* Although they provide for entry of TCNs, the purpose of "D" visas in Europe varies from country to country. See EMN, *Visa Policy*, pp. 23–27. EU data on visas limited to these years. Also see Bernd Parusel and Jan Schneider, *Visa Policy as Migration Channel* (Berlin: German Federal Office for Migration and Refugees, 2012), Table 3; *Visa Policy as Migration Channel, Spain* (Madrid: Permanent Observatory for Immigration, 2011), p. 59; *UK Entry Clearance, Visa Applications and Resolution by Category* (London: Home Office, UK Immigration Statistics, 2014), Table be-02.

*This total is about 30% higher than other government figures in UK *Official Statistics: Entry Clearance Visas by Length*, 2014 (London: Home Office, UK Immigration Statistics, 2014), https://www.gov.uk/government/publications/entry-clearance-visas-by-length/entry-clearance-visas-by-length, p. 3; *Les Chiffres de la politique de l'immigration et de l'intégration, 2011* (Paris: la Documentation Française, 2012), p. 20.

and Germany and the United Kingdom on the high end. However, particularly if we account for family entries in the United States, it does not appear to be more difficult to obtain an entry visa for the United States than for Europe.

The Border Is Here

Among the applicants for entry indicated in Table 4.2, many have already received visas. Nevertheless, as we can also see in Table 4.2, rejections at the borders of Europe have been generally higher than those for the United States.

The most important difference between Europe and the United States was the beginning of the movement of refugees across the Mediterranean in 2010 and 2011, and then across land borders in Eastern Europe after 2013. Normally most crossings into the EU through its external border had been through airports, but by 2014 there was mounting evidence that land entries had become far more important than before.[9] As the pressure of this movement began to build there was a marked decline of the rejection rate for those who were officially processed, a pattern that appeared to be different from the past, when increases in demands for asylum resulted in increased rejection rates.[10]

Table 4.2 **Rejection at the External Border for TCNs**

	2008	*2010*	*2011*	*2014*
Applications at border				
EU TCN	1,873,481	1,754,389	1,743,678	1,860,748
US	1,331,805	1,272,945	1,276,648	1,194,533*
Italy TCN applications				
for admission	143,964	177,400	155,209	122,949
UK TCN applications				
for admission	330,801	337,994	329,764	302,645
Spain TCN applications				
for admission	858,281	446,031	381,248	277,089
Rejections at border				
EU TCN	636,330	396,115	344,165	286,805
US	224,705	231,045	215,248	204,633*
Italy TCN rejections	6405	4215	8635	7005
UK TCN rejections	23,640	16,365	16,150	15,905
Spain TCN rejections	510,010	290,045	227,655	172,185
Rejection rates				
EU	34.0%	22.6%	19.7%	15.4%
US	16.9%	18.2%	16.9%	17.1%*
Italy rejection rates	4.4	2.4	5.6	5.7
UK rejections	7.1	4.8	4.9	5.2
Spain rejection rates	59.4	65.0	59.7	62.1

TCN applications are estimated from Eurostat data in the following way: total admissions – admissions of migrants with European citizenship + number of rejections. For both Europe and the US, applications are calculated as long-term admissions + rejections at the border. Rejection rates are rejections as a percentage of long-term applicants.

Source: **US**: Lisa Seghetti, "Border Security: Immigration Inspections at Ports of Entry," US Congressional Research Service, January 26, 2015, pp. 15–16; and US Customs and Border Protection reports, https://www.cbp.gov/document/annual-report. Organization for Economic Cooperation and Development statistics, https://stats.oecd.org/. **EU**: Data from Eurostat data explorer, European Commission, Eurostat Database for the European Union, http://appsso.eurostat.ec.europa.eu/nui/;.http://epp.eurostat.ec.europa.ey/portal/page/portal/statistics/search_database.

*Data from 2013

However, higher rejection patterns in Europe can be accounted for by patterns at localized land borders. Eighty percent or more of those who are refused entry to Europe each year are turned away from land entry points, with relatively few at airports and fewer yet at seaports. The pattern of land rejections has been set primarily by Spain, and in this sense the Spanish land border has been the most important border in Europe in terms of blocking entry. Although its rejection rates for long-term visas at consulates abroad has been one of the lowest in Europe (less than 5 percent),[11] Spain contradictorily rejects entry at the highest rate in Europe.

Just as the United Kingdom and Italy have been exceptional in terms of easy entry at the border, Spain has been exceptional in terms of patterns of rejection. Between 2007 and 2011 (the beginning and the beginning of the end of the financial crisis, which was particularly severe in Spain), the vast majority of those turned away from European borders were rejected in Spain—for the most part at their North African enclaves of Ceuta and Melilla (see Table 4.3). The best way to understand the unique Spanish case is that Spain remains the only EU country with part of its territory on the south side of the Mediterranean. Ceuta and Malila remain a consistent target for economic migrants, as well as those fleeing the violence and disorder to the south and the east of these Spanish enclaves.

As requests for entry at the borders of the Spanish enclaves diminished between 2007 and 2012, rejections at other EU land borders—particularly those of Poland and Greece—began to increase. In 2012, Poland rejected for entry almost 30,000 applicants, all but a few hundred by land. By 2015, Poland accounted for more than 10 percent of TCNs refused entry to the EU. Similarly, Greece rejected almost 10,000 also, almost all by land. For both Poland and Greece, these rejections represented increases of more than 100 percent of what they had been in 2008. Nevertheless, Spain still remained the most important land bastion of Europe.

Table 4.3 **Entries and Rejections at the Spanish Borders**

TCNs	*2008*	*2010*	*2011*	*2014*
Total entries into Spain	348,271	155,986	153,593	104,904
% of all TCN entries into EU	28.2%	11.5%	10.9%	6.7%
Total rejections at Spanish borders	510,010	290,045	227,655	172,185
% of all rejections at EU borders	80.1%	73.2%	66.1%	60.0%

Source: Data from Eurostat data explorer, European Commission, *Eurostat* Database for the European Union, http://appsso.eurostat.ec.europa.eu/nui/.http://epp.eurostat.ec.europa.ey/portal/page/portal/statistics/search_database.

Overall, since 2008, the fall in the number of TCNs rejected at all European borders can be accounted for by diminishing rejections at land borders. By 2012 these rejections were half what they had been four years before. In part, this can be accounted for by the fall in the rejection rate at the Spanish border, which was reduced by more than 60 percent. Given the relatively small number of legal entries into the European area by sea, even the spikes of entries into Italy in 2011–2012, and since had only a small impact on the overall pattern of declining rejection rates.

For most countries in Europe, the consulates are overwhelmingly the principle gates of entry, but not the only ones. In 2010, 4.9 percent of TCNs were refused entry at border crossings (mostly at airports) into France, about a quarter for invalid residence permits or visas.[12] The percentage of refusal of visa applications at consulates, however, was more than double that (9.8 percent). Similarly, the rejection rate for visas at the borders of the United Kingdom was 3.8 percent in 2010, compared with 15.5 percent at consulates.

Differences in visa rejection rates can also be attributed to national policies in the sense that different countries attempt to use visa policy as a tool to manage entry for different purposes and different priorities. The United Kingdom has prioritized entry for work, family, and study, roughly in that order; France has attempted to attract highly skilled immigrants; and, more recently, Italy has used long-term visas for humanitarian purposes for migrants arriving from North Africa, or perhaps to supply these arrivals with papers with which they can then move on to France or Germany.[13]

The policies, however, are clearer than the results. In part because visa policy provides only incentives and disincentives, it has only partial control over outcomes of actual immigration. Follow-up studies for a large project on visa policy reveal correlations between the liberalization for visas from some countries (presumably those from which there is significant demand) and the flow from there, but not for others.[14] Not surprisingly, visa policies meant to prevent entry are more effective than those meant to attract migrants. Moreover, what countries say they want (or do not want) is often very different from what they get. The British say that they want skilled migrants who contribute to the economy; in practice, they have gotten entry for study, work, and family, in that order. The French want the same, but only a small proportion of visa entries into France are highly skilled immigrants, and the largest proportion is generally for family unification.[15]

The difference in total rejection rates, however, seems to be more of a function of where migrants arrive. In those countries in which migrants arrive principally at airports, there are relatively low rejection rates, which reflect the success of prescreening of visas in their home countries, and the difficulty of boarding an aircraft without valid papers. In those few countries where migrants arrive by sea and land, rejection rates are high.

But where migrants arrive is often related to why they claim entry. Those who arrive by land and sea in Europe most often claim to be seeking asylum, and their numbers tend to reflect the pressures from evolving wars and failed states. Few are refused entry because they do not have a valid visa or residency permit or valid travel documents, the most important criteria for legal entry.[16] In fact, for most of those who are refused entry at land borders, no clear reason is given by border authorities.

Border authorities have often argued that large numbers of migrants who are refused entry then apply for asylum. If this were true, then an increase of refusal for entry should be followed by an increase in applications for asylum. However, between 2008 and 2015 refusal of entry declined from 635,000 to 298,000 in Europe, and the rates of rejection fell by half; at the same time, applications for asylum tripled, from 222,000 to 627,000. Rather than being related to the normal fluctuation of acceptance and rejection rates at the border, this increase of asylum applications appears to have reflected the breakdown of state authority in Africa and the Middle East. The documented rejection patterns at the borders in the United States are similar to those in Europe. Rejection is also concentrated overwhelmingly at the land and sea borders with Mexico and Canada (about 79 percent).[17] Fewer than 20 percent of applicants are rejected at airports from year to year. And, as in Europe, where migrants arrive is often related to why they arrive. Aside from the continuing issues of undocumented migrants, which I will discuss later, many of those who have arrived at the southern border of the United States have claimed asylum from rising levels of violence in Central America. As in Europe, increasing numbers of asylum seekers have driven a changing political debate about immigration, as some political leaders have attempted to differentiate issues of immigration from those of asylum.

But why and how does it matter where decisions on entry are made? On the European side, decisions on entry vary considerably from country to country. While in general the rates of rejection for visas in consulates of sending countries in Europe are lower in those of the United States, these rates are far from uniform. For example, rejection rates of the United Kingdom, Germany, and France tend to hover around the European mean of 15 percent, while Poland and the Slovak Republic refuse fewer than 2 percent of visa applicants.

Rejections, however, provide only part of the picture; the absolute number of acceptances may be important as well. The United Kingdom has issued the greatest number of long-term visas among the EU countries, almost 2 million in 2009, for example. Italy stands out in the same way. It reviewed 1.5 million applications at consulates in 2009, but rejected only 4.8 percent. The United

Kingdom also stands out as one of three EU countries issuing the largest number of residency permits since 2012 (together with Poland and Germany).[18] In addition, both the United Kingdom and Italy have border rejection rates that are far below those of the EU as a whole (see Table 4.2).

In which country migrants seek admission is also important because each admitting country has demonstrated different priorities for admission, priorities that are more evident in the process and results of granting visas and border admission than in legislated rules. For example, although visas for family unification are generally required as a result of court decisions, EU directives, and treaties, we have seen in chapter 3 that policies vary considerably, and we will see in chapters 6 and 7 that applications for family unification have become generally more difficult.[19] Nevertheless, in France, where family unification visas have been under attack as *immigration subie* (unwanted immigration), family remains the primary purpose for entry. In the United Kingdom, where the entry of TCN students has been an important political issue, most visas issued are for education.

Perhaps more to the point, because there are almost no legislated priorities in Europe, the purposes for which visas are given vary radically among different EU countries. Belgium and Sweden strongly favor family visas, while Italy varies, from year to year, between family and employment. The United Kingdom, Poland, and Hungary, on the other hand, grant relatively few visas for family unification, but many for employment.[20] Therefore, where migrants seek entry may be influenced by which criteria they can fulfill, whether they have family ties in one country or another, and whether they have the kinds of work skills that will be favored in one country or another. It may also be influenced by the sharp differences among receiving countries with regard to admissions and rejections of applicants from different sending countries.

Who?

In the previous sections I examined overall visa acceptance and rejection in Europe and the United States. Here I will look more closely at choices that are made on both sides of the Atlantic by receiving states among applicants. Patterns of acceptance and rejection by receiving states often reflect clear choices about applicants from different countries, and may represent an attempt to manage immigration, but not always in ways indicated by official policy. In general, major immigration recipient countries in Europe are most apt to reject applications from most countries in Africa (including North Africa), with Asian and Middle Eastern countries generally ranking second jin rejections (including Turkey; see Table 4.4). Even if we consider visitor visas, applications for only 7 percent of which are rejected by EU states, more than 35 percent

Table 4.4 **Applications and Rejections for Visas in 2010 in Europe and the United States**

	From Africa		From Asia		From Mexico	
	Applications (th.)	Rejections (%)	Applications (th.)	Rejections (%)	Applications (th.)	Rejections (%)
France	497.1	18.3	256.3	4.7	NA	NA
UK	118.8	22	217.4	16.0	NA	NA
Germany	72.3	37.7	53.5	3.3	NA	NA
US	320.9	36.1	2,019.0	28.8	73.7	11.1

For France, the UK, and Germany, the number of applications and the percentage of rejections is for all visas; for the United States, these figures are for visitors' ("B") visas only.

Sources: *Les Chiffres de la Politique de l'Immigration et de l'Intégration, Année 2011* (Paris: la Documentation Française, 2012), pp. 20–27; UK, Home Office, Immigration Statistics, Entry Clearance of Visa Applications and Resolution, by Country and Nationality, https://www.gov.uk/government/publications/immigration-statistics-april-to-june-2013/immigration-statistics-april-to-june-2013; EMN, *Visa Policy as Migration Channel* (Brussels: European Commission, 2012), p. 2; Bernd Parusel and Jan Schneider, *Visa Policy as Migration Channel* (Berlin: German Federal Office for Migration and Refugees, 2012), Tables 9 and 10; US Department of State, Bureau of Consular Affairs, http://travel.state.gov/content/visas/english/law-and-policy/statistics/annual-reports/report-of-the-visa-office-2010.html; http://travel.state.gov/content/dam/visas/Statistics/Non-Immigrant-Statistics/RefusalRates/FY08.pdf.

are rejected for applicants from Pakistan, Afghanistan, Eretria, and Nigeria (see Table 4.5).

2010 French rejection rates are consistently the highest from consulates in Africa, where the rate of rejection is as high as 45 percent in Guinea and 30 percent for Algeria. On the other hand, the rate of rejection of applicants from the United States and Canada hovers around 3 percent. Similarly, the high rejection rates for the United Kingdom in 2010 are largely explained by rejection rates as high as 35 percent for countries in Africa (22 percent on average) and Asia (16 percent), as well as former British colonies in the Caribbean (25 percent). Germany follows a similar pattern (see Table 4.4).

The rejection rates for the United States are similar. Although there are relatively few applications for visas from Africa for entry, the rejection rates tend to be higher than those for Europe. The rates of rejection from Asia are also relatively high, but tend to reflect the very high rates of visa rejection from Pakistan (42%), India (27%), and Bangladesh (36%), as well as the smaller countries from Southeast Asia, rather than China. China accounts for more than 40 percent of visa applications from Asia, about 750,000, with a lower rejection rate of 13 percent.

Table 4.5 **Entering Europe: Short-Term Visa vs. Asylum**

Top 10 Nationalities Claiming Asylum in the EU in 2015 (in Order)	Rejection Rate for Schengen Visitor Visa (2016) %	Rejection Rate for Asylum (2015) %	% Difference in Favor of Asylum or Visa Application
Syria	26.5	5.3	+21.2 Asylum
Afghanistan	39.4	33.0	+6.4 Asylum
Kosovo	19.7	97.4	+77.7 Visa
Eritrea	46.5	11.0	+35.5 Asylum
Serbia	1.3	98.8	+97.5 Visa
Pakistan	35.4	71.5	+36.1 Visa
Iraq	20.7	15.0	+5.7 Asylum
Nigeria	39.4	71.5	+32.1 Visa
Russia	1.2	77.0	+75.8 Visa
Albania	4.2	92.3	+88.1 Visa
EU Average	**6.9**	**53.8**	**+46.9 Visa**

Sources: Visa: https://ec.europa.eu/home-affairs/what-we-do/policies/borders-and-visas/visa-policy#stats; Asylum: Oliver Hawkins, Asylum Statistics, Briefing Paper Number SN01403, UK House of Commons Library, September 23, 2015, Table 7: https://researchbriefings.files.parliament.uk/documents/SN01403/SN01403.pdf.

However, for the United States, the Western Hemisphere is by far the largest source of visa requests, both for visits and for immigration. Over 40 percent of all visas issued in the United States in 2010 were granted to applicants from the Western Hemisphere, and 56 percent of those were issued to applicants from Mexico and the Dominican Republic. Relatively few of these applications are turned down for Mexico (11 percent), but the rate is much higher for the Dominican Republic (31 percent). Much higher rates of rejection are also typical for applicants from Central America and the Caribbean. Most Canadians arriving in the United States benefit from a special visa waiver agreement with the United States, and are able to cross the border with the United States with a secure identity card, and are able to remain for up to six months; Mexicans can obtain a border-crossing card in lieu of a visa for multiple crossings, but it is valid for a more limited stay and more limited travel.[21]

Rejection rates that persist over time indicate a pattern of selection that is not necessarily related to overall immigration policies. Neither the United States nor Europe has a policy of selection by country, although the United States places a ceiling of 7 percent of total immigration each year from any one country. These patterns represent real choices made by state authorities, but they do not tell much about overall openness at the gates, since the rates of entry of migrants into both Europe and the United States are now historically high at a time when the instruments of restriction have grown both more effective and more numerous.

Rates of refusal often have an unanticipated impact, one that is very different from imposing quotas on entry by nationality. French policy rhetoric and rejection rates, for example, indicate an attempt to limit entries from North African countries. They accounted for only 19 percent of total visas granted for entry into France in 2010.[22] Visa applications from North African countries were 21 percent of all demands in 2010, and rejection rates were 27 percent. Nevertheless, actual inflows for long-term stays or settlement for applicants from North Africa in 2010 was 34 percent of those admitted (136,000), the largest single group of entries.[23] Similarly, the United Kingdom rejected 16 percent of visa applicants from Asia in 2010, but Asians still represented 45 percent of all visas issued for entry that year, and almost 30 percent of the actual entries.[24] The gap between the rejection rates for some countries and regions and the high entry rates nevertheless is explained in part by the high volume of applications from these areas.

In general, then, it appears that high rejection rates for visas are a poor indicator of who will actually enter the European border through the external frontiers of the member states. North Africans (Algerians, above all) continue to be the largest group to enter France each year; Indians, Pakistanis, and Chinese immigrants dominate inflows into the United Kingdom; immigrants from Poland and Romania are the largest groups entering Germany, far ahead of the declining number of Turks who enter each year.

Moreover, intra-European migration, over which member states have only limited control, is an important component of those who are considered immigrants within member states. Although the overall flow of intra-European migration is generally a half, or more, each year in Europe (see Table 2.1), in some member states, migration from other European countries tends to dominate. Romanians are among the largest nationality immigrating into Spain, as well as Italy, with TCNs far behind.

This does not mean that visa policy has failed, but it does tell us something about the strength of selection criteria in force, which can limit but not exclude entry from countries of origin. The number of actual entries depends on criteria such as rules of family migration mandated by court decisions, and the volume of applications from each source country.

Here, it is useful to return to return to the question of open borders versus fortress Europe and America. In fact, for those who wish to enter, and are willing to engage in the process, access to Europe and the United States is relatively open, regardless of the political rhetoric on both sides of the Atlantic. The stock of immigrants has continued to grow, and the number of people who legally enter has grown as well. Indeed, from this perspective, Europe and the United States appear to be similar, despite very different policies and vastly different political rhetoric (see Table 4.1).

Migrants who arrive via the asylum route, however, present a more complicated story, primarily because the rules of entry and selection are constrained by treaty and are formally less controlled by national rules of immigration. They are, however, administered nationally.

4.2 How: Asylum

How migrants arrive, and how they define their entry, is particularly important in the case of asylum seekers, since, as we have seen in chapter 3, the rules of entry are quite different for them. In fact, the asylum gate is controlled in a way that is subject not only to external push forces, but also to treaty rules that are relatively open-ended.

The definitions of asylum seekers and refugees are often unclear, and the terms have been confused, often for political purposes. Under the rules summarized by the United Nations High Commissioner for Refugees, an asylum seeker is someone who claims refugee status, " . . . and unable to return to their country owing to a well-founded fear of being persecuted for reasons of race, religion, nationality, membership of a particularly social group, or political opinion." Recognition for asylum is not a grant of refugee status, but it does convey permission to stay. The granting of refugee status is then an acceptance of that status by the state.[25] In this sense, asylum-seekers may be refused entry (or expelled) at several different stages. They may simply be refused entry; they may be refused recognition for asylum, after consideration; they may be refused recognition for refugee status.

Claims for asylum have been seen in two very different ways. On the one hand, these claims have been understood in terms of human rights, and the "shameful unwillingness" of Europe or America to deal with an obvious outpouring from war zones of migrants with little choice.[26]

> When people take their children into leaking rubber dinghies in the dark
> to cross rough seas, knowing how many die every night, there is nothing
> "bogus" about their desperation. Once arrived, restored to dignity as the
> people they were, with stories and families, most with qualifications, we
> see them eye to eye and know them to be people like us.[27]

On the other hand, asylum claims have been seen as simply another way of entering through the restricted border; of using a claim for asylum to seek entry under more favorable rules.[28] As a result of international agreements:

Most states or their courts have articulated complex and lengthy legal procedures for processing and appeal, which make full asylum processing both time-consuming and expensive. When asylum seekers are legitimate refugees, there is little the states can or should want to do about it. This is, however, typically not the case. Recognition rates . . . in Europe rarely exceed 10 percent. Even when including nonconvention statuses, they usually hover around 30 percent and never top 50 percent.[29]

In fact, migration from war zones, as well as individuals from otherwise safe countries who may themselves have a well-founded fear of persecution, present a complex landscape that often varies from the general pattern. If we compare the rates of acceptance of EU visa applicants at consulates abroad and at land, sea, and air border crossings, with the rates of those recognized as asylum seekers, in general, admission by asylum is the most difficult of all routes for entry (see Figures 4.1 and 4.2).

If we focus on visitor visas, by country, which will enable a potential asylum seeker to buy an air ticket, then enter, and perhaps remain as a visa overstayer, the picture is more complicated. In both Europe and the United States, the rejection rate for these visas is generally far lower than the rejection rates for asylum. However, it varies significantly for particular countries. For those trying to enter Europe from Syria, Eritrea and Iraq, claiming asylum appears to be a better alternative, since the rejection rate for short-stay visas is higher than for asylum. For every country in Africa, however, the rejection rate for these visas is far above the 6.9 percent EU average, but the rejection rates for asylum are also well above the average (see Table 4.5).

For the United States, it seems pretty clear that those from countries most at risk outside of the Western Hemisphere, and seeking to enter, are probably better off applying for refugee visas from the United States through the United Nations High Commissioner for Refugees (UNHCR), for which 75 to 80% are granted refugee visas after considerable vetting (see the following section). If we look at the ten countries from which most refugees were admitted in 2015, eight of the ten posted refusal rates for short-stay visas of greater than 40 percen (see Figure 4.2). At least until 2016, the United States, more consistently than Europe, denied vistitor visas, but favored refugee status for those seeking entry through UNHCR (see Table 4.6). Claiming asylum at U.S. borders and within the country is a different story, however, and presents a pattern similar to Europe. Fewer than 20 percent of asylum claims are granted to asylum-seekers from those countries in the Western Hemisphere that make the most claims (El Savador, Honduras, Guatamala and Haiti); but visitor visas are also denied at levels above 40 percent.

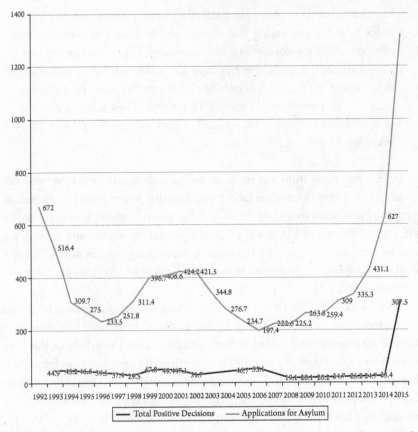

Figure 4.1 EU Applications for Asylum and Number Granted Recognition (thousands), 1992–2015. Source: UNHCR Population Statistics, Data, Asylum Seekers, http://unhcr.org/en/asylum_seekers.

Why, then, has there been a "refugee crisis" that has endured in Europe since 2010, and periodic crises in the United States since 2010? I will argue that the refugee crisis and the surge of migration, while certainly related to world events, have been deeply shaped by policy in Europe and the United States. Although policy has often been understood as reactive, it has also actively created and shaped these crises because of the way that it has defined access for making asylum claims. Both Europe and the United States have established rules and procedures that would enable them to conform to the requirements of international law to which they have agreed. At the same time, they have developed laws and policies to discourage migrants from claiming asylum or refugee status. On both sides of the Atlantic, claims are based on the Convention Relating to the Status of Refugees signed in Geneva in 1951, amended by the Protocol relating to the Status of Refugees of 1967 (see chapter 3).

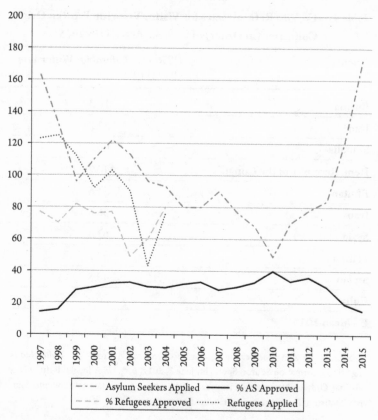

Figure 4.2 Applicants for Asylum and Refugee Settlement in the United States, and Percentage of Asylum Seekers Who Were Approved, Compared with the Percentage of Refugees Approved for Settlement, 1997–2015 (Applications × 1,000). "Approved" means application to and approval by the US Citizenship and Immigration Services (USIC)—an "affirmative" request and approval—or, after removal procedures have begun, approval by an immigration court of the Executive Office for Immigration Review (EOIR)—a "defensive" request. Generally, affirmative requests are granted more often than defensive requests. Sources: William A. Kandel and Ruth Ellen Wasem, *U.S. Immigration Policy: Chart Book of Key Trends* (Washington, DC: Congressional Research Service, March 14, 2016), p. 10; Department of Homeland Security, *2015 Yearbook of Immigration Statistics*, Table 16, https://www.dhs.gov/immigration-statistics/yearbook/2015; UNHCR, *Asylum Trends in Industrialized Countries*, Table 1, "Asylum Applications Submitted in Europe and Selected Non-European Countries," http://popstats.unhcr.org/en/asylum_seekers_monthly.

But the question is, how does one make a claim? Essentially, for most claimants, you must be in to get in. For the claimant there must be someplace to arrive, and for the state to which the demand is being made, there must be someplace to receive and process the application. Logically, that place should be ports of entry, and indeed border police at two of the main airports in France

Table 4.6 **US Visa Refusal Rates for Visitor Visas for Top Ten Origin Countries (in Order) of Refugee Arrivals in 2015**

Country	US Rate of Refusal for Visitor Visa (B1/2) (%)
Burma	16.3
Iraq	52.8
Somalia	64.6
Dem. Republic of the Congo	40.7
Bhutan	54.6
Iran	38.6
Syria	63.4
Eritrea	55.7
Sudan	40.5
Cuba	76
US Mean 2015	23.4

Sources: Jie Zong and Jeanne Batalova, *Refugees and Asylees in the United States*, Migration Information Source, Spotlight, June 7, 2017, p. 6; US Adjusted Refusal Rate - B-Visas Only by Nationality, Fiscal Year 2015, http://travel.state.gov/content/dam/visas/Statistics/Non-Immigrant-Statistics/RefusalRates/FY15.pdf.

and the United Kingdom argue that since there is no penalty for dubious claims for asylum, claims are routine among migrants who are detained and have exhausted all other means of entry.[30]

Nevertheless, the UK Home Office has documented that in 2012 the percentage of claims made at ports of entry was only 12 percent of all claims, and that percentage had been declining since 2001.[31] The French Ministry of the Interior has also acknowledged that their main process for dealing with migrants in "irregular situations," who claim regularization either for asylum or for other reasons (generally, visa overstayers), is at local prefectures. The ministry points out that restrictions on applications were significantly eased with an administrative circulaire of November 28, 2012. The circulaire specifies a number of exceptions to the existing legal restrictions on regularization (particularly for private and family life), and in some significant ways makes it easier to demonstrate a need to remain.[32]

Indeed, the difficulty facing asylum seekers is magnified by need to enter the country without valid documents, or to remain with invalid documents before demanding asylum. Inevitably, this relates the question of asylum to illegal immigration. Italian and Greek authorities were severely criticized by the British and French governments for not adequately blocking the entry of thousands of asylum seekers by sea and land in 2013 (see chapter 5). However, it appears that neither the United Kingdom nor France has been able to prevent claimants from passing through their ports of entry. In the French case, this is partially related to the more porous Schengen border with Italy, at least after 2011, but this cannot explain the British case.

The accepted rules make it difficult to demonstrate a well-founded fear of persecution to justify recognition; however, once an asylum seeker has crossed the border to make a claim, expulsion by the state is difficult as well. Therefore, receiving states have generally made access difficult, and claimants have attempted simply to gain access, even if their claims are weak or if they are economic migrants. Receiving states tend to define claimants, as much as possible, as economic migrants or simply as undocumented migrants; claimants define themselves, as much as possible, as people who are fleeing something. However, in this competition for framing, the states have the advantage.

Asylum in Europe

Almost all claims for asylum in Europe are made within the borders of member states, primarily because in both Europe and the United States carrier sanctions imposed on airlines (and shipping lines) permit only passengers with valid travel documents, such as passports and valid visas, to board. In the case of the EU, these prohibitions are enshrined in Article 26 of the Convention implementing the Schengen Agreement, as well as the Council Directive of 2001 to harmonize carrier sanctions. The directive notes that it is "without prejudice to the obligations resulting from the Geneva Convention," but clearly states that its objective is aimed at "curbing migration flows and combatting immigration."[33]

In effect, it aims to do for asylum what remote control does for immigration, but it is far stronger. It is meant to prevent asylum claims from reaching the borders of member states, and ensures that the route to these claims for TCNs is both expensive and dangerous. Since 1986, there have been proposals in Europe for the establishment of external processing centers in the sending countries, or the regions from which asylum seekers originate. One proposal—a British proposal in 2003—also recommended that asylum seekers be sent to closed reception centers in one or two member states, from which, if recognized, they would be distributed among other EU countries. None of these proposals was ever enacted, although the agreements between Italy and Libya in 2004 and 2009, and the Spanish agreements with Morocco, Senegal, Mauretania, and Cape Verde during the same period, were meant to prevent asylum seekers from reaching European shores.[34]

In fact, the movement of asylum seekers into Europe has been strongly influenced by Turkish passenger restriction on air and sea travel. Until January 2016, Syrian citizens were able to enter Turkey from Syria, Jordan, or Lebanon without having to obtain a visa beforehand, making Turkey the primary first destination for entry into Europe. This was then rescinded by the Turkish government.[35]

More recently the Macron government opened a small French mission in Niger, below the border with Libya, to review applications for asylum. Even before the mission was opened, the flow from Africa into Libya had reversed, with more migrants moving south than moving north. The French effort appeared to be only one of several member states' attempts to further externalize applications for asylum, with the cooperation of the UN International Office for Migration. The UN effort was also focused on moving asylum seekers out of a more dangerous situation in Libya.[36] Of course, it would be far less expensive and far less dangerous if those seeking asylum were able simply to buy an air ticket and board a plane.

Claims for asylum can also be registered with the UNHCR, and most refugees accepted by the United States gain access in this way. In Europe, however, only Norway has accepted a significant number of these as refugees.

Beyond carrier sanctions, during operations to interdict small craft on the high seas, such as Frontex Operation Trident in 2014, followed by Operation Sophia (both of which I will analyze in the next chapter), migrants "are treated as if they were all illegal immigrants. No provision is made for the potential asylum seekers amongst them, which can lead to situations where the EU member states do not fully respect their international obligations."[37] For both Europe and the United States, this is certainly true if those who are intercepted are forced to return to their port or country of origin because they lack proper papers to enter.

Why, then, is there a crisis of asylum in Europe? As I noted in chapter 3, in Europe the Dublin Regulation mandated that the claims would be made in the first member state country in which the claimant arrived. For those arriving by land or sea, only a few of the member states would be responsible for resolving these claims. Although the EU agreed on some guidelines for making these decisions, they would finally be made by national authorities, using national criteria.

However, the presumption behind the Geneva Convention and the Dublin Regulation was always that the number of asylum seekers would remain relatively small, and that crisis situations would be dealt with through special agreements. Indeed, before 2010, each time that there had been a large inflow of asylum seekers there was either an international conference to deal with issues of distribution, or the passage of special legislation to deal with the real or anticipated flood. The asylum movement that has developed since 2010 has been the most important worldwide movement of population since the postwar period of 1945–1952, but there has not been any international conference to set out an international plan. Even within Europe, proposals made by the European Commission have not been implemented. As Randall Hansen sums it up:

> The world is facing a global refugee crisis unprecedented since the 1945–1952 period, when nation-state formation and the shifting of national borders provoked the flight or expulsion of tens of millions of people. There are currently at least 19.5 million refugees globally; by 2014, 3.8 million people had fled Syria alone. Overall, there were by mid-2015 59.5 million forcibly displaced persons worldwide, a historical high. It is a humanitarian disaster of immense proportions.[38]

For Europe, the numbers alone do not convey the impact. The root of the crisis has been the rapidity with which migrants have arrived. As we can see from Figure 4.1, the number of asylum applications to Europe in 2014 was about the same as in 1992, at the height of the wars in the former Yugoslavia. After 2014, however, the number of applicants doubled, and the number of applicants that were granted recognition and leave to stay in Europe increased by a factor of twelve. Well before decisions were made on recognition, 1.3 million claimants in 2015 were within the borders of the EU, having arrived by perilous and expensive journeys by sea and land.

Even before the spike of arrivals in 2015 there was a "wind of panic," as the European press was filled with stories of hundreds of deaths by migrants attempting to cross the Mediterranean every week (see Table 3.2).[39] In 2015 alone, 3,771 were registered as having died crossing the Mediterranean, a record for a single year.

This surge of asylum has generally been seen as the source of the destabilization of the European system of border control. However, this is a crisis that has been brewing since the inception of the Dublin system, indeed before. As the novelist John Le Carré described the years before 1989:

> For five years the refugees of Eastern Europe had been pouring into Austria through every fast-closing gap in the barbed wire: crashing frontiers in Skoda cars and lorries, across minefields, clinging to the undercarriages of trains. . . . They came from Hungary and Romania and Poland and Czechoslovakia and Yugoslavia and sometimes Russia, and they hoped they were on their way to Canada and Australia and Palestine. They had travelled by devious routes and often for devious reasons. They were doctors and scientists and bricklayers. They were treacherous thieves, acrobats, publishers, rapists and architects.[40]

Now these East European countries themselves had become the gateway for those seeking asylum in Europe and beyond, and, although Le Carré's description of their journey looks hauntingly applicable to this new wave, these refugees have been met with increasingly militant rejection. The new surge did not create the problem, but it did magnify the weaknesses of the border control system that had been there all along. The institutional structures, regulations, and rules that were constructed under the Schengen and Dublin agreements have been dependent on one another, but they have never quite worked, and, indeed, lacked an enforcement mechanism.

Although the Dublin regulations noted in chapter 3 established an obligation of countries of first arrival to register asylum seekers, this obligation was limited in time, and made provision for other countries to register asylum seekers residing in those member states.[41] In addition, there was no legal obligation on the part of the asylum seeker to register in the first country of arrival, and in practice, those who arrive have had considerable control over where they register their applications. Even before the surge, more than 20 percent of asylum claims in the EU were made in Germany and Sweden, far from the external border of Europe. By 2012, claims in these two countries alone comprised 38 percent of those in the EU, and by 2015, almost half.

At first, most of the vast number of migrant arrivals by sea who touched down in Italy made their way north, some to France, but most to Germany and Austria and Sweden. Applications for asylum in Italy steadily increased as well, as France and Austria reinstituted controls at their Schengen borders. By 2015 Greece had become the most frequent entry point to Europe, but most of the migrants who came by land and sea to Greece also moved on, and the number of applications in Greece remained steady between 2010 and 2015.

As the migration pattern shifted from Italy as a first point of entry to Greece, and then on to the Balkans, Hungary became the center of the land migration in 2014–2015. Relative to the size of the population, Hungary had the largest number of asylum applicants in the EU (Sweden was second, ahead of Austria and Germany). Normally, Hungary would have been required to register, recognize, or reject these applicants. However, the Orban government quickly decided to build a secure fence on the border with Serbia in 2015 to prevent entry into Hungary; the prime minister then announced plans to reinforce and extend the barrier in 2016.[42] He also rejected EU Commission plans for distribution of asylum seekers among EU countries, in order to alleviate the pressure on those countries responsible for the external borders of Europe.

Most of the twenty-eight countries of the EU remained only modestly touched by the recent asylum crisis. Asylum applications in the United Kingdom increased only slightly (less than the EU mean), as did those in France, Belgium, and most countries in Eastern Europe.[43] More than 90 percent of the applications for asylum in 2015 can be accounted for by those in Germany, Hungary, Sweden, Italy, and France (in that order). The 33,000 asylum applications in the United Kingdom in 2015 were far below the level of 100,000 in 2002.[44]

In addition, although the increase in asylum applications has been massive and the pressure for asylum has grown, the granting of asylum has remained firmly under the control of member states. As we can see in Figure 4.1, the number of asylum applicants accepted—given refugee status or leave for protection or leave to remain from year to year—has been only a small percentage of those who enter and apply. In 2015, there were about 1.3 million asylum applications made among the EU28. Decisions were made on fewer than half (593,000), of which about 308,000 were granted some form of recognition— about 52 percent of the actual decisions (but only 24 percent of those who applied). These decisions were not all for those who posted their applications in 2015. Nevertheless, this recognition rate has increased substantially, from 22 percent between 2002 and 2006 to 34 percent in 2013 to 52 percent in 2015, a reflection of the outpouring of forced migration from war zones to which it would be difficult to return. Almost 60 percent of formal recognition or grants of protection in Europe in 2014 were given to applicants from Syria (37%), Eritrea, Afghanistan, and Iraq.

Since asylum is decided by each member state, it is important to note that the patterns of acceptance and rejection by member states have been very different. Almost half of the 308,000 grants of recognition in 2015 were in Germany; Sweden, France, Italy, and the Netherlands account for most of the rest. Hungary granted recognition to only 500 applicants (8 percent of those who applied). A decade before, Hungary had granted recognition to 35 percent.[45] Among the countries in Europe which are responsible for the external land and sea access points, only Italy is both the country of first official arrival and the country where large numbers of decisions on recognition have been made.

The core of the Dublin system is the rapid registration of those who seek asylum in the country in which they first touch down, followed by rapid decisions on the validity of their claims. That country, in turn, has had a right to return an asylum seeker to an external country, if that country had been designated a safe third country (STC) or a safe country of origin (SCO).[46] In fact, very few migrants claiming asylum have ever been returned to a second EU country. Requests for "Dublin transfers" increased after 2008, but the percentage of requests actually fulfilled fell from about 25 percent to 10 percent in 2015 (see Table 4.7). Part of the problem is the conflict between Dublin and the requirements of the European Convention on Human Rights. In 2011, the European Court of Human Rights (ECHR) found that Belgium was in violation of the European Convention in attempting to return a refugee from Afghanistan to Greece, because the conditions of detention in Greece violated the ECHR.[47]

Table 4.7 **Total Requests for Outgoing Transfers of Asylum Seekers and Actual Transfers, 2008–2015**

Year	2008	2009	2010	2011	2012	2013	2014	2015
"Outgoing" requests	32,313	51,110	48,363	43,924	53,495	78,612	91,895	131,124
"Outgoing" transfers	7,527	13,840	13,574	12,722	14,409	16,841	14,278	13,348
Percentage transferred	23.3%	27.0%	28.0%	29.0%	26.9%	21.4%	15.5%	10.2%

Source: Eurostat data. Some of these data are summarized in "Dublin Statistics on Countries Responsible for Asylum Application," http://ec.europa.eu/eurostat/statistics-explained/index.php/Dublin_statistics_on_countries_responsible_for_asylum_application. Also see Susan Fratzke, "Not Adding Up: The Fading Promise of Europe's Dublin System" (Brussels: Migration Policy Institute, Europe, 2015), https://www.migrationpolicy.org/research/not-adding-fading-promise-europes-dublin-system.

By 2015, with the vast increase of asylum seekers, the pattern of arrivals to Europe had shifted to sea ports in Italy and land access in the Balkans. Therefore, it is hardly surprising that between 2010 and 2015 Dublin requests for "take-backs" directed to Italy increased four times, and were almost a third of the requests in Europe. Seventy-five percent of these requests originated from just five countries: Germany, Austria, Switzerland, Sweden, and France. These were the primary countries beyond the periphery of Europe to which migrants had moved to claim asylum (mostly from Italy), and these were the countries that invoked the Dublin Regulation on responsibility for the examination and decision of asylum applications.

Even before the onset of the refugee crisis, these requests resulted in few actual transfers—about a third of the transfers indicated earlier went to Italy. Indeed, after 2013 both the number of transfers, as well as the percentage of the "outgoing requests," declined. Much of the problem has been that there is no way to authenticate where migrants had first touched down.

The best tool available is the Eurodac database of asylum seekers. In 2014 it held the fingerprints of almost 2.3 million people, and appeared to be an effective tool for policing the movement of migrants throughout the EU.

The aim of this database is to assist in determining which state is responsible for considering an application for asylum according to the mechanism and criteria set up by the "Dublin Convention." . . . It is therefore an important tool in the development of the Common

European Asylum System called for by the European Council at its meeting in Tampere (Finland), in October 1999.[48]

However, the database depends on prompt insertion of the fingerprints of asylum seekers at their port of entry into the EU, and even when individual data is entered, it has not always been used in an effective manner. Although Eurodac was supposed to prevent asylum shopping, its limits can be seen by the now documented increase in multiple submissions since 2003, and the jump in these submissions since 2010.[49] Indeed, missing Eurodac evidence has sometimes been used to prevent the acceptance of takebacks by member states.[50]

The second pillar of the Dublin system is equally problematic in practice. In theory, an application for asylum should be rejected if the applicant is arriving from an STC or SCO. In fact, the establishment of this cordon sanitaire has been understood as a core element of fortress Europe.[51] In practice, however, the enforcement of the cordon sanitaire for asylum has proven to be difficult at best.[52]

First, there has never been any agreement on which countries constitute the cordon sanitaire. Definitions of what constitutes either have been almost impossible to apply, at least in a way that is consistent with the 1951 Convention.[53] The EU has struggled to develop a common list of safe countries, although each member state is regarded as an SCO by other member states "as regards applications for asylum made by their nationals."[54] After the 2005 Asylum Procedures Directive to adopt a common list was annulled by the European Court of Justice in 2008 on procedural grounds, a new directive was adopted in 2015 that contained a deep explanation for a short list of seven SCOs (all of them candidates for EU membership), which included Turkey.[55]

Indeed, member states have adopted their own lists, not all of them compatible with the others, and not all of them published or available. In 2014 the European Migration Network (financed by the European Commission) conducted an ad-hoc query on safe countries of origin (SCOs) and STCs approved by member states. It received responses back from twenty-five countries. Of those countries that responded, thirteen noted that they either had lists that were kept confidential, could not be published, or did not exist. Eight declared that they simply followed criteria for "safe" that were consistent with the those of the European Convention of Human Rights, the Geneva (1951) Refugee Convention, the Convention for the Protection of Human Rights and Fundamental Freedoms, and the Convention Against Torture and Other Cruel, Inhumane or Degrading Treatment or Punishment. The most frequent countries named as safe were those in the European Economic Area, and those now seeking membership in the EU, including Albania, Bosnia-Herzegovina, Iceland, Macedonia, and Serbia.

Still, there were some surprising results that did not appear to be entirely consistent with the criteria developed in Commission proposals. Seventeen countries also named as safe by at least one of the respondents included those in Africa with a serious history of conflict and human rights abuses: Algeria, Kenya, Liberia, Ethiopia, and Mali. In addition, at least one country named China, Turkey, Georgia, Russia, and Ukraine.[56] At least until now, the considerable differences among member states is an important barrier to the development of a common asylum policy among the member states of the Schengen zone. It is also one more factor that encourages venue shopping among asylum seekers, and is one more unworkable aspect of the Dublin system.

Second, this somewhat ad hoc process has failed to serve as a deterrent for migrants from these countries to enter Europe to claim asylum. In theory, access to asylum from an SCO or STC should be difficult, and return to these countries should be easy. Nevertheless, among the top twenty nationalities of countries of those applying for asylum in the EU between 2013 and 2015 were those from Kosovo, Serbia, Macedonia, and Albania, all of them proposed on the list of the European Commission report on SCOs. It can be argued, on the other hand, that the system has worked, since applications from these countries are far more likely to fail than applications from other third countries. In 2015, for example, the recognition rate for all nationalities was 47.2 percent, compared with 2.6 percent for those of Kosovo, 1.2 percent from Serbia, 7.7 percent from Albania, and 0.7 percent for those from Macedonia.[57]

The strong possibility of migrants from safe countries being returned does not, however, appear to have been much of a deterrence to prevent them from coming in the first place. There are many indications that they still have opportunities to remain in Europe, and in some countries these opportunities are better than others. A German parliamentary report in 2016 (before the attack on the Christmas market in Berlin in December) noted that about 550,000 rejected asylum seekers were still in Germany, among whom were 69,000 from Kosovo and 51,000 from Serbia.[58] Indeed, after the terrorist attack on the Berlin Christmas Market, it became clear that even the expulsion of suspected terrorists could be difficult. Germany is not unique. A lengthy report by BBC news noted that the greatest impediments for returns are the legal system and the destruction of identity documents by asylum seekers or others, which makes them "effectively unreturnable."[59]

This problem is indicated by the gap between the numbers of migrants who are detained for expulsion, compared with the numbers who are actually expelled each year. Table 4.8 indicates that each year only about 40 percent of those who are detained, either because they have been denied asylum or because they have been determined to be in the country without proper documents, are effectively expelled each year.[60]

Table 4.8 Percentages of TCNs Ordered to Leave Member States' Territories Who Are Finally Returned, 2008–2015

	2008	2009	2010	2011	2012	2013	2014	2015
Total TCN % returned	40.10%	42.51%	41.74%	39.51%	42.73%	50.15%	41.75%	42.52%
Returned to:								
Albania % returned	88.10%	91.41%	91.92%	53.07%	67.57%	106.22%*	87.14%	87.58%
Serbia % returned	66.33%	63.35%	66.73%	74.08%	73.41%	92.34%	82.24%	97.00%
Bosnia % returned	50.98%	58.54%	47.16%	49.57%	60.55%	63.60%	67.62%	80.58%
Kosovo % returned	xxxxxxx	80.21%	69.99%	51.29%	49.60%	58.45%	54.36%	88.48%
Macedonia % returned	72.30%	51.69%	70.50%	59.23%	98.83%	49.01%	113.17%*

Source: European Commission, Eurostat Database for the European Union, http://appsso.eurostat.ec.europa.eu/nui/http://epp.eurostat.ec.europa.ey/portal/page/portal/statistics/search_database.

*Greater than 100% because returns are not necessarily from expulsion orders of the same year.

In comparison with the general rates of return, those for the few countries that have been broadly accepted as SCOs/STCs have been far higher. Thus, it can be argued that even if the Dublin cordon sanitaire is not much of a deterrent for keeping asylum seekers beyond the borders of Europe, it is an effective tool for excluding them once they have arrived. Perhaps, but a small window is left open for migrants from seemingly safe countries who continue to arrive each year.

As the flow across the land borders in the Balkans developed into a flood in 2015, the EU finally took action in three ways. First, it agreed on a distribution of asylum seekers already in Europe. It then agreed to further externalize policing of the Eastern border through a fragile agreement with Turkey (see the following section). Finally, it took measures to augment the policing and monitoring of the Greek islands with EU border agents. Each of these decisions recognized the breakdown of the Dublin system, and each was meant to be at least a temporary remedy.

The EU Council decision in 2015[61] for the emergency distribution of asylum seekers within its borders was widely ignored, however. In December 2016, the European Commission reported that more than 90,000 of the 160,000 emergency places called for still had not been allocated.[62] Ironically, the distribution of asylum seekers has not overburdened the states that have governed the external border, but not because of EU policy. Most asylum seekers have self-relocated among the countries of the EU following their own evaluation of where they would be most easily accepted, which countries were most easily accessible, and where they would find a supportive network.[63] The result has been an emerging system of sorts, but not the system envisioned by the Dublin Regulation.

Confronted with the effective rejection of the burden-sharing agreement, the Commission and Council, under the leadership of Germany, developed an agreement to externalize the problem through an agreement with Turkey. It offered Turkey financial assistance to support asylum seekers, and liberalized visas for Turkish nationals, in return for Turkey accepting the return of asylum seekers from Greece. The EU also committed to receiving additional applicants for consideration in a one to one exchange for those returned, and to aid the resettlement of Syrian refugees in Turkey. Essentially, the agreement was a new twist on the Dublin Regulation, on safe countries from which asylum seekers cannot claim protection in Europe. Turkey, with over 2 million refugees, had been the most important continuing source of the current wave of migration to Europe. Prior to this agreement, Turkey had made no commitment to safeguard or offer asylum to any of the refugees passing through its territory, and few of those refugees had sought asylum in Turkey. Indeed, since it imposed a geographic limitation when it signed the 1967 protocol of the 1951 Geneva Refugee Convention (1951/1967), Turkey had no obligation to recognize any of these refugees from outside of Europe.

To do this, in a decision widely criticized by human rights groups, the EU had to certify that Turkey was a STC:

> The Commission . . . finds that the legal framework in Turkey which establishes the protection status granted to Syrians . . . appears as sufficient protection or protection equivalent to that foreseen by the Geneva Convention. The Commission assesses that Turkey has taken all the necessary measures in order to allow Greece to declare . . . an application for asylum inadmissible in accordance with the Asylum Procedures Directive. . . . Moreover, at the meeting of the Justice and Home Affairs Council on 20 May 2016, Member States indicated that they share this assessment.[64]

Until 2016, only two countries, Bulgaria and Luxembourg, considered Turkey to be either a "safe country of origin" or a "safe third country," legal terms in international law that denote that a country is either safe for its own citizens (in terms of a variety of protections), or a safe haven where asylum seekers are adequately protected. The fragile agreement of 2016 however, gives Turkey the distinction of being the only non-European country that is effectively recognized by all members of the EU as a "safe third country" under European law, to which asylum seekers can be returned after they are considered for asylum.

By the winter of 2016, the system appeared to be working more or less as planned. The number of migrants arriving by sea from North Africa had declined by two-thirds compared with 2015; on the other hand, there was a 20 percent increase of arrivals from Africa in the central Mediterranean.[65] In a less publicized agreement with Afghanistan, signed in October 2016, the Afghan government agreed to accept an unlimited number of rejected Afghan asylum seekers from Europe in return for a considerable increase in financial assistance.[66] The agreement overrode considerations of the ongoing war and violence in favor of reducing asylum pressure on Europe from Afghanistan, the second largest source of asylum seekers.

The EU has, therefore, attempted to minimize pressure from asylum on its borders by externalizing the problem in a variety of ways. At the same time, it has, at least temporarily, strengthened the governance of the border by effectively removing sole authority from member states. As part of the agreement with Turkey, member states of the EU have sent border control personnel to Greece. By the fall of 2016 there were almost 700 police under the auspices of Frontex, and an additional 150 experts and interpreters. In an important way this erodes one of the assumptions about the Dublin system: that member states would still control their portions of the external border of Europe. Although these are emergency measures, this emergency may last a long time.

Refugees and Asylum in the United States

As we have seen in chapter 3, the regulation of refugee admission in the United States is now integrated into the Immigration and Nationality Act. In general, this system is far less complicated, less challenging, and can be seen as far more stable than that of the EU. As I elaborated in chapter 3, however, the United States has a two-track system, one in which the UNHCR works with the United States to select refugees for resettlement; the other for those who seek asylum both within the United States and at the border. In the first case, refugee status is determined before entry; in the second, it is considered after asylum is granted.

The decisions on the ceilings on refugee visas proposed by the president to Congress, and other aspects of refugee resettlement, have sometimes been contentious. In 2016, for example, President Obama's recommendations for an increased ceiling to settle larger numbers of Syrian refugees provoked House committee approval of legislation that would have revised presidential power to recommend ceilings.[67] Nevertheless, each year until 2017, the vast majority of those proposed for resettlement by the UNHCR to the United States have been accepted by the United States.

These lists of refugees are long and growing. The UNHCR has reported that by the end of 2015, about 65 million people were displaced worldwide; of these, 3.2 million people were waiting for some official decision on their application for settlement, and the number was increasing each week. This population of displaced persons was divided among the 21 million refugees living under United Nations mandate, the 134,000 submitted by the UNHCR for possible settlement, and millions of others who had not registered or officially applied for asylum. Of the 134,000 in 2015, 107,000 refugees were accepted for resettlement, worldwide; 82,500 names had been submitted to the United States, of which about 80 percent were accepted for settlement.[68]

The process for the establishment of ceilings set in 1980 was intended to build a stable procedure for the admission of refugees. Nevertheless, both the ceilings and admission of refugees to the United States have varied considerably since 1980, and have generally tracked wars and conflicts far from American shores that have been recognized as important for American interests. Admissions were 146,000 entries in 1978, and then moved as high as 231,000 in 1980. These were the years of the end of the war in Vietnam and the Indo-China refugee crisis, the Mariel Boatlift, and the admission of large numbers of Soviet Jews, an increasing number of whom chose to emigrate to the United States rather than Israel. Refugee admissions then fell until 1988, and rose with the fall of the Soviet Union and the onset of the Balkan wars. In 2002–2003 the number of refugees entering the United States fell sharply, far below the authorized levels, as entries were first suspended and then reduced by more demands for post-9/11 security vetting. In fact, it was only after 2008 that entries began to approach annual authorizations.[69]

But the peaks in the acceptance of refugees were the result of specific American policies and American problems. Reluctantly, the United States, together with Canada, Australia, and France, took the leadership in organizing the Geneva conference in 1979 (which reconvened in 1989), with the cooperation of the Vietnamese Government, which resulted in the orderly resettlement of more than 2.5 million Indo-Chinese refugees. Of these, more than half were resettled in the United States.[70] Nevertheless, this exit appears to be more orderly than it was in reality. UNHCR estimates that of the 2.5 million refugees, perhaps 400,000 had died at sea by 1997.[71]

Similarly, more than any other country in Latin America, Cubans have benefited from special rules that have enabled them to qualify for refugee and special status in the United States (see chapter 3). Since 1980, the overwhelming percentages of refugees from the Western Hemisphere, resettled in the United States (about 99 percent), have been from Cuba.[72]

In fact, the new rules, since the Clinton administration, which somewhat diminished the comparative advantage for Cuban refugees, did not appear to discourage those determined to leave. Indeed, this route continued to be the preferred way to gain entry from Cuba.

> In FY 2013, 82 percent of the 32,219 Cuban individuals granted permanent residence received green cards under the "refugee" category, a much higher percentage compared to all lawful permanent residents (LPRs) (12 percent). They were much less likely than the overall LPR population to gain green cards as immediate relatives of U.S. citizens (10 percent versus 44 percent), or through family-sponsored preferences (8 percent versus 21 percent).[73]

The beginning of the normalization process in 2014 prompted a surge of Cuban arrivals by sea during the following two years, an increase of 80 percent. At the same time, Cuban arrivals by land, across the southwest border of the United States, increased fivefold between 2009 and 2016.[74]

With the exception of Cubans, however, those who have been able to enter as refugees have been overwhelmingly from Africa and Asia. As the refugee crisis emerged after 2010, with the civil wars in North Africa and the Middle East—especially Syria—pressure began to build in Europe. Unlike previous international refugee crises, however, this surge had only a small impact on the number of refugees accepted for resettlement in the United States. Between 2013 and 2015, the number of admissions increased to almost 70,000, and matched the legal authorization. However, the authorization had been reduced by 10,000 between 2011 and 2013. Entries from war zones in the Near East and Asia remained remarkably stable, even as the Syrian civil war heated up.

Nevertheless, the priorities of admissions did change. Those granted refugee visas from countries still at war (Iraq and Somalia), countries in which the United Nations has intervened over a long period with peacekeepers (the Democratic Republic of the Congo), and countries with a recent history of human rights violations against a large minority (Burma) increased dramatically, even as overall arrivals remained stable. Refugees who arrived for settlement from these four countries alone accounted for almost 70 percent of admissions to the United States after 2010.

The process of refugee acceptance by the United States is remarkable insofar as the UNHCR plays a large role in selection. In 2014, the United States had accepted more than 70 percent of those who had been proposed by UNHCR. Indeed, this would account for almost all of refugees accepted under the first (highest) priority, and 43 percent of all acceptances. Most of the Priority 2 selections (53 percent)—groups of special humanitarian concern—overlap with UNHCR priorities as well. Nevertheless, as I noted earlier, the numbers have been small. In 2014 UNHCR proposed fewer than 104,000 people for resettlement, of whom 73,000 finally departed and 49,000 of whom went to the United States, far more than those who went to Europe. Indeed, in Europe, only Norway figured among those countries accepting a large number of UNHCR refugees (2,400).[75]

The stability of the program is indicated by rates of approval for refugee status. With little variation, the approval rate between 1980 and 2000 was about 80 percent, although the rates dipped slightly lower, to about 76 percent between 1996 and 2000. In 2002–2003, in the aftermath of the 9/11 attacks, approval rates fell as low as 49 percent, but rebounded to 80 percent by 2004 (the last year for which the US Department of Homeland Security (USDHS) has released figures; see Figure 4.2).

At first glance, this high rate of approval, combined with the relative generosity of American acceptance of those proposed for resettlement by UNHCR, seems to indicate a clear path of access to the United States by refugees. However, the only path to refugee access is beyond the borders of the United States, and, with only a few exceptions, in a third country that is not their own. Double vetting, first by the UN then by US officials, very much limits who will make it on to the UNHCR list and then be accepted by the United States. It is important to keep in mind that the 66,500 UNHCR refugees accepted for resettlement in 2015 in the United States are a miniscule proportion—2 percent—of the 3.2 million awaiting a decision on their application for asylum that same year, or the more than 21 million refugees under the mandate of the UN. In fact, very few make it through the increasingly demanding and lengthy vetting process by UNHCR and the USDHS in the United States.

If the entry of refugees has been externalized and more or less stabilized by the rules put in place in 1980, the path of asylum entry at the borders and within the country has looked very different. Generally, the number of people granted asylum each year in the United States (that is, permission to stay, and ultimately refugee status) is about a third to half of those granted refugee status from abroad. In addition, although the criteria are similar for both, the process is quite different, and involves different government agencies.

The percentage of asylum applications approved per year has varied between 15 and 40 percent, and has tended to be lower as the number of applicants has been higher. As a result, the total admitted has been pretty flat since 1996, at about 25,000 (see Figure 4.2).

The most important spike in asylum applications since 1997 was due to the movement of unaccompanied and undocumented children (UAC) across the Mexican border that began in 2011. It was unanticipated, and was related both to civil unrest in Central America and the peculiarities of American law. Between 2011 and 2014, the number of UAC increased from 6,560 to an estimated 60,000; between October 2013 and July 2014 alone, an estimated 52,000 children arrived. Rather than avoid border authorities, most of these children presented themselves to them as the first step for a claim for protection.[76] By mid-2015 the arrivals had begun to recede, primarily because Mexican authorities began to take a much more active role in blocking the movement of children from Guatemala, Honduras, and El Salvador. The Mexicans also increased deportations despite protests from human rights advocates.[77]

These children and their advocates claimed protection under the Trafficking Victims Protection Reauthorization Act. Clearly the trafficking legislation did not anticipate the tens of thousands of applications that accumulated in 2014. Preliminary studies of those arriving during the summer of 2014 provided evidence that between 40 and 60 percent had experiences that would fit the requirements of the 2008 legislation. Nevertheless, others were sent in the hope that they would simply not be sent back. If the former had claims of protection from traffickers, it could be claimed that the latter were simply illegal aliens, exploited by traffickers but without valid claims for asylum.[78] Therefore, as with the surge of people crossing from North Africa to Europe was defined, there were two ways of framing the issue politically, both of which had some support.

Most Democrats tended to frame the problem as an asylum crisis, and therefore quite different from the normal border problem. Senator Diane Feinstein, who helped write the 2008 legislation, compared the crisis to American refusal to accept Jewish refugees from Nazi Germany.[79] Most Republicans framed the issue as an example of the porous border, and blamed the president for creating the problem, "saying he provided a lure by instituting a program that deferred deportation for some immigrants who entered the nation illegally as children" (DACA).[80]

In contrast to refugee admission from abroad, almost none of the asylees admitted to the United States since 2000 were Cuban nationals. The largest number, more than half, were from Asia, mostly from China. A smaller number were from Latin America, with a growing number from El Salvador and Honduras, and a diminishing number from Haiti. Generally, these were undocumented migrants who had crossed the southwestern border, although some of the Haitians had arrived by sea. This was a very different population than those who arrived as refugees, who were vetted outside the United States. Asylees were admitted through a required legal process that has been dubbed by a major study as "refugee roulette."[81] The rules for admission are generally the same as those for refugee status, but the outcomes appear to be far more random, even chaotic. Each year immigration courts render decisions that admit about 25,000 asylum seekers to the United States.

Considered together, refugee and asylum consideration are only a limited means of gaining access to Europe or the United States. The United States considers and accepts far more refugees proposed by UNHCR than any country in Europe, but only a small percentage of those who apply for asylum at its borders or within the country. Moreover, the process appears to have worked to the advantage of those considered from abroad, and proposed by UNHCR, the vast percentage of whom are granted recognition.

Consideration for asylum at the borders and within, on the other hand, has been similarly chaotic in Europe and the United States. Surges in applications for asylum have resulted in elevated levels of rejection, and in the United States, studies have indicated a high level of arbitrary decision-making. Although the rules of entry for those claiming asylum appear to be reasonably clear, the gaps between refugee and asylum rejection have not been clearly explained. In fact, claiming asylum appears to offer the poorest chance of gaining access to either Europe or the United States. Visa application rejection rates in Europe (see Table 4.1) have been about 15 percent, compared with asylum rejection at an average of 55 percent. American visa rejection rates are lower than 20 percent, compared with asylum rejection rates (at the border and within the country) of more than 80 percent, although no more than 30 percent of the thoroughly vetted refugee applications from abroad have been rejected (see Figure 4.2).

This conclusion may be mitigated by the fact that applicants for asylum in Europe are most often from regions of the world with high rejection rates for visas. Even in these cases, however, visa rejection rates for applicants from Africa and Asia are less than 38 percent, compared with asylum rejections of greater than 45 percent in Europe. For the United States, the largest number of asylum applications is from Mexico, from which more than 95 percent of the applications are rejected, compared with only 11 percent of visa applications. The one exception is the very low rejection rate (9%) of asylum applicants from Syria in Europe since 2011.[82]

Conclusion

In this chapter I have analyzed the implementation of border control policies in Europe and the United States. I have found both contradictions with formal policy, and more importantly, implementation that implies more elaborate policies than those indicated by law, or even administrative rules. I have also found unexpected similarities and differences between Europe and the United States. There is a considerable difference between the policy and (especially) the rhetoric of border control and how controls are used to shape migration patterns.

The place where decisions are made about migrant entry is linked to the process of acceptance of different kinds of migrants for long-term stays. People seeking asylum in Europe, rather than settlement for family or work, are un- likely to make their request in their home country, and are most likely to attempt to present themselves at land and sea ports, where they are least likely to gain admission.

Whether by chance or design, by most measures, the chances of legally en- tering fortress Europe are greater than those of entering what is often considered the more open United States. Rejection rates for long-term visas at European consulates are generally lower than those at American consulates where applications are registered. However, there is considerable variation within Europe, which helps us to understand the relationship between the choices that migrants make and the pattern of decisions on entry made by administra- tive officials at consulates and at the border. Acceptances for settlement of third country nationals proposed by UNHCR are higher for the United Kingdom and Italy than for most other European countries, even though successive British governments have taken a hard line against immigration.[83]

There are also unanticipated results of decisions that are made. Although neither Europe nor the United States has established formal priorities for immigrants from some countries, rather than others, visa rejection rates clearly indicate a bias against applicants from Africa, Asia, and the Near East. Nevertheless, if we examine where immigrants actually come from, this chapter indicates that what you want is not always what you get. Regional preferences have been overridden by other considerations for admission: family ties to cit- izens and residents, as opposed to the needs of the labor market; a desire to admit students and those more likely to integrate appear to sometimes override labor market preferences; a need for unskilled workers often appears to override the desire for skilled workers and professionals, who in any case, may prefer to go somewhere else. A preference for migrants who are more likely to integrate socially may override the need for those who may more easily integrate economically. These priorities are more explicit in the United States, because the legislation that defines the rules of entry is far more comprehensive than that in Europe, where real preferences are indicated more clearly through visa approval.

One category of entry appears to override choices implied by visa selection. The treaty-based general rules governing the entry of those seeking asylum tend to focus on the needs of the applicant, rather than the needs of the state. Nevertheless, despite the political rhetoric to the contrary, entry through claims for asylum is generally far more difficult than gaining entry through normal channels, even when demands for asylum emanate from real crises of war and violence. Although those seeking asylum may be able to make their claims in countries other than their country of origin or their country of destination, actual rules make this very difficult to do. For most people, it is almost impossible to purchase air tickets without a visa in hand, and with few exceptions, anyone who seeks to claim asylum must approach the border, or cross the border without authorization.

One problem for Europe is that European rules and practices make it almost impossible to gain entry from a country that has been designated a STC or SCO. The alternative is to cross through a dangerous passage that has resulted in a loss of life that far exceeds a similar passage through the Mexican–US border. The other problem is that most asylum seekers arrive in countries on the periphery of Europe by land and sea. The result is that the rules of the Dublin regulations create an overwhelming burden for those countries that threaten to undermine the carefully constructed Schengen zone.

The United States has differentiated between refugees vetted at consulates abroad and granted visas, and asylum seekers vetted at or within the borders of the country. The surge of asylum seekers at European borders since 2011, a large percentage of whom have been granted recognition as refugees or been given temporary leave to remain, has created an illusion of easy acceptance into Europe. In fact, the UNHCR data indicate that normally, entry is granted to no more than 25,000 applicants in all of Europe. By contrast, the United States has normally accepted about 80,000 refugees, as well as more than 20,000 asylum seekers. Nevertheless, there is a complex disparity between the formal rules and the reality of how asylum seekers enter and are admitted on both sides of the Atlantic.

It is not surprising that patterns of immigration control have political consequences. The gap between the political rhetoric of governments and their enforcement policy on the ground has provided grist for the mill of the radical right in Europe for many years, and the failure to close the US border with Mexico has been an important political issue in the United States since the 1990s. The seeming gap in the regulation of asylum has also become an issue around which the Left has mobilized, claiming that the clear requirement of the Geneva Agreements are consistently violated by governments seeking to reduce entry. These inconsistencies are often presented as the clear unwillingness of public authorities to enforce the law. Policies may provide the basis for enforcement, but, as I have argued, in the end, patterns of control shape the reality of what policies really do.

5

The Hard Arm of the State

Policing the Border

In contrast to the orderly control of entry that follows policies and rules, the state must also deal with the breakdown of policy, and the failure to maintain its priorities. In this chapter I look at "the hard arm" of border control, and the instruments that have been used to deal with the enforcement and breakdown of policy.

I begin by examining how the border is policed, and policing deals with undocumented entry. I then look at attempts to enhance the policing of the border with passenger name records and entry/exit systems. I will then examine increasingly widespread construction of fences and walls on both sides of the Atlantic. Finally, I explore detention and expulsion.

5.1 Policing the External Frontier

Even with compensatory measures that have coincided with the implementation of Schengen, the SIS, and other cooperative efforts described later in the chapter, the buildup of police forces on the external border of Europe has been relatively modest and ad hoc. Until the influx of refugees after 2010, European countries had been far more concerned with perceived problems of integration than with problems of unauthorized entry.

In the United States, by contrast, there has been an impressive—even historic—buildup of the police forces which control the land, air, and sea borders of the United States since the 1990s. What has been termed the "formidable" increase in the number of police, especially since 2001, moreover, has been enhanced by an expansion of their mission. The control of immigration is now defined "principally in terms of national security and public safety," and the combined border forces have become the largest and the most active federal police forces in terms of arrest and prosecution.[1]

At the core of this buildup has been the Border Patrol. Although the primary mission of the Border Patrol has been understood in security terms since it was first organized in 1924, the objects of security have changed. With the onset of the Depression, unauthorized Mexican workers were excluded. Then, before and immediately after World War II, the government was most concerned with the movement of Chinese and European migrants across the southern border. During the war, the focus was on "enemy agents." What has changed since the 1990s is that migrants themselves have now become the security threat, and the priority of that threat is indicated by the relative budgetary importance of the border force.[2] According to calculations made by the Migration Policy Institute (cited in note 1, above), "The US government spends more on its immigration enforcement agencies than on all its other principle criminal federal law enforcement agencies combined" (see chapter 7).[3] Perhaps most striking is that There are far more border agents (TSA and customs agents at airports and ports of entry) employed now—more than 137,000—than were ever employed during the period when immigration was far more restricted before 1965.

One way to understand border policing is to consider the number of agents compared with the number of crossing points (land, sea, and air) for which they are responsible. Of course these are rough comparisons, since the configuration of entry points varies considerably. In Germany, France, and the United Kingdom, the most numerous ports of entry for TCNs are airports; the United Kingdom, however, has far fewer international airports than either Germany or France. Italy, by far, has the largest number of seaports for international entry. The number of land crossings in the United States is far larger than the number of international airports (see Table 5.1).

Europe

In Europe, the land and sea ports have been relatively less manned compared with airports, although there has been a buildup of border police forces along the eastern border of Germany and the Sahara border of Spain. On the German–Polish border, the police force of about 400 in 1990–1991 was increased to 3,300 by 1996. Most of the guards along this frontier, whose job is now to keep people out, had been East German guards whose job had been to keep people in.[4] By 2007, after the admission of Poland and the Czech Republic to the EU and the Schengen area, Germany was no longer responsible for policing the eastern border of the EU. Nevertheless, the German–Polish border has remained important, as Germany temporarily reimposed controls at the Polish border in 2014 (and then with Austria a year later).[5]

Table 5.1 **Border Control Agents and Crossings in the United States and Europe**

	Border Police*	International Border Crossings (land, sea, and air)*	Ratio of Border Staff/Border Crossings
US	137,380	341	416**
Germany	40,310	274	147
Italy	24,000	182	132
France	10,008	226	44
UK	20,000	140	143

Source: Commission of the European Communities, *COM (2004), Proposal for a Council Regulation establishing a Community Code on the rules governing the movement of persons across borders*, Annex: http://eur-lex.europa.eu/legal-content/EN/TXT/PDF/?uri=CELEX:52004PC0391&from=EN.   Joseph Chamie and Luca Dall'Oglio, *International Migration and Development, Continuing the Dialogue: Legal and Policy Perspectives* (Geneva: International Organization for Migration, 2008), p. 128.

*The border police include both actual police as well as staff for border agencies—equivalent agencies for each country—for 2008-2016. The crossings are land, sea, and air with non-EU countries, including Switzerland for Germany, Italy, and France as specified in the EU Commission document as well as the UKBF published documents.

**The US total includes CBP, TSA, and ICE, all of which are part of USDHS.

Spain was admitted to the EU in 1985 and Schengen in 1991, thus making Spain the steward of Europe's only land border with Africa. Although the border at Ceuta and Melilla was then more carefully monitored by an augmented force of Spanish police, controls largely depended on the construction of a wall in 1995. The effectiveness of these controls, however, has largely depended on co-operation with Moroccan authorities.[6]

The UK Border Agency, the comparable agency to the US Border Patrol and the TSA, was broken up into three separate agencies under the Home Office in 2013. The combined force had over 20,000 agents in 2014 concentrated primarily at the largest airports. In contrast to the United States, the budgets of these agencies and personnel were reduced after 2011, reductions that were scheduled to go much further through 2015, as a result of a highly critical parliamentary report. Interestingly, the report did not criticize the border force and its parent agency for letting too many people through the gates, but for delaying entry and operating inefficiently.[7] Britain's only significant land border is the frontier with the Republic of Ireland (just over 310 miles). Since 2011 the UK and Ireland have comprised a Common Travel Area. In fact, the 2011 agreement formalized what had been informal since the 1998 Good Friday Agreement—a "soft," lightly patrolled area of more or less free movement.[8]

The future of these arrangements is part of the ongoing Brexit negotiations. The future of this border is a particularly sensitive matter for the future of the peace agreement signed in 1998 and approved by referendum in 1999. As a report by the European Parliament noted in 2018:

> A bilateral bespoke deal between the UK and Irish governments to maintain the Customs Union between the two states—which would continue to render invisible Northern Ireland's frontier with the Irish Republic—would require EU approval. The UK government has listed tariff-free trade across borders, via a special agreement with the EU, as a priority. Failure to conclude such a deal will impact significantly upon Northern Ireland as a site of tariff checks.[9]

Of course Brexit also has implications for the free movement of people across this "invisible" land border, a problem of deep concern for families and workers, whether or not citizens of the United Kingdom and the Republic of Ireland, who are now able to cross on a daily basis. Therefore, one of the guiding principles for the EU has been to preserve this fluid border:

> Issues unique to Ireland include the protection of the gains of the peace process and of the Good Friday Agreement ("Belfast Agreement") in all its parts, the maintenance of existing bilateral agreements and arrangements between the United Kingdom and Ireland including the Common Travel Area, and specific issues arising from Ireland's unique geographic situation, including the aim of avoiding a hard border between Ireland and Northern Ireland. The invisible border on the island of Ireland is one of the major achievements and societal benefits of the Peace Process. Border issues are broader than economic questions. The physical border itself was a symbol of division and conflict.[10]

The problem, of course, is how to maintain an "invisible border" for people even while imposing a hard border for commerce. One additional complication is that citizens on either side of the border are currently permitted to obtain dual citizenship, thereby enabling citizens of Northern Ireland to retain their European citizenship. This does not, however, eliminate a hard border with passport checks.

For the United Kingdom, a surge in demands for asylum between 1998 and 2003 was more important than the recent asylum crisis for reorganizing the asylum system. The political reaction against asylum (which I will discuss in the next chapter) provoked not so much an expansion of the immigration force, but a reorganization that would demonstrate clear control of the border.

The predecessors of the existing agencies had already expanded their focus from ports of entry to significant internal control of immigration after 2000, with an increased focus on unauthorized immigrants within the country.[11] This capacity was developed only after many of the constraints on immigration agents operating within the country had been legally removed. The Home Office summarized its efforts after 2003 as the development of "a system that balances ability to process cases efficiently, with a high quality determination process: quickly identifying those who need our protection and providing it, whilst also deterring unfounded claims and ensuring there are consequences for those who do make unmeritorious claims."[12]

Perhaps the most important change in the organization of immigration policing in the United Kingdom has been the establishment of the Immigration Compliance and Enforcement agency (ICE), previously part of the UK Border Agency, as a separate police force within the Home Office. Although the British version of ICE is smaller than its American counterpart, it is far larger in proportion to the total personnel engaged in immigration control and enforcement. The mission of UK-ICE, with nineteen teams permanently established throughout the country, ranges from policing of sham marriages to workplace enforcement raids.[13]

Like its counterparts in Britain and the United States, in 1999 the French Ministry of the Interior created a dedicated police unit, primarily to deal with undocumented entry of TCNs: the Central Directorate of Frontier Police (DCPAF).[14] The actual number of police personnel was increased only modestly to about 5,500, but most of the increased numbers of police were posted in the interior of the country. Almost half of the DCPAF are posted at airports, with 30 percent at land and maritime ports. Soon after the unit was formed, the DCPAF took on a greater role in neighborhood policing, coordinated with regular police, as well as with the Central Office for the Suppression of Irregular Immigration and the Employment of Foreigners Without Papers (OCRIEST). By 2013, the total personnel of the DCPAF had doubled to 10,008, but its mission and responsibilities had remained about the same.[15]

Similar to the US and British, the DCPAF has a dedicated arm that deals with migrants within the country. OCRIEST has its own dedicated police force that coordinates with local police under the direction of the Ministry of the Interior. The DCPAF iws now involved in urban settings in the struggle against channels of illegal immigration, and actively participates in the removal of undocumented foreigners.. Its connections with counterparts on the European level have also grown with a focus on asylum-seekers and terrorists.[16] In France, policymakers appear to have generally dealt with increases in applications for asylum by decreasing the recognition rate. The recognition rate (the rate of acceptance of asylum applications) dropped by almost two-thirds after 1987, as the number of requests for asylum almost doubled.[17]

In Europe, as in the United States, the police buildup at the external land and sea borders resulted from both patterns of migration and asylum movement, as well as a developing securitized framing of migration. This has played out in different ways, both for individual countries and for the development of European cooperation on border control. If the United States has responded to an increase of migration across the southern border by devoting large and growing resources to the long land frontier, the response in Europe has been quite different. The British have devoted more modest, even diminishing resources primarily to airports. The French initially increased the personnel devoted to border control and investigation and coordinated activities with local police. However, after 2012, there are reports that indicate a freezing or even a diminishing number of police overall.[18]

Instead of dramatically increasing their resources, with the exception of some countries on the eastern frontier, European countries have moved toward increased cooperation. Harmonization and cooperation have appeared to be strengthening border policing in different ways in Europe, and this cooperation has been intensified with the refugee crisis since 2010. Perhaps the most intense cooperation (and conflict) among border forces in Europe has been at the sea border between France and the United Kingdom.

UK–French Cooperation

The Channel ports are relatively lightly patrolled, but the link between the two countries provided by the channel tunnel, opened in 1994, has proven to be complicated for several reasons. Since the United Kingdom is not a signatory to the Schengen Agreement the tunnel is a hard border, controlled on both ends. It is also the entry point, on the French side, for unauthorized migrants attempting to gain access to the United Kingdom.

By 2004, a legal basis had been agreed to that enabled the presence of the UK Border Force (UKBF) at seven points in France and Belgium with "juxtaposed controls" of British and French–Belgian border forces at access points to Eurostar or cross-channel ferries on both sides of the Channel. Three of these points are not close to the physical frontier (Paris, Brussels, and Lille). These agreements also provided for control zones, within which laws and regulations of the adjoining state (the UK in France and Belgium; France in the UK) may be applied.

Through the conventions with the EU and other bilateral arrangements, the United Kingdom is able to check passports in France and Belgium, can join in operations of Frontex far from its borders, cooperate with EU police operations against smuggling, and participate in the SIS.[19] Thus, Britain has externalized its border controls within Schengen in ways that enable the UKBF to maintain a presence in the rest of Europe. The UKBF maintains a link with the French border police (DCPAF), for example, through a special advisor.

Therefore, on the French and Belgian side, there is a British border. This border between the United Kingdom and the continent is at once one of the most challenged and best organized in Europe, with far more cooperation among national border police than at any of the external borders, controlled by national police alone. Nevertheless, the area around the entrance to the Eurotunnel near Calais has been a focal point of considerable chaos since 1997, as thousands of asylum seekers have converged on the area seeking access to the United Kingdom. Under this pressure, cooperative arrangements have been challenged, but have also expanded in content.

For almost two decades, there has been a problem of a buildup of asylum seekers at the juxtaposed controls on French soil. The British have complained that the French have refused to detain and register asylum seekers coming through their territory, as they are obliged to do under the Dublin regulations, while the French have complained that the British expect them to act as agents for the United Kingdom.[20] Both sides appear to be more or less correct. Nevertheless, the French have made the same (British) argument against the Italians at the Ventimiglia–Menton (Schengen) border on the Mediterranean, where the Italian government threatened to issue three-month tourist Schengen visas to asylum seekers after the French attempted to return six thousand migrants to Italy.[21]

The tensions in Calais and Ventimiglia are both a result of the rules governing the Schengen arrangements and rules of asylum agreed to under the Dublin regulations. For the French, the growing presence of asylum seekers is a challenge to the established rules, both because France probably was not the first country to which most of these migrants arrived, and is not the country in which they wish to claim asylum. In any case, France has shown little interest in registering them.

In 2010 and 2011, only 5 percent of asylum seekers in France claimed asylum at the frontier, and almost all of these at the two Paris airports, Charles de Gaulle and Orly.[22] Since most migrants seeking asylum in France do so after having entered the country, evidently with short-stay visas, responsibility for processing these demands is first assumed by prefects in each department, then by a special administrative agency, then by the French Office for the Protection of Refugees and Stateless People (OFPRA) supervised by the Ministry of the Interior, and finally by a special administrative court. These officials retain the power to enforce the border by ordering either recognition or expulsion. But these decisions vary considerably among different centers. This variation appears to be due less to the arbitrariness of judicial decisions, as they are in the American case, than to the vagueness of the criteria themselves, which leaves room for the impact of dynamics of representative bureaucracy (noted in chapter 1). However, the variation is also related to the intervention of NGOs. The French Ministry of the Interior has acknowledged that the intervention of and cooperation with NGOs has also been important in resolving cases for regularization where there have been concentrations of undocumented immigrants.[23]

Normally, according to the rules of the Dublin regulations, the French would be responsible for processing asylum claims, unless of course the asylum seekers arrived either from another European country or from a STC or SCO, in which case they could be returned to that country. However, very few of the claimants have been willing to register with the French authorities, and it is frequently difficult to ascertain from where these asylum seekers have arrived. Because of juxtaposed controls, the UK entry border is in fact a few hundred yards past the French exit border. Normally, as well, those seeking asylum in the United Kingdom could be processed in the UK control area, but under the bilateral agreements with France, they cannot be processed at this port of entry as they would at other ports of entry to the United Kingdom.[24]

Therefore, the juxtaposed controls that are now established at Calais have not been a normal process of border control, but have become a hard barrier for preventing access to the United Kingdom. Facing this increasing buildup of French and British paramilitary forces, a succession of encampments have been established, beginning with the opening of a Red Cross refugee camp at Sangatte in 1999. Sangatte was closed in 2002 by the French Ministry of the Interior, only to be replaced by an unofficial camp closer to the entrance to the Eurotunnel that had eight thousand or more inhabitants by 2015. It was quickly baptized "the Jungle."

The tensions in Calais in 2015 finally resulted in enhanced French–British police cooperation around the port and the entrance to the tunnel. In August 2015, both countries signed a joint ministerial agreement that increased police presence by both countries, and that established a joint command center. The agreement also included commitments by the French to establish more posts for more rapid expulsions.[25]

Within a year, the French government ordered the destruction of the camp, and the distribution of its inhabitants to detention facilities in other parts of France.[26] They warned that those who refused to be registered and processed would be deported. Attempts to reach an agreement with the British authorities about acceptance were largely unsuccessful, although a few hundred children were admitted to the United Kingdom in early 2017. Nevertheless, the French were left with the complex problem of dealing with a large and often vulnerable population of children and young women, as well as families and men.[27]

Although the registration and processing of asylum seekers in an orderly fashion has never been resolved, the juxtaposed controls seemed to work relatively well as a barrier to prevent access to the United Kingdom. A British report demonstrates both the chaos and cooperation. It estimates that during one year (September 2011–August 2012), about eight thousand people had been stopped attempting to cross, and few attempts had been successful.[28]

EU Police Cooperation

Unlike the external frontiers of the United States, which have been under the legal control of the federal government since 1876, there is no European authority that maintains similar control over the Schengen frontier. The alternative has been a modest commitment to cooperation on border control.

> Since no checks are carried out at the borders between Schengen states,
> EU States have decided to join forces to attain the dual objective of
> improving security through more efficient external border controls,
> while facilitating access of those having a legitimate interest to enter the
> EU territory.[29]

At the European level, some added common protections for asylum seekers and others entering the EU, combined with more muscular means of exclusion, increased the agreed-upon border governance even without a common border authority.[30] Nevertheless, the refugee crises, as well as terrorist attacks, have accentuated the border vulnerability. As a result, cooperative efforts to secure the common border have increased, primarily through augmented joint military operations.

The initial reaction to the surge in asylum seekers, Operation Mare Nostrum, was initiated by the Italian government in October 2013, largely in reaction to the growing number of deaths in the Mediterranean between Libya and the Italian island of Lampedusa. With a small subsidy from the European Commission, the Italian government devoted considerable resources primarily to search and rescue operation off the coast of Libya. Within six months, the financial pressure on the already weak Italian government forced them to request additional resources from the EU.

These requests were generally discussed but ignored, particularly by the British and the French, who were reported to oppose Mare Nostrum because, they argued, it encouraged continued undocumented migration.[31] Although the Italian operation was successful in rescuing almost 150,000 people at sea, as well as seizing motherships of smugglers and traffickers, it mostly terminated operations a year later and yielded to a newly organized Frontex operation.

Frontex is by no means a federal border police force comparable to the US Border Patrol. The mission of Frontex is to coordinate member state activity, and it is only modestly financed. It mostly monitors land and sea crossings. Beyond this normal activity, Frontex, at its core, is an emergency tool, driven by a succession of limited emergency operations (including search and rescue) that largely depend on temporary contributions of equipment (including ships and planes) by member states. One advantage of cooperation through Frontex is that joint operations do not require the participation of all member states. Thus, each operation represents a different coalition of countries, and generally avoids conflicting interests within the EU.

The shifting priorities of these operations can be seen through the lens of Frontex budget allocations for joint operations that focus on emerging problems (see Table 5.2). The evolution of budget allocations reflect the development of Frontex as a joint instrument used primarily by those member states to move EU priorities from search and rescue at sea to a focus on capture and disposal of vessels used by those identified as smugglers and traffickers. The total budget almost doubled between 2010 and 2011, with equally large increases (as percentages) going to land and sea crossing points under pressure; however, as the refugee crisis grew, by far the largest amount of money was allocated to sea operations. As the movement of migrants shifted to land crossings in 2012, the budgetary allocations also shifted, with more emphasis on land than sea. Spending at airports remained small, with an emphasis on support for member states' cooperative efforts.

Frontex's Operation Triton was smaller than the Italian Mare Nostrum, which operated freely up to the Libyan coast. Triton operated at a distance of only thirty miles off the European coast. Although its objectives remained

Table 5.2 **Financing Frontex Joint Border Operations, 2010–2015 (in Million Euros)**

	2010	2011	2012	2014	2015
Land ports	4.2	8.6	5.0	9.1	9.2
Seaports	26.5	50.0	25.1	21.4	31.1
Airports	2.7	2.8	2.2	2.1	2.5
Total	42.7	73.3	42.5	42.1	52.3

Source: *Frontex Programme of Work*
2010: www.europarl.europa.eu/document/activities/cont/.../20110720ATT24564EN.pdf (p. 40),
2012: http://www.statewatch.org/news/2012/jan/eu-frontex-2012-wp.pdf (p. 32),
2014: http://www.statewatch.org/news/2014/mar/eu-frontex-wp-2014.pdf (p. 32),
2015: http://www.statewatch.org/news/2015/jan/eu-frontex-2015-work-programme.pdf (p. 8).

search and rescue, it patrolled a smaller portion of the Mediterranean and Aegean, and focused more intensely on capturing smugglers.[32] By mid-2015, the focus of border control efforts gradually shifted to Operation Sophia. This operation was no longer under the control of Frontex, but was transformed into a military operation authorized by the EU Political and Security Committee, responsible for crisis management operations on the international level. Indeed, because it operated under the auspices of the Common Security and Defense Policy, Sophia directly linked border management to questions of internal security, and became an operation with only secondary commitment to search and rescue. Instead, the objectives were clearly "the identification, capture and disposal of vessels used or suspected of being used by migrants' smugglers or traffickers." Nevertheless "the operation has saved more than 22,000 lives and has supported other organisations in the rescue of more than 36,000 persons."[33]

So, since 2000, the policing of the common European border has been strengthened in fits and starts in reaction to perceived crises. The resources devoted to the border, however, have been temporary, and have not been the result of significantly larger forces or a shift of resources by the member states that are ultimately responsible for their parts of the border.

The Entry/Exit Problem in Europe

An important indicator of the weakness of European cooperation on border control is the entry/exit problem. There appear to be no reliable ways of determining whether people who have entered the EU for short-term visits have actually left on time—or left at all. Essentially, this means reliance on internal policing—checks on employment and identity checks.

Monitoring visa overstayers in Europe is uneven and is far more complicated than in the United States. Thirteen member states have their own national entry/exit systems (none electronic as of 2016), but the data is not shared on the European level, nor is it entered into the SIS. Moreover, the only large country of migration included in this group is Spain.

> To the extent that a person lawfully exits the same Member State through which he or she entered, an overstay would be detected by these systems. Beyond that, the possibilities for using such systems to detect overstayers are none, as entry and exit records cannot be matched when persons leave the Schengen area through another Member State than the one from which they entered and in which their entry was recorded.[34]

The first of many proposals was made by the Commission in 2008 to address this issue. A shared electronic entry/exit system, a 2013 report argues, would enhance the capabilities of internal policing, by providing a check on whether a person being questioned had overstayed his or her short-term visa, and providing a tool for calculating the number of visa overstayers in the European area. Of course, this system would also provide a tool for tracking natives as well as TCNs suspected of terrorist activity, by indicating when either a native or a TCN leaves one country for a war zone but returns through another European country. In 2017, revised proposals were still being discussed.

The United States

Policing the external frontier has become a major preoccupation of American policy. This concern was initially related to "the war on drugs," but, as the control of migration from Mexico came under immigration legislation, it quickly connected to the movement of people. In the United States, there has been a far more substantial buildup of police resources at the border than we have seen in Europe.

In the United States, the reorganization of border policing in 2003 resulted in a larger workforce for the agency primarily responsible for land and sea borders (Customs and Border Protection, CBP, formed from combining the Immigration and Naturalization Service and the Customs Service in 2003) than for airport controls (the TSA). Until the decade of the 1990s, there were relatively few border police manning the land crossings. Since then, the buildup has been most pronounced at these crossings, but the longest border (Canada) is still policed by only about 10 percent of the 20,000 Border Patrol agents (part of CBP). CBP agents are at all ports of entry, and the Border Patrol operates in the land areas between ports of entry. In 2016, CBP was the largest single border agency, with a budget equal to that of the TSA and Immigration and Customs Enforcement Police (ICE) combined.[35] In addition, almost 20,000 ICE agents now operate within the country, and are responsible for tracing and detaining undocumented migrants and conducting raids on places of employment.

During the first two years of the Obama administration—from 2009 to 2011—resources to reinforce the land border increased rapidly. The budget for the Border Patrol grew by more than 50 percent during this short period, while the number of agents increased from 17,500 to over 20,000 (see Table 5.3). Between 2005 and 2010, the budget for detention of illegal immigrants doubled. By 2011 there were 84 detention centers.[36] In May 2010, President Obama also sent 1,200 National Guard troops, double the number sent by President Bush, to the border to support the Border Patrol. Therefore it may not seem surprising

Table 5.3 **United States Border Patrol Agents and Budget, 1992–2016**

	Number of Agents	Budget (th. dollars)
1992	4139	$326,234
2000	9212	$1,055,444
2008	17,499	$2,245,261
2011	21,444	$3,549,295
2016	19828	$3,642,820

Source: US Border Patrol, US Border Patrol Fiscal Year Staffing Statistics (FY 1992–
FY 2017), https://www.cbp.gov/document/stats/us-border-patrol-fiscal-year-staffing-
statistics-fy-1992-fy-2017

that the budget of the border agency that deals with land crossing is almost twice
as large as the agency responsible for security at airports.[37]

US Police Cooperation

The buildup at the border in the United States should also been seen in terms of
internal policing of immigration, and the buildup and restructuring of the internal
police capacity. The federal government has attempted to recruit local police to
cooperate in internal immigration control. Through a network of programs, ICE,
the internal immigration police of the US Department of Homeland Security,
has developed a collaborative capacity with state and local police forces.

In a federal system in which most police are local, this has created a multiplier
effect for policing immigration. As Julie L. Myers, Homeland Security Assistant
Secretary for ICE explained in 2008, "Interoperability will create a virtual ICE
presence at every local jail, allowing us to identify and ultimately remove dangerous incarcerated criminal aliens."[38] In fact, she was talking about the technological component of the Secure Communities program, initiated in 2008,
which requires local police officials to share fingerprints of arrestees with ICE
(see below).

But Secure Communities was only the latest component of a more elaborate network of cooperation that had been in place since 1988, the objective of
which was to encourage or require local police to work either as agents for immigration enforcement, or to enhance the capabilities of ICE agents. The deepest
cooperation—known as Article 287(g)—was authorized under the Immigration
and Nationality Act of 1996. Under this program, ICE signs agreements with
local law enforcement authorities known as joint Memorandums of Agreement
(MOAs), under which local police receive "delegated authority for immigration

enforcement within their jurisdictions." Under these agreements local police receive limited training, and legally operate under the supervision of ICE officers. They can make federal arrests and can screen prisoners (generally before conviction) with regard to immigration status. In 2016, there were thirty-seven agreements in force in fourteen states. All of these agreements in 2016 operated in jails, but the legislation provides for broader cooperation. Nevertheless, this program has been limited, and the number of agreements in 2016 was only half those in force in 2011.[39] As we shall see in chapter 7, there has been considerable resistance, especially from police forces in larger cities, to this kind of cooperation.

In addition to 287(g), the federal-local partnership that is responsible for the largest number of arrests and detentions is the Criminal Alien Program (CAP). This program, initiated (under a different name) in 1988, is now responsible for the vast majority of detentions and removals in the United States. In contrast to 287(g), without "delegated authority" local police screen arrestees, and report to ICE those they believe are undocumented. ICE agents then perform a more formal screening. In March 2008, ICE reported that agreements were in place with all federal and state facilities, as well as with about 310 local jails.[40]

Secure Communities is the best known—and, as we shall see in chapter 7, the most challenged—federal partnership. It provides for more widespread information sharing between ICE and local authorities on those arrested. On the basis of the information provided, ICE then issues detainers. Secure Communities is data-driven, and remotely controlled. It depends on widespread input of data on all of those arrested, not just those who are suspect and reported. In effect, under this program, every inmate who is jailed is subject to immigration review by federal authorities. Secure Communities was initiated as a pilot program; then, according to ICE, expanded to all 3,181 jurisdictions by 2013.[41] The data that is gathered is primarily fingerprints, which localities already share with the FBI, which are then shared with Homeland Security and ICE. Therefore, as we shall see in chapter 7, it is difficult for states and localities to opt out of the program.[42] Secure Communities was modified in 2014 and replaced by a program that called for a slightly more restrictive collection of data (the Priority Enforcement Program) that was more consistent with President Obama's focus on deporting undocumented migrants convicted of serious offenses. The original program was reinstated by executive order on January 25, 2017.

These programs generally overlap, and have a great deal in common. Each has the objective of bridging the gap between limited federal police personnel and states and localities where the manpower is based. The 287(g) program effectively deputizes local police to serve as federal agents. The CAP program permits federal ICE officers to work in local jails, and screen prisoners, with the cooperation of local authorities. Secure Communities is the most removed, but

gathers the broadest range of data, which is then screened and analyzed at remote locations. Taken as a whole, these programs have created what Beer has
called a technocratic network that is a formidable force of national and local police engaged in internal immigration control.

The Entry/Exit Problem in the United States

American efforts to develop a reliable entry/exit system have also fallen short
of expectations. Part of the problem, as in Europe, is the sheer volume of those
arriving and leaving. Of course the United States does not have to deal with mul-
tinational administration of border controls. As in Europe, most of the data on
entrance and exit originates with passenger carrier manifests, both for incoming
and outgoing passengers, and now enhanced with biometric information.

The number of people both arriving and departing the United States through
land ports of entry is much greater than in Europe, and the USDHS has argued
that "there are major physical, infrastructure, logistical, and operational hurdles
to collect an individual's biographical and biometric data upon departure." This
appears to be due in part to the various modes of transportation that are used on
land crossings. However, even at airports, exit processing appears to be difficult.
"The United States did not build its border, aviation and immigration infrastructure with exit processing in mind. Consequently, United States airports do not
have designated areas exclusively for travelers leaving the United States."[43]

Despite the limitations, the USDHS has established estimates of short-term
visa overstayers for 2014 and 2015, based on matches of manifest information.
The number of overstayers was estimated as 534,342 for 2014, and 527,127 for
2015. Far more than half each year are from outside the Western Hemisphere,
and for each year, the numbers are less than 2 percent of the total of those who
have arrived.

5.2 Comparing Tools of Internal Policing

Therefore, in both the United States and Europe (at the member state and the
EU levels), there have been growing efforts to coordinate national immigration
police with local police forces. This coordination has been constrained by the
limits of federalism. US Homeland Security is able to work directly with local
police in a limited and defined way. Cooperation in the EU is essentially intergovernmental, filtered through member state decision-making. Nevertheless,
as the balance has changed among the population of unauthorized migrants,
between undocumented border-crossers and visa overstayers, the importance

and weakness of internal border policing has become more apparent. As internal border control has become more important, Europe and the United States have augmented the resources committed to these controls. Internal policing, however, has been approached very differently in Europe and the United States, and in many respects controls have been far stronger in Europe. I would argue that these controls explain a great deal about the lower levels of unauthorized migrants present in Europe, compared with the United States.

Coordination among national police forces is more difficult to arrange in Europe. Nevertheless, within member states policing appears to be more effective compared with the United States. The weakness of internal controls is indicated by the lack of coordination at the European level, and among the member states. In the United States, however, fewer resources have been devoted to internal controls. As a result, there has been far greater dependence on local and state police. Although I have estimated the total number of various kinds of border agents in the United States as over 137,000 (Table 5.1), only about 20,000 are involved in internal policing (ICE); of these, fewer than six thousand are enforcement agents who focus on unauthorized immigrants and worksite inspection.[44]

Employer Sanctions and Internal Policing

Perhaps the most important difference between Europe abnd the United States has been control over access to the labor market, which has been historically far greater in Europe than in the United States. Since the 1970s these controls have increased in Europe in three ways. First, more robust police instruments have been put in place; second, this has been linked to more frequent inspections, particularly in sectors more likely to employ immigrant labor; and finally, greater penalties have focused on employer responsibility, and include high fines and criminal penalties. In addition, employer sanctions have been Europeanized.

The Europeanization of employer sanctions dates from a directive in 2009 that requires minimum standards for sanctions against employers who employ undocumented workers. In fact, by the time the directive was passed, twenty-six of the EU member states already had their own laws sanctioning employers of undocumented workers. Of those, nineteen imposed criminal sanctions under certain circumstances. The purpose of the directive was to create a minimum, baseline set of disincentives for the employment of undocumented immigrants (most of whom were visa overstayers), while recognizing that illegal employment is related to labor-market pull. Therefore, the directive notes that sanctions should be directed against employers rather than workers employed illegally, and provides for numerous protections for those employed.[45] Nevertheless, it is clear that the most important burden is on the workers who, even if their rights are enhanced, will be deported outside of the EU.

By 2012, a year after member states were required to have transposed the directive into national law, it was evident that its effectiveness was related to mechanisms for enforcement. These mechanisms, initiated through inspections, included high employer fines for each worker employed, as well as criminal penalties for employers who violated the laws in place. In 2014 the European Commission issued its first report on some of the actions taken by the member states under this directive. Transposition was required by 2011, but it was delayed by as many as twenty of the member states.[46] Nevertheless, by 2012 reports were available on some actions that had been undertaken, particularly inspections that anticipated results.

Twenty-four countries submitted data to the European Commission for its 2014 report, and the number of inspections varied considerably from almost 244,000 in Italy to a mere 79 in Estonia. However, in total, there were 609,000 for the 24 countries. While the number of companies and the number of employees in these countries is greater than that of the United States, the number of inspections in the EU countries was two hundred times greater than the United States in 2012 (see Table 5.5).[47] The Commission report makes clear that in every country inspections were in targeted "risk sectors," but in a few countries, most notably Italy, all sectors were covered.

The EC report on the French case for 2012 is incomplete, but in 2015 French Prime Minister Valls announced that France would strengthen its system of inspections for undocumented workers with the formation of joint inspection units that would include labor inspectors, as well police and border officers, in effect a strengthening of internal border controls. He declared a goal of 30,000 joint inspections, half of all worksite operations against undocumented workers. In fact, the Ministry of Labor cites "combat against illegal employment" as its first priority, higher than its traditional mission of inspections for hazardous working conditions.[48]

In the United Kingdom, worksite inspections have been robust even without the pressure of the EU directive. A Home Office report notes that during the six years between 2009 and 2014, Home Office ICE teams carried out more than 36,000 (about 6,000 per year) "illegal working visits" throughout the country.[49] While this is far higher than the United States, it is lower than Italy, Germany, France, Spain, and Belgium. In contrast to most of the EU inspections, the UK process in 2014–2015 was supposed to be a cooperative effort with employers to encourage undocumented workers to leave voluntarily. French labor inspectors, however, have more of an adversarial relationship with employers, may demand additional documentation, and may enter the premises without any prior authorization.

In comparison with the United States, reports indicate that worksite inspections in most European countries have been far more extensive and demanding. As we can see in Table 5.4, even after worksite inspections were increased in the United States (see the next section), they were undertaken far less frequently than those in Europe. While the focus in Europe has been on the responsibility of employers (the pull factor), the focus in the United States has been far more ambiguous.

The emphasis on worksite inspections in the United States is relatively recent. The Immigration and Nationality Act of 1952 prohibits employers from knowingly hiring unauthorized workers, but the law was never enforced, and, indeed, was interpreted in a way to make it unenforceable.[50] Worksite inspections with penalties for employers were not integrated into the law until 1986. The 1986 Immigration Reform and Control Act (IRCA) was the end product of bipartisan efforts by Congress that had begun in 1972, and was viewed as a more effective way to deal with the pull of illegal immigration.

The core of the law, and its most controversial provision, provided for employer sanctions, which had been recommended by various commissions for many years. Penalties would be imposed on *employers* who knowingly employed

Table 5.4 **Inspections for Undocumented Immigrants Reported in 2012 in the EU, the UK, and the US**

European Union: 24 Countries Reporting		**608,999**
of which:	Germany	122,577
	Italy	243,847
	Spain	53,671
	Austria	32,765
	France (est. 2015)	60,000
	UK (2012)	5,365
United States (I-9 inspections in 2012)		**3,000**

Source: Communication from the Commission to the European Parliament and Council on the Application of Directive 2009/52/EC of 18 June 2009, COM(2014) final, May 22, 2014, Table 3, "Inspections carried out in 2012";

An Inspection of How the Home Office Tackles Illegal Working: http://icinspector. independent.gov.uk/wp-content/uploads/2015/12/ICIBI-Report-on-illegal-working-17.12.2015.pdf.

For French estimates, see: www.gouvernement.fr/en/the-fight-against-illegal-employment, February 12, 2015; US Department of Homeland Security data; Immigration and Customs Enforcement (ICE), Worksite Enforcement FY 2014 Annual Report: https://www.dhs.gov/sites/default/ files/publications/OCFO/Immigration%20and%20Customs%20Enforcement%20(ICE)%20-%20Worksite%20Enforcement%20FY%202014%20Annual%20Report.pdf.

aliens who were not authorized to work in the United States. However, no identification system was established under the law, and the sanctions program had
little political support. [51] IRCA also provided additional funding for expansion
of the Border Patrol.[52]

The number of undocumented immigrants continued to grow undeterred by
the provisions of IRCA.[53] In fact, the section of the legislation that proved to
be least effective was the section most directly related to its original intentions,
sanctions for employing illegal immigrants. Although this provision was popular
in public opinion, its actual enforcement was difficult for political reasons that
I will examine in chapter 6.

Since 1986, the approach to enforcement evolved in ways consistent with the
limited resources devoted to it. Before 2001 the Immigration and Naturalization
Service focused on "criminal employer cases," in which there was a pattern or
practice of knowingly employing unauthorized workers.[54] The resources devoted
to this effort, however, were unimpressive. Wayne Cornelius wrote that the internal enforcement side of the border enforcement strategy that was initiated in
1994 was the collapse of employer sanctions and worksite enforcement. While
there were almost 10,000 agents at the border in 2001, he argues, only 124 immigration agents were assigned to enforcement at the workplace. "This token level
of worksite enforcement is the fundamental reason why much tougher border
controls in the last 10 years have had such a weak deterrent effect."[55]

After 2001, the new Department of Homeland Security focused its attention on unauthorized workers in key security and infrastructure facilities, but
periodically on high-profile raids in support of the president's proposals for
immigration reform (see chapter 7). In 2004, the government won 46 criminal
convictions against employers; in 2005 it was 127. There was a surge of raids
in 2006–2007, each of which resulted in arrests of employers and deportation
of workers.[56] But in 2007, only 92 employers were arrested as a result of 1,100
investigations, and only 27,000 dollars in fines were assessed.

Enforcement increased, however, during the Obama administration. In 2009,
the first year, there was once again an important shift in strategy. The government continued to focus on employers, but with softer alternative tools. Rather
than high-profile raids, the new strategy was meant to be less aggressive, but with
broader application. According to ICE Deputy Director Kumar Kibble, "We
carry out this strategy with the robust use of Form I-9 inspections, civil fines and
debarment, and by promoting compliance tools like E-Verify through the ICE
Mutual Agreement between the Government and Employers (IMAGE) program."[57] This approach resulted in a significant increase of criminal investigations
(almost 4,000 by 2013), a growth in employer arrests (240 by 2012), and a very
large increase in fines assessed (almost 9 million dollars in 2013) (see Table 5.5).

Table 5.5 **Employer Audits (I-9), Employer Arrests, and Fines Assessed in the US**

Year	Number of Audits	Investigations Initiated	Employers Criminal Arrests	Fines Assessed (th. dollars)
1990	10,000			
2003	2,200	1,093	92	26.6
2008	503	1,191	135	496.6
2009	1,400	1,461	114	1,063.6
2010	2,200	2,746	196	5,824.1
2011	2,496	3,291	221	8,083.5
2012	3,000	3,904	240	8,315.5
2013	3,127	3,903	179	8,942.4
2014	1,320	2,022	172	7,331.0

Source: Peter Brownell, *The Declining Enforcement of Employer Sanctions* (Washington, DC: Migration Policy Institute, September 2005); Immigration and Customs Enforcement (ICE), *Worksite Enforcement FY 2014 Annual Report*.

Nevertheless, the American effort continued to be weaker than that of most countries in Europe. The number of audits and investigations was far smaller than in the larger European countries, and was only a small fraction of those in Europe as a whole (see Table 5.4). In addition, the criminal penalties available in most European countries are far stronger than those in the United States and the level of fines per unauthorized worker are far higher.

Does this effort make any difference, however? Is there any evidence on either side of the Atlantic that worksite enforcement has reduced unauthorized employment, and is there any relationship between the effort and the resources expended and the results obtained? Most studies have been inconclusive. Indeed, just prior to the passage of the 1986 legislation, Congress had commissioned a report from the General Accounting Office to evaluate employer sanctions in nineteen other countries; the report concluded that sanctions were "largely ineffective" in reducing the employment of unauthorized workers.[58]

These conclusions were confirmed by additional studies a decade later that essentially argued that employer sanctions, though potentially effective forms of control, were difficult to enforce.[59] Even when penalties were increased in Europe, after the implementation of the 2009 EU directive, one study concluded that "It remains to be proven if the employers' sanctions regime can have an

impact on both reducing irregular migration, as well as addressing the labor exploitation of undocumented workers."[60]

However, it is also clear that the impact on unauthorized workers is far more
consequential than on those who have employed them. The probability of detention and expulsion is also far greater for these workers in Europe than it is for
those in the United States.

5.3 The Failure of Border Controls: Fences and Walls

By current estimates, it appears that Europe will soon have more physical barriers
on its national borders than it did during the Cold War. On the other side of the
Atlantic, the president of the United States declared over and over that he would
"build a great wall—and nobody builds walls better than me."[61] Indeed, during
the years after the end of the Cold War, more new fences, walls, and militarized
boundaries were built (63 in 2016) than during the height of the Cold War in
the 1950s. The numbers grew even before the attacks of September 11, 2001, but
then skyrocketed after.[62]

The new walls were built not for protection against invasion, as they sometimes were until World War II, or to keep people in, as they were during the Cold
War, but primarily to keep migrants out. Essentially, the vast number of walls
built in the twenty-first century represents a policy failure, the inability of the
state to control the frontier any other way. This failure has been largely attributed
to push factors that drive the migrants themselves, rather than the pull factors
that both attract and facilitate their crossing. Walls or militarized frontiers as
barriers to entry have a singular advantage over other frontier controls: they provide a hard barrier against many of the pull factors of law and the labor market.
They have two disadvantages: they are costly,[63] and they are fixed defenses, and,
like most fixed defenses, they can often be circumvented.[64]

Europe

Most of the reported walls and fences were outside of Europe and the United
States. The longest was in western Brazil. India and Burma have virtually encircled
Bangladesh, and Algeria began building walls and reinforced fences against
Morocco in 1954. When it completes its wall along the Jordanian border, Israel will
be completely surrounded. In Europe the trend had begun well before the asylum
crisis, and was accelerated by the wave of asylum-seekers that moved across the
Balkans and Eastern Europe overland from Turkey and through Greece.

Each fence, wall, and barrier that has been built has been meant to provide a solution to a politically constructed policy problem, but the policy problem has varied both within Europe, and between Europe and the United States. The first new militarized border fence in Europe in fact was built in North Africa in 1993, along the Spanish–Moroccan border in the Spanish enclaves of Ceuta and Melilla. The fencing, which has been reinforced many times, was an attempt to stem the flow of migrants by land from sub-Saharan Africa. It coincided with the admission of Spain into the Schengen system, and it can be understood as one of the compensatory measures negotiated with Spain.[65] Because these enclaves were now the southernmost external border of Europe, the EU pressured Spain to assume greater control of the border, and it financed 75 percent of the costs of the project in 1995 and 2000.

The militarization of the border was a complicated issue for both Spain and the EU. Morocco does not recognize the sovereignty of Spain over Ceuta and Melilla, and has been reluctant to cooperate with the Spanish authorities in controlling the flow of migrants. At the same time, the EU has sought Moroccan cooperation in broader Euro-Mediterranean partnership, the goals of which include economic, cultural, and security cooperation. However, at the core of the Mediterranean partnership, as well as the broader European Neighbors' Policy, is an attempt to gain cooperation to secure the external border of Europe. As one scholar has put it, this is a way "to make good neighbors through 'good' fences":

> The fences of the two enclaves can be considered as a form of externalizing the problem of irregular migration . . . [of] exporting internal migration and asylum problems to the other neighboring countries and in particular the countries geographically closest in order to relieve the burden of undesired immigration in Europe.[66]

In fact, the reinforced fencing did not become an obvious deterrent for migrants. Ceuta and Melilla continued to be the principle land entry points into Europe, and the site where the vast majority of all rejections took place. A report by an EU mission to investigate continuing illegal immigration in 2005 addressed both the Spanish responsibility for the border, and the continuing demands by Morocco for increased aid from the EU.[67] By 2007 Spain was pressing the EU to take greater responsibility for this border, and requested increased financing from the EU.[68]

The construction of fences, walls, and barriers that followed those in North Africa was done much more hastily, in reaction to similar surges of migration, and with similar objectives. However, in contrast to the pressure from the EU on the Spanish government in 1993–1995, the fences and militarized barriers constructed after 2012 were built without the cooperation of EU authorities, and were often criticized by the UNHCR and the European Commission as violations of European human rights standards. The countries that constructed these new barriers argued that they were doing the work for Europe, and preventing migrants from using their countries as entry points to Northern and Western Europe.

In 2012 Greece and Bulgaria erected fences on their borders with Turkey to prevent a growing surge of migrants, and in 2015 Hungary completed a 109-mile fence on its border with Serbia that was later reinforced and extended 216 miles to Croatia. Slovenia then followed by building a barrier of its own on the Croatian border. Since Hungary and Slovenia are members of the Schengen zone, and Croatia is pledged to join, these fences seriously compromise the commitment to free movement within the Schengen zone.

The simple story is that the hard boundaries were constructed in reaction to the surge of migrants as the pathway for asylum seekers to Europe moved from sea to land routes. The more complicated story, however, is related to the rules of how asylum is obtained in Europe as regulated by the rules of Dublin and Schengen. The right-wing Orban government in Hungary, for example, has argued that it is attempting to enforce Dublin regulations and protect the European external border. It has insisted that there are legal ways to enter the country, and that they will only admit migrants who formally claim asylum (and are therefore registered) in Hungary.[69] They also argue that Serbia is recognized as a STC by Hungary, and therefore they are not obliged to recognize any claims from asylum seekers entering from there. Of course, this logic, supported by the Dublin Regulation, applies to all of Hungary's borders (see chapter 3). Additional hard barriers have been constructed between Macedonia and Greece and at the Austrian borders with Slovenia and Italy, all of them justified in the name of the Dublin regulations, and all of these countries are members of Schengen. Finally, this domino game of responsibility extends to the network of barriers that have been built around the Calais entrance to the Eurotunnel, which amounts to a militarized fence between France and the United Kingdom, largely financed by the United Kingdom (as discussed earlier in this chapter). In all of these cases, the erection of walls, fences, or hard boundaries is related to the tension between the open borders of Schengen, and the requirements for enforcing the Dublin regulations to keep people out. In some cases walls seem to have worked to prevent entry, at least at the site of the wall. The movement of migrants across the Hungarian border and the Greek–Macedonian border has more or less ground to a halt, no doubt aided by the EU agreement with Turkey; the success of the barriers at Calais is less certain. But this does not mean that the barriers have worked on the EU level. There is no evidence that entries into the EU have been prevented, or even deterred.

As the land routes were blocked in 2015, arrivals through the sea routes of the Mediterranean reached record levels in 2015 and 2016, but deaths reached record levels as well. There were 5,096 deaths in the Mediterranean in 2016. This was notably high even compared with the number of deaths on all routes to Europe noted in Table 3.2.[70]

The United States

In the run-up to the presidential election of 2016 candidate Trump promised, in a position paper on immigration, that "there must be a wall across the southern border" of the United States.[71] In subsequent speeches and interviews—as a candidate, as president-elect, and as president—President Trump made it clear that the wall was a project of first priority, needed to prevent illegal immigration and for the security of the country. In March 2017, US Customs and Border Protection announced a competition for designs for a "solid concrete wall."[72] In June it announced that it would fund the building of several prototypes, although there was not yet any funding from Congress.[73]

The attempt to build a barrier between the United States and Mexico is not new. The first attempt to prevent the movement of migrants across the border was Mexico's effort in 1830 to prevent illegal movement from the United States. Mexico ultimately lost, and by the end of the nineteenth century migration was flowing the other way. The more recent effort to construct a hard boundary is related to the politicization of immigration from Mexico, constructed around the war on drugs during the Nixon era, the Chicano civil rights movement, and the rise of immigration from Mexico. Immigration from Mexico had begun to rise in the 1950s, relatively unrestricted by immigration legislation in place. In addition, after 1968 Mexicans were particularly well positioned to take advantage of the family preference of the 1965 legislation that benefited spouses and unmarried children, and the fifth preference, that gave preference to brothers and sisters of US citizens. Therefore, one result of the change in the immigration regime inaugurated by the law of 1965 was a continued growth of legal immigration from Mexico and the rest of Latin America.[74]

However, because of the new limits on Mexican entry, a second result was to encourage undocumented immigration and settlement from Mexico. For fear of not being able to reenter the U.S., when the Immigration Act of 1965 was applied to the Western Hemisphere after 1968, many of the Mexican immigrants who had moved back and forth before were now more reluctant to return to Mexico. The immigration system had changed after 1968, but the push and pull factors had not. The new legislation now required more systematic border controls that had not existed before. With the establishment of defined categories and

numerical limits on immigration, the definition of legal and illegal migration had
changed; and in this context, the increase of unauthorized immigration across
the southern border was politicized as a growing economic and security crisis
(see chapter 7).[75]

The creation of a physical barrier between Mexico and the United States was
first initiated in 1990, with the construction of a metal fence along fourteen
miles of the border in the San Diego sector. This steel fence was extended and
reinforced in the years that followed. Other limited barriers followed, some to
prevent the entry of vehicles, rather than people, in wilderness areas. In 2004, for
example, a strong fence was completed along the southern border of Organ Pipe
Cactus National Monument in Arizona.

The first comprehensive effort to build a barrier, however, was the Secure
Fence Act of 2006, which ultimately authorized the construction of about 700
miles of fencing along the 2,000-mile border. The legislation was amended in
2007 to give the Secretary of Homeland Security the power to decide what kind
of barrier was appropriate for various parts of the border. By January 2009 the
USDHS announced that almost 600 miles of fencing had been completed, although this included various kinds of barriers, including "virtual" fences.[76]
Then, midway through President Obama's first term, the president announced
that the fence along the Mexican border was "basically complete." The 649 miles
of barriers included 299 miles of vehicle barriers and 350 miles of fencing for
people.[77] However, the lengthening and deepening of the fence system continued to be an unsettled political issue that divided local governments in the
southwest, as well as state officials from both political parties (see chapter 7).

The general balance between apprehension and removal seemed to indicate
that the border was never out of control, but was controlled in a particular way.
For many years, those crossing illegally were not prevented from crossing, but
were generally apprehended after they had already crossed, overwhelmingly in
the area just north of the southwestern border with the United States. They were
then "voluntarily" returned to Mexico, although many often returned to the
United States again. Voluntary returns or departures (often derisively referred to
as "catch and release") have covered a variety of procedures, but they are rarely
voluntary without pressures or threats.[78] They have included migrants caught
at the border (before entry) and then simply returned, as well as those who are
in removal proceedings that were not going well, who then decided to return
voluntarily. In general, the ability to choose voluntary return rather than formal
removal depended more on border policy, rather than migrant will.

The increase in resources was reflected in an increase of border control activity, and in a dramatic change in the pattern of expulsions. Until 2006, most
expulsions were voluntary, and there were few obstacles for those who were
expelled to return. After 2006, the number of formal (documented) removals

rose rapidly, and doubled to about 350,000 per year during the last years of the Bush administration, and then to almost 400,000 under Obama, a figure that was approaching the number of voluntary departures.

5.4 Detention and Expulsion

The most important assertion of the ability of the state to control its borders is the detention and expulsion of unauthorized immigrants. These include those who entered illegally, despite policing, fences, and walls, as well as visa overstayers mostly interned as a result of internal policing. In fact the widespread and growing use of detention and expulsion, as well as walls, is relatively recent and in general does not reflect an increased weakness of border controls.

In Europe there are far more detention camps than in the United States, but fewer migrants actually detained (see Table 5.6). A report from the EU in 2007 estimated 220 detention camps for immigrants within the twenty-five countries of the EU. Another authoritative report, by the European Migration Network, counts 128 dedicated detention (more narrowly defined) facilities in 2014.[79] Finally, as Table 5.6 indicates, the Global Detention Project lists more than 347 centers in Europe that were open between 2013 and 2016.[80] Of these, more than a hundred were in Switzerland and Germany, with France and Greece a close third and fourth on their list. Although the Return Directive and the Reception Conditions Directive[81] generally regulates the detention condition of migrants, limits the number of days in detention, and would appear to limit the use of jails

Table 5.6 **Detention Facilities and Detained Migrants in Europe and the US**

	Detention Facilities	Migrants Detained		Percent TCN Population	Percent of Undocumented Entries	Percent of Estimated Undocumented Population
	2013–2015	2009	2013	2013	2013	2009
Europe	347	116,371	92,875	.26%	32.7%	3.1%
US	220	383,524	441,000	.96%	90.6%	3.4%

Source: Global Detention Project: https://www.globaldetentionproject.org/countries/ and https://www.globaldetentionproject.org/detention-centers/list-view.

European Migration Network (EMN), The Use of Detention and Alternatives to Detention in the Context of Immigration Policies, https://ec.europa.eu/home-affairs/sites/homeaffairs/files/what-we-do/networks/european_migration_network/reports/docs/emn-studies/emn_study_detention_alternatives_to_detention_synthesis_report_en.pdf.

and other ad hoc centers, only about a third of the detention centers in Europe appear to be dedicated, long-term centers.

Many of these, particularly in the United Kingdom, are run by private for-profit security companies, which have sometimes been criticized for violating EU norms. Moreover, the United Kingdom and Ireland are the only EU countries that have opted out of the Return Directive (although, unlike the UK, which has no formal on detention, Ireland has imposed a limit of 21 days).[82] Most of these detention centers were created in and after the 1990s, although they were first established in France somewhat earlier, between 1981 and 1992.[83] Their creation does not appear to be related to a surge in immigration or undocumented migration, but rather to the politics of immigration in major receiving countries in Europe.

In France, the legal concept of administrative retention goes back to 1810. More recently, *zones d'attente* (waiting zones) and the *centres de rétention* (detention centers for foreigners waiting to be admitted or deported, where they can be held for up to forty-five days)[84] were created in 1981 and formalized in 1992 by socialist governments. In the 1980s there were reported to be seven or eight centers; by 2007 the number had risen to twenty-eight; the most recent estimate is at least thirty-seven: ten in the Paris region, and twenty-seven around the entire periphery of the country.[85] Some of them already existed in the 1930s or the 1950s, but the newest version was an attempt to prevent asylum seekers from claiming rights that they would have had once they formally entered French territory, or to hold undocumented immigrants and applicants for asylum whose applications have been refused, but whose cases may be under appeal.

The number of migrants detained in Europe remained stable or declined between 2007 and 2012. Although the number of asylum seekers entering Europe increased after 2010, the number of migrants in detention declined by about 5 percent per year from 2009 to 2013. There were two notable exceptions to this trend—Hungary and Bulgaria—both of which experienced a large and rapid influx of refugees.[86] Within Europe, the total number of TCNs in detention in France each year between 2009 and 2013 was far higher than any other country. More than 38,000 people were detained in 2013. This was, however, a 35 percent decrease from the high in 2010. In the United Kingdom, about 30,000 people entered the detention system in 2013, a small increase over 2009.[87]

The number of detention camps in the United States is smaller than in Europe, but the number of migrants detained is far higher from year to year. The Global Detention Project lists 220 immigrant detention facilities in the United States that were opened between 2013 and 2016, with an additional 400 that had been previously open but had been closed down. More than half were privatized, and many more were simply county jails in which migrants were held for some period of time under "civil detainers" requested by federal immigration authorities.

Many of these facilities that mix detained migrants with a criminal population are formally banned in Europe.[88] A critical report on immigration detention presented to ICE in 2009 noted:

> With only a few exceptions, the facilities that ICE uses to detain aliens were built, and operate, as jails and prisons to confine pre-trial and sentenced felons. ICE relies primarily on correctional incarceration standards designed for pre-trial felons and on correctional principles of care, custody, and control. These standards impose more restrictions and carry more costs than are necessary to effectively manage the majority of the detained population. . . . [Moreover] ICE is comprised primarily of law enforcement personnel with extensive expertise performing removal functions, but not in the design and delivery of detention facilities and community-based alternatives.[89]

The US detention population was relatively stable between 2000 and 2005 at just over 200,000 per year. Then the number of detainees in the United States increased at the same time as the comparable population in Europe decreased. The number peaked at about 480,000 in 2012, roughly four times the detention population in Europe, but about the same percentage of the estimated undocumented population of the United States in 2009. As we can see in Table 5.6, in 2013 the proportion of TCNs detained in the United States was more than three times that of the ten most important immigrant-receiving countries in Europe. Documents indicate that in 2011 there were between 84 and 364 detention centers that on an average day held more than 33,000 immigrants.[90] The total number of detainees exceeded 400,000 in 2014, an 86 percent increase over 2006, when the use of detention began to grow rapidly each year.[91]

At least until the spike of entries in Europe after 2013, about as many migrants were being detained each year in Europe and the United States as were apprehended or detected for entering without proper documentation. In Europe detention had long been related to internal policing of immigration. In the United States, after 2006, detention increased at the same time as the apprehension of undocumented entries steadily declined (see Figure 7.2). This was related to an increased use of internal policing of the stock of undocumented immigrants, rather than simply enhanced controls at the border.

Indeed, this was a long-term trend that had begun in the 1990s. Between 1994 and 1998 internal immigration arrests doubled, then doubled again during the next eight years, and doubled once again between 2006 and 2013. Between 1998 and 2012 there was a 145 percent increase of prisoners entering federal facilities for immigration offenses. By some measures, immigration control has become the most important preoccupation of federal law-enforcement. More than half of all federal arrests in 2013 were for violations of immigration laws, far more than for any other offense (including drug possession and sales). Although 60 percent of these arrests were in border states of the southwest, the remaining arrests were in other parts of the country.

The increase of detainees has also been inflated by the requirements of mandatory detention, a requirement that was first enacted in 1988, increased in 1996, and then further expanded in 2001.[92] Detention before trial is required for all asylum seekers pending final "credible fear determination," all noncitizens who have been placed in removal proceedings, and undocumented noncitizens with criminal records. Nevertheless,

> Immigration proceedings are civil proceedings and immigration detention is not punishment. Zadvydas v. Davis, 533 U.S. 678, 609 (2001).... Although ICE has no criminal detention authority, ICE has administrative authority pursuant to the Immigration and Nationality Act to detain aliens during the removal process.[93]

On the other hand, to re-enter the country after having been removed is a now a felony, a criminal charge that can be pursued by the Department of Justice. Most migrants in detention are held for re-entering. Many others, however, are detained while they are awaiting hearings for illegal entry or are awaiting removal. Still others are detained by state and local authorities at the request of federal authorities under civil detainers.

On average, 90 percent of those detained by federal authorities for migration offenses are held until trial, a much higher percentage than those being detained for any other offense, including violent crimes. Indeed, as increasing numbers of migrants have been detained, the line between immigration detention and criminal incarceration has blurred, and, from the list of US detention facilities, it is clear that prisons are the principal means of detention in most parts of the country. This is particularly true since Operation Streamline was initiated in 2005 by the Departments of Homeland Security and Justice, which focused on enforcing the imprisonment provisions for unauthorized entry, as well as formal removal.[94]

Locked detention facilities in Europe are generally used for migrants who are subject to deportation, while open facilities, such as the now closed center in Calais, are often used to house migrants and asylum seekers whose fate has not yet been decided. These centers fall under EU directives, although, since the surge of asylum seekers after 2012, the line dividing the two has not always been so clear. Nevertheless, the rules appear to have been more constraining on state authorities in most parts of Europe than in the United States.

In Europe, the rules that govern these anomalous zones have changed over time, and vary from country to country. What Tinsley House Removal Centre at Gatwick Airport near London and the Zone d'Attente at Charles De Gaulle Airport near Paris have in common is that they are neither prisons for migrants and asylum seekers, nor are those who are detained free to leave (except to leave the country). Different types of the extraterritorial facilities operate under different rules that have changed over time, and they often have somewhat different functions. As one researcher has said, they are "zones of law, but not of freedom."[95] They do not operate outside of the law, but under different laws. In particular, the rules that govern those seeking asylum and those who are simply undocumented are different, although in practice claiming asylum is often the final prerogative of migrants who have been refused entry.

The complexities of detention in France are specified in an information sheet given to those detained at Charles de Gaulle Airport (Zone d'Attente de Roissy).[96] The document makes clear that the detainee is being held either because the border police concluded that "you do not meet the conditions to enter France or any other state of the Schengen area," or because "you filed a request for entry as a refugee."[97] If a migrant has been refused entry, he or she has a right to a see a doctor (present at the airport), to be aided by a translator, to communicate with a lawyer (or any other person), and the right to leave for any country for which he or she has documents and an air ticket. It is interesting that the rights specified for asylum seekers are more extensive, including the right to appeal to an immigration judge, if a representative of the Office for the Protection of Refugees and Stateless People (OFPRA) decides that the case is unfounded.

At Charles De Gaulle Airport, access to translators, doctors, and preliminary administrative interviews, as well as representatives of authorized NGOs, is generally available at the facility. Although many of these same rights can be claimed at Tinsley House Removal Centre at Gatwick Airport in the United Kingdom, they are far more difficult to access. Both of these are locked facilities.[98]

The French system also has a large and growing network of open reception centers for migrants who have filed asylum claims. By 2017, there were almost 30,000 claimants housed in more than three hundred centers while their claims were being considered. These are more like welfare centers than the closed airport facility, and generally accommodate asylum seekers who have entered French territory by land, rather than through airports.[99] The British system also provides for subsidized accommodations, but they are both privatized and provided by local authorities.[100]

The use of open facilities for asylum seekers in the United States has been far more limited and sporadic. Most recently, this approach was used to deal with the 60,000 asylum seekers (mostly children) who crossed the southern border in 2011 and 2014 (see chapter 4). In 2017 these open centers were shut down, primarily to discourage asylum seekers from crossing the border.[101]

The construction of walls along the eastern borders of Europe, and the chaotic movement of asylum seekers across the Mediterranean and the Aegean, has created the impression of an emerging fortress Europe. If we look at patterns of detention, however, the United States appears to have developed a more effective barrier, even without the great wall advocated by President Trump. The United States has detained far more migrants than Europe, and while detentions in Europe were decreasing, at least until the surge of asylum seekers after 2013, detentions in the United States were increasing at the same time that undocumented border crossings were declining. The United States recognizes a limit on detention (180 days) that is far higher than every European country, at least until 2018, with the exception of the United Kingdom. Finally, the American system of detention is far harder than that of Europe. It has tended to criminalize unauthorized presence by migrants, both through the "interoperability" programs of cooperation with local police, in place since 1988, and the use of criminal holding facilities to detain migrants. Perhaps more to the point, the criminalization of immigrant detention has become the norm in the United States, supported in law and practice.

Expulsion

Patterns of expulsion accentuate this comparison. We would expect that levels of expulsion in Europe would be higher than in the United States, primarily because of the organization of internal enforcement is better. Indeed, as we can see in Table 5.7, the number of undocumented TCNs apprehended from year to year in Europe is considerably lower than those apprehended in the United States, except for 2014 and 2015. However, the number (and percentage) of those apprehended who actually leave is generally far lower in Europe since 2010.

In both Europe and the United States, even when returns and removals are actually ordered by judicial authorities, they often are not carried out. In Europe, generally no more than 45 percent of those ordered to return actually do so.[102] For the United States, there are no comparable statistics. However, in 2016, there was testimony from the acting director of ICE/USDHS that almost a million aliens with orders for removal were still in the United States, the vast majority of whom were not detained.[103] Nevertheless, the percentage of those apprehended who are then removed is far greater in the United States than in Europe, and has increased dramatically since 2009 (see Table 5.7).

For Europe this appears to be related to the growing number of asylum seekers. Those who apply for asylum are generally not detained in locked facilities, and

Table 5.7 **Undocumented Immigrants Apprehended and Returned from Europe and the US, 2008–2015**

Year	2008	2009	2010	2011	2012	2013	2014	2015
Europe								
Apprehended	580	564	505	469	433	452	672	2155
Returned*	242	253	225	194	207	216	196	227
Percent	41.7	44.9	44.6	41.4	47.8	47.8	29.2	10.5
United States								
Apprehended	1044	889	797	678	671	662	680	462
Removed	360	391	381	386	416	434	407	333
Percent	34.5	44.0	47.8	56.9	62.0	65.6	59.9	72.1

Sources: For Europe, these statistics are reported annually by Eurostat European Commission, *Eurostat* Database for the European Union: http://appsso.eurostat.ec.europa.eu/nui/.http://epp.eurostat.ec.europa.ey/portal/page/portal/statistics/search_database.

For the United States, apprehensions and removals are reported by fiscal year by the Department of Homeland Security, Yearbook of Immigration Statistics: https://www.dhs.gov/immigration-statistics/yearbook, Table 39.

*Formal removals in the United States are the equivalent of returns in Europe. In both cases they are based on formal orders of removal. On both sides of the Atlantic, apprehensions are generally made by immigration police in Europe, and by ICE in the United States.

often cannot be found to be expelled. In addition, orders for expulsion often cannot be applied to migrants who are refused asylum, because the countries from which they arrived will not accept them back, or are war zones to which they cannot be expelled. Not surprisingly, the actual numbers of those expelled each year is far closer to the number of those actually detained than to those against whom orders are issued. In Italy, Sweden, and especially France (which issued the largest number of expulsion orders), the percentage who actually are expelled after receiving an order of expulsion was less than 20 percent between 2010 and 2016, compared with 75 percent in the United Kingdom and more than 80 percent in Germany.[104]

For the United States, statements from ICE tend to explain that the backlog in expulsions is due to insufficient space in detention facilities, the resistance of local authorities, and the protections that the courts have given to undocumented migrants.[105] This is similar to the arguments that have been made in Europe.

There also appears to be little relationship between changes in the volume of apprehensions and changes in the volume of expulsions. Even when apprehensions increased in 2014 and 2015 in Europe, the number of those returned remained about the same. When apprehensions in the United States declined during this same period, removals declined, but far less than apprehensions. What varied the most in each case have been apprehensions, rather than returns and removals.

In both Europe and the United States, increases and reductions in apprehensions are easier to alter through policy than are formal expulsions that are generally subject to judicial actions. Indeed, on both sides of the Atlantic, apprehensions and expulsions are related, but are on different bureaucratic tracks. In Europe, apprehension is pursued by police, often special immigration and frontier police. Orders for exclusion or deportation, though usually ordered by the Home or Interior ministries, may be either administrative or judicial, and are generally subject to review by judicial authorities. Although the success of these reviews has been limited, they usually involve considerable time and delays.[106] Nevertheless, the difference between apprehension and ultimate expulsion appears to reflect policy decisions. Apprehension reports can be used as an indication of government determination to clamp down on undocumented immigrants, regardless of the outcome.

In the United States, the complexity of the asylum process ensures that only expedited and voluntary returns will proceed relatively rapidly. Even as the Trump administration increased ICE roundups of undocumented immigrants in 2017 by 40 percent compared with 2016, the number of removals actually declined by 12 percent, compared with the year before.[107] In addition, the arrests and deportations during the first few months of the Trump presidency were lower than comparable periods at the beginning of Obama's second term in 2013 and 2014, when arrests were more than 50 percent higher than those in 2017, and removals were 38 percent higher. These differences have been somewhat muted by more sympathetic policies promoted by Obama in 2015–2016, as well as by the very different ways that these policies were framed in each case.

However, the conventional wisdom is that expulsions have risen dramatically in the United States, and expulsion appears to be a more important issue in American politics compared to Europe. In fact, some kinds of expulsions (formal removals) have indeed increased, while others ("voluntary" returns) have declined (see below, Figure 7.2. The result has been a net decline in annual expulsions since 2000, but at the same time, expulsion has become harsher. An expedited removal process that provided for administrative removals without appeal in certain cases, administered by the Department of Justice, was authorized by Congress in 1996. In 2004, the program was transferred to Homeland Security, and its application was expanded. By 2013 the number of expedited removals peaked at 193,000, four times what they had been in 2004, and represented 44 percent of all removals. The numbers diminished somewhat over the next two years, but the percentage remained the same.[108] In addition, another third have been reinstatements of old orders, or returns of those who had previously entered undocumented and had been previously removed or returned. Therefore, by 2016, two-thirds of removals from the United States were subject to limited or no review by administrative courts.[109]

In Europe, despite the lower percentages of actual expulsions relative to orders to return, the system of expulsion, by some measures, has been more effective than in the United States. If we look at the number of returns in Table 5.7, the percentage of deportations each year from Europe have been over 5 percent of the undocumented population (Table 3.1). Even at the highest levels from the United States, in 2013, removals represented less than 4 percent of the estimated undocumented population.

Patterns of expulsion in Europe have begun to change as the coordinated effort to harmonize and coordinate returns from the various member states grows, based on the Return Directive of 2009.[110] Several aspects of this Directive provide an important comparison with the United States, all of which provide common criteria for expulsion. The first is the commitment to encourage member states to establish more robust systems for voluntary departure (Article 7). A commission report in 2014 notes that although there had been only a few "assisted voluntary return" programs before the directive went into effect in 2010, these programs have become more extensive, and by 2012, they accounted for 44 percent of returns (compared with 36 percent in the United States).[111]

Furthermore, this percentage—as it has in the United Kingdom[112]—is likely to increase over time, as the comparable percentage in the United States declines. Second, the directive has initiated an effort to reverse the widespread criminalization of irregular entry or stay in Europe, at the same time as the dynamic appears to be moving in the other direction in the United States. Although the directive seeks to soften and regulate some aspects of expulsion, it also attempts to harden the border by requiring member states to issue a limited re-entry ban—with some exceptions—for migrants who are returned, similar to the ban in the United States. The Commission report in 2014 noted that "The concern expressed by some Member States at the time of its adoption, that its protective provisions would undermine the efficiency of return procedures has not materialized." Until the surge of refugees, which peaked in 2014–2015, the percentage of those apprehended who were returned remained steady at more than 40 percent.

Far more than in Europe, however, the patterns of expulsion in the United States have changed, indicating a policy to harden the border that began even before 2001. During the second Clinton administration, there was a rapid increase in both voluntary departures as well as formal removals. After 2000, under President Bush, formal removals continued to increase, but voluntary departures dropped rapidly (see Figure 7.2). By Bush's second term, however, voluntary departures once again increased, but formal removals almost doubled. Finally, under Obama, formal removals increased once again (less dramatically than they had during the second Bush term). Voluntary departures, on the other hand, declined rapidly after 2004, even before the onset of the Great Recession. Figure 7.2 demonstrates that the policy of voluntary returns accounted for the overwhelming number of expulsions until 2003. The stability of this policy is indicated by the close proximity of apprehensions and expulsions. By 2011, however, formal removals accounted for the majority of expulsions from the United States.

Thus, by the end of Obama's second term, policy had clearly turned toward formal and recorded removals that prohibited any return to the United States for at least five years, and that criminalized any unauthorized return (see chapter 7).[113] The number of formal removals of undocumented migrants from the United States steadily grew after 2005 to over 400,000 in 2013, and stronger penalties have been imposed on employers, implying greater labor market controls. Because voluntary departures have diminished at the same time, the total number of expulsions since 2000 has steadily declined, from almost 2 million expulsions in 2000 to just fewer than 500,000 in 2015.

Conclusion: Walls Are Not Enough

The hard arm of the state in Europe and the United States has been directed primarily against unauthorized immigrants, many of whom have been resident for a long time. This represents a far larger population in the United States than in Europe, as well as a larger flow from year to year.[114] Nevertheless, police resources in Europe have generally been concentrated internally, while the United States mostly concentrated on border areas, primarily the southern border with Mexico.

During the past decade, increasing resources have been spent on walls to keep migrants out. The wall of the US–Mexican border has been a work in progress for decades. The walls in southeastern Europe and North Africa are more recent. In each case they are a hardening of land borders of some, but limited, effectiveness. There have been more effective ways that the border has been hardened, however, that have been more offensive than defensive.

In the evolving system of expulsions of undocumented migrants from the United States, the border itself has become increasingly important, even as movement across the border has slowed, and even reversed. The new system has created a harder border, with far more severe penalties for crossing. Until about 2000, the border was more fluid, and almost all expulsions were voluntary returns. Of course they were not really voluntary, but they were also less consequential. As border policy has become more politicized, expulsions have become more formal, and more consequential, even as the total number has declined dramatically.

At the same time, even as internal enforcement has increased, resources and policing have been more heavily concentrated on the border, in part because US law makes expulsions at the border and the area nearby far easier than expulsions of migrants apprehended and detained further inland. Aliens detained under expedited removal and reinstatement of removal procedures are easiest to apprehend in border areas, and can claim few legal protections or rights. Until 2001 they probably would have been voluntarily returned across the Mexican border. Now they are formally removed. Even with the decreased apprehensions, the border has been hardened by the increase of formal removals.

Europe has tended to concentrate policing resources further inland, with mostly sporadic operations at the land and sea borders. Of course, this is related to where unauthorized migrants are concentrated, but it is also related to the weak federal structure of the EU. The external land and sea borders are controlled by the member states, and policing is difficult to coordinate. Internal policing is easier for the member states to control and finance, but also difficult to coordinate and harmonize under EU directives.

Nevertheless, even with the constraints of weak federal authority, European member states have together deported proportionately large numbers of unauthorized aliens, more than the United States. Moreover, like the United States, they have agreed on rules that make it difficult—and illegal—for those whom they have expelled to return. In this way, the borders of Europe too have become harder.

6

The Politics of Border Control in Europe

Policy Failure and Border Pressure

In this chapter and the next I will examine the growing politicization of border control policy in Europe and the United States. Richard Bellamy, Joseph Lacey, and Kalypso Nicolaïdes provide a focus by presenting a typology of boundary politics that include boundary-making, boundary-crossing, and boundary-unbundling (the acceptance of some policies but not others).[1] The politics of border control, at their core, are about the opening of some borders, which almost always involves the closing of others. The result is the inclusion of some people and the exclusion of others based on citizenship, but also defined privilege, and sometimes-exclusionary bigotry. Borders may be relatively soft, in the sense that they can be crossed easily by most people (like the internal borders of the Schengen area, or the interstate borders of the United States), or hard, in the sense that they are militarized, and can be crossed only by some, under the most demanding controls (like the Cold War borders in Europe).

The stakes in borders are generally high because they shape relations of power and privilege by organizing inclusion and exclusion. They magnify the power of some interests and disperse the power of others.[2] This is the focus of Grant McConnell's classic study of American politics, in which he argues that the smaller, relatively protected space of state and local government tends to magnify the political power of local and private interests.[3] McConnell stresses the defensive capability that this protected local space affords to these interests. However, this space can also give them influence at the national level, well out of proportion to their population or size.

As effective barriers, borders are nevertheless variable and constantly being redefined. Even when they are not contested, their governance is constructed, constantly subject to debate and change. In previous chapters

I analyzed border policy and variations of enforcement. In this chapter I examine the political dynamics of the process itself, and the evolution of policy change.

I first look at why the border has become important at all at a time when some have argued (see chapter 1) that borders are increasingly less relevant. After all, the dynamics of increasingly free trade, combined with the reaction to the hard borders of the Cold War, appeared to be leading to an era of open borders, or at least softer borders, increasingly less politically salient. The relatively easy movement of migrants into Europe until the 1970s was matched by the easy movement across the soft northern and southern borders of the United States at the same time. How, then, did the issue of the border become increasingly salient and consequential on both sides of the Atlantic, and how did the borders become more significant barriers to movement for some migrants, if not for others?

I argue here that the developing political salience of the border has been the principle result of the reframing of the question of immigration by political party leaders as a failure by the state to control boundary crossing on both sides of the Atlantic. Party leaders and electoral competition have then mobilized public opinion around issues of border control as a political priority. This has taken place in the context of cross-border population movements within Europe, by movements of undocumented migrants across the southern border of the United States, and by increased numbers of asylum seekers seeking entry into Europe, and to a far lesser extent, the United States. The border has also become a focus of interest for groups seeking to protect cross-border migrants and asylum seekers, to prevent or promote their entry, or to engage in and profit from the buildup of border security.

The analysis of policy failure has created a lively debate among analysts and social scientists about which objective criteria best help us to evaluate success and failure of public policies.[4] However, these objective evaluations may finally be contradicted by a political evaluation that "squarely pertains to the world of impressions: lived experiences, stories, frames, counter-frames, heroes, villains." These are constructed in the way policies are being perceived and debated among their stakeholders, in the media, and in the forums where policymakers are held to account, such as citizen and institutional watchdogs, legislatures, and courts.[5] Indeed, political and objective evaluations of success and failure may be worlds apart, but for the framing of a political issue, political evaluation is the place to begin.[6] This political failure has had a different meaning on either side of the Atlantic, and has mobilized different political forces. The perceived sense of failure has been politicized, and has driven the politics of border control in different ways.

6.1 The Salience of the Border: Perceptions of Failure and Governance

The driver of change in Europe, one that has sometimes been noted in the literature on the development of federalism in the United States, is what Fritz Scharpf has called "the problem-solving gap." This is a gap that tends to exist "in policy areas where the EU generates problems and constrains solutions at national levels, while effective solutions at the European level are blocked by political conflicts among member governments."[7] The gap between problems created by boundary unbundling and the resistance of the member states can be a creative tension within which institutional change takes place.

Perceptions of Policy Failure at the Member State Level: Integration and the Border

On both sides of the Atlantic there is widespread perception of policy failure both at the elite and mass levels, largely driven by concerns about policy objectives and outcomes, concerns about integration, and growing concerns about security. The focus on the border in Europe began with the way that political leaders in Europe framed the issue of immigration as a failure of integration. Even at the moment that the gates were closed in Europe, there were several common themes in how the issue was framed. The first was the assumption that the balance of immigration had changed in ways that made integration of the new wave of immigrants far more challenging and difficult. The second was that immigrants were no longer needed for labor. The first was far more important.

The policy outcomes in Europe have been more frequently criticized since serious entry controls were first imposed in the 1970s, and particularly since immigration was framed in terms of identity and integration. The sense of failure was rooted in political arguments that traditional—less interventionist—modes of integration had failed to produce desired results. In some ways, this pessimism was similar to the debates in the United States before the First World War that finally led to the passage of the Johnson–Reed Act of 1924.[8] Although perceptions of policy failure on integration have not been particularly politically salient for the United States, they have been salient for the French, Germans, Dutch, and British.

For the French, the political rhetoric of failure began in the early 1980s, but was rooted in a debate among policymakers that went back to the 1950s. In France, there had been a fierce debate about framing the issue of immigration that had begun at the end of the Second World War. It reflected a deep conflict about the meaning and consequences of the shifting demography of immigration, but it remained hidden from public view, confined to a process of administrative decision-making. Immigration did not become a partisan electoral issue until the late 1970s, but that did not mean that it was not politicized. By the mid-1950s, administrative authorities were clearly seeking "immigration of Latin-Christian origin," with less and less success as the economies of Spain and Portugal began to grow. It was only in the 1980s that the number of Portuguese resident immigrants began to fall. Despite widespread perceptions to the contrary, it would not be until the 1982 census that the number of resident European immigrants would be slightly outnumbered by those from Africa and Asia, and not until 1990 that the stock of African (primarily North African) immigrants would absolutely outnumber those from Europe.[9]

Therefore, although the public framing of the question of immigration during the postwar period was that France needed immigrant labor for reconstruction (a continuation of labor immigration of the 1920s), administrative authorities had a parallel agenda based on considerations of integration. The result was what appeared to be a period of unregulated entry and posthoc regularization, a policy designed to balance out the free movement of Algerians (when Algeria was still part of France) without legislation or public debates.[10] Policy evolved through a problem-solving approach that was what Alexis Spire has called "the hidden face of the state."[11]

For three decades, the several hundred *circulaires* issued by state agencies— internal directives, rather than documents with the force of law dealing with immigration—altered the way the problem was defined. These *circulaires* and other documents effectively reframed immigration policy as one focused on a concern about ethnic balances, then a deep concern about integration, and finally—in 1974—on a view that "undesirable" immigration should be suspended, constituting a shift of thinking among policymakers about non-European immigration.[12]

In the United Kingdom, the reframing of the discourse around the immigration issue began as early as the late 1950s, with the Conservative Party's shift away from its historic commitment to Empire/Commonwealth subjectship toward a focus on immigration from the New Commonwealth (generally India, Pakisan and Bengladesh) as a challenge to British identity. Over a period of two decades, Conservative and Labour governments abandoned an inclusive immigration empire citizenship regime that made access to the United Kingdom possible for most subjects of the empire and the Commonwealth. By 1981, privileged access was effectively limited to those with familial roots in the United Kingdom; that is, generally white "patrials." Others, generally subjects from the colonies and the "New (nonwhite) Commonwealth," were admitted under rules that applied to TCNs from outside of the EU. The reframing signaled a strong movement toward exclusion that gradually took on more overtly racist aspects than the parallel French policy. By changing the definition of citizenship—and who could freely enter as a citizen, and who was a foreigner—legislation between 1962 and 1981 changed the boundaries of the United Kingdom.[13]

In refocusing the question of Commonwealth citizenship to one of identity, the Conservative government introduced the Commonwealth Immigrants Act of 1962, generally portrayed as a turning point toward restrictive immigration in the United Kingdom. The legislation restricted the entry of all subjects from the Commonwealth, and thereby created a new category of immigrants. Subsequent legislation in 1968 and 1971 then eased access for migrants from the Old Commonwealth, by permitting entry (and ultimately citizenship) to those who were able to establish their ancestry in the United Kingdom proper ("patrials"), and excluding those British subjects whose ancestry was in the colonies and the Commonwealth. It also affirmed the difference between British subjects whose passports were issued under the authority of HM Government *in* the United Kingdom (who had free entry into the UK) from British subjects whose passports were issued under the authority of a colonial Government, who would no longer have free access.[14]

The 1962 act was deeply opposed by the Labour opposition. Nevertheless, having first promised to repeal it when in opposition, the Labour government in fact accelerated this trend, implementing more demanding administrative controls after returning to power in 1964.[15] It also sponsored the Nationality Act of 1964, initiating a process that privileged white migrants, which was confirmed in 1971.[16] The subsequent 1968 Commonwealth Immigrants Act, passed under a Labour government that denied entry to British passport holders from East Africa who did not have ancestry in the United Kingdom, finally confirmed an overall policy consensus between the two major parties. Under the British Nationality Act of 1981, most of the ambiguity of UK citizenship was resolved with the exclusion of Commonwealth citizens from free entry, with the exception of those who could establish UK ancestry. There were only citizens of the United Kingdom, all of whom had the right to enter and abode—and others. By the 1980s, a common understanding of immigration between the two major parties made it possible to regulate entry administratively based on the interests of business, labor, and ethnic minorities already domiciled in the United Kingdom. Thus, while there is no specific reference to race, the patrial aspects of the 1971 legislation facilitated entry and citizenship for those born in the Old Commonwealth, while making it more difficult for NCW citizens and Asians in the colonies.

This two-decade series of elaborate legislative efforts was meant to discourage and minimize[17] the migration of TCNs into the United Kingdom. Indeed, it was meant to be a solution to what were perceived to be the disruptive effects of third world immigration. In fact, after 1996 there was a strong growth of entry of migrants from outside of Europe, and after 2004 this growth was supplemented by an equally strong growth of immigration through EU free movement. Much of this growth has been attributed to a combination of labor needs, the growth of the British economy from the mid-1990s until 2008, and the foreign policy and economic advantages offered to eight countries in Eastern Europe by the enlargement of the EU in 2004. In addition, the Labour government after 1997 further accelerated immigration by quietly shifting the initiative for labor migration from the state to employers. *The Economist*, looking back on immigration policy after 2000, concluded that:

> Over the past five years, the government has quietly liberalized the work-permit system: businesses, which used to have a tough time getting permits for foreigners, now find that applications go through pretty much on the nod. By and large, it is the employers who determine what kind of immigrants get jobs. They ask for permits, and the government responds, usually positively.[18]

However, by 2005, with an election approaching, the Blair government came under severe criticism for the increase of immigration, which now appeared to be "out of control," particularly because the number of asylum seekers was growing rapidly as well, and because of the attacks in London at the same time.[19] A sharp turn in policy[20] did little to assuage public opinion and the pervasive sense of failure.

For the British, the perception of failure grew in intensity after the suicide attacks in the London Underground and buses in July 2005. Home Secretary Charles Clarke, focusing on the failures of British multiculturalism, noted that he supported a more muscular integration contract that would ensure that "new immigrants live up to the values of our society," and that they could be expelled if they did not.[21] Clarke, in a different context, emphasized in 2011 that this was not just a problem for the United Kingdom, but that all governments in the EU need "to give priority to finding the best ways to form more harmonious societies from different communities."[22] These ideas were then integrated into the Borders, Citizenship and Immigration Act of 2009 with a more demanding "pathway" to citizenship. This approach, now dubbed "muscular liberalism," was given greater emphasis by the Tory-Liberal-Democratic government of David Cameron after 2010, who called on the government to bar state aid to groups that did not share Britain's liberal values.[23] In this, he was supported by the leaders of France and Germany.

For the Germans, the rhetoric of failure has become the core of how Chancellor Merkel has defined the problem of integration. In a speech before the youth group of her conservative Christian Democratic Union in October

2010, she famously declared that multiculturalism in Germany had "utterly failed," and that it was an illusion to think that Germans and foreign workers could "live happily side by side."[24]

Christian Joppke points out that political leaders tended to frame Germany as an "ethnic nation," well before immigration was suspended in 1973. Foreigners, particularly nonprivileged foreigners (from outside of the EU), "could never be part of 'us' in an ethnic nation." Indeed, Turks were singled out as a frankly and particularly undesirable group, a depiction that went beyond whether or not they were assimilable.[25] Similarly, for the Dutch, there was a broad-based political perception by 2000 that traditional—less interventionist—modes of integration had failed to produce desired results.[26]

At the time when the gates were closed in Europe, governmental considerations of identity and integrability were strong, if not paramount, but in different ways. For the British, framing the problem was very much related to citizenship, since immigration from the Commonwealth could not be controlled without redefining citizenship. For France framing the problem was very much about immigration and settlement, initially about changing labor market needs, but increasingly about integration and identity. For Germany, the issue has been focused on the large Turkish presence, but increasingly on asylum seekers. In each case, the discourse implied an objective of making legal immigration exceptional—primarily to protect the national community—and the phrase "zero immigration" was frequently used.

However, it rapidly became clear that this would not be possible. The new regulations were weakened, if not undermined, by court decisions vastly limiting restrictions on family unification and the ability of the state to expel foreigners.[27] Although entry into the United Kingdom became highly restrictive for NCW citizens, once having established residence, those who could get through the gates rapidly acquired significant rights that were quite different from those in other European countries.

Commonwealth citizens, who established legal residence, obtained a surprising number of citizenship privileges that sharply differentiated them from aliens from other countries in the United Kingdom. The usual requirement for registration with the police for these immigrants was dropped in committee during consideration of the 1971 Immigration Act. Once they registered to vote, Commonwealth citizens, citizens of the United Kingdom and colonies, and citizens of the Irish Republic resident in the United Kingdom were eligible to vote in all UK elections, as well as for deputies for the European Parliament. Another way to understand this is that citizens from fifty-four Commonwealth countries and Ireland, as well as immigrants from fifteen dependent territories, could vote (and run for office) in the United Kingdom. Although Commonwealth immigrants remained citizens of their home countries, they gained these British citizenship rights by virtue of residence in the United Kingdom.

The perception of failure in Europe has also been extended to the system of free movement, in part because it has been disproportionately employed by the new accession states of Eastern Europe. From year to year, free movement accounts for a third to half of all immigration movement in Europe, and European citizens represent more than a third of resident immigrant populations in the EU (see Table 3.1).[28] Most notable was the initiative that was enacted in Switzerland in February 2014, Against Mass Migration, which limits immigration from other Schengen states (Croatia was immediately affected). In reaction, the European Commission has proposed Swiss exclusion from the Erasmus + student exchange program, as well as Horizon 2020, the new European research program. But political tension over free movement has been widespread in Europe since the full accession of Romania and Bulgaria in January 2014. The government of the United Kingdom has been most vocal about the importance of limiting free movement within the EU, but other member states have echoed some of the UK concerns.

In the fall of 2013 both Home Secretary Theresa May and Prime Minister David Cameron began to advocate limits on free movement from poorer EU countries by imposing caps on movement based on per capita national income. Cameron also noted that there was a growing problem of "benefits tourism," and said that the government would impose restrictions and reductions of benefits for other EU citizens resident in the United Kingdom. To this was added the argument against "social dumping," the movement of workers from low-wage EU countries to worksites in high-wage countries, but with wages and benefits from their home countries.[29] If the campaign by the UK government to cap movement drew no support from other governments (by May 2014, Cameron argued that he had no plan to implement this proposal), the problem of social dumping had been invoked by other countries, including France, Belgium, and Germany.[30] In important ways, the political discourse throughout Europe by 2015 almost equated the free movement from European countries Eastern Europe to the problem of illegal immigration. In each case borders were being penetrated by unwanted and uncontrolled migrants, and governments discussed proposals that would greatly limit what appeared to be the established rights of immigrants from within the EU.

On the other hand, there is evidence that EU free-movement policy is consistently the most approved of policy of the EU in public opinion, and, despite recent reactions by member state governments, it has become more popular since 2015. In its annual report on public opinion in the EU in May 2017, Eurobarometer asked respondents' opinion on a set of policy priorities. By far, support for "the free movement of EU citizens who can live, work, study and do business anywhere in the EU" was the highest, at 81 percent, higher than in 2015 and 2016. It is perhaps more telling that support in the United Kingdom increased from 64 to 70 percent after the Brexit vote in 2016, in which free movement had been a major issue.[31]

Nevertheless, by framing the more restrictive policies in terms of identity and integration, perception of policy failure was built into the framing of the policy itself. By the 1980s, perceptions of policy failure on integration had become widespread and politically salient for French, German, Dutch, and British leaders.

Perceptions of Failure of Asylum Governance

Proposals for managing asylum proved to be more elusive. Demands for asylum increased more than 80 percent between 1996 and 2002, and then began to decline until 2011, when they vastly increased once again. Nevertheless, until the spike in the arrival of refugees after 2011, the governance of the external border of Europe appeared to be working reasonably well. From 1993 until 2014, the actual number of applicants granted recognition each year remained stable. Indeed, after 2006 the number went down, even though the number of applications went up (see Figure 4.1).

As we saw in chapter 4, however, the process of governance was weak. It presumed that border controls on the external frontier of Europe could be maintained primarily by the member states whose frontiers coincided with the external EU border. It also presumed that the governance of the external border would be compatible with the open internal borders of Schengen. As long as these assumptions held, the question of asylum could be framed as a question to be dealt with primarily by the member states. The Common European Asylum System, first initiated in 1999, was meant to establish minimum standards and prevent asylum shopping but did not deal with questions of actually controlling the external border. Indeed, it generally presumed that asylum applications would take place at the border. These arrangements were both extended and deepened after 2000, although proposed protections for asylum seekers were mostly rejected.[32] Other proposals to reorganize and externalize the processing of asylum seekers were also considered.

In March 2003, British Prime Minister Tony Blair submitted a proposal to the European Council to create what he called "external asylum processing centres" in order to better manage to asylum process. Under this plan, asylum seekers from "designated countries of origin," upon arrival within EU territory, would be sent to closed reception centers located in one or two member states.

They would then be given a fast-track review, and those who were approved would be distributed around the EU, and the remainder would be sent back to their country of origin under "EU imposed readmission agreements, or to detention centers in the region." This comprehensive proposal would have altered the Dublin system, and would have required unprecedented cooperation among member states for the placement and then distribution of those recognized as refugees or approved for protection. It would have also required agreement with countries of origin, as well as assurances of protection in regions of origin. For the United Kingdom, which was outside of the Schengen system, it would have required a much deeper involvement in European border governance. In fact, the proposal gathered a surprising amount of support, including a positive reception from the European Commission and a surprisingly warm reception from the UN High Commissioner for Refugees, but was never passed.[33]

The breakdown of the management of land and sea external borders of Europe became more evident after 2011. The crisis of the asylum system has laid bare the broader problems of the weak management of the external borders of Europe. Although the European Commission concluded that what is necessary is "restoring order," and that this "requires swift coordinated European action to address the immediate failings as well as to reduce the scale of the migratory inflows themselves," it did not bring into question that the "building blocks of a sustainable system of migration management are now in place."[34]

In fact, the building blocks themselves were deeply flawed in several ways. The real burden of financing the control of entry into Europe had been forced on member states that control parts of the external EU boundary, often with significant pressure from other member states. Although the collective financing by the member states appears to be short of the 18 billion dollars spent by the United States in 2012 (see the next section), different countries in Europe seemed to emphasize different aspects of border control in their big-ticket expenses. In Eastern Europe and in Spanish North Africa, the land border had been reinforced with walls and barbed wire, and militarized in some areas. Italy has relied mostly on reinforced sea patrols, and France and Germany strengthened internal policing.

From the very beginning of the current crisis, the limits of the Dublin–Schengen system were apparent. If the burden of policing the European frontier fell perhaps unfairly on the peripheral and poorer states of Europe, the real burden of dealing with asylum applications ultimately fell disproportionately on the wealthier member states.

During the 2011 Lampedusa crisis, France imposed border controls for a short time, and then Denmark imposed controls, until a government change the following year. Then both France and Italy supported modifications to the

Schengen border code that would make it easier for member states to reinstate border controls for periods of time. Ultimately, some order was reimposed on the system when the (EU) Council of Ministers first strengthened the role of the Commission in the Schengen Evaluation Mechanism (SEM) (see the next section), and then codified and defined the specific circumstances under which internal border controls could be imposed.

As the external border of the EU came under greater pressure from the growing number of asylum seekers, there was an increasing sense of the failure of policy that provoked even more intense pressure in member states. By 2011 it was becoming evident that the dismantling of the internal frontiers under the Schengen Agreement made dealing with the increase of asylum seekers far more complicated. As long as receiving countries did not rapidly process applications under Dublin, the legitimacy of the dismantlement of internal borders under Schengen increasingly came into question.

Perceptions of Failure of Maintaining Security and Preventing Terrorism

Perceptions of failure were further strengthened and accelerated by urban violence and then homegrown Islamic terrorism that began in Europe in the late 1990s. The first major incidents by homegrown terrorists in France provoked a major debate and discussion.[35]

In the years that followed, the urgency over control of the external EU border was driven by member state concerns over security. Until the late 1990s, when the number of terrorist attacks in Western Europe peaked, Europol reports make clear that most were perpetrated by domestic separatist and extremist groups of the Left and the Right. After the late 1990s "jihadist" incidents gained increased notice, although domestic conflict remained important.[36] The number of attacks declined, but the origin of the attackers was increasingly from outside of Europe, thus raising concerns about the external border.[37] After deadly incidents in Spain in 2004 and London in 2005,[38] it became clear that jihadist terrorism had merged with home-grown terrorism, and reinforced concerns about the failure of immigrant integration, combined with critiques of multicultural approaches to policy formation.

Given these perceptions of the failure of integration, asylum, and the resistance to terrorism, European member states might have simply turned inward or reinforced their own frontiers. While some of this happened—by 2018, six Schengen countries had introduced temporary border controls under Article 25 of the Schengen Agreement—the logic of the single European market led to intense negotiations about how the easing of internal border controls could be balanced against the compensatory measures that would strengthen the external common frontier (see chapter 5).

6.2 The Driving Force of Politics: Public Opinion, Interest Intermediation, and Party Competition

The shaping of perceptions of failure, and the reactions to them, did not take place in a vacuum. In each case, the initiatives to define and control the entry of migrants into Europe have been driven by domestic electoral politics, and, to a large extent, the developing impact of parties of the radical right. At the member state level, both the framing of the issue of entry and its political priority emerged in the context of electoral campaigns. At the European level, questions of entry were then driven by those member states for whom questions of culture merged with questions of asylum and terrorism.

Public Opinion

A permissive consensus has developed about the importance of entry. For mass publics, the German Marshall Fund Transatlantic Survey indicates that concern about immigration is relatively low compared with concern about other issues. Mass publics on both sides of the Atlantic have been most concerned with the economy and unemployment, and generally only a small percentage have given priority to questions of immigration, even in the United States, with fewer than 8 percent of respondents in any country claiming immigration as their most important priority in 2011 (a year when immigration pressure appeared to be high because of the surge of asylum seekers).

However, among those who feel that immigration is the most important issue facing the country, there is a tendency to focus on the border. Respondents are far more concerned about migrants who have crossed the border illegally, rather than legal immigrants (see Figure 6.1). In fact, this concern is very high even where concern about immigration is relatively low (Germany and Spain). Americans, the French, and Italians are the least worried about legal immigration; British, German, and Spanish respondents the most. All of them, however, are overwhelmingly concerned about illegal immigration, defined as unauthorized border crossing.

From the perspective of public opinion, what is generally referred to as the crises of immigration appears to be largely, though not entirely, a crisis of border control. Fewer than 25 percent of US respondents who prioritize immigration claimed to

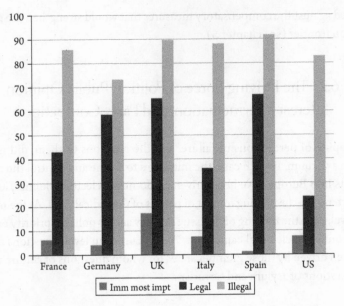

Figure 6.1 Among Respondents Who See Immigration as the Most Important
Issue Facing the Country, Percentage Who Are Most Worried about Legal/Illegal
Immigration. Source: German Marshall Fund, *Transatlantic Survey 2011:* Questions 1a, 4.1, 4.2,
http://www.gmfus.org/publications/transatlantic-trends-immigration-2011.

be worried about legal immigration, compared to more than 80 percent concerned
about illegal immigration. This difference has been less marked in Europe, where
the crisis of immigration is more often related to concerns about integration rather
than entry, but border crises have dominated the headlines, have become politically important in electoral politics, and have had an impact on public opinion.

In the results of the German Marshall Fund's Transatlantic Survey in 2011,
European concerns about illegal immigrants either equaled or exceeded that of
US respondents (see Table 6.1). In each case the concerns about illegal immigration far exceeded those about legal immigration. This is somewhat surprising,
since levels of illegal immigration are estimated to be far lower in Europe than
in the United States (see Table 3.1). Far more than the United States, European
governments have framed terrorism in terms of failures of integration rather than
border control as such. Illegal immigration has been linked to asylum and the
surge of asylum seekers after 2010. Nevertheless, concerns have been increased
by the linkage often made by European governments between terrorist incidents
and border control.

Although for European governments perceptions of failure have focused most
strongly on integration, for most Europeans (and most Americans), concern
about components of integration varies considerably from country to country.

Table 6.1 **The Most Important Precondition for Citizenship**

	Share Cultural Values	Speak National Language	Respect Political Institutions and Laws
NL	33	37	27
UK	17	34	32
Ger	8	49	37
FR	14	24	53
Sp	15	15	63
It	12	12	70
US	13	37	35

Source: German Marshall Fund of the United States, *Transatlantic Trends, Immigration* (Washington, DC, 2011), Q.10A, p. 22, http://trends.gmfus.org/files/2011/12/TTImmigration_final_web1.pdf.

For French respondents, respect for institutions and law is far more important than knowledge of language or shared cultural values; for British respondents, shared language and respect for political institutions and law dominate; and for Dutch respondents shared cultural values are far more important than in any other country in Europe.

In most respects, the importance of preconditions for citizenship varies little between left and right identities of the respondents within countries. Nevertheless, there are some differences in the UK and Germany. In the UK, shared cultural values are far more important for respondents who identify with the Right than those who identify with the Left.

Therefore, there seems to be a perception–policy gap. The policy process at the national level has focused on failure of integration (not always including language), while public concern has been greater about respect for law and institutions. The net results have been outcomes that are consistently disappointing to European voters, as well as many leaders. In the United States, support for the outcomes of policies on the entry of legal immigrants has been relatively strong (compared with Europe). Nevertheless, perception of policy failure has been directed against undocumented immigration.[39]

Public opinion in itself does not appear to drive governmental concerns about the border, I would argue. It does, however, become far more important when political groups, parties, and candidates mobilize voters around issues of identity. Its importance then becomes further focused in the politics of federalism, where the concerns of some member states become important—even magnified—in developing harmonized rules and laws.

The Importance of Interest Intermediation

Groups engaged in interest intermediation (associational groups that represent the interests of producers, workers, farmers, and other sectors of the economy, as well as religious groups, identity groups, and territorial groups) play an important role in the development of border policy in Europe and the United States.[40] In the European system, the primary question is not whether but where and how interest intermediation takes place. Indeed, how can we understand the structure of this intermediation, and how important is it?

The difference in process between Europe and the United States is that in Europe what Samuel Beer has called the "intergovernmental lobby" of territorial leaders (states and localities) tends to dominate the process, while the vertical networks of functional leaders—the technocracy (economic and identity-based interests) in key areas of public policy—are relatively weak (see below). Both of these networks have incorporated associational interest groups in different ways, but the groups associated with functional interests that tend to be national in scope in the United States, and European in scope in Europe, are far less influential in Europe. Nevertheless, depending on the policy arena, interest intermediation can influence policy at the European level by empowering member state governments or constraining them.[41]

Although there are abundant numbers of groups that are involved with various aspects of EU policy, they are only peripherally involved in actual questions of policy development. One scholar has noted that they do "interact with the Community's institutions in relatively unpredictable ways and at different points in the policy process." They do not, however, "work with government officials in structured ways to make policy."[42] Rather, they seem to be most involved with policy implementation, and the modification of policy as applied to individual cases.

But, as in the American federal system, there appear to be different patterns of interest intermediation in different policy arenas. In tightly knit and mutually supportive policy communities in agriculture and security, for example, they maintain stable relations with other state and administrative actors at the member state and EU levels. These interactions are important for both setting the agenda and developing the content of policy. Andrew Moravcsik has argued that policy positions by member states at the EU level are very much related to the mobilization capacity of groups within each state.[43] In other arenas, such as environmental policy, John Peterson has demonstrated that networks are looser, and interest groups are less effective in policy development.[44]

In migration, asylum, and border control, however, there is considerable evidence that interest groups may be consulted, but usually after policy has already been developed in order to build what Rubin Zaiotti has called "ex post facto political legitimacy" into the process.[45] As a result, policy at the EU level is strongly dependent on the ability of member states to reach agreements. At the same time, however, at least in the area of border control, there appears to be significant and continuing contact with some of the groups involved.

At the EU level in 2014 there were about 6,600 groups officially registered under the EU Transparency Register, about 3,000 of which represent business and trade groups. An additional 1,700 were NGOs or advocacy groups, almost all of which consult with the High Working Party on Immigration and Expulsion created by the Council of European Union in 1999. Of these, eight are transnational "Euro-groups," and all of these are either human rights organizations (i.e., the Migration Policy Group, the European Network Against Racism, the European Association for the Defense of Human Rights, the EU Rights Clinic, Human Rights Watch), or are organized for a specific human rights purpose (the European Network of Social Integration Enterprises to Fight Against Social Exclusion, the Association of Multiethnic Couples, the Platform for International Cooperation on Undocumented Immigrants).[46]

Few of these umbrella associations, that would normally play a strong role in policy development in the United States, play an important role in Europe. Part of the problem is the fragmentation of decision-making in EU institutions, where different directorates of the European Commission are responsible for different aspects of migration entry policy. Decision-making in the Council of Ministers is similarly fragmented. Moreover, there are few EU structures that bring together this fragmented decision-making.

The gap is particularly important between border control and asylum issues and issues of integration, discrimination, and rights of free movement. Groups involved with the latter are mostly committed to the protection of migrant rights. They have had considerable success in developing directives on discrimination, racism, and social exclusion, primarily by working with the Commission to define these issues in terms of social exclusion, linking migrant interests closely with those of member state minorities. Protected from electoral pressures, NGOs have been able to work with the Commission Directorate on Employment, Social Affairs and Inclusion (formerly Free Movement of Workers, Migrant Integration and Antiracism), a directorate that now focuses mostly on labor issues, and is far removed from DG (Directorate on) Migration and Home Affairs, which deals more with entry and border control issues.[47]

Groups working on the development of policy on border control have worked primarily with Interior and Justice intergovernmental groups that

largely exclude other EU agencies, except for DG Migration and Home Affairs.
As Virginie Guiraudon argues,

> The content of the emerging European regime is restrictive, emphasizing
> concerns about asylum fraud and smuggling rather than the importance
> of achieving internal free movement. This can be explained by the fact
> that Interior and Justice Officials were the first to define the meaning of
> a common "immigration policy" and continue to dominate.[48]

One way of understanding the development of policy on border control
is to focus on the development of a mutually supportive network of public
institutions and private structures into what some analysts have called the
"EU Security-Industrial Complex."[49] The impetus for this structure was the
commitments by the European Council to combine the strengthening of
the border against illegal immigrants, with larger considerations of security
after 9/11. These commitments were first made at the Laaken Council in
December 2001, then reaffirmed at the Seville Council the following year, and
formalized by a communication of the European Commission:

> In addition to the fight against illegal immigration, it [the European
> Council] proposes for the first time the most wide-ranging definition of
> "security of external borders," with the exception of military defence. It
> thus calls on Member States also to take into consideration at external
> borders the magnitude of crime, terrorism, crimes against children,
> arms trafficking, corruption and fraud in accordance with Article 29 of
> the European Union Treaty.[50]

The result was the development of a network of security institutions that now
include both public services and private companies, to which are outsourced or
contracted some functions (usually the management of detention centers, some
police functions, or the provision of specific kinds of services).

The model implies far more than outsourcing. It also refers to a mutually supportive system of public and private institutions engaged in this enterprise, and
the implication that this complex, like its counterparts—the military-industrial
complex or the interest-group liberalism networks in the United States analyzed
by Theodore Lowi—is important for the development of a public policy of
border control.[51]

While these networks have been established primarily on the member
state level, their policy recommendations and decisions have an impact on
policymaking at the European level as well. In 2003, a working group was set up
on the initiative of the European Commission to develop a European research

program on security. Together with the representatives of European institutions and researchers, eight companies specializing in security and defense from France, Italy, Spain, Germany, and Sweden participated in the group. The working group recommended that the EU allocate a budget of 1.3 billion euros per year to security.[52]

It also relates to other aspects of interest-group liberalism.[53] This partnership confers legitimacy and privilege by the EU for some private partners rather than others, and therefore for some approaches to border security rather than others. By developing a system of accommodating power, rather than countervailing power, the system then creates privileged access for private groups both for agenda-setting and policy making. It also muddies the waters of public responsibility. Contracting corporations are not government agencies, and may not be held to the same criteria of responsibility as the public service.[54] Analyses of the security-migration complex are generally limited to the emerging role of private security agencies, which have become agencies responsible for administering a more robust frontier.

NGOs that seek to protect migrants at the border are also part of the border network. Many of these associations have been legitimized by member states as privileged interlocutors, sometimes to the exclusion of others. They are represented in advisory councils, and may play a role in a larger decision-making process that shapes the implementation of entry policy. Moreover, as professed representatives of more open migration, they appear to be a countervailing force to the security corporations under contract with the state. From a larger, theoretical perspective, security and advocacy groups are linked to the same network, but act as countervailing forces at the border. They frame the issues differently, have different objectives, and relate differently to the decision-making process.

For example, advocacy groups in France are more or less integrated into the administrative networks that control entry and expulsion from the country. They are subsidized by the state, maintain offices at Charles de Gaulle Airport, and act as agents for migrant rights claims. In the United Kingdom, similar groups do not have a presence at airports, and are outside of the administrative agencies that control frontier policy. On the other hand, their lawyers are on call from airport detention facilities, and many of these same groups seem to be well connected to political parties as well as the press, and play a critical role in exposing problems in the system.

The so-called security-industrial complex has directly collaborated with state officials at the member state level, as well as with the working group established at the EU level. Nevertheless, the ability to develop border policy at the European level is very much limited by the ability and willingness of member states to agree on common border policies.

NGOs are poorly represented in the policymaking process on the border and at the EU level, where Interior and Justice Officials dominate, even when common visa and border guard standards are in place (see chapter 3). Nevertheless, at the level of policy implementation, they appear to have some influence in overseeing individual cases of entry, and establishing and overseeing rights at the border.[55]

Party Competition and Electoral Politics

If public opinion creates political opportunities, party competition may or may not attempt to exploit those opportunities through the electoral process. Let us consider the cases of France, Britain, and the Netherlands. In each case perceptions of failure of integration have been driven by electoral politics, in which political parties attempt to use public opinion to mobilize voters in different ways.

France

In the French presidential election of 2002, Jean Marie Le Pen, the candidate for the radical right National Front, presented the presence of a growing Muslim community in France as a challenge to French identity and a danger for the security of the French Republic.[56] Indeed, with growing electoral support, the Le Pen and the National Front had been focusing on these issues for more than a decade. Because the vote for the Left was splintered among several candidates in the first round of the presidential elections of 2002, this time Le Pen managed to come in second. The center right was divided as well, with the result that Jacques Chirac, the outgoing president of the center right, placed first, but with the lowest percentage of votes of any leading candidate in the history of the Fifth Republic, and only 2 percent ahead of Le Pen. In the second round, Chirac won with the support of the Left, and was elected with more than 81 percent of the vote. Nevertheless, Le Pen had succeeded in defining immigration as the overriding issue of the campaign.

For the center right the electoral lesson seemed clear: to never in the future permit the National Front to use opposition to immigration and questions about French identity to draw voters from the established parties of the center right. Their reading of public opinion underscored their electoral problem. The Transatlantic Trends data show virtually no difference on issues of integration between voters of the center right and those committed to the radical right. The differences are far more dramatic, however, with regard to *the priority* of immigration and integration. These issues are a priority for only 1 percent of those committed to the center left and 9 percent of those committed to the center right, but for 44 percent of those committed to the far right.[57] For the National Front, the challenge was to alter these priorities; for the center right the question became whether they could deal with these issues in ways that would both speak to the concerns of their voters, but remain different from the National Front.

Thus, in the years that followed 2002, the party competition was around the priorities of the political agenda and the importance of immigration, integration, and the maintenance of the frontier on that agenda. The strategy of the Right to deal with the challenge of the National Front included a combination of hard policy and actions that would demonstrate the effectiveness of the state in dealing with illegal immigration.

While he was Minister of the Interior, Nicolas Sarkozy periodically employed extreme Right discourse and also took action that would indicate that his government was serious about controlling the frontier. By 2005, Sarkozy was given credit by officials of the majority right for the relatively poor showing of the National Front in elections at the end of 2004 and early 2005.[58]

However, within a year after the 2007 electoral victories for President Sarkozy and the center right majority, the political climate changed rapidly. The Left did well in the municipal elections of 2008, and the president's popularity fell. Then the electoral advances of the Left were confirmed in the regional elections in 2010. In the (indirect) elections for the Senate in 2011, the Left gained a majority for the first time under the Fifth Republic. Perhaps far worse, from the point of view of the president, was the new spurt of support for the National Front in 2010, since the window of opportunity that had been opened by his success in attracting far right voters in 2007 now appeared to be closing.

Sarkozy's reaction was to move further to the right on a variety of issues of integration and border control. For the first time, the government expanded its law and order stance to target free movement of EU citizens. The most extreme action was an assertion of control of the border, punctuated by considerations of law and order, consistent with the strongest concerns of French voters. After an incident involving Roma during the Bastille Day holiday in 2010, Sarkozy shifted the focus to Roma (mostly Romanian citizens, but some Bulgarian as well) residing in France. In a major speech by the president in Grenoble at the end of July, he linked Roma to crime and immigration. This was followed by a *circulaire* of the Ministry of the Interior that directed prefects and the police to rapidly seek judicial action to dismantle three hundred illegal encampments ("those of the Roma *a priori*"), to prevent the establishment of new camps, and to prevent them from simply moving somewhere else. By September, more than 8,000 Roma had been deported (evidently for having overstayed their three-month entry permits).[59]

Just prior to the Roma incident, in 2009, the government initiated a campaign against the rare number of Muslim women who wore a burqa (full body covering) in public. This was largely a reaction to an initiative by the Communist deputy and former mayor of Vénissieux, André Gerin. With Sarkozy's cooperation, a special commission of the National Assembly was created to investigate the problem, chaired by Gerin. By October, a ban on wearing face coverings in public places had been passed (with only one opposing vote in the National Assembly), and affirmed by the Constitutional Council. The ban was justified in terms of law and order by the government (of the Right), but supported in the name of the rights of women by the Left. For both it was a way to strengthen the border against unacceptable practices. Although the result appeared to be consensus, it was the result of a struggle between Right and Left this time, framed in terms that were attractive to the Left that was the driving force that elevated a relatively unimportant problem to an issue of priority.

The complexity of the issue of integration for the Left is demonstrated by an incident in October 2013. A young Roma high School student was removed from a school bus in France on its way to a class outing, and then deported together with her family to Kosovo. The family had been refused a request for residence after they had resided in France without documents for about five years. Although there were widespread protests in their favor throughout France, the decision was quickly confirmed by the courts on multiple appeals.[60]

Nevertheless, Socialist President Holland confirmed a policy that was widely known (and confirmed to the author in interviews at the Ministry of the Interior) that children were not to be seized at schools for deportation. The president then opened the border to the girl and invited her to return to complete her education: "With regards to the case of this young girl, Leonarda, if she makes a request, given the circumstances, and if she wants to continue her schooling in France, a place will be made for her, and for her alone" (the girl refused).

Three months later a French administrative court confirmed the deportation, but, by accepting the argument of the prefect, focused on reasons other than those of insufficient grounds for asylum:

> "It's a succession of elements concerning the weakness of the social, professional and linguistic integration of the family that led to the refusal by the prefect to issue a residence permit in the country," recalls the lawyer [for the prefect], for whom the family has not shown "a real willingness to integrate."[61]

The case appeared to demonstrate the fluidity of legal entrance. It seemed to differentiate the young woman from her family, and, at the same time, emphasize "a real willingness to integrate" as a key criterion for entry.

The United Kingdom

In no country in Western Europe has immigration been of more concern than in the United Kingdom. As we have seen, this concern is most focused on undocumented migrants, generally understood as including asylum seekers. In a survey commissioned by *The Economist* in 2004, the results were similar to the Transatlantic Trends survey in 2011. Only 7 percent of those who thought that there were too many immigrants cited those who entered with employment permits, while 85 percent cited asylum seekers and those in the country illegally.[62] The reaction was largely due to the sharp rise in asylum applications between 1996 and 2002. These applications then sharply declined after 2002.

By 2005, with surveys indicating that voter concerns about illegal immigrants were on the rise,[63] more restrictive conditions were being considered by both the Labour government and the Conservative opposition in the name of respect for law. The Immigration, Asylum and Nationality Act of 2006 (presented by the Labour government) focused on controlling and reducing undocumented immigration by limiting the right of appeal for dependents (as well as for students and visitors) who are refused entry. The act also introduced heavy civil fines for employers who hired undocumented immigrants. The most controversial part of the new legislation, however, was the broad power that it gave to the Home Secretary to deprive a dual national of his or her British citizenship if the Home Secretary concluded that it is "conducive to the public good." Between 2006 and 2010, six people lost their British citizenship under this act.[64]

With the approach of another election in 2010, a weakened Labour government focused on another aspect of immigration policy about which there had been growing concern since the attacks on the London underground in 2005: multiculturalism and integration policy. The Borders, Citizenship and Immigration Act of 2009 reflected these concerns with the concept of "earned citizenship": steps toward citizenship were to be earned through a points system, linked to time spent working, learning, and doing community volunteer work, that was parallel to the system for entry. In effect the pathway to citizenship became more demanding, longer, and more complicated, with an obligation imposed on applicants to demonstrate their commitment to the United Kingdom.

These government-sponsored efforts were continued, even reinforced, under the Labour government of Gordon Brown, who placed emphasis on the importance of civic education programs at his first press conference in July 2007. In 2012, it was estimated that 100,000 children attend religious education classes at mosques, and civic education had been integrated into religious classes.

The government also pursued cooperation at the EU level that began with the French initiative at the meeting of interior ministers (G6) in March 2006. This approach, now dubbed "muscular liberalism," was given greater emphasis by the Tory-Liberal-Democratic government of David Cameron after 2010, who called on the government to bar state aid to groups that do not share Britain's liberal values.

By 2015 the Conservative Party had become increasingly concerned about the growing challenge from the radical right United Kingdom Independence Party (UKIP). From 1.5 percent of the vote in 2001, the party gained 28 percent of the vote in the European Parliament election in 2014, and then almost 13 percent in the UK parliamentary elections of 2015. Like the French National Front, UKIP attracted voters from the traditional Right, but also working-class voters who would normally vote Labour. In this way, the party challenge from the right increasingly became the force that drove border policy.

The Cameron government's response to the UKIP challenge was first to focus on the links between immigration (particularly free movement within the EU), and the exploitation of welfare-state benefits, and then to emphasize the importance of greater control over the border. While France's discourse on the Roma had emphasized crime, Britain's has emphasized employment and the exploitation of welfare state benefits. David Cameron's major immigration speech in March of 2013, assuring the British public that immigrants would not be awarded public housing, was an effort to avoid the defection of his supporters to UKIP. As the Queen stated in her annual speech marking the opening of Parliament, articulating the government's position, new immigration legislation would aim to "ensure that this country attracts people who will contribute, and deter those who will not."[65]

Certainly, the 2014 electoral success of UKIP generated much debate over questions of foreign (read EU) "welfare cheats" and of "Englishness."[66] After the Tory unanticipated victory in 2015, Cameron restated his position: "Under the free movement rules, national welfare systems can provide an unintended additional incentive for large migratory movements. . . . Changes to welfare to cut EU migration will be an absolute requirement in the renegotiation [with the EU]."[67] The UKIP increase of 2015 was in part responsible for the decision of the Cameron government to hold the Brexit referendum in 2016.[68]

The Netherlands

The turn toward integration policy in 2006 was the culmination of a series of chaotic changes in party politics in the Netherlands that had begun with the emergence of Pim Fortuyn in the run-up to the 2002 legislative elections. In the European context, Fortuyn was difficult to define. He was an openly gay professor of sociology who first moved from Marxism to the center left, and finally formed his own political party—the Pim Fortuyn List (LPF)—during the months before the election. He rejected the far right label, but strongly opposed Muslim immigration and the Dutch model of multiculturalism in the name of open social values. His assassination nine days before the election did not prevent his party from gaining 17 percent of the vote and entering into government. Although the electoral fortunes of LPF collapsed by 2006, the conflict around integration and multiculturalism remained very much on the political agenda, carried by the Party for Freedom (PVV) led by Geert Wilders.[69]

The immigration/integration debate had become less important by the time of the 2006 legislative elections, but part of the reason was the policy shift toward more demanding criteria for integration. By 2006 all major political parties had agreed on such issues as mandatory language tests, as well as more demanding integration programs for both new immigrants entering the country and resident aliens. For Dutch voters, the overwhelming concern with shared cultural values has had a special meaning in a European context.

> That there exists a wider cultural gap between Muslims and natives in the Netherlands than in most other European countries is not due to non-interfering multicultural policies but to the increasingly monocultural nature of native Dutch citizens. This rather homogeneous, progressive nature explains the cultural gap with Muslim inhabitants, who adhere to conservative morals in the Netherlands as they do elsewhere in Europe.[70]

Nevertheless, a deepening concern about polarization among Dutch political parties on how to deal with policies of cultural integration, asylum, and immigration, both at the border and within the country, became evident by the November elections.[71]

By 2017 the emphasis on the border to limit entry to the Netherlands by focusing on questions of integration was still being driven by party competition. It was considered an important victory against the populist radical right when the right-wing People's Party for Freedom and Democracy (VVD) of Mark Rutte defeated the radical right Party for Freedom (PVV) of Geert Wilders. However, although Rutte's rhetoric was softer than that of Wilders—who has been accused of inciting hatred against Dutch Moroccans[72]—it was only slightly less extreme. The leaders of both parties campaigned to reinforce the border, to defend Dutch values and those of the Christian West against the threat of Islam and Muslims, as well as against the secular Left.[73]

In different ways, electoral conflict within member states became a driver of immigration policies that increasingly focused on border control. However,

within the complex federal system of the EU, control over internal borders involved control over the external border as well.

The Political Construction of Reactions to Policy Failure at the EU Level: Strengthening the Commitment to Cultural Integration

Much of the reaction to the sense of failure of integration was focused by
member states on the border, particularly questions of entry. During the past
decade, major European countries have been moving toward linking entry
with narrowing concepts of integration that would tend to ensure cultural
stability and minimize challenges to the cultural status quo from immigration.[74] In effect, European countries have reinforced the externalized border
by setting criteria of integration as a standard for entry. Thus, requirements for
entry in the Netherlands, France, Germany, and (to a lesser extent) the United
Kingdom have increasingly demanded conformity with national social norms.
Many European countries have developed explicit policies for immigrant
entry that are consistent with their more muscular integration requirements,
and there have been attempts to Europeanize this approach to immigration
since 2006.[75]

The most demanding (and controversial) program for entry was initiated in
the Netherlands in 2006. Immigrants seeking a residency visa were required to
pass a civic-integration examination as a condition of entering the Netherlands.
The examination consisted of a Dutch language test, as well as an examination
that tested their understanding of Dutch liberal values. The most publicized
part of the exam was a film that featured pictures of a nude beach and gay
couples kissing. The point was that these scenes are part of normal life in the
Netherlands. Since most of those taking the examination would be people entering under family unification, the intention was to target spouses and potential
spouses, and to discourage resident Muslim immigrants from importing wives
from their home countries. Although the government has denied this interpretation, it is reinforced by the exemptions of immigrants from counties such
as the United States, Canada, Japan, South Korea, Estonia, Latvia, Lithuania,
Australia, and New Zealand (as well as the parliamentary debate on the legislation). Although 90 percent of those who actually took the examination during
the first year passed, the number of applicants for family unification per year was
cut in half after the examination was imposed in 2007.[76]

The Dutch initiative has been followed throughout Europe in various
ways. France has tightened admission requirements even for those seemingly

eligible for family unification.[77] Since 2007, those applying for residency and family unification have been required to take a two-month course of language training, as well as a civics course on the values of the secular French Republic. Success in the program constitutes the basis for granting long-term residence.[78] Similar programs (with different criteria) were developed in Germany in 2007 (for residence) and the United Kingdom in 2009 (as a step toward citizenship).[79]

Directives passed by the EU have been largely limited to establishing rights of migrants already resident in member state countries.[80] One exception has been the 2003 Directive on the Right to Family Unification, which contains numerous exceptions, including those based on integration criteria. A major study done for the European Commission in 2007 of the transposition of this directive into national law found that six of twenty-seven EU countries imposed important limits on family unification based on fulfillment of integration criteria, among which were some of the most important immigration countries in the EU (Austria, Denmark, France, Germany, Latvia, and the Netherlands).[81]

Thus, concerns about integration also resulted in more intensive efforts at the EU level to develop common criteria for integration that corresponded with the stronger criteria for entry. The development of a policy of civic integration was moved to the EU (intergovernmental) level at the initiative of Nicolas Sarkozy, then French Minister of the Interior. In March 2006, the interior ministers of the six largest EU countries (the G6) agreed to pursue the idea of an "integration contract," effectively bypassing the Commission and using the French model as a starting point. The initial step was to create a committee of experts to investigate the procedures used in all member states. They then proposed such a policy to the other nineteen countries of the EU.[82]

One of the first initiatives of the French presidency in 2008 was to propose a comprehensive, compulsory EU integration program. The compulsory aspect was finally dropped in June, but the European Pact on Immigration and Asylum was passed by the European Council in October 2008. Three criteria were accepted for acceptance and integration in Europe (according to the French Government): language mastery of the receiving country, knowledge and commitment to the values of the receiving country, and access to employment.[83]

The European context, rather than constraining states in Europe, has enhanced their abilities both to control immigrant entry and to develop more forceful policies on integration, essentially defined at the member state level. These policies have then spread through Europe through increasingly institutionalized intergovernmental consultations.

6.3 The Politics of Federalism: Securing
the External Border

The dynamics of federalism around issues of border control have had an impact on the power of all levels of territorial government in Europe. Samuel Beer has argued that two kinds of bureaucratic networks have become a main feature of American federalism. In key areas of public policy, people in government service—the technocracy—form a vertical network that tends to initiate policy, and forms alliances with their functional counterparts in state and local government. Their territorial check and counterpart has been the intergovernmental lobby of governors, mayors, and other local office-holders—elected officials who exercise general territorial responsibilities in state and local governments and meet in horizontal organizations. Each of these networks has incorporated associational interest groups in different ways. The technocracy has incorporated groups associated with functional interests that tend to be national in scope; the intergovernmental lobby has incorporated groups associated with defense of territorial interests at the local level, what one scholar has called "urban lobbies."

If the interests of the technocracy vary by the function of government for which they work, the intergovernmental lobby focuses on how policy costs and benefits are distributed among territorial units. From the perspective of federalism, this evolution was both centralizing, because it created a national network for local elected officials with territorial interests, and decentralizing, because it enhanced the ability of local officials to defend their local interests at and from the national level.[84]

Beer's analysis is not dissimilar to much scholarship on the development of multilevel governance in Europe:

> My thesis [he argues] is that more important than any shifts of power or function between levels of government has been the emergence of new arenas of mutual influence among levels of government. Within the field of intergovernmental relations a new and powerful system of representation has arisen, as the federal government [in the United States] has made a vast new use of state and local governments, and these governments in turn have asserted a new direct influence on the federal government.[85]

In contrast with the United States, where national officials have profited from the evolution of the federal system, in the EU, member state leaders have maintained a key role. In effect, they have maintained this role either through the equivalent of the intergovernmental lobby, or more directly through intergovernmental conferences and their role in the legislative process. As Adam Scheingate has noted, member states sometimes retain the right of veto even in the administrative process.[86]

Problem-solving deficits that have resulted from the difficulty for any one country to control entry from third countries have encouraged the development of European border policy. The problem has been understood as the need to reinforce the external border, and strengthen the will of countries that had been less prone (or less inclined) to maintain restrictive rules.

Another way to understand this policy frame is to examine how agreement was reached on the Schengen system. One of the few studies of the road to Schengen, by Ruben Zaiotti, emphasizes the process and growing agreement among high-level policymakers about a restructuring of the borders of the EU to provide for free movement of goods and people across the internal borders of Europe. The core of the ultimately successful process involved agreement among the ministries of interior/home affairs and the ministries of foreign affairs.[87]

Zaiotti argues that from the very beginning, one goal was the elimination of internal border controls, but a more important goal was the securitization of the external frontier. As we have seen, the dismantling of intra-European border controls was developed with compensatory measures that would make entry into the Schengen area more difficult and that would strengthen the ability of the police to track those who entered. The language of the Schengen Agreement was a direct reflection of that balance.

Two of the most demanding articles in the Schengen (application) Convention of 1990 involved the governance of the external border. Although the convention was an intergovernmental agreement, Articles 6 and 7, later incorporated into the Amsterdam Treaty, required the establishment of "uniform principles" for crossing the external border, as well as a commitment by the contracting states "to deploy enough appropriate officers to conduct checks and maintain surveillance along external borders" (Article 4). Moreover, to support what would inevitably be an evolving balance, implementation would be monitored by an executive committee.[88]

This framing of the Schengen Convention was understood as a tool for gaining more collective control over the external borders of the "softer" member states. The system was understood as creating opportunities for member states to influence the internal politics of their neighbors, generally in ways that would strengthen external border enforcement. In this sense, Schengen was a common victory for more secure borders that would be expanded to the remainder of the EU when the convention was incorporated into the Amsterdam Treaty, and would be then be applied to the accession states as they were accepted into the Schengen zone. This framing of border governance by a limited number of EU states would be the framework for the expanding union. When the Schengen

Convention was integrated into the formal EU structure under the Treaty of Amsterdam in 1997, border governance was framed as community responsibility (the "third pillar"), which established a new community basis for understanding, if not actual control over, what had to be done.

The reaction in the European Council was indeed to give more attention to the common border. An increasingly dense set of intergovernmental working groups was formed under the aegis of the Council to flesh out a collective approach to border responsibilities that included a Schengen working group to monitor the evolving SIS.[89] During the years that followed, additional compensatory measures at the external borders and beyond were all understood in terms of the original agreements about the complex system of Schengen border management by interdependent member states. The border of Europe was the external border, responsibility for which was distributed among the relevant member states. In turn, these member states were responsible for enforcing less than harmonized border policies under the watchful eyes of the SEM. The opening of the internal borders was always coupled with the strengthening of the governance of the external border under the Dublin Regulation.

This coupling was made easier by the fact that at least until the refugee crisis, entry of undocumented immigrants had not been a central problem in Europe in the way that it had been in the United States. The complexity that Dublin and Schengen imposed upon the member states, however, focused concerns squarely on unresolved questions of EU federalism and border control. In 2011, driven by the pressures of the electoral cycle, French President Sarkozy once again focused on the relationship between immigration control and border control. Although these two issues had been linked in the negotiations that put Schengen in place in 1995, and appeared to be a settled question, Sarkozy now reopened the question not as an emergency under Article 25, but as an institutional problem similar to that of governing the euro zone: "We must be able to sanction, suspend or exclude from Schengen any state that fails [to act], in the same way that we can sanction a state in the euro zone."[90] In other words, if states failed to meet their obligations under the Dublin Regulation, they should be sanctioned under the Schengen Agreement.

The enforcement of the Dublin Regulation could be facilitated by the data provided by the SIS. By 1999, at the Tampere summit meeting of heads of state, the EU seemed prepared to reinforce its commitment through a more coherent approach to management of the common border by establishing a European border agency. Over the next five years proposals were advanced by the European Commission that ranged from the establishment of an operational European border force, to more modest proposals for cooperation and harmonization. By 2004, agreement was reached on the establishment of a new agency, the European Agency for the Management of Operational Cooperation at the

External Borders of the member states of the EU, better known as Frontex. As we noted in Chapter 3, the mission of the new agency was modest. Nevertheless, with its emphasis on securitization of the border, it became an element of what was understood as a more or less coherent framework of open internal borders and more intensive controls at the external frontier.

The SEM had been set up by Council decision in 1999 to oversee the governance of the Schengen–Dublin system, and had been attributed to a Schengen evaluation working group, then to committees of experts named by member states. These committees produced a series of confidential reports (with recommendations) on how Schengen borders were being controlled in a technical sense by member states. The SEM was not a political priority, however, and these recommendations tended to be increasingly diluted as the Council sought consensus for approval—the usual process.

This time, the provisional settlement of the Schengen crisis involved a greater prospect of direct member state input into the governance of the Schengen border. By December 2011 the European Council (Justice and Home Affairs) had recommended "an effective and reliable monitoring and evaluation system . . . which should be EU-based." It would also involve experts from the member states, as well as the Commission and "competent agencies."[91] A year later, the Council adopted two regulations that reinforced the evaluation mechanism in two ways: first, by giving the Commission the primary role of investigation; second, by expanding the justification for reimposing border controls by member states if there are "serious and persistent deficiencies" in controls over the external border.[92]

On the one hand, these regulations certainly reinforce the power of some member states to impose their will on others by claiming serious and persistent deficiencies. On the other hand, the replacement of the technical committees of experts by the Commission may create more critical evaluations of member state behavior on the common border. Indeed, those who will be responsible for border issues in the Commission have anticipated that the net impact will be stronger EU border governance, because the Commission will be able to make coherent recommendations and will be able to follow through on them.[93] Unable to establish a mechanism of effective border governance through cooperation, the Council has not so much ceded authority as it has increased the weight and influence of the Commission to help impose the will of some states on others—a new solution to an old story in international relations.

Schengen, however, may also be important in itself for legitimizing the assertion of influence by some member states over others, a process that goes beyond the states that are within the Schengen area. There is now evidence that although the United Kingdom is not within the Schengen zone, it has successfully forced Schengen countries—the French (who are in the Schengen zone) in particular—to strengthen their Channel border, and to prevent the crossing of asylum seekers and undocumented migrants.[94]

The governance of the external border of Europe has been generally framed as a member state problem related to the Schengen system. At the same time, because of the Schengen system, there has developed an unprecedented relationship of interdependence among member states for border control that creates a dynamic for expanding intergovernmental controls.

Conclusions

In this context, policies of border control became increasingly important. First, at the member state level, criteria for entry were hardened to make it more difficult for those deemed difficult to assimilate to enter, and instruments were created to effectively harden the border. Second, there was an effort to harmonize these integration policies at the European level through greater coordination among Ministers of the Interior. Finally, the asylum crisis forced a (still ongoing) reevaluation of the governing of the European frontier through the Dublin regulations and the governing of the Schengen zone.

The governance of European borders is still a work in progress. But, like the United States, the politics of border definition and border control are shaping governance in reaction to perceptions of failure and the challenges of asylum and migration. Political parties have mobilized and shaped public opinion on the border and migrant entry through electoral politics, and, increasingly, voters are being motivated by reactions to movements of asylum seekers as well as by internal migration within the EU. Although interest groups appear to play only a small role in the development of political priorities, they seem to play a much stronger role in shaping how the border is governed. Migration, far more than trade, is dominating the politics of the border, and shaping the policies of control.

The Politics of Border Control in the United States

Policy Failure and Border Pressure

The shift in border policy in the United States emerged with what was framed as "the surge" of undocumented immigration after 1980, and the securitization of what had been the circulation of workers from Mexico to and from the United States. The perception of failure of immigration policy emerged not from a widespread reaction to a sense of failed integration, but to the increased political focus on undocumented crossings of the southern border. It was given impetus by the growth of the population of undocumented immigrants. The progressive reinforcement of the border, particularly after 1992, had the perverse effect of providing an incentive for migrants to remain on the US side of the border in larger numbers than ever before.

> The principal substantive finding of our analysis is that border enforcement was not an efficacious strategy for controlling Mexican immigration to the United States, to say the least. Indeed, it backfired by cutting off a long-standing tradition of migratory circulation and promoting the large-scale settlement of undocumented migrants who otherwise would have continued moving back and forth across the border. This outcome occurred because the strategy of border enforcement was not grounded in any realistic appraisal of undocumented migration itself but in the social construction of a border crisis for purposes of resource acquisition and political mobilization. . . . The shift from sojourning to settling as a prevailing migration strategy is thus most evident in decisions to undertake and return from first trips.[1]

The growth of the undocumented population weighed on the political process in three ways.

First, it fed a growing perception of failure of the adequacy of southern border controls. Second, as the issue of the border became politicized, it began to undermine stable understandings of policy within the policy network on immigration. Third, the border became a growing focus for intra- and interpolitical party conflict, and was accelerated by federal dynamics.

7.1 The Salience of the Border: Perception of Failure

In the context of American politics, the focus on failure has been directed toward the southern border and the flow of undocumented immigrants. Although the borders of the United States—above all the borders with Mexico—have become increasingly militarized, both the flow and the stock of undocumented immigrants have been far higher in the United States than in Europe.

All recent attempts to pass legislation on immigration control have been preoccupied with undocumented immigration. The failure to check the flow of undocumented immigrants to the United States—indeed the doubling of the stock of illegal immigrants after 1996—has become the focus of immigration politics that have resulted in three failed legislative proposals for comprehensive immigration reform that have been considered since 2006, including the bill passed by the United States Senate in June 2013. When Americans discuss immigration, they generally mean undocumented or illegal entries, how the border with Mexico can be more effectively controlled, and what should be done about the stock of 11 million undocumented residents in the United States.[2]

The increase of the undocumented population was largely the result of the new restrictions imposed by the 1965 immigration act. The law established limits on legal immigration from the Western Hemisphere for the first time, and, more importantly, a per-country limit of no more than 7 percent of the total number of visas to natives of any one independent country in a fiscal year. For Mexico the change was dramatic. In the late 1950s, when there were few legal restrictions on entry from the Western Hemisphere, there were about 50,000 entries per year from Mexico for permanent settlement, and about 450,000 people who entered for temporary work. After 1965 legal entry for most purposes was limited to about 20,000, with no provision for temporary work. By 1979, however, levels of actual entry per year had increased to those that prevailed in the late 1950s, primarily because what had been legal now became illegal border crossing.[3]

Framing the Issues

The first serious indication of a perception of failure of immigration policy in the United States was summarized in the report of the Select Commission on Immigration and Refugee Policy (SCIRP). The commission had been organized in 1978, in the aftermath of the refugee crisis engendered by the chaotic end of the war in Vietnam. The focus on Illegal immigration appeared to be the leading edge for the mobilization of a new restrictionist movement, and the formation of SCIRP was the government reaction to the growing restrictionist support in public opinion.[4] The final report in 1981, "Immigration Policy and the National Interest," was written by a commission that strongly supported both an expansive immigration policy and a compassionate refugee policy in the national interest. However, the report argued that the most important failure of US immigration policy was a failure to adequately control the southern border. It condemned the adverse impact of illegal entries, and urged that such entries be dealt with through strong employer sanctions, border enforcement, and the initiation of a national identity card.

It argued that "illegality erodes confidence in the law generally, and immigration law specifically." The precondition for increasing legal immigration was to effectively control illegal entry. The commission agreed—on the basis of existing studies—that there appeared to be 3.5 to 5 million illegal immigrants in the country, less than half of whom were from Mexico; that these immigrants were attracted by employment opportunities, and that they earned above the minimum wage; that they tended to depress the wages of those on the lowest end of the wage scale; and that while they paid payroll taxes, they tended not to benefit from social services. On the other hand, the commission took a strong stand on the consequences of permitting illegal immigration to continue. Illegal immigration had to be curbed not because of its social or economic consequences, but because "illegality breeds illegality."[5]

The Commission made the case that this illegal flow, which was encouraged by employers created an underclass of workers who feared apprehension and deportation: "Undocumented/illegal migrants, at the mercy of unscrupulous employers and coyotes who smuggle them across the border, cannot or will not avail themselves of the protection of US laws. Not only do they suffer, but so too does US society."

Most serious, as Tichenor notes, the Commission argued that the presence of a substantial number of undocumented and illegal aliens in the United States resulted not only in a disregard for immigration law but in the breaking of minimum wage and occupational safety laws, and statutes against smuggling as well. As long as undocumented migration flouts US immigration law, its most devastating impact may be the disregard it breeds for other US laws:

> The select commission holds the view that the existence of a large undocumented/illegal migrant population should not be tolerated. . . . Society is harmed every time an undocumented alien is afraid to testify as a witness in a legal proceeding, to report an illness that may constitute a public health hazard or disclose a violation of U.S. labor laws.[6]

Therefore, the commission recommended stronger controls at the border and enforcement at the workplace, as well as a program of legalization for illegal immigrants then present in the United States. However, stronger controls were seen as a precondition for legalization: "that legalization begin when appropriate enforcement mechanisms have been instituted." In the end, the most important impact of the SCIRP report was to separate out the policy tracks of legal and illegal immigration, which made it far more difficult for restrictionists to use one against the other.[7] Daniel Tichenor argues that during the two decades that followed, supporters of immigration would attempt to maintain this "decoupling," while restrictionists would attempt to fuse the two. In general, the supporters were successful. By the early 1980s, the understanding of the immigration issue was that there should be broad acceptance of legal immigration— supported by public opinion—combined with a commitment to dealing with illegal immigration in some way.

The problem of illegal immigration then became increasingly reframed as a menace to national security and a growing crisis during Reagan administration. As Massy, Durand and Pren notes:

> The most prominent politician contributing to the Latino threat narrative was President Ronald Reagan, who in 1985 declared undocumented migration to be 'a threat to national security' and warned that 'terrorists and subversives [are] just two days driving time from [the border crossing at] Harlingen, Texas' and that Communist agents were ready 'to feed on the anger and frustration of recent Central and South American immigrants who will not realize their own version of the American dream.'[8]

In fact, as Massey et. al. point out, not much had changed in terms of migrant movement into the United States, but the law had changed, and those who had entered legally before 1965 were now illegal. The flow had stabilized by the late 1970s and was no longer rising, but the undocumented population of the United States continued to increase as return migration slowed down. Moreover, as in

Europe, the now more stable resident population evolved from single workers to families with children. The perception of a surge was largely based on this growing population of undocumented migrants.

The perception of a generally successful policy of immigration, combined with failure at the border, was once again confirmed by another presidential commission, the Jordan Commission, but this time in the context of a broader political movement to stem the tide of illegal immigration. The Commission on Immigration Reform had been established by the 1990 Immigration Act, and it issued reports in 1994, 1995, and a final report in 1997. Its agenda was, therefore, strongly molded by this reaction of the 1990s. In addition, the composition of the commission was quite different from the SCIRP. In addition to supporters of immigration, the commissioners included strong restrictionists, and its reports represented a much broader compromise than the report in 1981. Although it recommended the maintenance of the principles of the existing system, it also recommended more important changes than had been previously addressed: a reduction of legal immigration, strengthened employer sanctions, and a well-supported program of "Americanization." Far more than SCIRP, the Jordan Commission questioned the dynamics of the existing system:

> The Commission supports the basic framework of current policy—family unification, employment-based immigration, and refugee admissions. We considered alternative frameworks, particularly a point system, but rejected these approaches. . . . At the same time, the Commission is convinced that our current immigration system must undergo major reform to ensure that admission continue to serve our national interests. Hence, the Commission recommends a significant redefinition of priorities and a reallocation of existing numbers to fulfill more effectively the objectives of our immigration policy.[9]

Many of the Commission's recommendations with regard to illegal aliens would seem quite familiar today. It recommended strengthened border controls based on 'Operation Hold the Line,' then in its early stages, but also the use of new technologies to enhance security at airport ports of entry.

Finally, for the first time since World War II, the Commission focused on integration policy. It placed considerable emphasis on new programs of Americanization as a way toward a more robust system of integration: "The Commission reiterated its call for the Americanization of new immigrants that is the cultivation of a shared commitment to the American values of liberty, democracy and equal opportunity."[10] Although it did not recommend specific

programs, it did call on governments at all levels of the federal system to provide leadership and resources to educate immigrants in the English language and
"core civic values." The Jordan Commission's hearings and reports spanned the
years of the strongest negative reaction to immigration. By the time its final report came out in 1997, the reaction to the reaction had begun to emerge. As a
result, general support for continued immigration was affirmed by the Clinton
administration, but the more controversial recommendations for reductions in
legal immigration—proposals that amounted to a reversal of the trend of immigration policy since 1965—were never implemented. Its recommendations on
illegal immigration, however, which echoed those of the SCIRP, are still part of
the immigration debate.

Thus, efforts over the years since 1965 to recast how the immigration issue
is framed have met with only limited success. All efforts until now to limit legal
immigration, and to alter the general framework of priorities for visas, have been
unsuccessful, and efforts to closely link illegal immigration to the legal frame
have been particularly unsuccessful. Nevertheless, the perceived failure to check
the flow of illegal immigrants to the United States, and the continued presence
of 11 million undocumented migrants, has become the focus of immigration
politics. Indeed, this failure has raised serious issues about the intentions of
immigration policy, or the contradiction between intentions and implementation. This was first propelled largely by a reaction to illegal immigration in
California, and fueled by the failure of the Immigration and Control Act of 1986
(IRCA). Indeed, the act ultimately authorized the legalization of about 3 million
people and criminalized employment of undocumented workers, but without
legislating effective employer sanctions or successfully halting the arrival of illegal immigrants.

The relationship between perceptions of failure and security has been generally linked to the southern border since the Reagan administration, and then
reinforced after the attacks of September 11, 2001. The importance of asylum
and the arrival of refugees, however, has been perceived differently compared
to Europe. The vast influx from Cuba (90% of those arriving for asylum from
the Western Hemisphere) was both accepted and supported by special legislation since the 1960s. The arrival of unaccompanied children after 2011, on
the other hand, was the object of a partisan war of framing (see chapter 4).
The question was whether this spike in asylum demands was just a different
kind of illegal immigration, or was more comparable to the much larger and
legal Cuban influx. Therefore, while lapses in security have been perceived as
a policy failure, the largest arrivals of refugees (Cuban) has been understood
as a policy success.

7.2 The Driving Force of Politics: Public Opinion, Interest Intermediation, and Party Competition

As an electoral issue, undocumented immigration has become as potentially potent in Europe as it is in the United States, perhaps more so.

Public Opinion

Figure 6.1 indicates that concern in public opinion about illegal immigration is strong on both sides of the Atlantic. The difference, however, is the gap between relatively little concern about legal immigration and great concern about illegal immigration, a gap that is greater in the United States than in any major European country.

As a partisan issue there is no difference between concerns of respondents on legal immigration in the United States, whether they identify as Democrats or Republicans (see Table 7.1). In each case, only 18 percent are worried. On illegal immigration the concerns are much greater in each case, but far greater for Republican identifiers (76%) than Democrats (49%). This pattern is verified by other surveys that ask questions about spending. In 2008, a national survey found that 87 percent of voters approved spending on tightening border security to prevent illegal immigration. Two years later, two-thirds of those surveyed agreed that United States should always welcome all or most legal immigrants. Legal immigration has not divided Democrats from Republicans in the United States, providing room for a more open policy. More than 80 percent of respondents from both parties have claimed to be not worried about a steady

Table 7.1 **Percentage on Left and Right Worried about Legal and Illegal Immigration in the US and Europe**

	Legal Immigrants	Illegal Immigrants
US Democratic identifiers	18%	49%
US Republican identifiers	19%	76%
Europe Left identifiers	17%	52%
Europe Right identifiers	30%	80%

Source: German Marshall Fund of the United States, *Transatlantic Trends, Immigration* (Washington, DC, 2011), Q.D3, D7, 4.1, 4.2, http://trends.gmfus.org/files/2011/12/TTImmigration_final_web1.pdf.

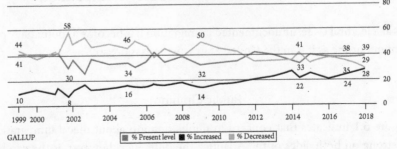

Americans' Views on Immigration in the U.S. Since 1999

Thinking now about immigrants–that is, people who come from other countries to live here in the United States, in your view, should immigration be kept at its present level, increased or decreased?

GALLUP

% Present level   % Increased   % Decreased

Figure 7.1 Americans' Views on Immigration in the United States since 1999. Source: Megan Brenan, Record-High 75% of Americans Say Immigration Is Good Thing, Gallup, June 21, 2018, https://news.gallup.com/poll/235793/record-high-americans-say-immigration-good-thing.aspx.

influx of legal immigration. In fact, there has been a steady increase of support since 2002 for *increased* legal immigration, as well as steady support in public opinion for the maintenance of present levels of immigration (see Figure 7.1). In 2018, after more than a year of strong anti-immigration rhetoric from the White House, support for decreased immigration levels declined to 29 percent, half of what it had been in 2002.[11] The pattern is very different when respondents are asked about illegal immigration.[12] A slim majority of Democrats are not worried, compared with only 22 percent of Republicans. It is not simply the negative opinion about illegal immigrants, but the partisan difference, that fuels the politics of the border in the United States.

Therefore, dealing with unauthorized entry and strengthening the border qualifies as a consensus issue in the United States, while approval for most legal immigration is strong, regardless of political affiliation. In terms of salience, dealing with the issue of illegal immigration was a top or important priority for more than 85 percent of voters surveyed in 2011—more than reducing crime, changing the federal tax system, and dealing with global trade issues. In voter opinion in the United States, legal and illegal immigration appear to be very separate issues for voters of both parties, but with strong priority support for dealing with the border and illegal immigration.[13]

Interest Intermediation

Far more than in Europe, the framing of policy and legislative success (and failure) in the United States is linked to interest intermediation. Although much of the political debate has centered on failed efforts at comprehensive immigration reform, most of the lobbying efforts have been in support of the system as it exists or in support of marginal changes in the existing system.

Most proposals that deal with immigration are not comprehensive, but focus on the authorization of a relatively small number of visas for specific needs. Lobbying efforts among insulated elites, within congressional committees and beyond the purview of mass publics, have focused largely on the distribution of the limited number of visas that authorize legal employment, generally fewer than 15 percent of those who enter the United States legally each year. These proposals are relatively uncontroversial because their benefits are broadly distributed.

In an analysis of lobbying efforts between 2008 and 2012 (a period during which no comprehensive legislation was passed by the United States Congress), 915 (noncomprehensive) bills relating to immigration were proposed. More than three thousand lobbyists reported that they were engaged by 718 clients in attempting to influence the outcomes of these proposals. Among the eighteen most active groups of lobbyists (rated by the number of interventions they report making on proposed legislation), more than half intervened on some question of work visas, six on some aspect of immigrant rights and protection (primarily the Dream Act—a proposal to permit about 800,000 undocumented young people who arrived with their parents), as children, and five on issues involving the border and border enforcement.[14] The efforts of each group of lobbyists were highly concentrated on their own specific interests, although there were some overlapping networks of interests (some employment visa proponents and support for the Dream Act, for example). However, the overall effect on policy has been to drive up the number of visas granted overall.[15]

Groups representing minority and ethnic groups, and advocates for immigrant rights and protections, intervene more than other single employment advocates, but their interventions are fewer than 15 percent of the total. Their efforts tend to be dispersed among a range of legislative proposals that deal mostly with rights and protections, and do not seem to drive up the overall level of legal immigration. Nevertheless, because their proposals are regulatory (changing rules to reunite families or for the passage of the Dream Act, proposals that have united most rights advocates), they are often more controversial. They bring government into a direct and coercive relationship with groups and sectors, and imply a general rule applicable to an entire group or sector. Indeed, specific groups are most often the force behind the development of new regulations, while others are organized to defend against them. The stability of regulatory power is based upon the ability of state agencies to negotiate an understanding (a balance of power) between groups or sectors, with implementation by the state in ways that generally minimizes public coercion and conflict. These agreements among political intermediaries are often referred to as "neo-corporatist" or (in Lowi's terms) "interest-group liberalism."[16]

Groups advocating more comprehensive changes in the immigration system—advocates of "redistributive" policy in Lowi's terms—are less numerous and less successful. They range from those seeking either to reduce immigration or alter the priorities that authorize the overwhelming number of visas (generally more than 70% each year) to family members of US citizens or legal permanent residents. Within the framework of the immigration system in place since 1965, interest groups have had considerable success in driving a broad distribution of entry, and even some aspects of regulation. The system of legal entry, however, has remained stable and intact, at least until now.

However, within this context, there has been an impressive expansion of interest group activity that focuses on border enforcement and security. The combination of distributive and regulatory policy involving state action has grown considerably. Like the European security-industrial complex, there are groups surveyed by US studies that have paid particular attention to border reinforcement and security, primarily related to jobs and military contracts.[17] The most active are data processing and computer services that provide services to the Department of Homeland Security, specifically for border control. The building trades (companies and unions) have a particular interest in building detention centers and facilities for the border: "The 'criminal alien' prisons set up to hold border crossers are almost exclusively run by private companies, led by Corrections Corporation of America [CCA] and the Geo Group."

Although "CCA and Geo have spent $17m and $2.7m respectively on lobbying in the past decade," in the United States, "both say they do not try to shape policy." Nevertheless, they acknowledge that lobbying activities represent an attempt to educate Congress and influence spending on border facilities in the United States. Prison contracts from the US Bureau of Prisons, and Immigration and Customs Enforcement (ICE) represented 24 percent of CCA revenue in the United States in 2011. Both CCA and Geo have warned their stockholders that any reforms that would reduce the imprisonment of illegal immigrants would "materially adversely impact us."[18] Geo Group also manages some of the largest immigrant detention centers in the United Kingdom. The company, however, had had little to worry about. By 2013, congressional appropriation for the border was also being driven by presidential priorities. In 2012, the federal government of the United States spent more on agencies enforcing and regulating immigration ($18 billion) than on all other principle federal law enforcement agencies combined.[19] As the border has become increasingly militarized, defense contractors have benefited with lucrative contracts for equipment. The proposed surge of spending on military equipment for the border in June 2013 was part of a package to support comprehensive immigration reform. Although the comprehensive bill died in the House of Representatives, it did pass the Senate with millions of dollars earmarked for defense contractors.[20]

The growth and distribution of border protection resources appeared to have little to do with security and the attacks of 2001 as such, and was related far more to the politics of immigration reform and the need to attract sufficient congressional support for broader reform proposals. The reporting on the spending surge in 2013 noted that the focus on border security was necessary to attract Republican votes for comprehensive legislation that would also deal with a pathway to citizenship for undocumented immigrants in the United States:

> The language was included in a $46 billion border security package the Senate approved last week as part of a comprehensive immigration bill. The so-called border surge—an additional $38 billion in spending—was added in the final week of negotiations to attract more GOP support for the measure, which passed with 68 votes, including 14 from Republicans.[21]

One particularly noteworthy aspect of the amendment that was passed was that major contracts were awarded directly to named companies through legislative stipulation, without competitive bidding.[22] This suggested that favorable votes were in states that would benefit from these specific awards.

Despite considerable opposition, the surge also legislated 30 billion dollars to double the size of the Border Patrol. By 2013 the Border Patrol and its union, the National Border Patrol Council (NBPC), had become a political force capable of promoting its own expansion and its own mission, and had resisted outside control of both its priorities and its actions by the Obama administration. For the only time in their history, the NBPC supported a presidential candidate—Donald Trump—in 2016. Within days after Trump's inauguration, the chief of the Border Patrol, a former agent of the FBI who had been named six months earlier "to change what is considered even by law enforcement standards, to be an insular culture," was forced to resign. He was replaced by an insider supported by the union. In a remarkable statement, the union noted that:

> We are unlike any other law enforcement agency in the world. We operate marine, land, and air units in every climate, and every environment. The previous administration's attempts to treat the Border Patrol like any law enforcement agency resulted in leadership that was reactive and in constant crisis. As we begin to implement President Trump's plan to secure the border and protect our communities, Mr. Vitiello's [the new Chief] experience will be invaluable. . . . The men and women of ICE and Border Patrol will work tirelessly to keep criminals, terrorists, and public safety threats out of this country, which remains the number one target in the world—and President Trump's actions now empower

us to fulfil this life saving mission, and it will indeed save thousands of lives and billions of dollars.[23]

In effect, because of its uniqueness, the union was claiming a high level of discretion for its agents. "Before we used be told 'You can't arrest those people,' and 'we'd be disciplined for being insubordinate if we did,' said a 10-year veteran of the agency.... Now those people are priorities again. And there are a lot of them here."[24] In fact, the Secretary of Homeland Security noted that the president intended to "take the shackles off" the agents of the Border Patrol and ICE. In the weeks after, USDHS issued two memos that erased the hierarchy of priorities that governed how enforcement was carried out both on the physical border and at airports and ports of entry to the United States. In effect, criteria for rounding up those suspected of being unauthorized were left in the hands of individual agents, sometimes with consequences that appeared to be arbitrary.[25]

There is is a network of political forces that support strong border enforcement for different reasons. Border enforcement is a building project, a customer for the arms and equipment industry, and a challenge for new technology, as well as a trade-off for comprehensive immigration reform. Most of all, political resistance to strengthened border control and enforcement is weak.

At the same time, political support for the current system of immigration has proven to be surprisingly strong. In an impact report of major groups that lobby Congress for and against immigration, the Lobbyists.info website cites only two groups (Federation for Immigration Reform and NumbersUSA) that have lobbied against the current system inside the beltway. There are several other conservative and more moderate groups that seek (sometimes important) changes, and still others that focus on illegal immigration (the Christian Coalition and the US Border Patrol), but the most virulent groups (listed by the Southern Poverty Law Center, some of which probably qualify as hate groups) are not lobbyists, and play no direct role in shaping legislation. "In fact," argues Lobbyists.info, "over the past few years, the most vocal opponents have been Congressional Republicans."[26]

While ethnic and employment interests that support immigration are similar in the way that they are dispersed, border enforcement has brought together "iron triangles" of private interests, administrative (or police) agencies, and congressional committees. These groups are concentrated and mutually reinforcea more muscular border policy.

The resistance to a hard border policy, however, can be strong as well. Free (or at least freer) movement across the border has historically benefited agribusiness and food processing. It has also benefited other business interests that have depended on cheap and flexible labor. Meat processing businesses, farm organizations, and chambers of commerce have lobbied against such programs as E-Verify, but so have computer manufacturing and service companies that depend on the movement of products, services, and people across the border.[27]

The pattern of enforcement of border controls at the southern border was established decades ago, and was largely related to the relative benefits for American business interests. Legally, entry restrictions under the 1924 Johnson–Reed Act did not apply to the Western Hemisphere. Well before World War II two separate and different immigration regimes were in place. The first regime, which was controlled by the Department of State, screened Europeans who applied for entry under the quota system. The second, with relatively few restrictions, was controlled by the Immigration Bureau, and screened mostly Mexicans who entered as temporary labor for growing agribusiness. If immigration from Europe was framed in terms of identity and a challenge to Americanism, immigration from other countries in the Western Hemisphere was understood in terms of labor that was necessary for the stability of the American economy.[28] If anti-immigrant movements that emerged from state politics tended to oppose immigration from Southern and Eastern Europe (as well as Asia), often the same state interests, primarily agricultural, strongly supported temporary labor migration from Mexico, Central America, and South America. Indeed, the incentives in place tended to encourage, rather than restrict, this stream of immigration.

In fact, at least until the 1950s, the line between legal and illegal entry remained blurred, and the southern border remained only lightly patrolled. The efforts of the Border Patrol (established in 1924) were directed more toward undesirable Europeans and enforcement of prohibition, rather than against Mexicans. In general, migrant workers from Mexico were also encouraged to return home, through formal and informal means:

> Growers, ranchers, and other employers of low-skilled workers continued to enjoy an abundant supply of cheap labor. A powerful iron triangle [that supported immigration] ensured access to temporary Mexican labor, one animated by growers, Southern and Western Immigration Subcommittee chairs, and a malleable INS bureaucracy.[29]

This system remained remarkably stable until the mid-1950s, when legal immigration for settlement from Mexico and Latin America began to grow rapidly.[30]

At the same time, there was a parallel increase of illegal immigration. Although there was considerable resistance in Congress to react to either the legal or illegal surge, the Eisenhower administration, for political reasons I will analyze later, ordered a roundup of undocumented Mexicans in 1954, which was dubbed Operation Wetback. The INS claimed that more than a million illegal immigrants had been rounded up and sent back to Mexico. In fact, many of those rounded up were in the country legally, and still others were quietly permitted to remain as legal workers under the Bracero program.[31]

In any case, the number of Mexican immigrants (for settlement) and their proportion among total immigrants continued to grow, recruited by agribusiness in the southwest and attracted by the prospect of work and long-term settlement. Although the two systems of immigration control became more explicit and better coordinated after 1965, the labor-market incentives for undocumented entry, and the political system that supported these incentives, remained in place even after the new legislation was passed. Agribusiness continued to provide incentives for Mexicans and Latin Americans who arrived through Mexico, entering both legally and illegally. What has changed is that undocumented immigration is no longer temporary, and much of the immigration for settlement is undocumented.

Political Parties and Electoral Politics

The most important change in the politics of immigration in the United States, however, has been the re-emergence of political parties as the driving force in the politics of immigration. Since 1965 political parties have become increasingly important in the development of border policy, first as aggregators of a range of border interests but increasingly as initiators, as the border developed as an issue in electoral politics. However, the weakness of political parties has made them ineffective as agents of change. In this policy arena they have proven to be effective in agenda-setting but not decision-making, and presidential leadership has fallen short of success.

The first change in border policy, The Immigration Reform and Control Act of 1986 (IRCA), was a result of broad party agreement. As we have seen, in 1981 SCIRP had strongly recommended that the federal government make a stronger effort to combat the growing flow of undocumented immigrants across the southern border. Although most of its recommendations were ignored, in 1986 legislative action was taken for the first time that *dealt specifically with the border*. The legislation was the end product of bipartisan efforts by Congress under four presidents. Considering that SCIRP had made their recommendations in 1981, the 1986 legislation was surprisingly weak and virtually unenforceable. It provided for employer sanctions (certainly the most controversial provision), but the sanctions program had little support in Congress and the administration and was never fully funded under the Reagan administration, which was far more interested in deregulation of business than in imposing additional regulations. The law contained provisions that would grant the largest amnesty in American history (far larger, in fact, than has been granted by any European country), make it easier for aliens to become permanent residents, establish a new farm-worker program, and give greater legal protections to aliens working in the United States. Eventually more than 3 million illegal immigrants would benefit from IRCA, in part because the courts overruled attempts by the INS to establish restrictive rules of implementation.

The section of the legislation that proved to be least effective was the section most directly related to its original intentions, employer sanctions for employing illegal immigrants. Although this provision was popular in public opinion, its actual enforcement was difficult, and was strongly resisted by both pro-immigrant groups and by employers' associations. For both of these reasons, the issue would continue to reverberate, particularly because illegal immigration continued to grow in the decades after the passage of IRCA, and because the resident undocumented population grew as well.

In the 1990s the cutting edge of the politics of immigration in the United States moved sharply into electoral politics. Many of the elements seemed to be in place that provided energy for the anti-immigrant wing of the Republican Party. First, there was a resounding Republican victory in the congressional elections of 1994. Then, there was a political reaction in California in 1994, led by the suddenly restrictionist governor, Pete Wilson. Its most important success was the passage of Proposition 187, which limited access of the children of illegal immigrants to schools, hospitals, and welfare services. Indeed, there was growing popular and intellectual support to limit immigration, the arguments for which resembled those of the eugenics movement of the late nineteenth century. Dorothy Nelkin and Mark Michaels wrote at the time that

> the immigration discourse of the mid-1990s is assuming an ominous but familiar tone. We hear, for example, that "natural" laws support "territorial integrity," that certain groups are "genetically inferior," that immutable biological differences underlie social distinctions, and that immigration will weaken the American "gene pool" and result in "race suicide." Once again, arguments about race relations in America (*The Bell Curve*) have been linked to immigration (Brimelow, Rushton, and the statements issued by FAIR).[32]

After IRCA, two variations evolved in the politics of immigration. The politics of legal immigration continued to be dominated by powerful interest groups with distributive goals. At the same time, the politics of illegal immigration and border control were increasingly dominated by political parties, primarily at the initiative of Republican lawmakers. Indeed, as early as the 1980s voters identified the Republican Party as having primary ownership of questions of border security and the prevention of illegal immigration, and there have been sharp differences in preferences between Republican and Democratic identifiers who prioritize this issue.[33]

> Republicans for whom the issue of unauthorized immigration is extremely important hold views on immigration policy that are quite far to the right compared to the preferences of the typical American. But... for Democrats, partisans who care most about the issue of unauthorized immigration are located close to the center—in fact, they are actually slightly more moderate than their co-partisans.[34]

Moreover, there is abundant evidence that the core issues over which a party maintains ownership are part of the fabric that holds the party together:

> A party owns an issue to the extent that its members—whether they be party activists, party voters, or party elected officials in government—believe that the consensus goal associated with the issue should be prioritized with government action and federal spending.... [P]arties own issues because they prioritize them with their beliefs and actions. Quite simply, parties own issues because they make them priorities.[35]

And, indeed, unauthorized immigration and border control has become one of those issues for Republicans.

It has become a wedge issue *within* the Republican Party in a prolonged contest for leadership and domination. It has become one of a small group of issues that have solidified contacts among a new right coalition of legislators who have framed the issue, collaborated on key votes, and built a broader network that has gradually worked to undermine Republican business interests that have profited from a relatively open southern border.

A decade after IRCA was passed by a bipartisan coalition, that coalition began to break down. With the apparent success of Proposition 187 in California and the report of the Jordan Commission urging reduction of immigration ceilings, the country seemed to be going through a backlash against immigration, but the principal victims were illegal immigrants. The Illegal Immigration Reform and Responsibility Act, passed during the election campaign of 1996, was aimed at undocumented immigration and the border. It authorized more Border Patrol agents, tightened asylum procedures, and generally made life more difficult for undocumented aliens.

What went less noticed, however, was that the congressional votes on the legislation established a unity among the Republican majority that would endure. Only five of the 234 Republicans who cast votes in the House opposed the final vote; on a previous vote, only three Senate Republicans had opposed the bill. The Democrats were far more divided, although their support was not necessary for the final passage. Welfare legislation passed at the same time—the Personal Responsibility and Work Opportunity Act of 1996—blocked a range of welfare benefits for legal residents until five years after their arrival.

The political process that dealt with the border after 2001 changed rapidly, however. It focused, with increasing intensity, on what was called "immigration reform"; was increasingly linked to the open debate between and within congressional parties (rather than to the distributive decisions endorsed by congressional committees); and was increasingly connected with electoral politics.

As it evolved, the problem for the Republicans was a deepening partisan division about border issues. However within the Republican Party an additional issue was the division between more traditional business Republicans favorable to compromise reform proposals of (then) President Bush, and the growing group of more ideologically driven Republicans in the House, for whom security at the border was a priority issue. The partisan division separated the Republican president from his own House majority, and ultimately doomed any effort to resolve the contradictions of border policy. Pressures for more robust controls, both at the border and within the country, would impede entry of workers generally employed by employers close to the Republican Party; pressures for a formula that would resolve the fate of the 11 million undocumented migrants already in the country were met by opposition to any formula that would even imply amnesty. The fate of reform legislation in 2006 demonstrates how divisions within the Republican Party served to drive the politics of the border.

The partisan and intra-party divide is demonstrated by the fate of one failed proposal in 2005–2006. In December 2005, the Republican-controlled House passed legislation that would make illegal presence in the United States a criminal offense, eliminate diversity visas, and authorize the construction of additional barriers along the border with Mexico. It was proposed and strongly advocated by the Republican chair of the House Judiciary Committee, James Sensenbrenner Jr., and was passed by an overwhelming majority of Republicans (203) and a small minority of Democrats (36); it never passed the Senate, however, in part because it was linked to the more important question of President Bush's support for immigration reform in 2006.[36]

Hoping to get out in front of the issues of the border, the president proposed comprehensive legislation meant to attract a coalition of congressional Republicans and Democrats. At the heart of the president's proposal were some familiar ideas: a temporary worker program would be linked to an amnesty program. The temporary worker program would create a legal path for foreign workers to enter our country in an orderly way, for a limited period of time. This program would match willing foreign workers with willing American employers for jobs Americans are not doing.[37]

Finally, the president proposed a pathway to legality (he specifically denied that this would be the equivalent to amnesty) for those who met specific requirements, as a means of reducing the unprecedented number of illegal immigrants already in the country.[38]

The Sensenbrenner bill passed by the House Republicans contained none of the key provisions advocated by the president.[39] It was widely regarded as a way to undermine the compromise reform bill then being examined in the Senate, since it would criminalize virtually all of the 11 million undocumented immigrants then in the United States, making the president's proposed guest worker program more difficult, if not impossible to pass. Moreover, the vote in the House, in which the vast majority of the opposition Democrats tended to support a relatively unpopular Republican president, reflected a fissure in governance. The Sensenbrenner bill was never taken up by the Senate.

Five months later, the Republican-controlled Senate passed very different legislation—the Kennedy-McCain bill—that contained most of the president's ideas. However, as the midterm elections approached, no compromise appeared to be possible, and because of Republican opposition, the House never voted on the McCain-Kennedy bill. The Republican majority leader Tom Delay favored legislation only on border enforcement, and would not support any bipartisan effort to reconcile his proposed bill with Kennedy-McCain.

The president tried once again in 2007, with a somewhat more conservative compromise with the same Senate sponsors, but it died a slow death as the presidential race began in earnest. Even with the president's strong and active support, only twelve of forty-nine Republicans in the Senate were willing to support him on a procedural vote to end debate. This was the beginning of the mobilization of the Republican move to the right. Senator Jeff Sessions of Alabama, who opposed the bill, gave considerable credit to talk radio for its failure:

> [He] said that talk radio was "a big factor" in derailing the immigration bill. Supporters of the bill wanted to pass it quickly, "before Rush Limbaugh could tell the American people what was in it," Mr. Sessions said.[40]

One pro-reform advocate, Frank Sharry of America's Voice, noted that he thought that the possibility of the new Bush proposal would be helped by Democratic control of Congress. However, "Republicans were beginning what we might call the advent of the tea party—they started to lurch to the right, they wanted to give Bush a bloody nose, as the conservative media mobilized."[41] Then, in just over a month in 2006, the conservatives were victorious. Congress was able to pass, with an overwhelming vote, the Secure Fence Act, which authorized the construction of a 700-mile border fence; this was accepted by the president as a part of what he termed a larger compromise, "an important step toward immigration reform."[42] However, the larger compromise never evolved.

Thus by early 2007, the decoupling of legal and illegal immigration had led to a passionate and partisan debate about the rapidly increasing population of undocumented immigrants that even the conservative Republican House leadership agreed could not be deported.[43] On the other hand, these same Republicans were willing to defy their own president to prevent legislation that would contain even partial amnesty. The division within the congressional Republican Party had resulted in an effective veto of a presidential proposal by his own party in the House of Representatives.

These divisions within the Republican Party played out in a somewhat different way under a Democratic president in 2013. After his election in 2008 President Obama favored reviving the reform legislation, but this was not a priority before the 2010 congressional elections. The Republican victories in November 2010 seemed to eliminate that possibility at the national level. It also created more opportunities for other initiatives at the state and local level that we will explore later. Nevertheless, in 2013 there was once again a major bipartisan effort to restart immigration reform. This was, in important ways, a replay of 2005–2006. There were eight key bipartisan sponsors in the Senate (instead of four in 2006); there were some differences in the requirements for border security; the Senate was now under Democratic control; the president was a Democrat. But partisan divisions were sharper than they had been in 2006, and the Republican Party was still divided on this issue in many of the same ways.

The reform legislation was introduced in the Senate in April, and then passed with fourteen Republican votes in June. A month later, however, the Republican Speaker of the House, John Boehner, announced that the House would never take up the Senate bill, and indeed they did not.[44] At the same time that the Senate was passing the reform legislation the house was debating a rewrite of the 2005 legislation criminalizing undocumented immigrants in the United States, this time dubbed SAFE (the Strengthen and Fortify Enforcement Act). Although the bill was approved by committee and sent on to the full House, it was never voted on by the House of Representatives.[45]

What was driving the focus on the border and border control, then, was primarily internal conflict within the Republican Party—the same pattern of conflict that was evident in 2006–2007. At the congressional level, the conflict was similar to the historic divide between business Republicans, favorable to easy informal movement of workers across the southern border, and identity Republicans, more concerned with the unauthorized settlement of families within the United States. Their concern was both with legality and the lack of cultural fit of these immigrants from Mexico and Central America. Business Republicans in the Senate, and most in the House, supported the Bush initiative in 2005–2006 and collaborated with the Democrats in the Senate. Increasingly, however, they represented a shrinking group within each congressional caucus, and were unable to initiate or shape the Republican approach to the large population of unauthorized immigrants in the United States.

Instead, after 2005, the initiative was taken up by a growing minority of identity Republicans whose focus was consistently on border security. They maintained a veto over comprehensive legislation in the House, and were able to pressure the Bush and Obama administrations into symbolic and real action on border control. As we saw earlier, Republican voters' views on undocumented entry have been moving far to the right of the average voter. More important, the views among Republican voters who care most about unauthorized entry are much further to the right, even compared to their fellow partisans. This has given support and comfort to congressional Republicans who are determined to resist compromise legislation that would legalize the presence of unauthorized immigrants in the United States.

One indication of how far the machine of the Republican Party has moved on immigration and border control are the changes in the Heritage Foundation. The foundation has been the ideas and programmatic arm of the conservative movement since the Reagan administration—a driving force within the Republican Party.[46] Over the years it has worked closely, but has sometimes been in conflict with, the Republican Study Committee (RSC), which had organized a majority of the Republican House members into a conservative caucus. Until 2013, Heritage had privileged access to closed RSC meetings and provided the intellectual depth for Republican policy proposals. In 2012, an evaluation of the role of Heritage concluded that "the Heritage Foundation is where policy agendas are set and tactics are developed hand-in-hand with Hill staff." The article argued that its role grew more important after 1995:

This turn of events has become a pattern because in 1995, Congress lost much of its capacity to produce unbiased public-interest information—the facts that help legislators make decisions and craft sound policies. Under Gingrich, the system that supplied bipartisan information and analysis to Congress was disbanded—including the Office of Technology Assessment—the world's premier legislative advisory body on technology.[47]

The role of the foundation changed, however, as the House RSC moved further to the right after the Tea Party breakthrough in 2011, and the policy/ intellectual role of the foundation was largely displaced by the lobbying arm, Heritage Action for America. Heritage Action was established in 2010 to lobby for Heritage political priorities. In 2012 Senator Jim DeMint, sometimes described as "a Tea Party gladiator," left the Senate to become president of the Heritage Foundation. DeMint replaced the founding president who had focused on the development of policy alternatives, rather than advocacy. Under DeMint, the balance shifted decidedly toward advocacy, and Heritage Action became an important player for the development of priorities that would aid in fundraising.

Therefore, the evolving position of the Heritage Foundation on immigration is of considerable importance for understanding how the Republicans have been puzzling out this issue. Heritage had "a long history of supporting higher immigration levels and legalization of immigrants." Allied with the conservative business wing of the Republican Party, the foundation produced studies favoring increased immigration as a free market boost to the economy:

> In 1986, economist Julian Simon, then a Heritage senior fellow, took on the anti-immigration Federation for American Immigration Reform [FAIR] in a well-publicized debate. The tradition of support for comprehensive immigration reform continued in 2006 with a paper authored by Tim Kane, Heritage's director of international economics. "The century of globalization will see America either descend into timid isolation or affirm its openness," Kane concluded. "Throughout history, great nations have declined because they built up walls of insularity, but America has been the exception for over a century."[48]

This straightforward business argument changed in 2007, as Heritage shifted its focus from business and economics to concerns about the welfare state and identity. They recruited and published a long study by two specialists on welfare, "The Fiscal Cost of Low-Skill Immigrants to the U.S. Taxpayer" (strongly criticized by Kane), which rapidly became the institutional position against comprehensive immigration reform still supported by the administration.[49] By 2013 this position had become hardened, and then repeated in a second, stronger, Heritage document, widely criticized as a "political study" by Republican supporters of immigration reform.[50]

By then the Heritage Foundation had firmly allied itself with the Tea Party core of the Republican House caucus, and its center of gravity had moved from a conservative study think tank to a more militant advocacy group against immigration reform. The positions advocated by Heritage on a range of issues no longer represented a source of information for conservative lawmakers, and no

longer reflected a consensus of the Republican House caucus. Instead, under the
leadership of Jim DeMint, Heritage Action raised large amounts of money, and
forcefully lobbied for political positions that sometimes divided even the RSC.

In 2013, for example, the RSC barred Heritage staff from attending its weekly
meetings. The dispute itself (a somewhat arcane conflict about farm legislation)
was symbolic of a larger issue of strategy. If for forty years the think-tank approach provided conservative lawmakers with deeper understanding of the issues, the emphasis on lobbying made Heritage Action a player in the movement
to the right after 2010.

> If nothing else, the schism is symbolic, representing an emerging divide
> between some conservatives in Congress who argue for amassing small
> policy victories, and the conservative outside groups [like Heritage]
> that will settle for nothing less than outright ideological purity. As one
> conservative House aide put it, "We can't score touchdowns on every
> play; our job is to put points on the board. But all they want us to do is
> throw Hail Marys."[51]

The pattern of interest group politics generally defends the existing system of
legal immigration and border control. Evolving patterns of party conflict, however, presents a driving force for agenda-setting that presents new challenges
for border control, and could bring into question the existing system of legal
immigration.

The Federal Dynamic

The interactions of territorial institutions within the federal system, however,
demonstrate a different dynamic: the ability of the states to initiate policy, and
their limited capability to block federal action. Alberta Sbragia refers to federalism as "dispersed power" that benefits different actors in each territorial
system. The way power is dispersed also helps us to understand policy strategies
and policy outcomes. However, the dispersal of power and the dynamics that
flow from it have evolved in each system because of the way political actors have
exploited, used, and challenged institutions.[52]

In the United States, the development of immigration and border policy was
related to two dimensions of federal relations: the expansion of the range of
policymaking covered by *all levels* of government and the expansion of functions
of policymaking in which the national government dominated.[53] The real impulse
for extended federal control over entry came from two principal sources: first,
the states themselves (which had been prevented from acting independently by

the courts), and second, a federal-level reaction against the new wave of immigration from Eastern and Southern Europe that began in the 1880s.

Immigration control first became a national function as a result of court decisions that defined *where* the question had to be considered, but not *how*. How it was defined and considered was a result of a Senate initiative undertaken by a small but determined group of senators, primarily from New England. In 1890, with the establishment of the Senate Committee on Immigration, the Senate actually created an arena that favored the initiation of immigration control legislation.[54]

Built into the American federal structure is a territorial bias that permits states to develop defensive capacities over federal actions at the state level, as well as capacity to influence policy at the national level that gives disproportionate weight to the interests of smaller states. Throughout most of the twentieth century, this unequal capacity was exaggerated further by a congressional seniority system that gave power to representatives and senators from one-party districts and one-party states.

As federalism has evolved in the United States, relationships among territorial units have become increasingly complex. At the end of the nineteenth century, the influence appeared to flow predominantly up from the states. By the middle of the twentieth century, however, the power of the center over the periphery was more evident, in part because of the influence of a more powerful presidency in articulating national interests and functional interests over peripheral and territorial interests. In addition, the technocracy generally was allied with national interest groups, and developed a national policy perspective.

For the development of immigration policy, presidential leadership and the technocracy were crucial elements for explaining change after the Second World War. Between the end of the war and 1965, executive orders and special legislation supported by the president altered the execution of the restrictive 1924 legislation in fundamental ways. By the time that the new immigration regime was approved in 1965 (with the strong support of President Johnson), about 300,000 immigrants were arriving each year—double the number of the immediate postwar period, most of them nonquota, and an increasing proportion from outside of Europe, primarily from the Western Hemisphere. By 1965 fully two-thirds of the legal immigrants from Europe were nonquota. This significant rise of immigration was due in part to the admission of immediate relatives of US citizens, as well as to admissions of refugees and displaced persons (400,000 under the legislation of 1948 and 1950).[55]

But presidential leadership has been only one element of the federal dynamic. A second has been the tension between the federal government and the states and localities in the development and enforcement of policy, as well as the interests that influence them. Each often acts as a countervailing power against the other, and each is capable of mobilizing different coalitions of political interests to act and resist.

Cycles of Enforcement

One way that we can understand the interaction and tensions of functional and territorial interests in immigration politics is by examining cycles of border enforcement over time. Each cycle has usually begun either because the president would like to create pressure for related legislation (such as Eisenhower's Operation Wetback and support for employer sanctions in 1954); or in response to expanding local movements in opposition to immigration (such as Clinton's Operation Hold the Line in response to the passage of Proposition 187 in California in 1994); or as an attempt to demonstrate toughness on the southern border to generate congressional support for a solution to the problem of millions of undocumented immigrants residing in the United States (such as the buildup of the southern border, and the increase of expulsions after 2006, by Bush and Obama).

The cycles generally conclude with pressure from businesses whose interests have been hurt or undermined, or with reaction from states and localities whose constituents have been harmed by federal enforcement policies. The results of the compromise have sometimes been gains or additional benefits for migrants (as in the Eisenhower cycle), or diminished enforcement, or relief (as it seems happened in the Bush and Obama cycles).[56]

The surge of enforcement in 2006–2008 was both determined and brutal. The government focused on criminal charges against both employers and immigrant workers, and formal *removals* (that criminalized re-entry), as opposed to voluntary *returns*, increased by 12 percent in 2006.[57] As opposed to the crackdowns of the 1990s, the scope of these raids was national, and struck several different kinds of industries. At the beginning of December 2006, Swift and Co. meatpacker plants were raided in five states, and 10 percent of the workforce was arrested.[58] A few months later, in Illinois and Michigan, managers of two cleaning companies were arrested for criminal offenses and received significant jail time.[59] Small family farms were raided in western New York State; a job agency was raided in Baltimore and a company that manufactures backpacks for the US Army was raided in New Bedford, Massachusetts.[60]

As in other operations, many of the victims were legal immigrants. Legal children were separated from their illegal parents, and legal immigrants were mistakenly rounded up and sent back to Mexico. Immigration agents conducted announced and unannounced raids even on companies that had been cooperating with federal efforts to identify undocumented immigrants.[61] By the summer of 2007, the government was demonstrating its toughness and resolve by focusing more resources on holding employers responsible for ascertaining the legal status of the workers that they hire, with an emphasis on criminal charges against employers.[62] By 2008, large numbers of immigrant workers were forced to serve prison time before they were formally removed.[63] As in the past, however, this cycle of enforcement represented a limited effort, with a limited political objective. The not-so-hidden agenda of the Bush administration was to gain support for its immigration proposals by encouraging business interests to increase their pressure on Congress.

As the Secretary of Homeland Security expressed it, there was a direct link between the increased enforcement and the president's immigration proposals. He argued:

> It would be hard to sustain political support for vigorous work-site en-forcement if you don't give employers an avenue to hire their workers in a way that is legal, because you are basically saying, "You've got to go out of business." [Nevertheless] businesses need to understand if you don't . . . play by the rules, we're really going to come down on you.[64]

To reinforce this point, he told protesting farmer groups and employers that hired low-wage labor that they should focus their attention on Congress: "We can be very sure that we let Congress understand the consequences of the choices that Congress makes."[65]

Enforcement during the Obama years, after 2009, generally resembled that of the Bush years. Although apprehensions and voluntary departures continued to decline, formal removals continued to increase as they had during the Bush years (see Figure 7.2). However, in deference to the Hispanic constituencies of the Democratic Party, greater priority was given to expulsion of offenders with criminal convictions. In 2008, 29 percent of the 360,000 formally removed had criminal status. This percentage increased to 43 percent in 2010, and then 55 percent in 2011.[66] The new administration also focused on less public criminal investigations of employers, and moved away from sweeping raids and arrests of workers.[67] At the same time, it focused considerable effort on the Secure Communities Act, passed in 2008, to track and deport immigrants arrested and booked by local authorities (see chapter 5). Under the Obama administration this program was expanded to most of the country, with the result that almost half of those deported were from the interior of the country.[68]

These patterns of enforcement, however, did not alter the basic structure of the relatively open American labor market, as well as the willingness (or determination) of employers, agribusiness in particular, to employ undocumented

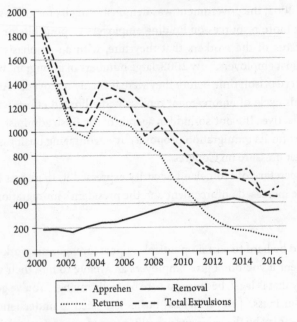

Figure 7.2 Changing Patterns of Enforcement: US Apprehensions and Expulsions, 2000–2015. Source: US Department of Homeland Security, Office of Immigration Statistics, *2010 Yearbook of Immigration Statistics* (Washington, DC: US Government Printing Office, 2011), pp. 91, 94.

workers. After Operation Wetback, the Bracero program was vastly expanded to appease agricultural interests. After the raids in 1998 and 1999, their scope was cut short as the agribusiness employers complained that plants were forced to close in the Midwest, and crops rotted in Georgia.[69]

In 2006–2008 press reports indicated that farmers would continue to hire illegal immigrants to fulfill their labor needs, given the very limited availability of guest workers.[70] Farmers openly said what they have always said about illegal Mexican labor: "We would rather use legal workers . . . but if we don't get a reasonable guest-worker program we are going to hire illegals."[71] In addition, there were indications, reminiscent of 1998–1999, that political coalitions that united business interests with human rights advocates could effectively block draconian enforcement—in Texas, for example.[72] In 2011 Republican lawmakers in Congress, generally reacting to constituency pressures and anticipating constituency pressures from Latino voters, began to propose legislation that would benefit discrete groups of immigrants, legal and illegal.[73] A bill proposed by Republicans in the House to require that all employers use the E-Verify system to confirm the legal status of all employees was blocked by a coalition of farm organizations, who are usually sympathetic to conservative causes.[74]

But resistance to federal action was also mobilized by state and local authorities themselves, often as a result of local interest group pressure. During the Obama years, some state and local governments began to systematically resist federal enforcement programs that had been put into place during the Bush administration. There was considerable resistance by local authorities to the enforcement of the Secure Communities Act. In the fall of 2011 cities and states had publicly declared that they would not participate in this program, both because they questioned the accuracy of the computer matches and because they argued that it sowed mistrust of law enforcement authorities in immigrant communities. By June, three states—Illinois, New York, and Massachusetts—had either suspended or cancelled participation, although the program continued to operate in forty-two states. In September a task force, organized to advise the administration on the program, issued a highly critical report and urged the administration to no longer deport immigrants who had committed minor violations. A month earlier, the Department of Homeland Security announced that it would review deportation orders issued for undocumented immigrants without criminal records (about 300,000 cases), particularly those who were young and in school.[75]

The actions of state governments since 2010 certainly demonstrate how divided the states are in their approach to attacking or defending immigrant populations. What is most striking, however, is how many states have taken some kind of action, successful or not. In all at least forty states have taken action one way or the other, and sometimes both ways (Texas and Florida, for example).[76]

The crisis of unaccompanied children, which peaked in 2015, focused on other elements of federalism. In this case, the continuing tension between the federal government and the states and localities emerged once again, but mostly around the framing of the issue. The federal government focused on its obligations under the 2008 legislation, but local protests emphasized both undocumented crossing of the border, as well as the unequal distribution of costs within the federal system: the likelihood that local authorities would be responsible for the education of large numbers of children who will be granted asylum.[77] The states and localities that feared the social and economic costs of migration, framing the surge as a breakdown in the federal management of the border, and charging that the government encouraged the influx, left responsibility entirely in the hands of the federal government. The federal government focused on the surge as a human rights crisis for which there was a collective, not territorial, responsibility. Indeed, this was not a question of the permeability of the border but the need to rescue children, in much the same way as the Mare Norstrum operation.

But the states have not simply resisted federal initiatives. They themselves have also initiated changes to develop policy in areas where they have considered that the federal government has been lax. Within a year after the Republican victories in the congressional elections of 2010, during Obama's first term, six states seized the initiative and passed legislation meant to deter undocumented immigrants from working or living in those states and to encourage those already there to leave. The first law, passed in Arizona before the 2010 elections, set a standard for those that followed. The key provision required police to verify the immigration status of anyone stopped for other reasons, and whom they suspected of being undocumented. Within months Alabama, Georgia, Utah, South Carolina, and Indiana passed similar provisions.

Alabama and Georgia then went much further, by making it a crime to harbor or employ an undocumented immigrant. Alabama made it illegal to rent property to or transport an illegal immigrant, required schools to check the immigration status of students, and declared all contracts signed by illegal immigrants to be null and void. In contrast, Utah passed legislation which, in addition to police powers similar to those of Arizona, created a guest worker program with a pathway to legal status.

But resistance to enforcement was evident on the state level as well, as groups and localities more favorable to immigration and immigrants began to mobilize. By late 2011 all of these laws had been vigorously challenged in federal court by numerous associations, as well as by the federal government. In most cases (with the exception of Alabama) the key provisions were suspended by the courts, but the cases then went forward on appeal. By 2012, fifty-three proposals were introduced, but only six were enacted and twenty-six had failed.[78]

One serious problem for advocates of anti-immigrant state legislation was the pushback from business groups in need of immigrant labor, as well as rights groups that have continued mostly successful legal challenges. Even in states where tough legislation had already been passed, business and agricultural interests began to push back. Under pressure from business, five new bills directed against undocumented immigrants were rejected by the Arizona State Senate in March 2011.[79]

Worksite enforcement also has been cyclical. Generally understood as a more acceptable alternative to more aggressive raids, employer audits have also had consequences. Between 1990 and 2002, employer I-9 audits (usually random investigations, but some as a result of a tipoff or lead) declined 77 percent from a previous high of 10,000. There was a similar drop in sanctions: warnings to employers dropped by 62 percent and fines by 82 percent. In 2003, only 124 employers received fines for employing illegal immigrants.[80] Criminal prosecutions declined from 182 in 1999 to 4 in 2003. Then, from a low of 503 in 2008, the last year of the Bush administration, the number of I-9 audits steadily rose to over 3,000 in 2012 during Obama's first term. They then declined significantly during his second term (see chapter 5, Table 5.5).

Although enforcement tended to follow a cyclical pattern, softening as business interests accelerated complaints, two long-term trends have emerged in the politics of the border. During the Bush and Obama years, border control moved decidedly toward more muscular enforcement somewhat masked by shifting patterns of expulsion (see Figure 7.2). After 2004 the total number of expulsions declined steadily, from 1.4 million to about 450,000 in 2016. At the same time, however, the number of returns (those returned across the border without any formal legal order) vastly diminished as a component of total expulsions: from 1.2 million in 2004 to 106,000 in 2016. Those expelled through returns were more or less free to cross the border again without consequence. The number of formal removals, however, continued to increase over this same period, to a peak of 433,000 in 2013. Previously, and more typically, during the 1980s, formal removals hovered around 20,000 per year.[81] Formal removals are based on a legal order, and "an alien who is removed has administrative or criminal consequences placed on subsequent reentry owing to the fact of the removal."

The shift toward a policy of formal removal represented part of the continuing attempt to secure congressional approval for reform legislation, but has rapidly become one of the principal means of reinforcing and hardening the southern border. Both Presidents Bush and Obama placed this shift in the context of continuing negotiations over immigration reform. In his 2013 State of the Union address to Congress, President Obama emphasized that a path to citizenship for undocumented immigrants now in the United States must be balanced with stronger border control at the southern border:

> And right now, leaders from the business, labor, law enforcement, faith communities—they all agree that the time has come to pass comprehensive immigration reform. Now is the time to do it. Now is the time to get it done. Now is the time to get it done.
>
> Real reform means strong border security, and we can build on the progress my administration has already made—putting more boots on the Southern border than at any time in our history and reducing illegal crossings to their lowest levels in 40 years.
>
> Real reform means establishing a responsible pathway to earned citizenship—a path that includes passing a background check, paying taxes and a meaningful penalty, learning English, and going to the back of the line behind the folks trying to come here legally.[82]

The president's argument was not new. It mirrored the basic case that had been presented since 2006—indeed in other ways since the Eisenhower administration—by both Bush and Obama, and provided a commitment to harden the southern border in a way that it had never been hardened before. The focus on *removals* was meant to prevent easy movement back and forth. A high level of *returns*, often characterized as "catch and release," was rapidly replaced by a higher level of *removals*.

In fact, it may be more useful to understand these cycles as an attempt to expand the scope of politics (or what Schattschneider called "the scope of conflict")[83] beyond the control of the understandings of insulated client politics, or to challenge (or appear to challenge) the constraints imposed by the agribusiness iron triangle. By going public, Eisenhower supported stronger employer sanctions, Clinton put California agribusiness on notice, and Bush challenged the congressional wing of the agribusiness of the iron triangle to support his proposals for immigration reform, while Obama continued to maintain pressure by balancing business interests against the interests of the Hispanic communities.

These dynamics, however, have resulted from the gradual weakening of the business wing of the congressional Republican Party. As the more ideologically rigid wing of the party has gained ascendency with the support of President Trump, enforcement has become an end in itself and is far less limited by resistance from business, or by considerations of the interests of Latino constituents. Moreover, at the end of the first year of the Trump administration, criteria of legal entry have also been brought into question. Although no detailed proposals have been made, President Trump has brought into question the core of the present immigration law, family preference.

Conclusion

As in Europe, the politics of the border in the United States have become increasingly salient as perceptions of policy failure have grown among political elites. The rhetoric of failure and border breakdown has been developed as the population of undocumented immigrants has grown, whether they have entered the country illegally or not (as visa overstayers), and even after undocumented border entry had begun to diminish. As in Europe, this rhetoric was supported by a virtual consensus in public opinion expressing concern about illegal immigration. Even among those most supportive of legal immigration, there is strong opposition to undocumented immigrants. In the United States, the immigration issue has become the question of undocumented immigrants and illegal entry.

Although interest group networks have stabilized the system put into place for immigration in 1965, ethnic associations and employers have also promoted an expansive distributive growth of legal immigrant entries. A growing part of this network, however, has also benefited from and promoted a border buildup. This includes private security companies that have increasingly managed detention facilities, as well as construction companies and unions that have built new facilities along the southern border and that have benefited from the increased budget allocations from the federal government. A particularly strong component of this border network has been the Border Patrol and its union. It has been a strong advocate that has developed an important relationship with both the executive branch and Congress.

Security and construction companies have also worked closely with advocates in the executive branch and Congress to promote, build, and manage the extended border and the federal facilities further inland. This interaction has sometimes been referred to as a security-industrial-complex, a mutually supportive network with limited checks and balances. Nevertheless, opposition to this increasing militarization has also been important, and includes industries dependent on immigrant labor as well as immigrant advocate organizations. This tension about the border has therefore resulted in the cycles of enforcement that have become characteristic of border enforcement policies.

The focus on the border has also been a result of intra- and interparty conflict at the national level. As the Republican Party has divided between its business supporters and its identity wing during the last twenty years, the border and border control has become an increasingly important and irreconcilable issue for them. Although presidential leadership has often been the key to dealing with problems of immigration, neither a Republican nor a Democratic president has been able to bridge this division. Thus, intra and inter-partisan divisions have been a driving force in defining and politicizing questions of the border in the United States, but the divisions and the issues are quite different than in Europe.

Similarly, the American case is a good illustration of how constraints within territorial units may operate differently at different times, and can be turned into opportunities. As in Europe, in the American federal system, actions at one level are linked to actions at other levels. The different arenas of the federal system are now unavoidably linked. Politically, initiatives taken at the state level can act as a springboard for action at the national level, while initiatives at the national level can sometimes be resisted at the state level.[84]

The initiatives taken by the states in the United States, either opposed or favorable to those who are undocumented, have been far more numerous than is generally understood. Although most of these initiatives have been turned back by federal court decisions, they reflect a continuing federal struggle over the unresolved rules for the control of the border and territorial space. Of course, many of these state initiatives are an attempt to force the federal government to militarize the border even more. On the other side, the federal government has attempted to convince (and even force) state officials to effectively multiply its border police force by expanding the police power of local and state police to include the internal policing of immigrants on their territory.

8

Conclusion

The Border Is Back

The border appears to be back with a vengeance as a focus of politics in Europe and the United States. Political issues that involve the border had never entirely disappeared. During the postwar period in Europe borders were central to the Cold War division, and then during the Balkan wars in the decade of the 1990s, border issues were at the center of the violence. In the United States, the war on drugs has been a focus of American relations with Mexico since 1971, as has the complex question of border control.[1]

The new focus on the border, however, has come in a context of important— and seemingly successful—efforts of international cooperation toward the removal of barriers to trade and the movement of people on both sides of the Atlantic. What has changed is that the shift toward harder controls at the border to keep people out has been moving from the margins of politics to the very top of the political agenda. The border is back as the core of state efforts to regulate the transnational movement of people in an effort to reassert national sovereignty. It is back in the context of the emergence of new radical right movement and political parties on both sides of the Atlantic. Borders are closing not because of economic protectionism (although that may emerge as well), but as a result of what Hansen and Gibney have called conflicting commitments of liberal democracies: rights-based and treaty-based immigration is running up against growing support for a reinforcement of national identity and border control.[2] Although there has consistently been significant opposition to immigration in the West, the increase in rights-based immigration on the borders of Europe, as well as unauthorized immigration on the southern border of the United States, has given this opposition political traction. In the context of electoral politics, political parties have driven border issues as political priorities. At the same time, groups supporting the link between national identity and stronger borders have gained greater attention, while those supporting rights of access have found their work more difficult.

8.1 A Harder Border

There is no question that policy and enforcement on both sides of the Atlantic have been moving toward tougher efforts at border control for the movement of people. To understand the reassertion of borders I have looked both at the evolution of policy, and then at the implementation and enforcement of policy. The development of both elements of policy is consistent with the argument supporting a growing fortress Europe and America.

A Western world without borders remains an elusive objective that applies far more to goods and services than to most people.[3] The reinforcement of borders, and the renewed proliferation of fences and walls, is directed against the movement of people. Although it is often presented as a reaction to a surge of unauthorized movement of migrants and asylum seekers, it began well before the surge in Europe, and is far more complicated in the United States. It is driven by a politically instrumentalized response fed by developing fears of strangers and loss of identity.

More Demanding Entry Policy

What is striking about the evolution of policy is the increased priority given to border policy over time, along with the hardening of policies of border controls for the movement of people. Until the 1980s the external borders of the EU were only lightly controlled at the physical frontiers. Indeed, until 1989, the borders on the east of the EU were most heavily controlled to keep people in by the Communist authorities. If there was concern about the border, it clearly was not to aid these states in their border control missions.

On both sides of the Atlantic, entry policy began to change in important ways in the 1970s. Entry into Europe from TCNs became increasingly demanding. Until the economic crisis that began in 1973 entry into Europe for TCNs had been relatively easy, and generally encouraged. Even after the suspension of immigration, restrictions were tempered by court decisions that validated family unification. Legal entry in the years that followed was below what it had been before, but levels of entry remained surprisingly robust.

In addition, public policy was not focused on the border or border control, except for airports. Entry into Europe was effectively controlled through the externalization to countries of origin of visa applications and authorization. Unauthorized entry was not a serious problem in Europe, and those migrants in Europe without residency permits were overwhelmingly those who overstayed temporary visas. Illegal stays were largely controlled through internal policing, and through a labor market in which administrative controls were far greater in Europe than in the United States.

Nevertheless, policy began to harden. Even as court decisions eased family unification, by the 1980s member states began to limit their effectiveness by applying more demanding requirements for citizenship and by developing a priori requirements for entry.[4] These requirements varied from country to country, but they have generally demanded that those migrants who otherwise would have a right to enter or to remain provide evidence of their potential for integration. Enhanced requirements that had begun with considerations of integration were multiplied in the 1990s, as terrorist incidents perpetrated by migrants who had entered Europe became more commonplace.[5] As I noted in chapter 2, studies now show that both the number and the variety of new measures to restrict entry have increased and become more complex in almost every country in Europe.[6]

As increased requirements were imposed, policymakers also shifted their attention to the border. The borders of Europe, however, had become complicated by the 1990s. The open borders of the countries that participated in the Schengen Agreement and then integrated into the Treaties on European Union, meant that the control of the external European border was an interdependent arrangement that attributed major responsibilities to those countries that controlled the external ports and frontiers.

Decision-making on authorization to enter and reside—visas—remained under the control of individual member states, although there were areas of cooperation at the EU level. This decision-making process that had been moved away from the physical land, sea, and air points where migrants actually arrive became better coordinated. By strengthening visa processing for legal entry at consulates in countries of origin and by developing rules that made it difficult for migrants to board aircraft, ships, or international trains in countries of origin without visas, the border was effectively moved away from the frontier. Nevertheless, as Schengen was applied, migrants who were able to enter into Schengen space did not find it difficult to move among European countries.

One aspect of border control in Europe has strongly resisted the movement toward the hardening of border controls, at least until recently. Free movement of European citizens, stipulated by the Treaties on European Union and not regulated by Schengen, is one of the fundamental freedoms guaranteed by Community law. It includes the right to live and work in another member state, and has been widely exploited. Almost half of immigration each year into the member states of the EU consists of citizens of other member states, and more than a third of foreign residents in the twenty-eight EU countries are citizens of other member states.

As we have seen, however, government opposition to free movement has been growing, particularly since the full accession of Romania and Bulgaria to the EU in 2014. The government of the United Kingdom has been most vocal about the importance of limiting free movement within the EU, but other member states have echoed many of the UK concerns.

Beginning in 2007, French President Nicolas Sarkozy began to question the exploitation of free movement by Roma from Romania and Bulgaria (even though free movement was not extended until 2014), a campaign that continued in 2010. But it was in the United Kingdom that free movement was transformed into a major political issue, which culminated in the Brexit campaign in 2016. In the fall of 2013 both Home Minister Theresa May and Prime Minister David Cameron began to advocate limits on free movement from poorer EU countries by imposing caps on movement based on per capita national income of the sending country. Cameron focused on what he called "benefits tourism." He also added the argument against "social dumping," the movement of workers from low-wage EU countries to worksites in high-wage countries, but with wages and benefits from their home countries.

The political discourse throughout Europe by 2015 practically equated the free movement from Eastern European countries with the problem of illegal immigration. In each case borders were being penetrated by unwanted and uncontrolled migrants, and governments discussed proposals that would greatly limit what appeared to be the established rights of immigrants from within the EU.

By comparison, legal entry for the United States grew easier after 1965. The United States abandoned a highly restrictive policy of country quotas (except for the Western Hemisphere) and exclusion (from Asia), and replaced it with a broadly based visa entry policy based largely on family unification and labor needs. Compared with the European policies developed after the 1970s, American policy for entry seemed to be open and generous.

Even after the passage of harsh limits on immigration in 1924, most of these limits did not apply to the Western Hemisphere. American borders in the north with Canada and the south with Mexico were only lightly controlled, and in some areas, hardly controlled at all. Moreover, movement across these borders in both directions was an integral aspect of the labor market. It was strongly supported by American business groups that benefited from low-cost labor, and it also benefited from the weakening of agricultural unionization efforts.

The 1965 legislation and subsequent amendments, however, applied more restrictions on immigration from Latin America than had existed before. Ceilings were now placed on entry from each individual country,[7] and general visa requirements now applied to the Western Hemisphere (after 1978). Therefore, what appeared to be more open and generous for the rest of the world was now more restrictive as applied to the closest neighbors of the United States. These new and evolving policies also had other implications for the lightly patrolled southern and northern borders. The easy cycles of movement of migrants back and forth were now subject to more restrictive regulations that were imposed at the border.

Consequently, on both sides of the Atlantic, policy at the border has become harder and more demanding for entry, but in different ways. European rules increasingly focused on questions of potential for integration, accentuated by concerns with security. American rules were not concerned with integration, but with undocumented entry and unauthorized residence. Security (particularly after 2001) was also a concern, but was generally linked to the more general problem of undocumented entry at the southern border.[8]

Asylum entry has also become harder, but here too there have been differences between Europe and the United States. Entry for asylum in Europe and the United States is regulated by the obligations of signatories of the Convention Relating to the Status of Refugees signed in Geneva in 1951, amended by the Protocol relating to the Status of Refugees of 1967. In addition, European rules are also governed by the European Convention on Human Rights, ratified in 1952, but further defined by the series of Dublin regulations. All of these agreements recognize that asylum should be granted if there is a well-founded fear of persecution, which has been increasingly broadly defined since the original agreements were signed. But how are decisions made?

There are two core principles of Dublin. The first is to assign responsibility for decision-making to member states that first receive those seeking asylum, which appears to acknowledge that most claims for asylum will be made at the weakest patrolled entry points, sea and land ports on the periphery of Europe. Enforcement of the Dublin Regulation relies on decision-making at the member state level. Asylum seekers can be returned for registration to the EU state where they first arrived. In fact, the number of transfers increased between 2008 and 2015, but the actual numbers remained small compared to the number of requests. The second is that applicants cannot be considered if they arrive from an STC or a SCO. The problem is that there is no universally recognized list of countries that fit this category, and each country in Europe has its own list, sometimes secret and unpublished.

The countries in Eastern Europe that have hastily constructed fences and walls have claimed that they are doing the work of Europe and enforcing Dublin rules. The Hungarian government, for example, has refused to admit any asylum seekers from Serbia, a candidate for EU membership, which it has designated as an STC. The other problem is a broader complication with the asylum system itself. In practical terms, anyone seeking asylum in Europe must enter a European country illegally—you must first be there in order to claim asylum. Therefore, asylum in Europe is closely tied to undocumented entry or illegally overstaying a limited visa.

The United States has been complicated in a different way. Although similar rules apply, US law differentiates between refugee selection and asylum selection. Most entries are for those who have applied for settlement with refugee visas. These have been decided through procedures outside the United States, from lists formulated and vetted by the UN High Commission for Refugees. The admission of refugees has been a regularized process, built into the visa system of legal immigration. In fact, at least until the Trump administration slashed resettlement quotas, the United States has been relatively generous in admitting applicants through this route. Asylum seekers either apply at the border, as they enter, or to immigration authorities inside the the United States, after they have been detained. Of these, only a small percentage are generally granted asylum.

Although the rules that govern asylum in Europe and the United States have not changed a great deal, they have been altered through implementation. As the number of asylum seekers has increased in Europe, the implementation of these rules has grown more demanding, and the rules of the Dublin regulations have become more difficult to apply. The asylum process, moreover, has merged politically with questions of legal and illegal entry. In the United States entry through asylum has also merged with questions of illegal entry.

The important exception has been asylum seekers from Cuba who—under special legislation—have been automatically admitted if they have managed to place a dry foot on American soil. In the United States, the percentage admitted of those who claim asylum on American soil has tended to decline as the number of asylum seekers has gone up. In Europe, the percentage admitted has actually increased as the number of applicants has gone up in recent years.

Nevertheless, in both Europe and the United States there has been a public misperception, encouraged by political leaders, that claims for asylum have increased because asylum provides easier and less dangerous entry than other forms of immigration.[9] As we have seen, although there is considerable variation by country of origin, in general a far higher percentage of those who apply are granted long-term entry visas compared with the percentage of those granted recognition through the refugee or asylum process.

Stronger Implementation and Policing

Borders in Europe and the United States have been increasingly strengthened with more militarized police forces, and with instruments to prevent entry and force exit of unwanted migrants. On both sides of the Atlantic these buildups have constituted a response to different aspects of immigration: in Europe it was largely a response to the emerging politics of identity; in the United States it was a more complex part of the war on drugs, and then to the increase of unauthorized crossing at the southern border. In Europe, frontier police forces that operate within Europe, as well at the physical frontier, have been expanded. With the dismantling of most internal European borders, greater attention was given to the governance of the external borders, and to the entry of TCNs.

The border was also reinforced with the development of harsher enforcement procedures. Beginning in the 1980s, a network of detention centers was built throughout Europe to facilitate the deportation of migrants who had either attempted to enter without proper papers, or who had been detained by the police within European countries. The expansion of the number of detention centers, beginning in the 1990s, appeared to have little to do with either the growth of the population of undocumented migrants, or with the spike in asylum seekers (which would begin decades later).

The buildup at the southern border of the United States began slowly in the 1990s, but then more rapidly after 2001. This has represented an historic militarization of the police forces that control the land, air, and sea borders of the United States. What has been termed the formidable increase in the numbers of police has been enhanced by an expansion of their mission. The control of immigration is now defined largely in terms of national security and public safety, and these border forces have become the largest and the most active federal police forces in terms of arrest and prosecution. Moreover, as in Europe, border control has been extended internally by linking the police powers of ICE to local police. As we have seen, some indication of the priorities of border control can be understood by comparing the budgets of the border agency that deals with land crossing with the agency that deals with airport security. The budget of Customs and Border Protection is almost twice as large as the Transportation Security Administration.

As in Europe, the hardening of border control has been supported by the network of detention centers in which undocumented migrants are housed, often for long periods of time, before deportation. In addition, undocumented migrants are often detained in local jails under federal authorization. This network has grown incrementally since 2001.

Detention has become an important tool of border control, but more in the United States than in Europe. The network of detention centers in the United States is smaller than in Europe, but the number of those detained is considerably larger. This growth is in part a result of the emphasis on internal policing in the United States. If we look at the number detained as a proportion of the undocumented population on both sides of the Atlantic, however, the contrast disappears, because the undocumented population of the United States is three times that of Europe. By 2009, the percentage of the estimated undocumented population of those detained was about the same on both sides of the Atlantic.

Expulsion statistics paint a very different picture of enforcement. European countries apprehended fewer undocumented migrants than the United States, in part because there are fewer to apprehend. In addition, they have actually returned fewer than 50 percent of those apprehended. In the United States, apprehensions are increasingly among a large population of unauthorized and undocumented residents, relatively few of whom are able to make a credible case for asylum, and more of whom are actually expelled. How can we understand the low rates of expulsion in Europe? One way is to understand that apprehensions are police and administrative decisions, and the levels of apprehensions are often related to pressures from the ministries of the interior. Orders of expulsion, however, are subject to judicial review, and are therefore far more constrained. Orders of expulsion have increased substantially, and have been less constrained by immigration judges in the United States, even as the rules for expulsion have been expanded. The 330 judges are not part of an independent judicial system, but are supervised by the Attorney-General of the United States.

Finally, as if to accentuate the growing importance of the physical frontier, there has been an accelerated construction of fences and walls in both Europe and the United States. During the years after the end of the Cold War, more new fences, walls, and militarized boundaries were built than during the height of the Cold War in the 1950s. The numbers first grew even before the attacks of September 11, 2001, but have grown even more during the years since 2010. These new walls were built primarily to keep migrants out of Europe and the United States.

In Europe, the walls were built as the number of asylum seekers grew, and as their paths of entry into Europe shifted from the Mediterranean Sea to land routes through Greece, the Balkans, and Turkey. Although the first secure fences were constructed between Morocco and the Spanish enclaves of Ceuta and Melilla, they have since proliferated in Eastern Europe. The construction of these more recent fences and walls is directly related to the complexities of EU asylum policy and to the Dublin system.

The reasons given for the walls that have been constructed between the countries of Eastern Europe that control the eastern boundary of Europe, and the countries to the south and east, have focused on the Dublin contradiction. The forceful claim by the Hungarian government that it is protecting Schengen by excluding asylum seekers from Serbia and Croatia represents an unwillingness to take responsibility under Dublin. It may also be a recognition that given the experience of Italy after 2011, it is also likely that many will remain, either by choice or necessity.[10] Relative to its population, Hungary had the largest number of asylum applicants in the EU in 2014–2015.

Thus the case for a movement toward what has been called "the Wall around the West" is impressive.[11] Legal requirements for the entry into Europe by TCNs have multiplied, and new instruments have been created to enforce these changes. In the United States, laws and regulations have made legal entry from the Western Hemisphere more difficult. In addition, enforcement along the southern border has transformed what was once a relatively open border into the most militarized frontier in the Western world.

If we examine the process through which the border has changed in Europe and the United States, it is apparent that little attention has been given to how these actions might impede or interfere with the requirements of cross-border trade patterns. And indeed, in part because of the differences between where and how people and trade cross the border, the conflicts have been relatively rare. Nevertheless, continuing problems at the Calais crossing of the Eurostar in France, and some crossings at the Canadian and Mexican borders in the United States, indicate that the separation is not total. The border has grown harder, and in some ways less penetrable, but are we moving toward fortress Europe and fortress America?

8.2   The Border Is Soft

The larger picture is that the hardening of the border has had only limited impact, and has created neither a fortress Europe nor a fortress United States. Borders have been increasingly open to trade, and restrictions on immigration, whether imposed in home countries or at the physical border, have not inhibited a continuing growth of trade and immigration. Trade between the United States and Canada, and especially Mexico, has boomed at the same time as the border has been increasingly reinforced and militarized. During the period when internal border controls were being dismantled within the Schengen area and external borders were being strengthened, the total value of external trade actually increased more rapidly than the value of internal trade. On balance, it appears that the tightening of restrictions for the entry of people in Europe and the United States has not inhibited the flow of free trade, even in truck traffic across borders. Even where there has been a progressive enhancement of exclusionary policy, backed up by vastly increased human and material resources, trade has continued to grow.

Peter Andreas and Timothy Snyder got it about right when they wrote in 2000 that the requirements of free trade have not constrained the enhancement of the police functions at the border.[12] However, the border is not hard for everyone. Fortress Europe has its Eurostars, and legal access to the United States, though controlled, is relatively open by law. At the same time that the border has been hardened on both sides of the Atlantic, record numbers of immigrants have entered Europe and the United States, the largest number coming from the country on the other side of the wall, Mexico. Each year about a million immigrants settle in the United States, over three per thousand population (see Table 2.1). Indeed, for the United States the rates of entry and the settlement of immigrant populations are now approaching the levels experienced when there were few restrictions in place before World War I. This is not surprising, since American visa policy has been relatively generous. What is more surprising is that more than a million immigrants—TCNs from outside the EU—enter the countries of the EU each year, more than two per thousand of a much larger population. Moreover, if we include migrants within the EU who move to other EU countries through free movement, the number climbs to almost 2 million, or about four per thousand population.

Refusal rates for those applying for settlement in Europe are about the same as for the United States. The most important differences are with visa applicants from Africa and Asia, which are substantially higher for those seeking to enter Europe, compared with the United States. Nevertheless, the refusal rates reported in chapter 4 indicate that it is not overwhelmingly difficult to get a visa either for entry into the United States or into Europe. Of course this conclusion understates the difficulty of actually applying for a visa, or for the requirements that must be met to enter Europe, or for the long wait to obtain a visa to enter the United States. Nevertheless, the fortress analogy does not seem appropriate. Moreover, the degree to which the border is open or closed, or for whom it is open or closed, is related to the political process through which these decisions are made.

8.3 The Politics of the Border

The border is back because of the evolving dynamics of the political process in many of the member states of the EU, as well as in the United States. In somewhat different ways, a focus on the border has represented a political reaction to perceptions of state weakness, and to the inability of the state to defend what have been perceived as essential national values of identity and legality. In both symbolic and concrete ways, maintaining the border has been seen as an essential way of defining access and keeping others out.

Perceptions of Failure

Perceptions of failure of policies of border control and immigration policy were widespread in both Europe and the United States after the 1980s. In

Europe perceptions of failure began soon after immigration was stopped or suspended in the 1970s. As the gates were at least partially closed, European governments focused more intently on resident migrant populations, who were now more reluctant to return to their countries of origin. For those governments the problem quickly became questions of integration, or rather what they perceived as the resistance of these now new ethnic populations to cultural integration.

In countries such as France, which had a long tradition of immigration, the old institutions through which older immigrant communities became "French" appeared to have failed. This failure was punctuated by urban riots in the early 1980s, and by demands by assertive Muslim populations for community rights that had never been granted before to any immigrant group. Even in Britain, which was far more open to accepting multiculturalism and community rights deemed unacceptable in France, perceptions of failure among political elites were widespread after 2000. The perception of integration failure soon brought policies of entry into question. Policy quickly included criteria for integration, or requirements that those who entered either demonstrate values that would ease integration, or be willing to engage in programs to ensure integration.

Perceptions of failure among elites in the United States were sharply focused on the failure of controls at the southern border. By the 1980s several presidential commissions had warned about the movement of undocumented migrants across the border, and had recommended both more robust controls as well as tougher action against employers who hired these migrants. At the same time, the system of legal immigration in place since 1965 was politically separated from the question of illegal immigration and the growing population of undocumented migrants in the United States. This perception of failure, which had been growing among political elites of both major parties since the 1980s, had been linked to considerations of security by President Reagan, and was further tied to security after 2001.

Until the recent surge in asylum-seekers, illegal entry and presence has been far less of a problem in Europe than in the United States. Moreover, immigration has not generally been a priority in public opinion, either in Europe or the United States. Nevertheless, for voters on both sides of the Atlantic for whom immigration was a priority, concern about illegal migration was far stronger than about legal migration. Therefore, as a political issue around which voters could be mobilized, the perceived vulnerability of the border could be important. Thus, although public opinion was not the driving force of the politics of the border, it did provide an opportunity for mobilization by political elites.

Interest Intermediation

The activities of interest groups in the United States have played an important and continuing role in structuring and defining entry policy. I have found that most proposals that deal with entry are distributed among a wide variety of a relatively small number of visas for specific needs. Each proposal generally applies to fewer than 15 percent of those who enter the United States legally each year. These proposals are relatively uncontroversial because their benefits are broadly distributed among those groups making demands. While these efforts have generally avoided large questions of comprehensive legislation, the overall effect on policy has been to drive up the number of visas granted overall.

On a different track, there has been a security-industrial network that has grown along with the increased resources that have been devoted to border control. Concentrated on the border is a network of political forces that support strong border enforcement for different reasons. Public opinion has been strongly supportive of border enforcement, even among voters who otherwise support legal immigration. Expanded enforcement creates jobs, markets for goods and equipment, as well as a bargaining chip for immigration reform. The important involvement of interest groups in the development of entry and border policy in the United States is quite different from the more limited collaboration in Europe. What has sometimes been termed the European security-industrial complex has directly collaborated with state officials at the member state level, as well as with the working group established at the EU level, but this collaboration has not resulted in a major strengthening of the management of the common border. That is very much limited by the ability and willingness of member states to agree on an institutional expansion of the border regime. It has, however, contributed to the construction of increased detention facilities, and to the management of those facilities in some countries, notably the United Kingdom.

NGOs are poorly represented in the policymaking process on the border and at the EU level, where interior and justice officials dominate. At the level of policy implementation, however, their influence in overseeing individual cases of entry and establishing and overseeing rights at the border has been important, but entirely at the member state level.

Although group intermediation has been important on both sides of the Atlantic, there is evidence that in Europe, group influence has not been as critical for understanding the expansion of entry rights and numbers as it has been in the United States. The security-industrial network has clearly represented an expanded role for private security firms in Europe, but it does not appear to have played the kind of lobbying role that it has played in the United States, either for the deepening of border controls at the EU level or among the member states.

Party and Electoral Competition

By far, party and electoral competition have been the most important drivers for the changes in entry and border policy in Europe and the United States, but in different ways. In Europe, perceptions of failure that focused primarily on questions of integration established a context for augmenting entry requirements. In some European countries, such as France and the Netherlands, the focus on failure provided an electoral opening for the radical right, which in turn began to play an important role in agenda formation.

Limitations on rights of entry became important political issues after 2000, and were the objects of cooperation and harmonization at the EU level by 2006. These tentative efforts, however, were not matched by any serious attempt to cooperate on enforcing the common EU border. Instead, the asylum crisis after 2010 undermined the Dublin regulations, which were regularly ignored, and member states began to build their own barriers to movement of asylum seekers across their frontiers. They then reinforced their internal borders by temporarily suspending their commitments to Schengen. In this way, the greater political salience of entry and border issues, and more intense electoral competition among political parties, resulted in diminishing cooperation at the EU level.

In American party politics, entry policy and the border have become important in a different way. Hard positions on undocumented entry and unauthorized residence have become issues that the Republican Party has emphasized as their own, and their supporters in the electorate agree with them. Opposition to these hard positions has been claimed by the Democratic Party, and their electorate agrees with them as well. However, illegal entry and border control have become a wedge issue within the Republican Party in a prolonged contest for leadership and domination. For these reasons, the conflict within the Republican Party has driven the party further to the right, making it more difficult to develop an interparty coalition to pass comprehensive immigration border control legislation that would begin to deal with the problem of 11 million undocumented immigrants on American soil.

Thus in very different ways, party and electoral politics have elevated entry and border control to priority issues. For the United States the political salience of the border has been driven primarily within the Republican Party in a continuing factional struggle between ideological conservatives, who focus on identity, and centrist business Republicans, who tend to support more open immigration.

Federalism

The politics of the border has been structured by the political process, but federal relations within Europe and the United States provide another dimension for understanding this process. Federalism complicates the border. Because of the broad distribution of territorial power within the European and American federal systems, dispersed territorial decisions about border policy can substantially influence both policy and enforcement. Decisions that are made by Hungary have a strong impact on border politics in Austria, as well as other countries to the south and west of Hungary. Access to France for refugees on the move depends on decisions made in Italy.

Europe and Interstate Borders

Each member state can control the entry of immigrants and each has different criteria for entry developed within their own political process. They do not, however, have the same kind of control over the entry of asylum seekers. Because of the requirements of the Dublin regulations, all countries do not have equal responsibility for border governance and control. Asylum seekers are far less numerous at European airports. Because of the difficulty of boarding a flight to Europe without valid papers, asylum tends to be claimed at land crossings and seaports.

Sixteen of the twenty-eight countries of the EU have land or sea borders that comprise the external border, but few of these are important border crossings for asylum seekers or undocumented immigrants. Seaports in Italy and Greece, and land ports in the Balkans on the border with Turkey, have been the primary points of entry for most. In theory, countries on the external border, where asylum seekers arrive, have primary responsibility to register them and decide their fate. In practice, however, more than 90 percent of the applications for asylum in 2015 can be accounted for by those in Germany, Hungary, Sweden, Italy, and France. The tension between those member states on the external European border and those to which asylum seekers actually move has generated a problem-solving gap for which there is no easy policy solution.

The 2015 EU agreement on the distribution of asylum seekers was never applied, and member states continue to take actions that weaken the common Schengen area (the temporary re-establishment of border controls), that undermine the understanding of responsibilities under the Dublin Regulation, and that weaken human rights protections for those seeking asylum in Europe. The only important common border initiative that appears to have succeeded is the 2016 return agreement with Turkey, which has raised serious human rights questions. But member states have continued to pursue their own initiatives to externalize asylum: the Italians in Libya and the French in Niger. In the case of Europe, the federal dynamic has not resulted in greater common effort to control the common border.

We can understand this by focusing on three aspects of federal relations in Europe. The first is the domination of what Samuel Beer called the intergovernmental lobby. In establishing EU common border policy, intergovernmental alliances can either directly or indirectly prevent the establishment of policy, or—as in the case of the 2015 agreement on the distribution of asylum seekers—the implementation of policy that has been decided already. Second, without a strong executive authority, comparable to the presidency in the United States, there is no centralized institution capable of mobilizing support for coherent control over the frontier.

Third, in Europe, there is no real equivalent of what Beer has called the technocracy, networks of similar interests across state boundaries that are able to develop and lobby for coherent policies at the central level. The security-industrial complex has, from time to time, played some role in policy formation.[13] Human rights NGOs have been a countervailing force at the border and in some cases have received member state subventions. But like the security complex, they do not appear to play an important role in policy formation.

The domestic politics of member state policy formation have largely renationalized issues of border control. Even for countries in which the surge of asylum seekers has not been a serious problem, the dynamics of domestic politics have resulted in a movement to reassert the state frontier. In France, for example, a center left government in 2018 proposed a harder policy for asylum, as well as for undocumented migrants. For the first time, criminal penalties are proposed for crossing the frontier illegally.[14]

The problem for each of the member states is similar: the entry of migrants seeking asylum. However, the problem varies significantly among the twenty-eight EU countries. The interdependence of border control is inherent in the EU (free movement) and the Schengen area (open borders). This creates what Fritz Scharpf has termed a classic problem-solving gap: "where the EU generates problems and constrains solutions at national levels while effective solutions at the European level are blocked by political conflicts among member governments." To avoid undermining the output legitimacy of both national political systems and European integration, Scharpf has called for institutional reforms that would either increase the EU capacity for effective action, or that would restore national problem solving capabilities.[15] In fact the EU has not done either, and the legitimacy of the EU border has been deeply questioned.

The United States: Federalism and Cycles of Enforcement

Federal dynamics have taken on a different form in the United States. The dynamics of federal territorial relations can often be seen in what I have called cycles of enforcement. These are enforcement cycles since 1954 that generally begin with presidential actions meant to reinforce border control, and generally conclude with pressure from business and immigrant interests, often supported by state governments, to ease constraints.

The federal government is responsible for the crossing of the southern border by unauthorized immigrants, few of whom are asylum seekers. Illegal status is largely a product of the laws and regulations in force. Initially after the landmark legislation of 1965 came into force, migrants were attracted by the same market forces that had existed before the immigration legislation was passed. They were then discouraged from returning to their home countries, as they were mostly able to do before. The impact of their presence, however, is far from uniform among the fifty states. As in Europe, these undocumented migrants have had an important impact on the politics of some states, but little on others. The political influence of these states, however, is magnified by the federal system.

Although the 11 million unauthorized residents are generally concentrated in only six states,[16] about forty states have developed policies that are meant to influence federal entry policy, or its implementation, in various ways. Some states have taken actions meant to challenge the federal authorities for not acting more decisively to close the border (Arizona) or actions meant to protect the presence of undocumented migrants (California), or have done both at different points in time (California). Many of these efforts have been turned back by federal courts, but the states remain important ongoing actors in the enforcement of federal policy. In each case, state political systems have reflected the interests of organized economic groups (agribusiness), the interests of a growing immigrant population, or the opposition of voters to a growing immigrant population.

More recently, the efforts of some state and local authorities to support sanctuary cities and various other protective efforts for undocumented migrants since 2016, may or may not limit the determination of the federal authorities to deport larger numbers of undocumented migrants. They do, however, indicate the tensions of yet another cycle of enforcement. Court decisions have generally limited the authority of American state governments to make policy on immigration control, and have imposed on them obligations to provide some services and benefits even to undocumented immigrant populations. The states, however, have maintained considerable ability to constrain federal enforcement by limiting police cooperation and limiting the pooling of information.

As in Europe, the problems on the land borders of the United States have been largely produced by federal actions, which have then provoked reactions at state levels. As in Europe, there remains a problem-solving gap. The federal government has generated problems but constrains solutions at the state level, while effective solutions at the federal level are blocked by the veto power of mostly smaller states in Congress since 2005. In this way, the federal system has magnified the problem of the border.

8.4 The Border and the Politics of Immigration

In both the United States and Europe, perception of failure of migration and border policy has been one of the seedbeds from which has grown the salience of the border as an object of politics. Thus, tighter border control has been seen by governments and by mass publics as a solution to perceived problems of immigration, rights-based immigration in particular. Under pressure from political interests and political parties in the context of electoral politics, policy has tilted toward stronger borders and border controls.

The results have not been impressive. The costs of harsher border policies have been significant. In economic terms, the strengthening of the border and border forces has demanded increased resources. In human terms, the costs can be seen in the increase of deaths on the southern border of the United States and on the Mediterranean border of Europe. In value terms, the establishment of off-shore detention centers, as well as the growing archipelago of detention facilities within Europe and the United States, has created the image (if not the reality) of a vulnerable fortress.

Nevertheless, the flow of immigration has continued and even increased in Europe and the United States. How can we understand this? Only by examining the complex politics of immigration can we understand why walls go up, but they are far from constituting a fortress. Contrary to what we might expect, there remains considerable and steady support for legal immigration on both sides of the Atlantic. Indeed, European publics overwhelmingly support free movement, and maintain support for legal immigration. In the United States, support for increased immigration has grown dramatically since 2002, from 8 to 28 percent, while support for maintaining present levels has remained steady, at about 35 percent; in 2018 it increased to 39 percent.[17]

Business interests favor the availability of immigrant labor on both sides of the Atlantic; in contrast to their opposition to immigration, even after World War II, American trade unions (European unions as well) generally see immigration as a new source of membership, and are generally supportive of immigrant rights. As the current debate on Brexit seems to indicate, at least some sectors of the economy would suffer mightily if legal immigration were reduced significantly. Moreover, despite President Trump's anger about chain migration, there remains strong legal and political support for family unification. In the United States and in some European countries, immigrants and their descendants are not simply objects of politics, but are increasingly actors and potential actors as well.

Radical right political parties in Europe have gained votes by militating against immigration, and the electoral challenge that they have posed has served to move more mainstream parties closer to their positions, at least in the short run. The result, however, has not been to reduce immigration, but only to make it more difficult and more humiliating. This may happen in the United States as well.

The strengthening of the border is unlikely to be a solution to the vexing problems of poverty and war that have driven record numbers of refugees from their homelands toward Europe and America. Strong borders are construed to be fixed defenses against entry, but they have historically proven to be vulnerable, and costly in many ways. The more recent attempts to externalize the border are an effort to build a wall against exit, particularly in Africa. It is also an effort to move the political problem somewhere else. Somewhere else, however, is often to countries that are unstable and vulnerable themselves. For this reason, the short-term solution is the seedbed of the long-term problem.

The pull of Europe and the United States is likely to remain considerable, regardless of costly efforts to close the frontier. Nevertheless, what we can learn from the politics of the border in Europe and the United States is that even border policies that are doomed to fail may be deemed necessary in order to avoid even worse policies. We should not underestimate the problems that the border poses even for well-intentioned powerful political leaders, as the fate of German Chancellor Angela Merkel in the German federal elections 2017 (and since) demonstrates.[18]

Peter Andreas has argued that hard border policies are essentially "image management and image-creating," a political means of creating the appearance of effectiveness. This is not entirely true, since these policies have real consequences that deeply affect both the targeted populations as well as those who control the border. Nevertheless, to the extent that they create the appearance of a more secure and orderly border, they become a way of dealing with the political contradictions of the liberal paradox, of managing the tensions between liberal commitments to rights-based entry and democratic demands for stronger border control.[19]

NOTES

Chapter 1

1. Edward Wong, "As Interest Grows in Great Walls, an Ancient Chinese Fortress Beckons," *New York Times*, December 30, 2016, p. A4.
2. Peter Andreas and Timothy Snyder, eds., *The Wall Around the West: State Borders and Immigration Controls in North America and Europe* (Lanham, MD: Rowman & Littlefield, 2000), pp. 1 and 219.
3. "The New Political Divide," *The Economist*, July 30–August 5, 2016, pp. 7 and 16–18.
4. The data on walls was gathered by Élisabeth Vallet, Josselyn Guillarmou, and Zoé Barry of the University of Quebec, Montreal, and reported in a series of three special reports in the *Washington Post* on October 12, 14, and 17, 2017. Samuel Granados, Zoeann Murphy, Kevin Schaul, and Anthony Faiola, "Raising Barriers," "Fenced Out," and "Concrete Divisions", https://www.washingtonpost.com/graphics/world/border-barriers/global-illegal-immigration-prevention/.
5. Gary Freeman, "Modes of Immigration Politics in Liberal Democratic States," *International Migration Review* 29, no. 4 (Winter 1995), pp. 881–902.
6. Matthew J. Gibney and Randall Hansen, *Deportation and the Liberal State: The Forcible Return of Asylum Seekers and the Unlawful Migrants in Canada, Germany and the United Kingdom,* New Issues in Refugee Research, UNHCR, Working Paper No. 77 (New York: UNHCR, 2003), pp. 1–2.
7. See Vivian Yee, "Judge Threatens Sessions with Contempt over Deported Asylum Seekers," *New York Times*, August 9, 2018.
8. In 2013, Randall Hansen and Demetrious G. Papadimitriou published an edited volume titled *Managing Borders in an Increasingly Borderless World* (Washington, DC: Migration Policy Institute, 2013).
9. Hugh Heclo, *Modern Social Policies in Britain and Sweden* (New Haven, CT: Yale University Press, 1974), pp. 305–306. Also see Peter A. Hall, "Policy Paradigms, Social Learning, and the State: The Case of Economic Policymaking in Britain," *Comparative Politics* 25, no. 3 (April 1993), pp. 275–296.
10. See David Dixon and Julia Fellat, *Immigration Enforcement Spending since IRCA* (Washington, DC: Migration Policy Institute, 2005), pp. 2–4.
11. Peter Andreas, *Border Games*, 2nd ed. (Ithaca, NY: Cornell University Press, 2009), p. 121.
12. "Will Britain Leave the European Union?," lecture given by the Rt. Hon. Charles Clarke at the Munk School of the University of Toronto on Friday, March 22, 2013..
13. Richard Rosecrance, "The Rise of the Virtual State: Territory Becomes Passé," *Foreign Affairs,* July–August 1996, pp. 45–61.

14. Kenichi Ohmae, *The End of the Nation State: The Rise of Regional Economies* (New York: The Free Press, 1996); *The Borderless World: Power and Strategy in an Interlinked Economy*, rev. ed. (New York: HarperCollins, 1999).

15. Saskia Sassen, *Losing Control: Sovereignty in an Age of Globalization* (New York: Columbia University Press, 1996), chs. 1 and 3.

16. Ariane Chebel d'Appollonia, *Frontiers of Fear, Immigration and Insecurity in the United States and Europe* (Ithaca, NY: Cornell University Press, 2012).

17. James Hollifield, "The Emergence of the Migration State," *International Migration Review* 38 no. 3 (September 2004), p. 885.

18. Adrian Favell, *Eurostars: Free Movement and Mobility in an Integrated Europe* (Oxford: Blackwell, 2008), viii–ix.

19. James Hollifield, *Immigrants, Markets and States: The Political Economy of Postwar Europe* (Cambridge, MA: Harvard University Press, 1994).

20. Christian Joppke, ed., *Challenge to the Nation-State: Immigration in Western Europe and the United States* (Oxford: Oxford University Press, 1998), chapter 2.

21. Saskia Sassen, "The De Facto Transnationalizing of Immigration Policy," in Joppke, *Challenge to the Nation-State*, p. 68.

22. Freeman, "The Decline of Sovereignty? Politics and Immigration Restriction in Liberal States," in Joppke, *Challenge to the Nation-State*, pp. 101–104.

23. For example, see the common Schengen Manual, to be used by border authorities of the member states who are responsible for the common frontier: Council of the European Union, 13380/10, FRONT 125/COMIX 571, *A Practical Manual for Frontier-Guards*, C(2010) 5559 Final, September 8, 2010.

24. See Erin F. Delany, "Justifying Power: Federalism, Immigration and Foreign Affairs," *Duke Journal of Constitutional Law and Public Policy* 8, no. 1 (2013), pp. 164–165.

25. See Diego Acosta Arcarazo and Andrew Geddes, "The Development, Application and Implications of an EU Rule of Law in the Area of Migration Policy," *Journal of Common Market Studies* 51, no. 2 (2013), pp. 179–193.

26. Rey Koslowski, "European Union Migration Regimes, Established and Emergent," in Joppke, *Challenge to the Nation-State*, chapter 5.

27. John Torpey, *The Invention of the Passport* (Cambridge: Cambridge University Press, 2000).

28. See Didier Bigo, "Frontier Controls in the European Union," in *Controlling Frontiers: Free Movement into and within Europe*, ed. Didier Bigo and Elspeth Guild (Burlington, VT: Ashgate, 2005), pp. 55–57.

29. Gibney and Hansen, "Deportation and the Liberal State," pp. 1–2.

30. The normative aspects of this argument are explored by Matthew Gibney in "Liberal Democratic States and Responsibilities to Refugees," *American Political Science Review* (March 1999), pp. 169–181. It is also explored by Ryan Pevnick in *Immigration and the Constraints of Justice: Between Open Borders and Absolute Sovereignty* (New York: Cambridge University Press, 2014), chapter 4.

31. See, in particular, Andrew Geddes, *Immigration and European Immigration: Beyond Fortress Europe* (Manchester: Manchester University Press, 2008).

32. Karolina S. Follis, *Building Fortress Europe: The Polish–Ukrainian Frontier* (Philadelphia: University of Pennsylvania Press, 2011), p. 7.

33. Andreas, *Border Games*, p. 141.

34. Zygmunt Bauman, *Freedom (Concepts in Social Thought)* (Minneapolis: University of Minnesota Press, 1988), cited in Didier Bigo and Elspeth Guild, eds., *Controlling Frontiers: Free Movement into and Within Europe* (Aldershot: Ashgate Press, 2005), p. 3.

35. Bigo and Guild, eds., *Controlling Frontiers*, p. 4.

36. Ryan Pevnick, *Immigration and the Constraints of Justice: Between Open Borders and Absolute Sovereignty* (New York: Cambridge University Press, 2014), p. 174.

37. Elia Zureik and Mark B. Salter, "Global Surveillance and Policing Borders: Borders, Security, Identity," in *Global Surveillance and Policing Borders: Borders Security, Identity*, ed. Zureik and Salter (Cullompton, Devon: Willan Publishing, 2005), pp. 4–5.

38. Susan Martin, "Unauthorized Migration: US Policy Responses in Comparative Perspective," presentation at the 2007 annual conference of the International Studies Association, Chicago, Illinois, March 2, 2007.

39. See Marc Rosenblum, *Unaccompanied Child Migration to the United States: The Tension Between Protection and Prevention* (Washington, DC: Migration Policy Institute, 2015).

40. See European Agency for Management of Operation Coordination, *Frontex Annual Risk Analysis, 2014* (Warsaw: Frontex, 2014), p. 31.

41. See US Border Patrol, "Total Illegal Alien Apprehensions by Fiscal Year, 1992–2013," https://www.cbp.gov/sites/default/files/assets/documents/2017-Dec/BP%20Total%20Apps%20FY1925-FY2017.pdf.

42. Julia Preston, "Hoping for Asylum, Migrants Strain U.S. Border," *New York Times*, April 11, 2014.

43. Mable Berezin, "Territory, Emotion, and Identity: Spatial Recalibration in a New Europe," in *Europe Without Borders: Remapping Territory, Citizenship, and Identity in a Transnational Age*, ed. Mable Berezin and Martin Schain (Baltimore: Johns Hopkins University Press, 2003), pp. 2–6.

44. See Michael Skapinker, "The Conservatives' Battle over Immigration, Tourists and Students," *The Financial Times*, May 13, 2015.

45. For Andrew Geddes's analysis of the application of these concepts to British migration policies, see "Getting the Best of Both Worlds? Britain, the EU and Migration Policy," *International Affairs* 81, no. 4 (2005), pp. 723–740, 724–725.

46. Julie Mostov, *Soft Borders: Rethinking Sovereignty and Democracy* (New York: Palgrave, 2008), p. 124.

47. *The Economist*, November 8, 2014, p. 39.

48. The European Parliament estimates 220 closed detention camps within the countries of the EU 25 in 2007. See Directorate-General Internal Policies, Policy Department C, *The Conditions in Centres for Third Country Nationals* (Brussels: EP, Committee on Civil Liberties, Justice and Home Affairs, December 2007), p. 35.

49. The process was stipulated in chapter 7 (Articles 28–38) of the SIS of June 19, 1990, and later incorporated into the Dublin Convention of 1997, as well as the further development of the agreement in Dublin II and III.

50. Rey Koslowski, "Global Mobility and the Quest for an International Migration Regime," in *International Migration and Development: Continuing the Dialogue: Legal and Political Perspectives*, ed. Joseph Chamie and Luca Dall'Oglio (Geneva: International Organization for Migration, 2008), p. 127.

51. See Tara Brian and Frank Laczko, *Fatal Journeys: Tracking Lives Lost during Migration* (Geneva: International Organization for Migration, 2014), p. 24.

52. Cecile Ducourtieux and Julia Pascual, "Les mesures pour lutter contre le terrorisme one du mal à se concrétiser au niveau de l'UE," *Le Monde*, March 24, 2016.

53. See National Commission on Terrorist Attacks, *Final Report of the National Commission on Terrorist Attacks Upon the United States* (New York: W. W. Norton, 2004), chapter 8.

54. See Marion Panizzon, "Readmission Agreements of EU Member States: A Case for EU Subsidiarity or Dualism?" *Refugee Survey Quarterly* 31, no. 4 (2012), pp. 101–133.

55. For a counterargument, see Anand Menon, "The Limits of Comparative Politics: International Relations in the European Union," in *The United States and the European Union in Comparative Perspective*, ed. Anand Menon and Martin A. Schain (Oxford: Oxford University Press, 2006), pp. 35–59.

56. Norman K. Nicholson, "Arenas of Power, the Model," in *Arenas of Power*, ed. Theodore J. Lowi and intr. Norman K. Nicholson (Boulder, CO: Paradigm Publishers, 2009), p. 22.

57. Ruben Zaiotti, *Cultures of Border Control: Schengen and the Evolution of European Frontiers* (Chicago: University of Chicago Press, 2011), pp. x–xii.

58. In particular, see John W. Kingdon, *Agendas, Alternatives and Public Policies* (London: Longman Classics, 2003).

59. See Peter Hall, "Policy Paradigms, Social Learning and the State: The Case of Economic Policymaking in Britain," *Comparative Politics* 25, no. 3 (April 1993), pp. 275–296.

60. See John Peterson, "Policy Networks," in *European Integration Theory*, ed. Antje Wiener and Thomas Diez (Oxford: Oxford University Press, 2004), pp. 105–125.

61. For a discussion of representative bureaucracy, see the seminal study by J. Donald Kingsley, *Representative Bureaucracy* (Yellow Springs, OH: Antioch Press, 1944) and V. Subramaniam, "Representative Bureaucracy: A Reassessment," *American Political Science Review* 61, no. 4 (December 1967), pp. 1010–1019; for a discussion of principal-agent models, see Brian J.

Cook, "Principal-Agent Models of Political Control of Bureaucracy," *American Political Science Review* 83, no. 3 (September 1989), pp. 965–974. Bureaucratic patterns of independence are also analyzed in Alexis Spire, *Accueillir ou Reconduire: Enquête wur les Guichets de l'immigration* (Paris: Editions Raisons d'Agir, 2008).

62. Andreas, *Border Games*, p. 9.
63. See Barry Buzan, Ole Wæver, and Jaap De Wilde, *Security: A New Framework for Analysis* (Boulder, CO: Lynn Reinner Publications, 1998).
64. See Martin A. Schain, *The Politics of Immigration in France, Britain and the United States* (New York: Palgrave-Macmillan, 2012), chapters 2, 5, and 8. We should also note that securitization has been developed for a multitude of political goals. In the United States, for example, the Soviet launch of the Sputnik satellite in 1957 was used to generate support for federal support of education through the National Defense Education Act in 1958. For years, graduate fellowships provided under this legislation were fondly referred to as "Sputnik scholarships."
65. D'Appollonia, *Frontiers of Fear*, pp. 15–17.
66. Andreas, *Border Games*, p. 85.
67. E. E. Schattschneider, *The Semisovereign People* (New York: Holt, Rinehart and Winston, 1960), chapter 2. Also see Schain, *The Politics of Immigration*, pp. 23–24.
68. Although the Italian Navy withdrew from extended sea rescues in November 2014, the Italian Coast Guard continued more limited operations that went beyond the limits of the thirty nautical miles undertaken by the Triton Frontex mission.
69. Statements from representatives of the United Nations Refugee Agency. Mare Nostrum was credited with saving 100,000 lives. See Gaia Pianigiani, "Recued African Migrants Recount Ordeal in Mediterranean," *New York Times*, February 12, 2015, p. 9, and Reuters, "Italy to End Sea Rescue Mission that Saved 100,000 Migrants," by Steve Scherer and Massimiliano Di Giorgio, http://www.reuters.com/article/2014/10/31/us-italy-migrants-eu-idUSKBN0IK22220141031.
70. Samuel H. Beer, "Federalism, Nationalism and Democracy in America," *American Political Science Review* 72, no. 1 (1978), pp. 17–19.
71. Andrew Moravcsik, "Preferences and Power in the European Community: A Liberal Intergovernmentalist Approach," *Journal of Common Market Studies* 31, no. 4 (December 1993), pp. 481–517. Also see Andrew Moravcsik, *The Choice for Europe: Social Purpose and State Power from Messina to Maastricht* (Ithaca, NY: Cornell University Press, 1998), pp. 3–85.
72. Grant McConnell, *Private Power and American Democracy* (New York: Vintage Books, 1966), chapter 4.
73. Virginie Guiraudon, "The EU 'Garbage Can': Accounting for Policy Developments in the Immigration Domain," Paper presented at the 2001 Conference of the European Community Studies Association, Madison, WI, May 29–June 1, 2001, p. 7.
74. See Terri Givens and Adam Luedke, "The Politics of European Union Immigration Policy: Institutions, Salience and Harmonization," *Policy Studies Journal* 32, no. 1 (2004), pp. 145–165.
75. Andrew Geddes, *Immigration and European Integration* .
76. Antje Ellermann, *States Against Migrants: Deportation in Germany and the United States* (New York: Cambridge University Press, 2009), pp. 58–61.
77. Peterson, "Policy Networks," p. 8.
78. Virginie Guiraudon, "The EU 'Garbage Can': Accounting for Policy Developments in the Immigration Domain."
79. Joachim K. Blatter, "Debordering the World of States: Towards a Multi-Level System in Europe and a Multi-Polity System in North America? Insights from Border Regions," *European Journal of International Relations* 7, no. 2 (2001), pp. 175–209.
80. See Liesbet Hooghe and Gary Marks, "Unraveling the Central State, but How? Types of Multi-Level Governance," *American Political Science Review* 97, no. 2 (May 2003), esp. pp. 237–238. Also see Sabine Weyand, "Inter-Regional Associations and the European Integration Process," *Regional and Federal Studies* 6, no. 2 (1999), pp. 166–182.

Chapter 2

1. Moisés Naim, "Borderline: It's Not about Maps," *Washington Post*, May 28, 2006.

2. Calculated from estimates by Frontex, *Annual Risk Analysis 2014*, pp. 70–74, and Eurostat data: The European Commission, *Eurostat* Database for the European Union, http://appsso.eurostat.ec.europa.eu/nui/.

3. See statistics release by the US Department of Commerce for 2015, *International Visitation in the United States*, http://tinet.ita.doc.gov/outreachpages/download_data_table/2015_Visitation_Report.pdf.

4. Virginie Guiraudon and Gallya Lahav, "Comparative Perspective on Border Control: Away from the Border and Outside the State," in *The Wall Around the West: State Borders and Immigration Controls in North America and Europe*, ed. Peter Andreas and Timothy Snyder (Lanham, MD: Rowman & Littlefield, 2000), pp. 55–81; also by Guiraudon and Lahav, "The State Sovereignty Debate Revisited: The Case of Immigration Control," *Comparative Political Studies* 33, no. 2 (2000), pp. 163–195.

5. For example, applicants for long-term visas to France from the US must submit an FBI report to the French consulate.

6. Aristide Zolberg, "Matters of State: Theorizing Immigration Policy," in *Handbook of International Migration: The American Experience*, ed. Charles Hirschman, Philip Kasinitz, and Josh DeWind (New York: Russell Sage Foundation, 1999), pp. 71–93.

7. Guiraudon and Lahav, "The State Sovereignty Debate Revisited." The Schengen area now encompasses 23 of the 28 EU countries.

8. Saskia Bonjour, "The Transfer of Pre-departure Integration Requirements for Family Migrants Among Member States of the EU," *Comparative Migration Studies* 2, no. 2 (2014), pp. 203–226.

9. My thanks to M. Jean de Ceuster, Directorate General for Home Affairs, for pointing this out in an interview on December 9, 2013.

10. Gerald L. Neuman, "Anomalous Zones," *Stanford Law Review* 48, no. 5 (May 1996), pp. 1197–1234. Also see Virginie Guiraudon, "Enlisting Third Parties in Border Control: A Comparative Study of its Causes and Consequences," in *Borders and Security Governance*, ed. Marina Caparini and Otwin Marenin (Geneva: Geneva Center for the Democratic Control of the Armed Forces, 2006), pp. 79–94.

11. See The European Commission, *Eurostat* Database for the European Union, http://appsso.eurostat.ec.europa.eu/nui/; http://epp.eurostat.ec.europa.ey/portal/page/portal/statistics/search_database.

12. Jeffrey S. Passel, D'Vera Cohn, and Ana Gonzalez-Barrera, "Population Decline of Unauthorized Immigrants Stalls, May Have Reversed," Pew Research Center's Hispanic Trends Project, September 2013, p. 16, http://www.pewhispanic.org/2013/09/23/population-decline-of-unauthorized-immigrants-stalls-may-have-reversed/.

13. "Frontex and Managing the EU's Borders—Briefing," February 24, 2010, http://www.eubusiness.com/topics/living-in-eu/frontex-guide.10.

14. See Europa, *The Schengen Area and Cooperation* (2013), http://europa.eu/legislation_summaries/justice_freedom_security/free_movement_of_persons_asylum_immigration/l33020_en.htm.

15. See Menon, "The Limits of Comparative Politics," pp. 40–42; and Alberta Sbragia, "Comparing Two Sui Generis Systems," in *Comparative Federalism: The European Union and the United States in Comparative Perspective*, ed. Anand Menon and Martin A. Schain (Oxford: Oxford University Press, 2006), pp. 15–34 and pp. 35–58. Sbragia argues that "both the United States and the EU disperse power so widely that the term 'government' is not used in the United States in the way that is used in other advanced industrial democracies while 'governance without government' characterizes the EU."

16. These figures are Eurostat estimates. See Katya Vasileva, "Population and Social Conditions," *Eurostat Statistics in Focus*, 31/2012. The UK estimates for 2016 and 2017 indicate a growth in the number of UK citizens residing in other parts of Europe; see The U.K. in a Changing Europe, *How Many British Citizens Live in the EU?*http://ukandeu.ac.uk/fact-figures/how-many-british-citizens-livein-the-eu/.

17. See Anne Herm, "Recent Migration Trends: Citizens of EU-27 Member States Become Ever More Mobile While EU Remains Attractive to Non-EU Citizens," *Eurostat, Statistics in Focus,* 98/2008, pp. 1 and 3.

18. This was formerly Article 39 of the Treaty Establishing the European Community. See http://europa.eu/legislation_summaries/justice_freedom_security/free_movement_of_persons_asylum_immigration/l33152_en.htm, "Right of Union Citizens and Their Family Members to Move and Reside Freely Within the Territory of the Member States," judgment of May 7, 1991, C 340/89, *Vlassopoulou.* Numerous directives of the European Union have affirmed the right of free movement, the most important of which is "Directive 2004/38/EC of the European Parliament and of the Council of April 29, 2004, on the Right of Citizens of the Union and Their Family Members to Move and Reside Freely Within the Territory of the Member States."

19. See Bigo and Guild, *Controlling Frontiers,* esp. pp. 59–91. Free movement now applies to all countries in the EU; see *End of Restrictions on Free Movement of Workers from Bulgaria and Romania—Statement by László Andor, European Commissioner for Employment, Social Affairs and Inclusion,* Brussels, January 1, 2014. http://europa.eu/rapid/press-release_MEMO-14-1_en.htm.

    There are now 26 countries that are in the Schengen area, four of which are not members of the European Union (Iceland, Norway, Lichtenstein, and Switzerland). The UK and Ireland have opted out. Bulgaria, Romania, and Cyprus have not yet been admitted. See Jean-Pierre Stroobants, "Schengen: les vingt-septs crispés sur le contrôl de leurs frontières," *Le Monde,* June 11, 2011, p. 6.

20. These rights are codified in two directives: the 1996 "Posted Workers Directive" (Directive 96/71/EC of the European Parliament and of the Council of December 16, 1996, concerning the posting of workers in the framework of the provision of services), the details of which have been widely challenged; and the 2004 "Free Movement Directive" (Directive 2004/38/EC of The European Parliament and of the Council of April 29, 2004), which has been challenged by the UK but is broadly supported by other member states.

21. For the full list of temporary controls imposed under Article 25 of the Schengen borders code, see European Commission, *Temporary Reintroduction of Border Control* https://ec.europa.eu/home-affairs/sites/homeaffairs/files/what-we-do/policies/borders-and-visas/schengen/reintroduction-border-control/docs/ms_notifications_-_reintroduction_of_border_control_en.pdf.

22. See Nicos Trimikliniotis, "Migration and Freedom of Movement of Workers: EU Law, Crisis and the Cypriot States of Exception," *Laws* 2 no. 4 (2013), pp. 440–468.

23. See Bigo and Guild, *Controlling Frontiers,* esp. pp. 59–91.

24. In *Edwards v. California* (314 U.S. 160 /1941).

25. See statement by UK Prime Minister in George Parker, "David Cameron Launches Attack on EU Migration,"*Financial Times,* November 27, 2013.

26. Norman Williams, "Why Congress May Not Overrule the Dormant Commerce Clause," *UCLA Law Review* 53 (October 2005), pp. 2–3.

27. *Henderson et al. v. Mayor of the City of New York, and Commissioners of Immigration v. North German Lloyd,* 92 U.S. 259 (1875); and *Chy Lung v. Freeman,* 92 U.S. 275 (1875). Also see Schain, *The Politics of Immigration,* pp. 200–201.

28. Free movement of people was not constitutionally established in the US until 1941, when the US Supreme Court overturned a California depression-era law that made it a misdemeanor to bring into California "any indigent person who is not a resident of the State, knowing him to be an indigent person." In *Edwards v. California* (314 U.S. 160 /1941), the Court unanimously overturned the law. Also see *Saenz v. Roe,* 526 U.S. 489 (1999).

29. The challenges by state governments have either been attempts to force the federal government to take stronger action on the Mexican border (and states have claimed a right to "co-enforce" border controls) to eliminate illegal entry of people; or attempts to prevent the federal government from creating a more nuanced policy of border control. See *Arizona v. United States 567 US* (2012), and David Montgomery and Julia Preston, "Seventeen States Suing on Immigration," *New York Times,* December 3, 2014. Arizona has also worked to ease the entry of goods from Mexico "in keeping with how things are done in other states": Luis

F. Carrasco, "Border Truckers: Disproportionate U.S. Inspections Hurt Trade," *Arizona Daily Star*, May 23, 2015.

30. See Marc Rosenblum, *Unaccompanied Child Migration to the United States: The Tension Between Protection and Prevention* (Washington, DC: Migration Policy Institute, 2015).

31. Martin, "Unauthorized Migration."

32. See Randall Hansen and Demetrios G. Papademetriou, *Managing Borders in an Increasingly Borderless World* (Washington, DC: Migration Policy Institute, 2013), pp. 5–6.

33. James F. Hollifield, "The Emerging Migration State," *International Migration Review* 38, no. 3 (Fall, 2004), p. 887.

34. Hollifield, "The Emerging Migration State," p. 888, and Gibney and Hansen, "Deportation and the Liberal State," pp. 1–2.

35. See Maragret E. Peters, "Open Trade, Closed Borders: Immigration in the Era of Globalization," *World Politics* 67, no. 1 (2015), pp. 114–154.

36. Andreas, *Border Games*, p. 121.

37. "Communication from the Commission to the European Parliament and the Council: On the State of Play of the Implementation of the Priority Actions Under the European Agenda on Migration," COM (2016) 85, final, February 10, 2016, pp. 13–14, http://ec.europa.eu/dgs/home-affairs/what-we-do/policies/european-agenda-migration/proposal-implementation-package/docs/managing_the_refugee_crisis_state_of_play_20160210_en.pdf. Also, for estimates of the benefits for trade of open Schengen borders, and the costs of suspension of open borders, see the report of France Stratégie, Vincent Aussilloux and Boris Le Hir, "The Economic Cost of Rolling Back Schengen," https://www.strategie.gouv.fr/sites/strategie.gouv.fr/files/atoms/files/the_economic_cost_of_rolling_back_schengen.pdf, p. 7.

38. Stephen Castles and Mark Miller, quoted in Pevnick, *Immigration and Constraints of Justice*, p. 174.

39. See "The United States-Canadian Border: Undefended No More," *The Economist*, November 8, 2014, pp. 38–39.

40. For the best recent comparative analysis, see Ariane Chebel d'Appollonia, *Immigration and Insecurity in the United States and Europe* (Ithaca, NY: Cornell University Press, 2012).

41. See Schain, *The Politics of Immigration*; and Christopher Caldwell, *Reflections on the Revolution in Europe: Immigration, Islam and the West* (New York: Doubleday, 2009).

42. Martin, "Unauthorized Migration," p. 1.

43. Michel Beine, Justin Gest, Anna Boucher, Eiko Thielemann, Michel Hiscox, Patrick McGovern, Hillel Rapoport, and Brian Bergoon, "Comparing Immigration Policies: An Overview from the IMPALA Database," *International Migration Review* 50, no. 4 (2016), pp. 825–1076. This index is based on studies of seven European countries, as well as the US and Australia. However, the authors note that their results are generally consistent with the results of the MIPEX index, and with several other similar studies. MIPEX and other indices have been analyzed and criticized in Maarten Peter Vink and Marc Heibling, "The Use and Misuse of Policy Indices in the Domain of Citizenship and Integration," Special Issue, *Comparative European Politics* 11, no. 5 (September 2013), pp. 551–554. The IMPALA index is best at demonstrating both variation among countries, as well as intensity of restriction ("stringency"), and the movement of both over the decade from 1999 to 2008.

44. Laura Block and Saskia Bonjour, "Fortress Europe or Europe of Rights? The Europeanization of Family Unification Policies in France, Germany and the Netherlands," *European Journal of Migration and Law* 15, no. 2 (2013), pp. 203–224. For Visa data, see Anna Boucher and Justin Gest, *Crossroads: Comparative Immigration Regimes in A World of Demographic Change* (New York: Cambridge University Press, 2018, Tables 4.1 and 4.3.

45. There is also a country limit on immigrants, which limits the percentage of all immigrants that any one country can send. See the very good fact sheet issued by the American Immigration Council, https://www.americanimmigrationcouncil.org/sites/default/files/research/how_the_united_states_immigration_system_works.

46. US Department of State, Bureau of Consular Affairs, "U.S. Visas," https://travel.state.gov/content/travel/en/us-visas.html.

47. See the reports of the UN World Tourism Organization, Annual Report of the UNWTO, https://www.e-unwto.org/doi/book/10.18111/9789284418725.
48. Statistics release by the US Department of Commerce, International Trade Administration, Office of Travel and Tourism Industries for 2010, *Summary of International Travel to the United States October 2010 and Year to Date*, http://travel.trade.gov/research/programs/i94/October_2010_I-94_Report.pdf.

    The estimates from 1975 are from a Department of Commerce report, *Summary and Analysis of International Travel to the United States, 1975*, https://ia600304.us.archive.org/10/items/summarxxxx00unit/summarxxxx00unit.pdf.
49. See Department of Transportation, Bureau of Transportation Statistics, *2015 North American Freight Numbers*, Washington, DC, 2015, http://www.bts.gov.
50. The Eurostat measure is somewhat different than that for the United States. The EU measure is by weight and distance, in ton-kilometers.
51. European Commission, Communication from the Commission to the European Parliament and the Council: "On the State of Play of Implementation of the Priority Actions under the European Agenda on Migration," COM (2016) 85 Final, p. 14.
52. The analysis of border closings is from Sergio Carrera, Elspeth Guild, Massimo Merlino, and Joanna Parkin, *A Race Against Solidarity: The Schengen Regime and the Franco-Italian Affair*, Center for European Policy Studies, Liberty and Security in Europe, April 2011, Appendix. A follow-up CEPS analysis argues that "Schengen is here to stay," that the "crisis" has been exaggerated, and that the closings are legal under Articles 23–25 of the Schengen Border Code of 2006. See Elspeth Guild, Evelien Brouwer, Kees Groenendijk, and Sergio Carrera, *What Is Happening to the Schengen Borders*, CEPS Paper in Liberty and Security, No. 86, December 2015, Brussels, Center for European Policy Studies.
53. See Commission of the European Union, *EU Transport in Figures, Statistical Pocketbook 2014* (Brussels: European Commission, 2014), pp. 35–39.
54. EU-28 Imports, Exports and Trade Balance, 2000–2015, Eurostat, 2016, http://ec.europa.eu/eurostat/statistics-explained/index.php/File:EU-28_Imports,_exports_and_trade_balance,_2000-2015_(Index_2000_%3D_100).png.
55. Melodie Pellot-Hernandez, "Cargo Pre-Inspection Aims to Facilitate Trade Between Mexico, U.S.," *University of North Carolina Journal of International Law* blog, November 8, 2015, http://blogs.law.unc.edu/ncilj/2015/11/08/cargo-preinspection-aims-to-facilitate-trade-between-mexico-us/.

Chapter 3

1. Usually attributed to the great Yankee catcher Yogi Berra, although this may just be urban legend.
2. See John R. Bowen, "Working Schemas and Normative Models in French Governance of Islam," in *Comparative European Politics* 10, no. 3 (July 2012), Special Issue: The Problems with National Models of Integration, A Franco-Dutch Comparison, ed. Christophe Bertossi, Jan Willem Duyvendak, and Martin A. Schain, pp. 354–369.
3. See Robert Wuthnow, "Religion," in *Understanding America: The Anatomy of an Exceptional Nation*, ed. Peter Schuck and James Q. Wilson (New York: Public Affairs Press, 2008), chapter 10.
4. The best elaboration of the concept of international regimes is in Robert O. Keohane, *After Hegemony: Cooperation and Discord in the World Political Economy* (Princeton, NJ: Princeton University Press, 1984). Keohane also applied the concept to the European Union in an essay with Stanley Hoffmann, "Institutional Change in Europe in the 1980s," in *The New European Community: Decision-Making and Institutional Change*, ed. Robert O. Keohane and Stanley Hoffmann (Boulder, CO: Westview Press, 1991), pp. 1–39.
5. Thomas Nail, *Theory of the Border* (New York: Oxford University Press, 2016), Part III.
6. These were the *Tampere, The Hague*, and the *Stockholm* programs, each of which produced some convergence in policy and practice. These successive programs increasingly focused on cooperation to reduce irregular immigration, to control asylum seekers, and to cooperate around the return of unwanted arrivals. See Andrew Geddes, "Europe's Border Relationships

and International Migration Relations," *Journal of Common Market Studies* 43, no. 4 (2005), pp. 797–799.

7. See Goeffrey Evans and Anand Menon, *Brexit and British Politics* (Cambridge: Polity, 2017), p. 121 and chapter 4.

8. Council Directive 2004/82/EC of April 29, 2004, on the obligation of carriers to communicate passenger data.

   See Christian Kaunert, Sarah Leonard, and Adrienne Hériter, *The Development of the EU Asylum Policy: Revisiting the Venueshopping Argument*, European University Institute (EUI), Migration Working Group, Florence, 2010, https://www.eui.eu/Documents/RSCAS/Research/MWG/201011/10-27-Kaunert.pdf.

9. Beine et al., "Comparing Immigration Policies."

10. Patrick Weil, *La France et ses Etrangers: l'Aventure d'une Politique de l'Immigration de 1938 à nos Jours* (Paris: Gallimard, 2004), pp. 79–100.

11. See Leah Haus, *Unions, Immigration and Internationalization: New Challenges and Changing Coalitions in the United States and France* (New York: Palgrave, 2002).

12. See Paul Foot, *Immigration and Race in British Politics* (Harmondsworth: Penguin, 1965), p. 80. For statistics on net migration, see B. R. Mitchell, *International Historical Statistics, Europe, 1750–1993*, 4th ed. (London: Macmillan Reference, 1998), Table A9.

13. For recent figures see UK Home Office, "Immigration Statistics, April to June 2013," https://www.gov.uk/government/publications/immigration-statistics-april-to-june-2013/immigration-statistics-april-to-june-2013, October 8, 2013. Also see Schain, *The Politics of Immigration*, pp. 127–128.

14. Schain, *The Politics of Immigration*, p. 128.

15. Christian Joppke, *Immigration and the Nation-State: The United States, Germany, and Great Britain* (Oxford: Oxford University Press, 1999), pp. 196–207.

16. This argument is notably supported by the classic work by Ian R. G. Spencer, *British Immigration Policy Since 1939: The Making of Multi-Racial Britain* (London: Routledge, 1997).

17. See Christian Joppke, *Immigration and the Nation-State: The United States, Germany, and Great Britain* (New York: Oxford University Press, 1999), p. 65.

18. Regarding the Nazi *Ausländerpolizeiverordnung* of 1938 see Joppke, *Immigration and the Nation-State*, p. 66.

19. Peter Katzenstein, *Policy and Politics in West Germany* (Philadelphia: Temple University Press, 1987), p. 216.

20. See Philip Martin, "Germany: Managing Migration in the Twenty-first Century," in *Controlling Immigration: A Global Perspective*, ed. James F. Hollifield, Philip L. Martin, and Pia M. Orrenus (Palo Alto, CA: Stanford University Press, 2014), pp. 227–230.

21. See Deniz Göktürk, David Gambling, and Anton Kaes, eds., *Germany in Transit: Nation and Migration: 1955–2005* (Berkeley: University of California Press, 2007), Introduction, p. 11.

22. A good example is the reaction to the Marcellin-Fontanet circulars in 1972, administrative decrees that ended the long period of regularization of illegal immigrants. The Minister of Labor, George Gorce, faced with this opposition, reversed Marcellin-Fontanet in 1973, and granted amnesty to over 50,000 illegal immigrants. See Jeffrey Togman, *The Ramparts of Nations* (Westport, CT: Praeger, 2002), pp. 106–107.

23. See David Jacobson, *Rights Across Borders: Immigration and the Decline of Citizenship* (Baltimore: Johns Hopkins University Press, 1997), p. 30; and James F. Hollifield, *Immigration, Markets and States: The Political Economy of Postwar Europe* (Cambridge, MA: Harvard University Press, 1992), p. 76.

24. See Douglas Webber, "The Politics of Differentiated Integration in the European Union: Origins, Decision Making and Outcomes," Working Paper Series 2012/1, Monash University European and EU Centre, Melbourne, Australia, pp. 14–15.

25. Zaiotti, *Cultures of Border Control*, pp. 67–69.

26. *The Community Code on Visas, the Common Visa Policy for EU Visas*, Regulation (EC) no. 810/2009 of the European Parliament and the Council, July 13, 2009, provides for a common list of countries for which visas are required; the EU Visa Code specifies procedures for the granting of Schengen visas; and the *Common Consular Instructions on Visas for the Diplomatic Missions and Consular Posts* (2002/C313/01) provides more detailed regulation for the

management of Schengen visas. However, these harmonized procedures are all implemented by the consular authorities of the member states.

27. Council Directive 2011/98/EU of the European Parliament and of the Council of December 13, 2011 on a single application procedure for a single permit for third-country.

28. Council Directive 2003/86/EC of September 22, 2003 on the right to family reunification.

29. Council Directive of 2003/109/EC of November 25, 2003 concerning the status of third-country nationals who are long-term residents.

30. Council Directive 2004/114/EC of December 13, 2004 on the conditions of admission of third-country nationals for the purposes of studies, pupil exchange.

31. See Marco Velicogna, "Large Scale E-Justice Interoperability: The Case of the Schengen Information System, the Technological Backbone of the European Arrest Warrant and Surrender Procedures," Report prepared for the Building Interoperability for European Civil Proceedings Online (Bologna: IRSIG-CNR, May 2012).

32. For a list of the EU directives under which the system operates, see European Commission, Migration and Home Affairs, *The Schengen Information System*, February 6, 2019, https://ec.europa.eu/home-affairs/what-we-do/policies/borders-and-visas/schengen-information-system_en.

33. Malcolm Anderson, Monica Den Boer, Peter Cullen, William Gilmore, Charles Raab, and Neil Walker, *Policing the European Union* (New York: Oxford University Press, 1996), p. 61.

34. Council of the European Union, Amended Proposal for a Regulation of the European Parliament and of the Council on the Establishment of an Evaluation and Monitoring Mechanism to Verify the Application of the Schengen Acquis 18196/1/11, REV 1, December 9, 2011.

35. Council of the European Union, Council Regulation 10597/13 and PE-CONS30/13, The Schengen Governance Package.

36. Commission of the European Communities, "Communication from the Commission: Free Movement of Workers—Achieving the Full Benefits and Potential," COM (2002) 694 final, November 12, 2002, http://eurlex.europa.eu/LexUriServ/LexUriServ.do?uri=COM:2002:0694:FIN:EN:PDF.

37. These rights are codified in two directives: the 1996 Posted Workers Directive (Directive 96/71/EC of the European Parliament and of the Council of December 16, 1996, concerning the posting of workers in the framework of the provision of services), the details of which have been widely challenged; and the 2004 Free Movement Directive (Directive 2004/58/EC of the European Parliament and of The Council of April 29, 2004), which has been challenged by the UK but is broadly supported by other member states.

38. Commission of the European Communities, "Communication from the Commission: Free Movement of Workers—Achieving the Full Benefits and Potential," p. 9.

39. See Schain, *The Politics of Immigration*, pp. 201–210.

40. See Schain, *The Politics of Immigration*, pp. 220–222.

41. Elspeth Guild, "The Europeanisation of Europe's Asylum Policy," *International Journal of Refugee Law* 18, no. 3–4 (September 1, 2006), pp. 630–651.

42. The Dublin Convention was first signed in Dublin in 1990, outside of the formal treaties of the EU. It came into force in 1998 for all members of the EU, as well as Norway and Iceland. It was revised between 2003 and 2008 as Dublin II, and then again in 2013 as Dublin III. It is now a regulation under European law.

43. Council Regulation (EC) No 343/2003 of February 18, 2003, Establishing the Criteria and Mechanisms for Determining the Member State Responsible for Examining an Asylum Application Lodged in One of the Member States by a Third-Country National, http://eurlex.europa.eu/legalcontent/EN/TXT/PDF/?uri=CELEX:32003R0343&from=EN.

44. Council Directive 2005/85/EC of December 1, 2005, Article 36 (3); *European Parliament v. Council of the European Union*, C-133/06, European Union: European Court of Justice, May 6, 2008; COM (2016) 467 Final, 2016/0224 (COD), Proposal for a Regulation of the European Parliament and of the Council, Establishing a Common Procedure for International Protection in the Union. Recognition of the right of member states to send asylum seekers back to a third state has been retained in the succession of Dublin regulations, through Dublin III,

45. Council Regulation (EC) No 343/2003 Establishing the Criteria and Mechanisms for Determining the Member State Responsible for Examining an Asylum Application Lodged in One of the Member States by a Third-Country National, Preamble (2), February 18, 2003.

46. Daniel J. Tichenor has an excellent account of these exceptions in *Dividing Lines: The Politics of Immigration Control in America* (Princeton, NJ: Princeton University Press, 2002), pp. 221–224.

47. See Ruth Ellen Wasem, "*Cuban Migration to the United States: Policy and Trends,*" *Congressional Research Service*, June 2, 2009, pp. 1–5, https://fas.org/sgp/crs/row/R40566.pdf. Wasem notes that the Carter administration created a category of Cuban-Haitians that would enable the relatively few Haitians who arrived to benefit from the same assistance as the Cubans.

48. Wasem, *Cuban Migration to the United States*, p. 110.

49. See *Consolidated Version of the Treaty on European Union*, http://eur-lex.europa.eu/legal-content/EN/TXT/PDF/?uri=OJ:C:2016:202:FULL&from=EN.

50. *The Nationality, Immigration and Asylum Act 2002*, No. 2818 (Juxtaposed Controls) Order 2003. Legislation.gov.UK: https://www.legislation.gov.uk/uksi/2003/2818/contents/made.

51. Information provided to author by the Asylum Policy team, Immigration and Border Policy Directorate, UK Home office, June 13, 2013.

52. Secrétariat Général du Comité interministériel de contrôle de l'immigration, Rapport au Parlement, *Les Orientations de la politique de l'immigration*, troisieme rapport, 2007, p. 4, www.ladocumentationfrancaise.fr > Rapports publics.

53. See Martin A. Schain, "The Border: Europe, the Immigration Dilemma and the State in France, Straus Institute Working Paper Series (New York: New York University School of Law, 2011).

54. See Martin A. Schain, "The State Strikes Back: Immigration Policy in the European Union," *The European Journal of International Law* 20, no. 1 (February 2009), pp. 93–111.

55. Doris Meissner, Donald M. Kerwin, Muzaffar Chishti, and Claire Bergeron, *Immigration Enforcement in the United States: The Rise of a Formidable Machinery* (Washington, DC: Migration Policy Institute, 2013).

56. Koslowski, "Global Mobility and the Quest for an International Migration Regime," pp. 127–129. I believe that he has substantially undercounted the total number of police in the United States who work on the border. He counts only the CBP; I include CBP, TSA, and ICE.

57. Peter H. Schuck has defined success and failure somewhat differently, in terms of cost-benefit analysis. Nevertheless, his evaluation of US immigration policy is largely qualitative: negative in terms of undocumented immigration, but positive in terms of legal immigration. See his *Why Government Fails So Often and How It Can Do Better* (Princeton, NJ: Princeton University Press, 2014), pp. 243, 352.

58. Sarkozy was not alone. In January 2017 François Fillon, ultimately the losing candidate of Sarkozy's political party for the presidency in 2017, proposed legislation that would have given substance to Sarkozy's priorities. See Cédric Mathiot, "Quotas, choix des immigrés, par zones d'origine: la bombe du projet Fillon sur l'immigration," *Libération*, January 11, 2017, p. 1.

59. I have elaborated on this in Martin A. Schain, "Managing Difference: Immigration Integration in France, Britain and the United States," *Social Research*, 77, no.1 (Spring 2010), pp. 205–237.

60. See Schain, *The Politics of Immigration*, Table 9.8.

61. See the summary of the SCIRP report in the *New York Times*, February 28, 1981, section B, p. 5.

62. See Schain, *The Politics of Immigration*, pp. 258–262.

63. See "Why Is Chain Migration So Controversial?" *The Economist*, January 17, 2018.

64. Tichenor, *Dividing Lines*, p. 251.

65. My thanks to Marc R. Rosenblum, senior policy analyst at the Migration Policy Institute, for pointing this out.

66. Clandestino Research Project, European Commission, "Size and Development of Irregular Migration to the EU," October 2009, http://irregular-migration.net/typo3_upload/groups/31/4.Background_Information/4.2.Policy_Briefs_EN/ComparativePolicyBrief_SizeOfIrregularMigration_Clandestino_Nov09_2.pdf.

67. The Clandestino estimates, together with detailed country studies, can be found on their site (see note 66). In general, the comparison among France, Britain, and the United States—if not the exact figures—is confirmed in a massive report by the French Senate in Rapport de commission d'enquête n° 300 (2005–2006), *sur l'immigration clandestine*, Tomes I et II, de MM. Georges Othily et François-Noël Buffet, fait au nom de la commission d'enquête, déposé le 6 avril 2006. The report also deals with the complex problem of estimating the population of "irregular immigrants." In particular, see the testimony of François Héran in Volume II, and cited on p. 47 of Volume I. He also cites the United States as one of the countries where the informal labor market is most important. The data cited by the report (Vol. I, p. 47) indicate that no country in Europe has a lower rate of irregular immigration than France. Finally, there is an important difference between estimates of undocumented immigrants in each country and the much lower "number of TCNs found to be illegally present," which are officially published by Eurostat Migration Statistics (migr-eipre). For current working estimates by France and Germany, see Margot Desmas, "Loi asile et immigration: Que dit la législation chez nos voisins européens?," *Le Monde*, February 23, 2018.
68. See reports of French government officials in Schain, *The Politics of Immigration*, p. 70, and Bastian Vollmer, "Briefing: Irregular Migration in the UK: Definitions, Pathways and Scale," The Migration Observatory, Oxford University, November 7, 2011.
69. Reported in the Frontex, *Annual Risk Analysis*, https://reliefweb.int/report/world/frontex-annual-risk-analysis-2018.
70. See Passel et al., "Population Decline of Unauthorized Immigrants Stalls, May Have Reversed."
71. See Robert Warren and Donald Kerwin, "Beyond DAPA and DACA: Revisiting Legislative Reform in Light of Long-Term Trends in Unauthorized Immigration to the United States," *Journal on Migration and Human Security* 3, no. 1 (2015), pp. 80–108.
72. See Samuel Granados, "Why Trump's Wall Contradicts Today's Immigration Trends," *Washington Post*, April 12, 2017.

Chapter 4

1. Donald Trump, "Make America Great Again," 2016 https://www.donaldjtrump.com/positions/immigration-reform.
2. James F. Hollifield, *Immigration, Markets, and States: The Political Economy of Postwar Europe* (Cambridge, MA: Harvard University Press, 1992), pp. 6–10.
3. For a related argument see Claudio M. Radaelli, "Diffusion Without Convergence: How Political Context Shapes the Adoption of Regulatory Impact Assessment," Journal of European Public Policy 12, no. 5 (2005), pp. 924–943; and Natasha Zaun, "Why EU Asylum Standards Exceed the Lowest Common Denominator: The Role of Regulatory Expertise in EU Decision-Making," *Journal of European Public Policy* 3, no. 1 (2016), pp. 136–154.
4. See Paul Scheffer, *Immigrant Nations* (Cambridge: Polity Press, 2011), chapter 1; and Christopher Caldwell, *Reflections on the Revolution in Europe* (New York: Doubleday, 2009), chapter 12.
5. See Andreas and Snyder, *The Wall Around the West*; and Aviva Chomsky, *Undocumented: How Immigration Became Illegal* (Boston: Beacon Press, 2014).
6. Schengen visas are issued by member-state consulates under the Common Visa Code and the Common Visa Policy. See Regulation Number 810/2009 of the European Parliament and the Council of July 13, 2009, establishing a Community Code on Visas.
7. These refusal rates declined after 2013, to 12% in 2014, and then rose slightly after, as indicated by Tables I and XX of the State Department Visa Office: US Department of State, *Annual Reports of the Visa Office*, http://travel.state.gov/content/visas/english/law-and-policy/statistics/annual-reports/report-of-the-visa-office-2017.html.
8. In addition, the US visa system gives first preference to other family members of citizens and legal residents, whose numbers are counted in this table.
9. See the data from the UNHCR: UNHCR Population Statistics, http://popstats.unhcr.org/en/overview. Also see Frontex, *Annual Risk Analysis* 2014, p. 6.
10. See Schain, "The Border."
11. See European Migration Network, "Visa Policy as Migration Channel in Spain," December 2011, http://ec.europa.eu/dgs/home-affairs/what-we-do/networks/european_migration_

network/reports/docs/emn-studies/migration-channel/es_20120613_visapolicy_en_version_final_en.pdf, p. 59.

12. Data from Eurostat, Tables, Graphs and Maps Interface (TGM), Third Country Nationals Refused Entry at the External Borders—Annual Data, 2013, European Commission, *Eurostat* Database for the European Union, http://appsso.eurostat.ec.europa.eu/nui/.http://epp.eurostat.ec.europa.ey/portal/page/portal/statistics/search_database.

13. See the presentation of the European Migration Network, "Visa Policy as Migration Channel." The synthesis report of the study, along with the national reports from twenty-one member states, can be found on https://ec.europa.eu/home-affairs/sites/homeaffairs/files/what-we-do/networks/european_migration_network/reports/docs/emn-studies/migration-channel/00b._synthesis_report_visa_policy_as_migration_channel_final_april2013_en.pdf.

14. See Bernd Parusel and Jan Schneider, *Visa Policy as Migration Channel: The Impact of Visa Policy on Migration Control* (Berlin: German Federal Office for Migration and Refugees, 2012), pp. 5–6.

15. European Migration Network, "Visa Policy as Migration Channel," pp. 15–17.

16. Among the nine reasons for refusal of entry listed in the Schengen Borders Code, possession of a valid visa and residence permit are the most important. For data on reasons for refusal of entry, see European Commission, *Eurostat* Database for the European Union, http://appsso.eurostat.ec.europa.eu/nui/.http://epp.eurostat.ec.europa.ey/portal/page/portal/statistics/search_database.

17. See John Simanski and Lesley M. Sapp, "Immigration Enforcement Actions: 2012," *Annual Report 2012*, Department of Homeland Security, Washington, DC, September, 2013, p. 4, Table 3, https://www.dhs.gov/sites/default/files/publications/ois_enforcement_ar_2012_1.pdf.

18. See European Migration Network, "Visa Policy as Migration Channel," p. 15; and European Migration Network, "Visa Policy as Migration Channel in Italy" (Rome: Centro Studi e Ricerche IDOS, 2012), p. 40 https://www.researchgate.net/publication/264378868_Visa_policy_as_migration_channel_in_Italy.

19. For a recent study of policymaking in the EU, see Harry Ganzeboom and Johanne Søndergaard, "MIPi: A Better Index for Comparing Family Reunification Policies Across Europe," unpublished paper, p. 9.

20. European Migration Network, "Visa Policy as Migration Channel," p. 16.

21. See US Department of Homeland Security, US Customs and Border Protection, Entering the US—Documents Required for Foreign Nationals (International Travelers), https://help.cbp.gov/app/answers/detail/a_id/572/~/entering-the-u.s.---documents-required-for-foreign-nationals-(international.

22. Data on rates of refusal by country, obtained from the French Ministry of the Interior, Jean De Croon, Chef de Service, Adjoint au Directeur de l'Immigration. Other data are from Secretairiat Général du Comité de Contrôle de l'Immigration, Les Chiffres de la Politique de l'Immigration et de l'Intégration, 2011 (Paris: La Documentation Française, Décembre, 2012) pp. 19–28.

23. *Les Chiffres de la Politique de l'Immigration et de l'Intégration, Année 2011* (Paris: la Documentation Française, 2012), pp. 20–27.

24. See UK, Home Office, Immigration Statistics, Entry Clearance of Visa Applications and Resolution, by Country and Nationality, https://www.gov.uk/government/publications/immigration-statistics.

25. According to the interpretation by the UNHCR: "An asylum seeker is an individual who has sought international protection and whose claim for refugee status has not yet been determined. It is important to note, however, that a person is a refugee if he/she fulfils the criteria set out in the 1951 Convention Relating to the Status of Refugees. The formal recognition of someone through individual refugee status determination (RSD) does not establish refugee status, but rather confirms it." See UNHCR, *UNHCR Statistical Yearbook 2008*, p. 42,.https://www.unhcr.org/statistics/country/4bcc5bb79/unhcr-statistical-yearbook-2008.html.

26. See Gideon Rachman, "Refugees or Migrants? What's in a Word?" *The Financial Times*, September 3, 2015, http://blogs.ft.com/the-world/2015/09/refugees-or-migrants-whats-in-a-word/.

27. Polly Toynbee, "The UK's Stance on the Refugee Crisis Shames Us All," *The Guardian*, September 3, 2015, https://www.theguardian.com/commentisfree/2015/sep/03/david-cameron-shaming-britain-refugees-europe.

28. Saskia Sassen, *Losing Control? Sovereignty in an Age of Globalization* (New York: Columbia University Press, 1996), pp. 88–99.

29. Randall Hansen and Demetrios G. Papademetriou, "Securing Borders: The Intended, Unintended, and Perverse Consequences," in *Managing Borders in an Increasingly Borderless World*, ed. Randall Hansen and Demetrios G. Papademetriou (Washington, DC: Migration Policy Institute, 2013), p. 9.

30. Interviews with United Kingdom Border Agency and Managerial Staff at Tinsley House Immigration Removal Center, Gatwick Airport, UK, August 13, 2013. Interviews with the Direction de la Police aux Frontières, October 16, 2013.

31. Information provided by the Asylum Policy Team, Immigration and Border Directorate, Home Office, June 13, 2013.

32. Groupe d'Information et de Soutien des Immigré(e)s (GISTI), "*Régularisation: la circulaire 'Valls' du 28 novembre 2012 Analyse et mode d'emploi*," November 2012, http://www.gisti.org/IMG/pdf/np_circ_valls_nov2012.pdf.

33. Council Directive 2001/51/EC of June 28, 2001, supplementing the provisions of Article 26 of the Convention implementing the Schengen Agreement of June 14, 1985.

34. Advisory Commission on Migration Affairs, *External Processing: Conditions Applying to the Processing of Asylum Applications Outside the European Union* (The Hague: December, 2010), pp. 15–21. This is a report commissioned by the Netherlands State Secretary for Justice: https://acvz.org/wp-content/uploads/2015/09/Advies-ACVZ-NR32-ENG-2010.pdf. For the UK proposal, see Letter of March 10, 2003, Office of the Prime Minister, "New International Approaches to Asylum Processing and Protection," http://www.statewatch.org/news/2003/arr/blair-simitis-asile.pdf. Similar proposals, mostly by European ministries of the interior, have been circulating since 2015, but have been resisted by the European Commission. See Jacopo Barigazzi, "Malta Calls for New Ways to Send Back More Migrants," *Politico*, European edition, January 27, 2017, p. 1. https://www.politico.eu/article/malta-calls-for-new-ways-to-send-back-more-migrants-europeaan-commission-north-africa/.

35. See "Turkey's New Visa Law for Syrians Enters into Force," *Hurriyet Daily News*, January 10, 2016, http://www.hurriyetdailynews.com/turkeys-new-visa-law-for-syrians-enters-into-force.aspx?pageID=238&nID=93642&NewsCatID=352.

36. See Adam Nossiter, "Blocking Migrants Far Away," *New York Times International Edition*, February 27, 2018.

37. See Sarah Léonard, "EU Border Security and Migration into the European Union: FRONTEX and Securitisation Through Practices," *European Security* 19, no. 2 (2010), pp. 240–241.

38. Randall Hansen, "Population Displacement and the Global Refugee System 200 Years after the Congress of Vienna," report prepared for presentation at the Congress of Vienna 2015: In Search of Principles for a Stable World Order, Vienna, October 22–25, 2015, p. 1.

39. Philippe Ricard, "Migrants: vent de panique européen," *Le Monde*, November 7, 2015. For an excellent summary of this wave of migration, see Medecins Sans Frontieres, *Obstacle Course to Europe: A Policy-made Humanitarian Crisis at EU Borders*, December 2015, https://www.msf.org/sites/msf.org/files/msf_obstacle_course_to_europe_0.pdf.

40. John Le Carré, *The Perfect Spy* (London: Coronet Books, Hodder and Stoughton, 1986), p. 446.

41. Council Regulation (EC) No. 343/2003, Establishing the Criteria and Mechanisms for Determining the Member State Responsible for Examining an Asylum Application Lodged in One of the Member States by a Third-Country National, http://eurlex.europa.eu/legalcontent/EN/TXT/PDF/?uri=CELEX:32003R0343&from=EN, February 18, 2003.

42. See Lizzie Deardon, "Hungary Planning 'Massive' New Border Fence to Keep Out Refugees as PM Vows to 'Hold Them Back by Force,'" *The Independent*, August 27, 2016, http://www.independent.co.uk/news/world/europe/hungary-massive-new-border-fence-to-keep-out-refugees-prime-minister-orban-turkey-eu-hold-them-back-a7212696.html.

43. See *Asylum Statistics*, Briefing Paper Number SN01403, September 23, 2015, https://researchbriefings.parliament.uk/ResearchBriefing/Summary/SN06077, pp. 15–16.

44. The origins of the spike of refugees in 2002 vary, but for the UK, the largest number arrived from Iraq and Somalia. France also had a spike of applications at about the same time, but the number of applications after 2011 was far higher.

45. The 2002–2006 figures are from Timothy J. Hatton, *Seeking Asylum: Trends and Policies in the OECD* (London: CEPR Policy Portal), Table 6.1, p. 50, https://voxeu.org/article/seeking-asylum-trends-and-policies-oecd. More recent figures are reported in *Eurostat Regional Yearbook[s]*, 2009 (p. 173) and 2012 (p. 161), https://ec.europa.eu/eurostat/web/products-statistical-books/-/KS-HA-18-001.

46. A STC is considered safe for providing international protection; a SCO is safe to live in for its own citizens as well.

47. ECtHR—M.S.S. v Belgium and Greece [GC], Application No. 30696/09, Asylum Law Database, http://www.asylumlawdatabase.eu/en/content/ecthr-mss-v-belgium-and-greece-gc-application-no-3069609.

48. See European Commission Press Release Database, http://europa.eu/rapid/press-release_IP-03-37_en.htm.

49. See Chris Jones, "Analysis: 11 Years of Eurodac," *Statewatch*, January 2014, http://www.statewatch.org/analyses/no-235-eurodac.pdf.

50. Susan Fratzke, *Not Adding Up: The Fading Promise of Europe's Dublin System* (Brussels: MPI Europe, 2015), https://www.migrationpolicy.org/research/not-adding-fading-promise-europes-dublin-system, pp. 12–13.

51. See Gundrun Hentges, "Asylum Policy Influenced by Europeanization," in *Europe's New Racism: Causes, Manifestations and Solutions*, ed. Evans Foundation (New York: Berghahn Books, 2005), pp. 105–131; also Andreas, *Border Games*, pp. 117–126.

52. These problems have sometimes been noted by geographers and demographers. See Bernd Kasparele, "Implementation of Schengen: The Dublin System and the European Border," in *Immigration Policy and Practice: Interventions and Solutions*, ed. Harald Bauder, Christian Matheis, and Nora Crook (New York: Palgrave, 2016), pp. 1–19.

53. Directive 2013/32/EU of the European Parliament and of the Council of June 26, 2013 on Common Procedures for Granting and Withdrawing International Protection. The directive was originally passed in 2005.

54. This is the Protocol on Asylum for Nationals of the Member States incorporated into the Amsterdam Treaty in 1999. This was done at the initiative of the Spanish government after Spanish Basques had applied for asylum in Belgium. Of course, this protocol may sharply conflict with the Geneva Convention obligations as East European countries move to the right. See Elspeth Guild, "The Legal Framework: Who Is Entitled to Move?," in *Controlling Frontiers*, ed. Didier Bigo and Elspeth Guild (Burlington, VT: Ashgate, 2005), pp. 33–34.

55. There is no agreement on how a "safe" country is defined. For example, there is an important difference between a SCO, which is safe for its own citizens, and a STC, which provides adequate protection for those seeking asylum from some other country. The designation of STC is generally considered the stronger of the two for asylum seekers. See Sandra Lavenex, *Safe Third Countries: Extending the EU Asylum and Immigration Policies to Central and Eastern Europe* (Budapest: Central University Press, 1999), pp. 51–52.

56. See the European Migration Network, "Ad-Hoc Query on Safe Countries of Origin and Safe Third Countries," for both the questions and the responses, http://www.emn.fi/files/1172/Compilation_BG_EMN_NCP_AHQ_list_of_safe_countries_of_origin_and_safe_third_countries_WIDER.pdf. This was the most complete of a series of the queries, the most recent in 2015.

57. See Oliver Hawkins, Asylum Statistics, Briefing Paper, number SN01403, September 23, 2015, Table 7, p. 19, https://researchbriefings.parliament.uk/ResearchBriefing/Summary/SN01403 The data are from Eurostat.

58. Emma Anderson, "Over 500,000 Rejected Asylum Seekers Still Live in Germany," *The Local de*, German news in English, https://www.thelocal.de/20160922/550000-rejected-asylum-seekers-living-in-germany.

59. See Camila Ruz, "What Happens to Failed Asylum Seekers?," *BBC News Magazine*, August 13, 2015, http://www.bbc.com/news/magazine-33849593.

60. Although I have compared effective returns with orders to leave, in fact these are not the percentage of those given orders each year, since actual returns may take more than one year to be effectuated.

61. Council Decision 2015/1601 of September 22, 2015, "Establishing Provisional Measures in the Area of International Protection for the Benefit of Italy and Greece."

62. See European Commission, Migration and Home Affairs, *European Agenda on Migration—Factsheets*, https://ec.europa.eu/home-affairs/sites/homeaffairs/files/what-we-do/policies/european-agenda-migration/press-material/docs/state_of_play_-_relocation_en.pdf.

63. Elspeth Guild and Sergio Carrera, *Rethinking Asylum Distribution in the EU: Shall We Start with the Facts?*, Centre for European Policy Studies, June 17, 2016, https://www.ceps.eu/system/files/Rethinking%20asylum%20distribution%20in%20the%20EU_0.pdf.

64. Agreement Between the European Union and the Republic of Turkey on the Readmission of Persons Residing Without Authorisation, https://eur-lex.europa.eu/legal-content/EN/ALL/?uri=celex%3A22014A0507%2801%29

65. See The European Commission—Fact Sheet, *Implementing the EU-Turkey Statement—Questions and Answers*, http://europa.eu/rapid/press-release_MEMO-16-3204_en.htm. Also the European Union reports in "UE: le nombre de migrants arrivés par la mer en Grèce a chuté de deux tiers en 2016," *Le Monde*, January 6, 2017.

66. The initial reports of the agreement focused on the aid package. However, in a restricted report issued by the European Commission (and High Representative) it is clear that the primary objective was to force the Afghan government to accept the return of even unwilling Afghan citizens who had been refused asylum in Europe. See Council of the European Union, Joint Commission-EEAS, "Non-Paper on Enhancing Cooperation on Migration, Mobility and Readmission with Afghanistan" (restricted) http://statewatch.org/news/2016/mar/eu-council-afghanistan-6738-16.pdf; and "Europe Makes Deal to Send Afghans Home, Where War Awaits Them," by Rod Nordland and Mujib Mashal, *New York Times*, October 5, 2016, https://www.nytimes.com/2016/10/06/world/asia/afghanistan-eu-refugees-migrants.html?_r=0.

67. The House Judiciary Committee passed the Refugee Program Integrity Restoration Act (H. R. 4831) on March 16, 2016. The bill was not approved by Congress.

68. UNHCR, *Global Trends: Forced Displacement in 2015* (Geneva: UNHCR, 2016), https://www.unhcr.org/statistics/unhcrstats/576408cd7/unhcr-global-trends-2015.html.

69. Ceilings are published by the US Department of State, Bureau of Population, Refugees and Migration; the annual summary of refugee admissions (for settlement) is extracted by the Worldwide Refugee Admissions Processing System (WRAPS), *Admissions and Arrivals, 1975–Present*, http://www.wrapsnet.org/admissions-and-arrivals/.

70. See W. Courtland Robinson, *Terms of Refuge: The Indochinese Exodus, and the International Response* (New York: Zed Books, 1998).

71. Karl Miller, *From Humanitarian to Economic: The Changing Face of Vietnamese Migration* (Washington, DC: Migration Policy Institute, April, 2015).

72. See Joseph Russell and Jeanne Batalova, *Refugees and Asylees in the United States* (Washington, DC: Migration Policy Institute, September 27, 2012), p. 6.

73. Sylvia Rusin, Jie Zong, and Jeanne Batalova, *Cuban Immigrants in the United States* (Washington, DC: Migration Policy Institute, April 7, 2015).

74. See Julie Hirschfeld Davis and Frances Robles, "Obama Ends Exemption for Cubans Who Arrive Without Visas," *New York Times*, January 12, 2017.

75. UNHCR publishes a *Global Resettlement Statistical Report* each year. These figures are from the 2015 report, United Nations High Commissioner for Refugees (UNHCR), *Global Resettlement Statistical Report 2015*, p. 26, http://www.unhcr.org/en-us/statistics/unhcrstats/576408cd7/unhcr-global-trends-2015.html, 2015.

76. These figures are from the US Department of Health and Human Services, *HHS Budget in Brief: Strengthening Health and Opportunity for all Americans*, FY 2015, https://www.hhs.gov/about/budget/fy2015/budget-in-brief/index.html, pp. 5, 6, 108, 110.

77. See Ana Gonzales-Barrera and Jens Manuel Krogstad, "With Help from Mexico, Number of Child Migrants Crossing U.S. Border Falls," Pew Research Center, April 28, 2015 http://www.pewresearch.org/fact-tank/2015/04/28/child-migrants-border/.

78. Migration Policy Institute, "What Is the Right Policy Toward Unaccompanied Children at U.S. Borders?," https://www.migrationpolicy.org/news/what-right-policy-toward-unaccompanied-children-us-borders.

79. "Obama Challenges Perry to Rally Around Border Plan," *Boston Globe*, July 10, 2014.

80. Carle Hulse, "Immigrant Surge Rooted in Law to Curb Child Trafficking," *New York Times*, July 7, 2014.

81. Jaya Ramji-Nogales, Andrew I. Schoenholtz, and Philip G. Schrag, "Refugee Roulette: Disparities in Asylum Adjudication," *Stanford Law Review* 60 (November 2007), pp. 295–410.

82. For Europe, see Oliver Hawkins, "Asylum Statistics," UK House of Commons Library, briefing paper no. SN01403, Table 7, September 23, 2018, https://research-briefings. files.parliament.uk/documents/SN01403/SN01403.pdf. For the United States, see UNHCR, *Asylum Trends 2014*, Table 6, https://www.unhcr.org/en-us/statistics/unhcrstats/551128679/asylum-levels-trends-industrialized-countries-2014.html. The rejection percentages can be seen as minimal, since they are based on decisions actually taken. Not all applications for asylum reach this stage.

83. See UNHCR, *Resettlement at a Glance for 2017*, http://www.unhcr.org/5a9d507f7.

Chapter 5

1. Meissner et al., *Immigration Enforcement in the United States*.

2. See Joseph Nevins, *Operation Gatekeeper and Beyond: The War on "Illegals" and the Remaking of the U.S.–Mexico Boundary* (New York: Routledge, 2002), pp. 36–39.

3. Meissner et al., *Immigration Enforcement in the United States*.

4. See Andreas, *Border Games*, pp. 119–120.

5. "Europe Starts Putting Up Walls," *The Economist*, September 19, 2015.

6. Andreas, *Border Games*, pp. 126–128.

7. *The Work of the UK Border Agency (July–September 2012)—Home Affairs Committee*, http://www.publications.parliament.uk/pa/cm201213/cmselect/cmhaff/792/79207.htm. Also see *Fast and Fair?—Report on UK Border Agency by the Parliamentary Ombudsman*, published February 9, 2010, https://assets.publishing.service.gov.uk/government/uploads/system/uploads/attachment_data/file/247919/0329.pdf. Also see National Audit Office, Home Office, Report by the Comptroller and Auditor General, HC467, *The UK Border Agency and Border Force: Progress in Cutting Costs and Improving Performance*, July 17, 2012, https://www.nao.org.uk/wp-content/uploads/2012/07/1213467.pdf. The UKBA had been quasi-independent from the Home Office (an "executive agency") from 2008 until 2013, when its various functions were then brought back into the Home Office.

8. See "Joint Statement by Mr. Damian Green, Minister of State for Immigration, the United Kingdom's Home Department and Mr. Alan Shatter, Minister for Justice and Equality, Ireland's Department of Justice and Equality Regarding Co-Operation on Measures to Secure the External Common Travel Area Border," https://www.gov.uk/government/uploads/system/uploads/attachment_data/file/99045/21197-mea-sec-trav.pdf.

9. *The Impact and Consequences of Brexit for Northern Ireland* (The European Parliament, Commission on Constitutional Affairs, Policy Department C: Citizens' Rights and Constitutional Affairs, 2017), http://www.europarl.europa.eu/RegData/etudes/BRIE/2017/583116/IPOL_BRI(2017)583116_EN.pdf.

10. European Commission Task Force for the Preparation and Conduct of the Negotiations with the United Kingdom under Article 50 TEU, "Guiding Principles Transmitted to EU27 for the Dialogue on Ireland/Northern Ireland," September 6, 2017, https://ec.europa.eu/commission/sites/beta-political/files/guiding-principles-dialogue-ei-ni_en.pdf.

11. The effort to increase internal policing began to show significant results within a few years. By 2006, as many unauthorized immigrants were removed from within the country as at ports of entry. Information provided by the Asylum Policy team, Immigration and Border

Policy Directorate, Home Office, summarized in the internal document: *The UK's Approach to Humanitarian Migration*, March 2013.

12. *The UK's Approach to Humanitarian Migration*, March 2013.

13. National Audit Office, "Reforming the UK Border and Immigration System, Report by the Comptroller and Auditor-General," https://www.nao.org.uk/wp-content/uploads/2014/07/Reforming-the-UK-border-and-immigration-system.pdf, July 22, 2014, p. 44.

14. The DCPAF is responsible for border crossings at the largest ports of entry in France. Customs agents control the smaller entry points.

15. For an excellent analysis of the coordinating role of the PAF, see Claude-Valentin Marie, "Measures Taken to Combat the Employment of Undocumented Workers in France," in Organization for Economic Cooperation and Development (OECD), *Combating the Illegal Employment of Foreign Workers* (Paris: OECD, 2000), pp. 115–119.

16. The data from France are from the archives of the Ministry of the Interior, Police Nationale, *Rapport d'activité de la DCPAF*. The organization missions are from the report of 2003, p. 9.

17. These figures can be found in the annual Rapport d'activité of OPFRA, as well as in the report of the UNHCR, Asylum Levels and Trends in Industrialized Countries, 2009, Division of Programme Support and Management, March 23, 2010. I have organized the results in a table in "The Border," Table 2.

18. See the investigative report in Le Monde information, "Depuis 2012, les effectifs des forces de l'ordre ont diminué," *Le Monde*, November 18, 2015.

19. Information provided by the Immigration and Border Policy Directorate, UK Home Office, May 21, 2013.

20. Liza Schuster, "Sangatte: A False Crisis," *Global Dialogue* 4, no. 4 (Autumn 2002), pp. 57–68. Also see: Independent Chief Inspector of Borders and Immigration, *An Inspection of Juxtaposed Controls November 2012–March 2013*, John Vine CBE QPM, Independent Chief Inspector of Borders and Immigration, http://icinspector.independent.gov.uk/wp-content/uploads/2013/08/An-Inspection-of-Juxtaposed-Controls-Final.pdf.

21. Stephanie Kirchgaessner, "Italian Police Forcibly Remove Migrants Stranded Near French Border"; and Ian Traynor, "Italy Threatens to Give Schengen Visas to Migrants as EU Ministers Meet," *The Guardian*, June 16, 2015.

22. France, *Les Chiffres de la Politique de l'Immigration et de l'Intégration, Année 2011* (Paris: la Documentation Française, 2012), p. 110.

23. See the Asylum Information Database (AIDA), Regular Procedure France, https://www.asylumineurope.org/reports/country/france. Also see Alex Spire, *Accueillir ou Reconduire: Enquête sur les Guichets de l'Immigration* (Paris: Raisons d'Agir, 2009), chapters 2 and 3. Spire's argument was largely confirmed by Jean de Croon, Director Ajoint de l'Immigration of the ministry of the interior (September 5, 2013). De Croon noted the importance of protests in Lille between 2002–2008 of groups of undocumented immigrants for the creation of discussions and meetings with collectives to set priorities for regularization and expulsion. Although the process began in Lille (and is therefore referred to as "the Lille process") it is now widespread, de Croon argued, "anywhere where it is necessary." Some of the results of these negotiations were formalized as an administrative circulaire in November 2012: "Circulaire pour clarifier les critères de régularisations des étrangers sans papiers," November 22, 2012 (NORINTK1229185C). See Bertrand Guay, "Une circulaire pour clarifier les critères de régularisation des étrangers sans papiers," *Le Monde*, November 28, 2012.

24. Nor are asylum seekers permitted to apply in Belgium where there are also juxtaposed controls. In the case of France, this is stated in Article 4 of the Additional Protocol CM 5015 to the Protocol between the United Kingdom of Great Britain and Northern Ireland and the French Republic concerning Frontier Controls and Policing, Co-operation in Criminal Justice, Public Safety and Mutual Assistance relating to the Channel Fixed Link, Cm 2366, signed at Sangatte on November 25, 1991. It is not explicit in the Belgian agreement. See Asylum Information Database (AIDA), *Border Procedure (Border and Transit Zones) United Kingdom*, http://www.asylumineurope.org/reports/country/united-kingdom/asylum-procedure/procedures/border-procedure-border-and-transit-zones. The Sangatte Agreement to close the Sangatte refugee camp in 2003 reaffirmed the exclusion of asylum claims (Article 9). Nevertheless, as part of this agreement, 70% of those remaining in the

camp were accepted for asylum by the UK; See "Sangatte Refugee Camp to be Closed the Month," *The Irish Times*, December 3, 2002, https://www.irishtimes.com/news/sangatte-refugee-camp-to-be-closed-this-month-1.1104934.

25. See the joint declaration: UK, *Managing Migratory Flows in Calais: Joint Ministerial Declaration on UK/French Cooperation*, https://www.gov.uk/government/uploads/system/uploads/attachment_data/file/455162/Joint_declaration_20_August_2015.pdf.

26. See Alan Taylor, "France Dismantles 'The Jungle' in Calais," *The Atlantic*, October 26, 2016.

27. "What Does the Closure of the Calais Camp Mean for the Refugees?" *The Guardian*, October 24, 2016, https://www.theguardian.com/commentisfree/2016/oct/24/panel-calais-camp-france-demolition-refugees-migration.

28. Independent Chief Inspector of Borders and Immigration, *An Inspection of Juxtaposed Controls November 2012–March 2013*, John Vine CBE QPM, Independent Chief Inspector of Borders and Immigration, http://icinspector.independent.gov.uk/wp-content/uploads/2013/08/An-Inspection-of-Juxtaposed-Controls-Final.pdf, 2013.

29. European Commission, Migration and Home Affairs, "Border Crossing," http://ec.europa.eu/dgs/home-affairs/what-we-do/policies/borders-and-visas/border-crossing/, 2019.

30. See Eiko Thielemann and Nadine El-Enamy, "Beyond Fortress Europe? How European Cooperation Strengthens Refugee Protection." Presented at the 11th Conference of the European Union Studies Association, Los Angeles, California, April 22–25, 2009; Natascha Zaun, "Why EU Asylum Standards Exceed the Lowest Common Denominator," *Journal of European Public Policy* 3, no. 1 (2016), pp. 136–154; and Acosta and Geddes, "The Development, Application and Implementation of an EU Rule of Law in the Area of Immigration Policy," pp. 179–193.

31. This was reported by the International Organization for Migration, "IOM Applauds Italy's Life-Saving Mare Nostrum Operation: 'Not a Migrant Pull Factor,'" International Organization for Migration, 2017, http://missingmigrants.iom.int/iom-applauds-italy%E2%80%99s-life-saving-mare-nostrum-operation-%E2%80%9Cnot-migrant-pull-factor%E2%80%9D; it was also reported by Reuters: Steve Scherer and Ilaria Polleschi, "Italy in Talks with EU to Share Responsibility for Boat Migrants," http://www.reuters.com/article/us-eu-italy-migrants-idUSKBN0FD1YL20140708, July 8, 2014.

32. See European Commission, "Communication from the Commission to the European Parliament and the Council: On the State of Play of Implementation of the Priority Actions under the European Agenda on Migration," COM (2016) 85 Final, p. 4.

33. Council of the European Union, "EUNANFOR MED Operation Sophia Authorised to Start Two Additional Supporting Tasks," Press Release 491/16, August 30, 2016, https://www.consilium.europa.eu/en/press/press-releases/2016/08/30/eunavfor-med-sophia-op-add-supporting-tasks/. For an excellent article that deals with these various joint operations, see Peter Dombrowski and Simon Reich, "The EU's Emerging Grand Strategy of Retrenchment: Europe Is Coming Home, American 'Exceptionalism' Isn't," *International Affairs* 93, no. 5, (September 1, 2017), pp. 18–36.

34. European Commission, "Proposal for a Regulation of the European Parliament and of the Council Establishing an Entry/Exit System (EES) to Register Entry and Exit Data of Third Country Nationals Crossing the External Borders of the Member States of the European Union," COM (2013) 95 final, February 28, 2013, p. 2.

35. All three were included for purposes of comparison with major European countries. CBP is responsible for border checkpoints, TSA for airport controls, and ICE for internal investigation and policing. In 2016, CBP employed 62,450; TSA 55,600; and ICE 19,330. However, the budget of CBP was about the same as TSA and ICE combined. See USDHS, *FY 2016 Budget in Brief*, https://www.google.com/search?q=dhs+fy+2016+budget+in+brief&rlz=1C1GGRV_frFR786FR786&oq=FY+2016+Budget+in+Brief.&aqs=chrome.2.69i57j0l2.1351j0j8&sourceid=chrome&ie=UTF-8.

36. USDHS, *US Border Patrol Statistics*, http://www.cbp.gov/xp/cgov/border_security/border_patrol/usbp_statistics/. Also see USDHS, ICE, *Detention Facility Locator*, http://www.ice.gov/detention-facilities.

37. The FY budget for CPB was 12.8 billion dollars, compared with 7.3 billion for TSA. ICE, primarily responsible for internal enforcement and removals, had a budget of 5.4 billion dollars. See USDHS, *Budget in Brief, Fiscal Year 2016*, p. 10.

38. ICE report, "Wake County Sheriff's Office First of 4 Sites in North Carolina to Receive Full Interoperability Technology to Help Identify Criminal Aliens," November 12, 2008, https://www.ice.gov/news/releases/wake-county-sheriffs-office- first-4- sites-north-carolina-receive-full-interoperability.

39. See USDHS/ICE, Delegation of Immigration Authority Section 287(g) Immigration and Nationality Act, https://www.ice.gov/287g. For additional background, see Randy Capps, Marc Rosenblum, Cristina Rodriguez, and Muzaffar Chisti, *Delegation and Divergence: A Study of 287(g) State and Local Immigration Enforcement* (Washington, DC: Migration Policy Institute, 2011).

40. Melissa Keaney and Joan Friedland, "Overview of the Key ICE ACCESS Programs," National Immigration Law Center, November 2009, https://www.nilc.org/issues/immigration-enforcement/ice-access-2009-11-05/, p. 4.

41. See USDHS/ICE, *Secure Communities* www.ice.gov/secure-communities.

42. Kirk Semple and Julia Preston, "Deal to Share Fingerprints Is Dropped, Not Program," *New York Times*, August 6, 2011.

43. See USDHS, "Entry/Exit Overstay Report," Fiscal Year 2015, www.dhs.gov/publication/entryexit-overstay-report, pp. 8–22.

44. USDHS, *Budget in Brief 2016*, https://www.dhs.gov/sites/default/files/publications/FY_2016_DHS_Budget_in_Brief.pdf, p. 47.

45. Directive 2009/52/EC of the European Parliament and of the Council of 18 June 2009 providing for minimum standards on sanctions and measures against employers of illegally staying third-country nationals.

46. Denmark, Ireland, and the UK were not party to the directive.

47. See Communication from the Commission to the European Parliament and Council on the Application of Directive 2009/52/EC of June 18, 2009, COM (2014) final, May 22, 2014, Table 3, "Inspections Carried Out in 2012."

48. For the Valls statement, see GISTI, *Regularisation*. A similar pledge was made by President Macron in 2018: Bertrand Bissuel, "Seize mesures pour combattre le travail illegal," *Le Monde*, February 13, 2018.

49. UK, *An Inspection of How the Home Office Tackles Illegal Working*, http://icinspector.independent.gov.uk/wp-content/uploads/2015/12/ICIBI-Report-on-illegal-working-17.12.2015.pdf.

50. Unauthorized workers are migrants without work permits, although they may be in the United States legally (Immigration and Naturalization Act of 1952, chapter 477). The unenforceable part of the law was related to the so-called Texas Proviso, that legalized the harboring of unauthorized workers. See Peter Brownell, *The Declining Enforcement of Employer Sanctions* (Washington, DC: Migration Policy Institute, September 1, 2005).

51. See Daniel Tichenor, *Dividing Lines: The Politics of Immigration Control in America* (Princeton, NJ: Princeton University Press, 2002), pp. 362–363.

52. The law also provided for the largest amnesty in American history (far larger, in fact, than had been granted by any European country), that would make it easier for aliens to become permanent residents, would establish a new farmworker program, and would give greater legal protections to aliens working in the United States. Eventually, about 3 million undocumented aliens would benefit from the amnesty. See Schain, *The Politics of Immigration*, pp. 212–213.

53. See Tichenor, *Dividing Lines*, pp. 264–265.

54. See statement by the INS Associate Commissioner for Policy and Planning in US Congress, Committee on the Judiciary, Subcommittee on Immigration, *Immigration and Naturalization Service's Interior Enforcement Strategy*, 106th Congress, Session 1, July 1, 1999 (Washington, DC: GPO, 2000), p. 13, cited in Andorra Bruno, *Immigration-Related Worksite Enforcement: Performance Measures*, Congressional Research Service, 7-5700, August 7, 2013, www.crs.gov R40002.

55. Wayne Cornelius, *Evaluating Enhanced US Border Enforcement* (Washington, DC: Migration Policy Institute, 2004), p. 1.

56. Spencer Hsu and Kari Lydersen, "Illegal Hiring Is Rarely Penalized," *Washington Post*, June 19, 2006.

57. Statement by ICE Deputy Director Kumar Kibble for US Congress Judiciary Committee, Subcommittee on Immigration Policy and Enforcement, January 26, 2011:,:// judiciary.house.gov/hearings/pdf/Kibble01262011.pdf, cited in Bruno, "Immigration-Related Worksite Enforcement," 2013.

58. Brownell, *The Declining Enforcement of Employer Sanctions*, p. 2. This conclusion was not shared by the European Commission in its report on the application of the 2009 directive on employer sanctions.

59. Philip Martin and Mark Miller, *Employer Sanction: French, German and US Experiences*, International Migration Papers 36 (Geneva: International Labour Office, 2000).

60. Kadri Soova, Liliana Keith, and Michele LeVoy, *Employers' Sanctions: Impacts on Undocumented Migrant Workers' Rights in Four EU Countries* (Brussels: PICUM Platform for International Cooperation in Undocumented Migrants, April 2015), p. 11, http://picum.org/Documents/Publi/2015/EmployerSanctions.pdf.

61. See "More Neighbors Make More Fences," *The Economist*, Daily Chart, January 7, 2016; Julie Hirschfield Davis, David E. Sanger, and Maggie Haberman, "Trump to Order Mexican Border Wall and Curtail Immigration," *New York Times*, January 24, 2017.

62. The data on walls was gathered by Élisabeth Vallet, Josselyn Guillarmou, and Zoé Barry of the University of Quebec, Montreal, and reported in a series of three special reports in the *Washington Post* (www.washingtonpost.com), on October 12, 14, and 17, 2017 (see chapter 1, note 4).

63. US Senate, "Securing the Border: Fencing Infrastructure and Technology Force Multipliers," Committee on Homeland Security and Governmental Affairs, https://www.hsgac.senate.gov/hearings/securing-the-border-fencing-infrastructure-and-technology-force-multipliers, May 13, 2015.

64. Jaume Castan Pinos, "Building Fortress Europe? Schengen and the Cases of Ceuta and Melilla," School of Politics, International Studies and Philosophy, Queen's University Belfast, pp. 10–12, https://www.qub.ac.uk/research-centres/CentreforInternationalBordersResearch/Publications/WorkingPapers/CIBRWorkingPapers/Filetoupload,174398,en.pdf.

65. Jaume Castan Pinos, "Building Fortress Europe?"

66. Said Saddiki, "Ceuta and Melilla Fences: A EU Multidimensional Border?," https://www.cpsa-acsp.ca/papers-2010/Saddiki.pdf, p. 12.

67. European Commission, *Visit to Ceuta and Melilla—Mission Report: Technical Mission to Morocco on Illegal Immigration, 7th October-11th October 2005*, pp. 3–4, http://www.migreurop.org/IMG/pdf/rapport-ceuta-melilla-2.pdf.

68. See Ricard Zapata-Barrero and Nyne De Witte, "The Spanish Governance of EU Borders: Normative Questions," *Mediterranean Politics* 12, no. 1, March 2007, pp. 89–90.

69. See "Hungarian Crisis: UN Criticizes Hungary over Border Controls," BBC News, July 9, 2016, https://www.bbc.com/news/world-europe-36753648. Also see Alasdair Sandford, "Hungary Completes New Anti-Migrant Border Fence with Serbia," http://www.euronews.com/2017/04/28/hungary-completes-new-anti-migrant-border-fence-with-serbia.

70. Reports of the UN International Organization for Migration, https://www.iom.int/news/mediterranean-migrant-arrivals-top-363348-2016-deaths-sea-5079. Also see reports of the *Missing Migrants Project: Migrant Fatalities Recorded Worldwide*, https://missingmigrants.iom.int/.

71. See Donald Trump, "Immigration Reform That Will Make America Great Again," https://assets.donaldjtrump.com/Immigration-Reform-Trump.pdf.

72. See USDHS, US Customs and Border Protection, *CBP Requests Proposals for Border Wall Prototypes*, https://www.cbp.gov/newsroom/national-media-release/cbp-requests-proposals-border-wall-prototypes, March 17, 2017.

73. See John Bowden, "DHS to Start Building Border Wall Prototypes This Summer," *The Hill*, June 27, 2017, http://thehill.com/homenews/administration/339743-dhs-to-start-building-border-wall-prototypes-this-summer.

74. See Schain, *The Politics of Immigration*, pp. 223–224.

75. Joseph Nevins, *Operation Gatekeeper and Beyond: The War on "Illegals" and the Remaking of the U.S.–Mexican Boundary* (New York: Routledge, 2002), pp. 77–80.

76. Randal C. Archibold, "U.S. Plans Border 'Surge' Against Any Drug Wars," *New York Times*, January 7, 2009.

77. See Robert Farley, "Obama Says the Border Fence Is 'Now Basically Complete,'" *Politifact*, May 16, 2011, http://www.politifact.com/truth-o-meter/statements/2011/may/16/barack-obama/obama-says-border-fence-now-basically-complete/.

78. See Dara Lind, *Removals vs. Returns: How to Think About Obama's Deportation Record*, Vox News, April 11, 2014, https://www.vox.com/2014/4/11/5602272/removals-returns-and-deportations-a-very-short-history-of-immigration.

79. The European Parliament estimates 220 closed detention camps within the countries of the EU 25 in 2007. See European Parliament, Directorate-General Internal Policies, Policy Department C, Citizens' Rights and Constitutional Affairs, *The Conditions in Centres for Third Country Nationals*, p. 35, http://www.europarl.europa.eu/RegData/etudes/etudes/join/2007/393275/IPOL-LIBE_ET(2007)393275_EN.pdf, December 2007.

   The EMN report excludes Italy and Romania and Slovenia, and does not count the prisons used for detention in Ireland. See EMN, *The Use of Detention and Alternatives to Detention in the Context of Immigration Policies: Synthesis Report for the EMN Focussed Study 2014* (Brussels: The European Commission, 2015), https://ec.europa.eu/home-affairs/sites/homeaffairs/files/what-we-do/networks/european_migration_network/reports/docs/emn-studies/emn_study_detention_alternatives_to_detention_synthesis_report_en.pdf.

80. See *Global Detention Project* (Geneva, 2019), https://www.globaldetentionproject.org/detention-centers/list-view.

81. The "Return Directive," Directive 2008/115/EC of the European Parliament and of the Council of December 16, 2008 on common standards and procedures in Member States for returning illegally staying third-country nationals, is meant to regulate the detention of irregular migrants in view of their return, https://eur-lex.europa.eu/LexUriServ/LexUriServ.do?uri=OJ:L:2008:348:0098:0107:EN:PDF; the "Reception Conditions Directive," Directive 2013/33/EU of the European Parliament and of the Council of June 26, 2013, laying down standards for the reception of applicants for international protection (recast) is meant to regulate the conditions for receiving asylum seekers, https://www.refworld.org/docid/51d29db54.html.

82. An all-party parliamentary committee has severely criticized this lack of limits. See *UK, Report of the Inquiry into the Use of Immigration Detention in the United Kingdom*, 2015, https://detentioninquiry.files.wordpress.com/2015/03/immigration-detention-inquiry-executive-summary.pdf, p. 1.

83. For a more elaborate analysis of the French case, see Schain, "The Border."

84. The Macron government has proposed the extension of this limit to 90 days or more, together with other proposals to dissuade asylum seekers from entering France.

85. See the book by the Socialist senator Louis Mermaz, *Les Geôles de la République* (Paris: Stock, 2001). The figures for 2007 are from Secrétariat général du comité interministériel de contrôle de l'immigration, *Les Orientations de la politique de l'immigration*, 2007, Cinquième rapport établi en application de l'article l. 111-10 du code de l'entrée et du séjour des étrangers et du droit d'asile (Paris: La Documentation Française, 2008). The most recent figure of 37 is from the Council of Europe, The European Committee for the Prevention of Torture and Inhuman or Degrading Treatment or Punishment, https://www.coe.int/en/web/cpt, A far larger recent number (78) is reported in a European Parliament report, European Parliament, Directorate-General Internal Policies, Policy Department C, Citizens' Rights and Constitutional Affairs, *The Conditions in Centres for Third Country Nationals*, http://www.europarl.europa.eu/RegData/etudes/etudes/join/2007/393275/IPOL-LIBE_ET(2007)393275_EN.pdf, December 2007, p. 79. In addition, the EP report notes also 185 administrative detention facilities where TCNs can be held for periods of 48–96 hours.

86. See the European Migration Network, *The Use of Detention and Alternatives to Detention in the Context of Immigration Policies: Synthesis Report for the EMN Focussed Study 2014*, Annex 4 Statistics, Table A4.A.

87. The Migration Observatory, "Immigration Detention in the UK," February 16, 2015, http://migrationobservatory.ox.ac.uk/briefings/immigration-detention-uk. Please note these figures are higher than those reported in the EMN report, *The Use of Detention and Alternatives to Detention in the Context of Immigration Policies: Synthesis Report for the EMN Focussed Study 2014*, which mistakenly reported monthly totals in the British case, rather than the total number of TCNs entering into detention each year.

88. See *Global Detention Project: The United States Immigration Detention*, https://www.globaldetentionproject.org/countries/americas/united-states.

89. Dora Shriro, *Immigration Detention Overview and Recommendations*, ICE, Department of Homeland Security, October 7, 2009, https://www.ice.gov/doclib/about/offices/odpp/pdf/ice-detention-rpt.pdf.

90. USDHS, *US Customs and Border Protection, Border Patrol Statistics*, http://www.cbp.gov/xp/cgov/border_security/border_patrol/usbp_statistics/. Also see *US Immigration and Customs Enforcement, Detention Facility Locator*, http://www.ice.gov/detention-facilities. The difference depends on how a detention facility is defined. Such facilities range between actual prisons with a number of beds attributed to immigrant detention, to dedicated detention centers that are either public or private. One detailed report was issued by the Global Detention Project in 2009, most of which are prisons: *Global Detention Project: The United States Immigration Detention*.

91. See the report of the US Conference of Catholic Bishops and the Center for Migration Studies, *Unlocking Human Dignity: A Plan to Transform the U.S. Immigration Detention System*, May 2015, http://www.usccb.org/news/2015/15-074.cfm, pp. 7–9.

92. Aspects of migrant mandatory detention go back to previous waves of immigration as well. See Philip L. Torrey, "Rethinking Immigration's Mandatory Detention Regime: Politics, Profit and the Meaning of 'Custody,'" *University of Michigan Journal of Law Reform* 48, no. 4(2015), pp. 879–913.

93. Dora Schriro, *Immigration Detention*, fn p. 4.

94. See Cornell Law School, Legal Information Institute, "8 U.S. Code § 1325. Improper entry by alien,"https://www.law.cornell.edu/uscode/text/8/1325#a.

95. Claire Rodier, "Des Zones De Droit, Mais Non De Liberté," *Revue Projet*, 2009/1 (n° 308), pp. 57–61.

96. Obtained by the author at the *Zone d'Attente de Roissy*, Charles de Gaulle Airport, August 13, 2013.

97. *Information Note on the Maintenance of Immigrants in the Zone d'Attente de Roissy*, obtained from the director of the facility on August 13, 2013.

98. Based on visits to both facilities on August 13, 2013 (Roissy), and August 23, 2013 (Tinsley).

99. See the report of the French National Assembly (Assemblée Nationale), *Rapport d'Information sur la mise en œuvre des conclusions du rapport d'information (n° 1879) du 10 avril 2014 sur l'évaluation de la politique d'accueil des demandeurs d'asile*, http://www.assemblee-nationale.fr/14/pdf/rap-info/i4077.pdf, October 5, 2016.

100. Magnus Gittins and Laura Broomfield, *The Organisation of Reception Facilities for Asylum Seekers* (UK Home Office Report, 2013), https://ec.europa.eu/home-affairs/sites/homeaffairs/files/what-we-do/networks/european_migration_network/reports/docs/emn-studies/27.united_kingdom_national_report_receptionfacilities_en_version_jan2014_final.pdf.

101. Frank Bajak, "The Trump Administration Is Shutting Down the Least Restrictive Alternative to Detention Available to Asylum-Seekers Who Have Entered the U.S. Illegally," *Newsweek*, June 9, 2017, https://www.usnews.com/news/best-states/texas/articles/2017-06-09/ice-shutters-detention-alternate-for-asylum-seekers.

102. Statistics are available from Eurostat: "Eurostat Statistics Explained: Non-EU Citizens Subject to the Enforcement of Immigration Legislation in EU Member States," https://ec.europa.eu/eurostat/statistics-explained/index.php?title=File:Non-EU_citizens_subject_to_the_enforcement_of_immigration_legislation_in_EU_Member_States,_2008-2017_(number)_1.png&oldid=392384.

103. US Senate, "Declining Deportations and Increasing Criminal Alien Releases—The Lawless Immigration Policies of the Obama Administration," Judiciary Committee, Subcommittee on Immigration and the National Interest, https://www.judiciary.senate.gov/meetings/declining-deportations-and-increasing-criminal-alien-releases_the-lawless-immigration-policies-of-the-obama-administration, May 19, 2016.

    Testimony of Thomas Horman, Executive Associate Director (EAD) of ICE Enforcement and Removal Operations (ERO), https://www.judiciary.senate.gov/meetings/declining-deportations-and-increasing-criminal-alien-releases_the-lawless-immigration-policies-of-the-obama-administration.

104. See Margot Desmas, "Loi asile et immigration: que dit la législation chez nos voisins européens," *Le Monde*, February 23, 2018.

105. In particular, see the testimony of Thomas Horman in note 103. Also see the case articulated by Jessica M. Vaughan, "Deportation Number Unwrapped: Raw Statistics Reveal the Real Story of ICE Enforcement in Decline," *Center for Migration Studies*, October 2013, https://cis.org/Report/Deportation-Numbers-Unwrapped.

    She argues that the impact of the Supreme Court decision *Zadvydas v. Davis* has severely restricted the ability of the United States to deport migrants to "recalcitrant" countries that refuse to admit them, and also argues that between 2010 and 2013, 17,000 essentially un-removable aliens were released from detention (p. 13).

106. Expulsions are also complicated by whether they result from claims for asylum, from lack of documentation, from visa overstay, or from criminal or security issues. See Elspeth Guild and Paul Minderhoud, eds., *Security of Residence and Expulsion: Protection of Aliens in Europe* (The Hague: Kluwer Law International, 2001), especially chapter 9; and House of Lords/Commons, Joint Committee on Human Rights, *Legislative Scrutiny: Borders, Citizenship and Immigration Bill*, paper # HL62/HC375, 9th Session, 2008–2009, pp. 77–79.

107. Nick Miroff, "Deportations Slow Under Trump Despite Increase in Arrests by ICE," *Washington Post*, September 28, 2017.

108. See Bryan Baker and Christopher Williams, *Immigration Enforcement Actions: 2015*, Annual Report, Homeland Security, Office of Immigration Statistics, July 2017, p. 8.

109. See Alison Siskin, *Alien Removals and Returns: Overview and Trends, Congressional Research Service Report*, February 3, 2015, https://fas.org/sgp/crs/homesec/R43892.pdf pp. 8–10.

110. Directive 2008/115/EC of the European Parliament and of the Council of December 16, 2008 on common standards and procedures in Member States for returning illegally staying third-country nationals: https://eur-lex.europa.eu/LexUriServ/LexUriServ.do?uri=OJ:L:2008:348:0098:0107:EN:PDF.

111. European Commission, "Communication from the Commission to the Council and the European Parliament on EU Return Policy," March 28, 2014, COM (2014) 199 Final, https://eur-lex.europa.eu/procedure/EN/1041853, p. 5.

112. Scott Blinder, *Briefing: Deportations, Removals, and Voluntary Departures from the UK*, 4th revision, The Migration Observatory, University of Oxford, July 19, 2017, p. 5.

113. Until 1996, what are now called returns were voluntary removals. For the most part, this involved migrants who were unauthorized, and who had been apprehended close to the border. The number of returnees declined both because of policy changes and because fewer unauthorized migrants were entering the United States during the Great Recession. Removals generally involve a formal process that has far harsher consequences, and creates a paper trail. See Dara Lind, "Removals vs. Returns: How to Think About Obama's Deportation Record," *Vox*, April 11, 2014, https://www.vox.com/2014/4/11/5602272/removals-returns-and-deportations-a-very-short-history-of-immigration.

114. USDHS has only recently begun to produce reports on visa overstayers. They estimate that more than 416,000 visitors' visas ran out in 2015, in addition to the 350,000 migrants that Pew estimates entered the country illegally. See Jeffrey S. Passel and D'Vera Cohn, *Homeland Security Produces First Estimate of Foreign Visitors to U.S. Who Overstay Deadline to Leave*, Pew Research Center, February 3, 2016, http://www.pewresearch.org/fact-tank/2016/02/03/homeland-security-produces-first-estimate-of-foreign-visitors-to-u-s-who-overstay-deadline-to-leave/.

Chapter 6

1. See Richard Bellamy, Joseph Lacey, and Kalypso Nicolaïdes, "European Boundaries in Question," *Journal of European Integration* 39, no. 5 (2017), pp. 484–498.
2. In Adrienne Héritier's excellent study of policymaking in the EU her primary focus is on interest accommodation, but she also deals with the importance of European borders in shaping these interests, by protecting them from competition and magnifying their importance at the member state level. See Adrienne Héritier, *Policy-Making and Diversity in Europe: Escaping Deadlock* (New York: Cambridge University Press, 1999), chapter 3.
3. Grant McConnell, *Private Power and American Democracy* (New York: Vintage Books, 1966), chapter 4.
4. See Peter H. Schuck, *Why Government Fails So Often and How It Can Do Better* (Princeton, NJ: Princeton University Press, 2014), chapter 2.
5. Mark Bovens and Paul t'Hart, "Revisiting the Study of Policy Failures," *Journal of European Public Policy* 23, no. 5 (2016), p. 656.
6. See Mark Bovens, P. t'Hart, and B.G. Peters, eds., *Success and Failure in Public Governance: A Comparative Analysis* (Cheltenham: Edward Elgar, 2001).
7. Fritz W. Scharpf, "Problem-Solving Effectiveness and Democratic Accountability in the EU," MPIfG (Max Plank Institute for the Study of Societies) working paper no. 03/1, 2003, http://www.mpifg.de/pu/workpap/wp03-1/wp03-.
8. See Paul Scheffer, *Immigrant Nations* (Cambridge: Polity Press, 2011), pp. 325–333. For the debate that led up to the Johnson-Reed Act in 1924, see Schain, *The Politics of Immigration*, chapter 10.
9. Vincent Viet, *La France immigrée: Construction d'une politique 1914–1997* (Paris: Fayard, 1998), p. 27.
10. See Patrick Weil, *La France et ses étrangers*, p. 95.
11. Alexis Spire, *Etrangers à la carte: l'administration de l'immigration en France (1945–1975)* (Paris: Grasset, 2005), p. 13.
12. These documents were first summarized in a report published by Corentin Calvez for the Economic and Social Council in 1969. He distinguished "assimilable" Europeans who should be encouraged to become French citizens from "inassimilable" non-European workers. See Corentin Calvez, "Le Problème de travailleurs étrangers," *Journal Officiel de la Republique Française, Avis et Rapports du Conseil Economique et Social*, March 27, 1969, p. 315ff.
13. The best analysis of this shift is Randall Hansen, *Citizenship and Immigration in Post-war Britain* (Oxford: Oxford University Press, 2000).
14. As Hansen emphasizes, it was the *authority*, rather than the actual place of issue, that was crucial. See *Citizenship and Immigration*, pp. 109–110. Hansen's book is particularly good at analyzing the complexities of this evolving process.
15. Paul Gordon, *Policing Immigration: Britain's Internal Controls* (London: Pluto Press, 1985, pp. 16–17.
16. This is the point made by Ian Macdonald and Nicholas Blake in *Macdonald's Immigration Law*, 3rd edition (London: Butterworth's, 1991), pp. 11, 13–15. A variation of the Natal formula was first applied in South Africa in 1897.
17. In fact, Randall Hansen argued in 2004 that the UK perhaps represented the closest approximation in the EU to a successful zero immigration country. See "Commentary," in *Controlling Immigration: A Global Perspective*, 2nd ed., ed. W. A. Cornelius, T. Tsuda, P. L. Martin, and J. F. Hollifield (Palo Alto, CA: Stanford University Press, 2004), pp. 338–342.
18. *The Economist*, "Why the British Government's Plan for Controlling Immigration Is a Bad Idea," February 10, 2005.
19. See Chris F. Wright, "Policy Legacies, Visa Reform and the Resilience of Immigration Politics," *West European Politics* 35, no. 4 (2012), pp. 726–755.
20. UK Home Office, "A Points-Based System: Making Migration Work for Britain," presented to Parliament by the Secretary of State for the Home Department, by Command of Her Majesty, March 2006, Cm 6741.

21. Hugh Williamson, "EU Six Consider Introduction of 'Integration Contracts' for Immigrants," *The Financial Times*, March 24, 2006.
22. Charles Clarke, *The EU and Migration: A Call for Action* (London: The Center for European Reform, 2011), pp. 4–5.
23. Peter Hollinger, "Council of Europe Warns on Multiculturalism," *Financial Times*, https://www.ft.com/content/72c02d9a-39c6-11e0-8dba-00144feabdc0, February 16, 2011.
24. Chancellor Merkel's speech was reported in *Der Spiegel* on October 18, 2010. This pessimistic position was also supported by the normally pro-multiculturalist Council of Europe. See Hollinger, "Council of Europe Warns on Multiculturalism.". The sharp movement toward consensus and away from multiculturalism is summarized and analyzed in three recent articles in *Le Monde*, February 26, 2011, under the rubric "Le multiculturalisme, entre modèle et crise." Two articles of particular interest are Eric Fassin, "Nicolas Sarkozy en marche vers le 'monoculturalisme,'" and Béatrice Durand, "En Allemagne, un mot d'ordre bien plus qu'une politique: l'idée de la nécessité d'une culture de référence l'emporte," pp. 18–19.
25. Joppke, *Immigration and the Nation-State*, p. 76.
26. Paul Scheffer, *Immigrant Nations* (Cambridge: Polity Press, 2011). This is a follow-up of his influential essay in 2000 in the Dutch newspaper of record: "*Het multiculturele drama*" ("Multicultural Tragedy") jin *NRC Hanelsblad*, January 29, 2000.
27. For Germany, see Joppke, *Immigration and the Nation-State*, pp. 69–76. For France, see Schain, *The Politics of Immigration*, pp. 48–50.
28. By 2006, the largest numbers of EU citizens migrating to other member states were from Poland and Romania. By 2016, Polish citizens were the largest single nationality among EU-settled migrants in Germany, Ireland, Lithuania, Denmark, the Netherlands, the UK, and Norway; Romanians were the top EU nationality in Italy, Hungary, and Spain. See Anne Hern, "Recent Migration Trends: Citizens of EU-27 Member States Become Ever More Mobile While EU Remains Attractive to Non-EU Citizens," *Eurostat, Statistics in Focus*, 98/2008, p. 4; and Eurostat, Statistics Explained, "Migration and Migrant Population Statistics," October 2010, Table 2, https://ec.europa.eu/eurostat/statistics-explained/index.php?title=Special:ListFiles&sort=img_timestamp&limit=50&user=Marcumc&asc=1&desc=; and Eurostat, Statistics Explained, "Main Countries of Citizenship and Birth of the Foreign, Foreign-Born Population," January 1, 2016, https://ec.europa.eu/eurostat/statistics-explained/index.php?title=File:Main_countries_of_citizenship_and_birth_of_the_foreign_foreign-born_population,_1_January_2016_(%C2%B9)_(in_absolute_numbers_and_as_a_percentage_of_the_total_foreign_foreign-born_population).png&oldid=331054.
29. See David Cameron, "Free Movement within Europe Needs to Be Less Free," *Financial Times*, November 26, 2013.
30. See "Ryanair Fined 8m Euros by French Court," https://bbc.com/news/business-24371633, October 2, 2013.
31. See *Eurobarometer* (Standard) 84, National Report, Public Opinion in the European Union, United Kingdom, Autumn 2015, p. 5; *Eurobarometer* (Standard) 85, p. 58; *Eurobarometer* (Standard), First Results 87, pp. 31–32.
32. See the analysis by the NGO Statewatch: Steve Peers, *Statewatch Analysis, The Revised "Dublin" Rules on Responsibility for Asylum-Seekers: The Council's Failure to Fix a Broken System*, http://www.statewatch.org/analyses/no-173-dublin-III.pdf.
33. See the account of the process in Ruben Zaiotti, *Cultures of Border Control*, pp. 182–184, as well as Commission of the European Communities, "Towards More Accessible, Equitable and Managed Asylum Systems," COM [2003] 315 final, June 2003.
34. European Commission, "Communication from the Commission to the European Parliament and the Council: On the State of Play of Implementation of the Priority Actions under the European Agenda on Migration," COM (2016) 85 Final, February 10, 2016, p. 3.
35. See Dietmar Loch, "Moi, Khalel Kelkal," *Le Monde*, October 7, 1995; and Jean-Philippe Leclaire and Aziz Mouats, "Khaled Kelkal, premier djihadiste made in France," *Le Monde*, September 18, 2015, http://www.lemonde.fr/m-le-mag/article/2015/09/18/khaled-kelkal-premier-djihadiste-made-in-france_4762322_4500055.html#tDULTgeuZrReF8t0.99.

36. The Europol *EU Terrorism Situation and Trend Report 2017* classifies 13 of 142 attacks in 2016 as "Jihadist." See Annex 1, p. 49. https://www.europol.europa.eu/activities-services/main-reports/european-union-terrorism-situation-and-trend-report-2017-tesat-2017.

    France stands out as the European country before 2000 that suffered from a large number of terrorist attacks from foreign perpetrators (mostly from the Middle East) who entered the country from outside of Europe. See Martin A. Schain, "Immigration Policy and Reactions to Terrorism after September 11," in *Immigration, Integration, and Security America and Europe in Comparative Perspective,* ed. Ariane Chebel d'Appollonia and Simon Reich (Pittsburgh: University of Pittsburgh Press, 2008), pp. 111–130.

37. The data on terrorist attacks is from the Global Terrorism Database, University of Maryland National Consortium for the Study of Terrorism and Responses to Terrorism's Global Terrorism Database, https://www.start.umd.edu/pubs/START_GTD_Overview2017_July2018.pdf. The data on asylum is from Figure 4.5.

38. Nine of the twenty-eight accused terrorists in Spain were born in Spain, and all four of the attackers in London were raised in the UK.

39. For an excellent short analysis of the success and failure of the 1965 Hart–Cellar Act, see Schuck, *Why Government Fails So Often and How It Can Do Better,* pp. 243 and 350–353.

40. See Vivien Schmidt, "National Patterns of Governance under Siège: The Impact of European Integration," in *The Transformation of Governance in the European Union,* ed. Beate Kohler-Koch and Rainer Eising (London: Routledge, 1999), pp. 155–172.

41. The most original approach to the roles of interest groups in preference formation in the European Community can be found in Andrew Moravcsik, "Preferences and Power in the European Community: A Liberal Intergovernmentalist Approach," *Journal of Common Market Studies* 31, no. 4 (December 1993), pp. 482–524.

42. See Alberta Sbragia, "Politics in the European Union," in *European Politics Today,* 3rd ed., ed. Gabriel Almond, Bingham Powell Jr., Russell J. Dalton, and Kaare Strøm (New York: Pearson-Longman, 2006), pp. 485–486.

43. See Moravcsik, "Preferences and Power," p. 490.

44. See Mark Thatcher, "The Development of Policy Network Analysis, From Modest Origins to Overarching Frameworks," *Journal of Theoretical Politics* 10, no. 4 (1998), pp. 389–416; John Peterson, *Policy Networks,* Institute for Advanced Study, Vienna, Political Science Series 90, July 2003, pp. 4–9.

45. Here, Rubin Zaiotti is referring to the construction of Frontex, but also to the way that the Schengen system was developed. See Zaiotti, *Cultures of Border Control,* p. 169. This legitimating role of interest groups was carefully analyzed by Ezra Suleiman in *Politics, Power, and Bureaucracy in France: The Administrative Elite* (Princeton, NJ: Princeton University Press, 1974), chapter XII.

46. The EU Transparency Register contains a wealth of information about these groups, including their budgets, stated purpose, and activities. I have focused primarily on groups that have a presence in at least several EU countries. See http://ec.europa.eu/transparencyregister/public/homePage.do.

47. See Virginie Guiraudon, "Setting the Agenda on Immigration and Asylum in the EU: Experts and the Public," unpublished paper presented at the Annual Conference of the American Political Science Association, Boston, August 30, 2002, pp. 14–18.

48. Guiraudon, "Setting the Agenda on Immigration and Asylum in the EU," p. 15.

49. Nick Buxton and Fiona Dove, eds., *NeoConOpticon: The EU Security-Industrial Complex* (London: Transnational Institute/Statewatch, 2009).

50. Communication from the Commission to the Council and the European Parliament, Towards Integrated Management of the External Borders of the Member States of the European Union, COM/2002/0233 final, 2002, p. 1.

51. Theodore J. Lowi, *The End of Liberalism: The Second Republic of the United States,* 2nd ed. (New York: Norton, 1979).

52. Claire Rodier, *Xénophobie Business: à quoi servent les contrôles migratoires?* (Paris: la Découverte, 2012), pp. 34, 36–37.

53. Lowi, *The End of Liberalism,* pp. 59–64.

54. See Valsamis Mitsilegas, "Immigration Control in an Era of Globalization: Deflecting Foreigners, Weakening Citizens, Strengthening the State," *Indiana Journal of Global Legal Studies* 19, no. 1 (Winter 2012), pp. 42–45.

55. Interviews with the French Police de la Frontier (PAF) at the detention center at Charles de Gaulle Airport, August 13, 2013; and interviews with administrators of Tinsley detention Center at Gatwick Airport, UK, on August 23, 2013. See also interviews with Sarah Belaish, responsable des équipes "migrants" pour La Cimade, at CIMADE (French NGO) June 3, 2013.

56. Martin A. Schain, "The Extreme-Right and Immigration in Policy-Making: Measuring Direct and Indirect Effects," in *Immigration Policy in Europe: The Politics of Control*, ed. Virginie Guiraudon and Gallya Lahav (New York: Routledge, 2007), pp 70–91.

57. Based on two questions asked: ("the most important issue") and left-right-far right commitments.

58. "Nicolas Sarkozy tenté par le discours populiste," *Le Monde*, June 23, 2005.

59. Le Ministre de l'Intérieur, de l'Outre-mer et des Collectivités territoriales, *Circulaire IOC/K/1017881/J du 5 août 2010, "Evacuation des campements illicites."* Although this was not a public document, it was widely distributed: http://www.errc.org/uploads/upload_en/file/appendix-2.pdf. In fact, France had expelled about 10,000 Roma in 2009, but much more quietly. The *Circulaire* was modified (essentially withdrawn) in October, after a dialogue with the European Commission.

60. See Alissa J. Rubin, "France says Deportation of Roma Girl Was Legal but Badly Handled," *New York Times*, October 20, 2013, p. A12.

61. "Avis défavorable à la demande de séjour de la famille de Leonarda," *Le Monde*, January 7, 2014.

62. "Out with the New," *The Economist*, December 9, 2004.

63. See the report of the MORI (Market and Opinion Research International), "MORI Political Monitor, February, 2005," in the *Financial Times*, February 23, 2005.

64. "Howard's Way," *The Economist*, January 27, 2005.

65. "Queen's Speech: Immigrants Face Tougher Rules," *BBC News*, http://www.bbc.co.uk/news/uk-politics-22437884, May 8, 2013.

66. For a cogent and succinct discussion of the latter see Michael Kenny, "The English Question, Identity, Diversity and Nationhood in England," in *Democracy in Britain: Essays in Honor of James Cornford*, ed. Guy Lodge and Glenn Gottfried (London: Institute for Public Policy Research, 2014), pp. 133–144.

67. The speech was delivered on May 21, 2015.

68. Matthew Goodwin, "Ukip, the 2015 General Election and Britain's EU Referendum," *Parliamentary Insight* 6, no. 3 (2015), pp. 12–15.

69. See J. W. Duyvendak and Peter Scholten, "The Invention of the Dutch Multicultural Model and Its Effects on Integration Discourses in the Netherlands," *Perspectives on Europe* 40, no. 2 (2010), pp. 39–49.

70. Jan Willem Duyvendak, Tres Pels, and Rally Rujkschroeff, "A Multicultural Paradise? The Cultural Factor in Dutch Integration Policy," in *Bringing Outsiders In: Transatlantic Perspectives on Immigrant Political Incorporation*, ed. Jennifer L. Hochschild and John M. Mollenkopf (Ithaca, NY: Cornell University Press, 2009), chapter 9, pp. 129–139.

71. See Chavi Nana, "With Strict Policies in Place, Dutch Discourse on Integration Becomes More Inclusive," Migration Information Source, April 19, 2007, https://www.migrationpolicy.org/article/strict-policies-place-dutch-discourse-integration-becomes-more-inclusive.

72. Gordon Darroch, "Geert Wilders Found Guilty of Inciting Discrimination," *The Guardian*, December 9, 2016, https://www.theguardian.com/world/2016/dec/09/geert-wilders-found-guilty-in-hate-speech-trial-but-no-sentence-imposed.

73. Cas Mudde, "'Good' Populism Beat 'Bad' in Dutch Election," *The Guardian*, March 19, 2017, https://www.theguardian.com/world/2017/mar/19/dutch-election-rutte-wilders-good-populism-bad-. For an in-depth study of electoral trends, see Hilde Coffe and Job van den Berg, "Understanding Shifts in Voting Behavior Away from and Towards Radical Right Populist Parties: The Case of the PVV between 2007 and 2012," *Comparative European Politics* 15, no. 6 (2016), pp. 872–896.

74. Christopher Caldwell makes this argument in *Reflections on the Revolution in Europe* (New York: Anchor Books, 2010).

75. European Pact on Immigration and Asylum (13440/08), approved by the JHA Council on September 25 and adopted by the European Council. www.euractiv.com, November 12, 2008.

   For the development of integration requirements, see the summary in the *New York Times* by Liam Stack, "Burqa Bans Spreading from Europe to Canada," October 20, 2017.

76. Paul Scheffer, *Immigrant Nations*; Chavi Nana, "With Strict Policies in Place, Dutch Discourse on Integration Becomes More Inclusive" (Washington, DC: Migration Policy Institute, 2007).

77. The sharp movement toward reinforcing consensus is summarized and analyzed in the three articles in *Le Monde*, February 26, 2011, under the rubric "Le multiculturalisme, entre modèle et crise." Also see Hollinger, "Council of Europe Warns on Multiculturalism."

78. Schain, *The Politics of Immigration*, p. 57.

79. See the report of the French IFII on the "Welcome Contract," Les missions de l'ofii (Office Français de l'immigration et de l'intégration): EN 2013, http://www.ofii.fr/IMG/pdf/Rapport_activite_Missions_VERSION_internet.pdf; and Schain, *The Politics of Immigration* (see note 10), pp. 164–166. For a good summary of some of the evolving rules on family unification, see Yves Pascouau and Henri Labayle, *Conditions for Family Reunification under Strain: A Comparative Study in Nine EU Member States* (Brussels: King Baudouin Foundation, European Policy Centre, Odysseus Network, November 2011).

80. See European Commission, *Handbook on Integration for Policy-makers and Practitioners*, 3rd ed., 2010, pp. 15–16, http://euinfo.rs/files/biblioteka-srp/06_Vodic_kroz_inegracije.pdf.

81. Réseau Academique d'Etudes Juridiques sur l'Immigration et l'Asile en Europe, "Study on the Conformity by Member States of 10 EC Directives in The Sector of Asylum and Immigration," Directorate of Justice, Freedom and Security (DG JLS) of the European Commission, 2007, http://odysseus-network.eu/eu-directives/.

82. Hugh Williamson, "EU Six Consider Introduction of 'Integration Contracts' for Immigrants," *The Financial Times*, March 24, 2006.

83. See European Pact on Immigration and Asylum. http://register.consilium.europa.eu/doc/srv?l=EN&f=ST%2013440%202008%20INIT.

84. Beer, "Federalism, Nationalism and Democracy in America," pp. 17–19.

85. Beer, "Federalism, Nationalism and Democracy in America," p. 9.

86. Adam Sheingate, "Agricultural Biotechnology: Representative Federalism and Regulatory Capacity in the United States and European Union," in *The European Union and the United States in Comparative Perspective*, ed. Anand Menon and Martin A. Schain (Oxford: Oxford University Press, 2006).

87. Zaiotti, *Cultures of Border Control*, pp. 117–161.

88. See https://www.ucc.ie/archive/hdsp/Shengen-agreement_io.pdf.

89. These included the Strategic Committee on Immigration, Frontiers and Asylum (SCIFA) and the High Level Working Group on Asylum and Migration. See Zaiotti, *Cultures of Border Control*, pp. 154–158.

90. Arnaud Leparmentier and Jean-Pierre Stroobants, "Le candidat Sarkozy instrumentalise l'Europe," *Le Monde*, March 13, 2012.

91. Council of the European Union, Amended Proposal for a Regulation of the European Parliament and of the Council on the Establishment of an Evaluation and Monitoring Mechanism to Verify the Application of the Schengen Acquis 18196/1/11, REV 1, December 9, 2011.

92. Council of the European Union, Council Regulation 10597/13, Council Regulation Establishing an Evaluation and Monitoring Mechanism to Verify the Application of the Schengen Acquis and Repealing the Decision of the Executive Committee of 16 September 1998 Setting up a Standing Committee on the Evaluation and Implementation of Schengen, http://register.consilium.europa.eu/doc/srv?l=EN&f=ST%2010597%202013%20INIT.

93. Interviews by author at the European Commission, December 9, 2013.

94. See Gena Clayton, "The UK and Extraterritorial Immigration Control: Entry Clearance and Juxtaposed Control," pp. 397–431, and Elspeth Guild and Didier Bigo, "The Transformation

of European Border Control," pp. 257–281 in *Extraterritorial Immigration Control: Legal Challenges*, ed. Bernard Ryan and Valsamis Mitsilegas (Leiden: Martin Nijhoff, 2010).

Chapter 7

1. Douglas S. Massey, Jorge Durand, and Karen A. Pren, "Why Border Enforcement Backfired," *American Journal of Sociology* 121, no. 5 (March 2016): 1557–1600.
2. For a more extended account of the fate of immigration reform after 2006, see Schain, *The Politics of Immigration*, chapter 10.
3. Massey et al., "Why Border Enforcement Backfired," pp. 1557–1558.
4. David Reimers, *Still the Golden Door: The Third World Comes to America* (New York: Columbia University Press, 1985), pp. 235–237. A short version of the text of the SCIRP report can be found in *New York Times*, February 28, 1981, Section B, p. 5.
5. For an elaboration of this analysis, see Schain, The Politics of Immigration in France, Britain and the United States, chapter 10, pp. 256-257.]
6. Reported inTichenor, Dividing Lines, p. 251.]
7. Tichenor, *Dividing Lines*, p. 251-2.
8. Douglas Massey, Jorge Durand and Nolan Malone, *Beyond Smoke and Mirrors: Mexican Immigration in an Age of Economic Integration* (New York: Russell Sage, 2002), p. 87.
9. United States Commission on Immigration Reform (USCIR), Report to Congress, *U.S. Immigration Policy: Restoring Credibility* (Washington, DC: US Government Printing Office, 1994), p. 3.
10. [USCIR, Report to Congress, Becoming an American: Immigration and Immigrant Policy (Washington, DC: USGPO, 1997), pp. 26 and 29].
11. The tracking poll is produced by Gallup: see Megan Brenan, "Record High 75% of Americans Say Immigration Is a Good Thing," https://news.gallup.com/poll/235793/record-high-americans-say-immigration-good-thing.aspx, June 21, 2018.
12. For Europe, the differences are between respondents (the majority of voters) who identify as left or center-left and those who identify as center-right or right. For the United States, the differences are between Democratic and Republican identifiers.
13. The 2008 results are from the American National Election Studies; the 2011 results are from the CBS News/*New York Times* survey of April 2010. The survey on priorities was done by the Pew Research Center. All were reported by Patrick J. Egan, *Partisan Priorities: How Issue Ownership Drives and Distorts American Politics* (New York: Cambridge University Press, 2013), pp. 26–29.
14. "Untangling the Webs of Immigration Lobbying," by Lee Drutman and Alexander Furnas, the Sunlight Foundation, https://sunlightfoundation.com/2013/03/25/immigration/, March 25, 2013. This report is based on reports filed by registered lobbyists between 2008 and 2012.
15. This is similar to the way that Daniel Tichenor analyzes the primary dynamic for the expansion of immigration in the United States. See Tichenor, *Dividing Lines*, pp. 148–149 and 245–246.
16. Theodore Lowi argues that regulatory politics tend to be more conflictual. Theodore J. Lowi, *Arenas of Power*, ed. and intr. Norman K. Nicholson (Boulder, CO: Paradigm Publishers, 2009), p. 120.
17. For example, see Center for Responsive Politics Open Secrets database on lobbyists and lobbying in the United States, 2018, https://www.opensecrets.org/lobby/lobbyist.php?id=Y0000039775L.
18. Anna Fifield, "US Immigration Reform Draws 3,000 Lobbyists," *Financial Times*, March 20, 2013. The quotes and data are taken by Fifield from the annual reports and SEC reports filed by CCA and Geo, https://www.ft.com/content/83b39af0-9181-11e2-b839-00144feabdc0.
19. See Doris Meissner, Donald M. Kerwin, Muzaffar Chishti, and Claire Bergeron, *Immigration Enforcement in the United States: The Rise of a Formidable Machinery* (Washington, DC: Migration Policy Institute, 2014), p. 9.
20. Seung Min Kim, "Border Surge Amendment Approved," *Politico-pro*, June 23, 2013.
21. Matea Gold, "Immigration Deal Would Boost Defense Manufacturers," *Washington Post*, July 1, 2013.

22. "Goodies for Big Givers in Immigration Bill," Sunlight Foundation, https://sunlightfoundation.com/2013/07/02/goodies-big-givers-immigration-bill/, July 2, 2013.

23. National Border Patrol Council, "NBPC Statement on Selection of Ron Vitiello for Chief," NBPC press releases, February 2017, https://bpunion.org/press-releases/nbpc-statement-on-selection-of-ron-vitiello-for-chief/.

24. Nicholas Kulish, Caitlin Dickerson, and Ron Nixon, "Immigration Agents Discover New Freedom to Deport under Trump," New York Times, February 25, 2017.

25. See Jerry Markon, Lisa Rein, and Wesley Lowery, "Border Patrol Chief Removed from Post after Clashing with Powerful Union," Washington Post, January 26, 2017.

26. Lobbyists Information, Lobbying Impact Report: Immigration Legislation, 112 Congress. Available only directly from Lobbyists-info.

27. Drutman and Furnas, "Untangling the Webs of Immigration Lobbying."

28. Immigration from Canada was seen as generally benign, although the immigration of French-Canadians to work in factories in New England was sometimes posed in the same terms as migration from Mexico ("the Mexicans of the Northeast"). See Aristide Zolberg, Nation by Design, Immigration Policy in the Fashioning of America (Cambridge, MA: Harvard University Press, 2008), p. 256.

29. Tichenor, Dividing Lines, p. 202. Also see Kitty Calavita, Inside the State (New York: Routledge, 1992).

30. See Schain, The Politics of Immigration, pp. 222–225.

31. Tichenor, Dividing Lines, p. 202.

32. Dorothy Nelkin and Mark Michaels, "Biological Categories and Border Controls: The Revival of Eugenics in Anti-immigration Rhetoric," International Journal of Sociology and Social Policy 18, no. 5/6 (1998), p. 33. Also see Richard Herrnstein and Charles Murray, The Bell Curve (New York: Free Press, 1994); Seymour W. Itzkoff, The Decline of Intelligence in America (Westport, CT: Praeger, 1994); Philippe Rushton, Race, Evolution and Behavior (New Brunswick, NJ: Transaction Press, 1994).

33. See Egan, Partisan Priorities, p. 71.

34. Egan, Partisan Priorities, p. 187.

35. Egan, Partisan Priorities, pp. 143–144.

36. See Joel S. Fetzer, "Why Did House Members Vote for H.R. 4437?," International Migration Review 40, no. 3 (Fall 2006), pp. 698–706. See release of the President Bush's speech on May 15, 2006: http://www.whitehouse.gov/news/releases/2006/05/20060515_7.html.

37. See release of the President Bush's speech on May 15, 2006: http://www.whitehouse.gov/news/releases/2006/05/20060515_7.html.

38. See Schain, The Politics of Immigration, pp. 214–215.

39. "Border Protection, Antiterrorism, and Illegal Immigration Control Act," (the Sensenbrenner bill), reported by the National Conference of State Legislatures, http://www.ncsl.org/research/immigration/summary-of-the-sensenbrenner-immigration-bill.aspx.

40. Robert Pear and Carl Hulse, "Immigration Bill Fails to Survive Senate Vote," New York Times, June 28, 2007.

41. Quoted in Rachel Weiner, "The Fix: How Immigration Reform Failed, Over and Over," Washington Post, January 30, 2013. On the other hand, a number of Democrats voted against the legislation because the AFL-CIO opposed the guest worker proposal.

42. See HR 6061, The Secure Fence Act of 2006, https://www.govtrack.us/congress/bills/109/hr6061.

43. Harold Meyerson, "Out of the Shadows," Washington Post, April 12, 2006.

44. See David Nakamura and Ed O'Keefe, "Timeline: The Rise and Fall of Immigration Reform," Washington Post, June 26, 2014.

45. See Congress.Gov, "HR2278 SAFE Act, 113th Congress, 2013–14," https://www.congress.gov/bill/113th-congress/house-bill/2278.

46. Molly Ball, "The Fall of the Heritage Foundation and the Death of Republican Ideas," The Atlantic, September 25, 2013, https://www.theatlantic.com/politics/archive/2013/09/the-fall-of-the-heritage-foundation-and-the-death-of-republican-ideas/279955/.

47. Lorelei Kelly, "DeMint's Departure Is Just the Beginning," Roll Call, December 18, 2012, http://www.rollcall.com/news/kelly_demints_departure_is_just_the_beginning-220056-1.html?pg=1.

48. Ball, "The Fall," pp. 12–13.
49. Christine Kim and Robert Rector, "The Fiscal Cost of Low-Skill Immigrants to the U.S. Taxpayer," The Heritage Foundation, Washington, DC, http://www.heritage.org/immigration/report/the-fiscal-cost-low-skill-immigrants-the-us-taxpayer, May 22, 2007.
50. Reported by David Nakamura, "On Immigration Legislation, Fissures Emerge within Conservative Ranks," Washington Post, May 6, 2013.
51. See Tim Alberta, "Republican Lawmakers Retaliate Against Heritage Foundation," National Journal, August 28, 2013.
52. Sbragia, "Comparing Two Sui Generis Systems."
53. William Riker, Federalism (Boston: Little Brown, 1964), chapters 3 and 4.
54. Schain, The Politics of Immigration, chapter 8.
55. See Schain, The Politics of Immigration, p. 215, from US Bureau of the Census, Historical Statistics of the United States (Washington, DC: US Government Printing Office, 1975), pp. 105 and 113. The figures for family immigration are from Tichenor, Dividing Lines, p. 188. David Reimers gives a much higher figure of 700,000; see Still the Golden Door, p. x.
56. Cornelius, Evaluating Enhanced US Border Enforcement.
57. Julia Preston, "US Puts Onus on Employers of Immigrants," New York Times, July 31, 2006.
58. See Schain, The Politics of Immigration, p. 276.
59. Schain, The Politics of Immigration, p. 276.
60. Schain, The Politics of Immigration, p. 277.
61. Schain, The Politics of Immigration, pp. 277–278.
62. Julia Preston, "Government Set for a Crackdown on Illegal Hiring," New York Times, August 8, 2007.
63. See the report by Julia Preston, "270 Illegal Immigrants Sent to Prison in Federal Push," in the New York Times on May 24, 2008.
64. Hsu and Lydersen, "Illegal Hiring Is Rarely Penalized."
65. Julia Preston, "Farmers Call Crackdown on Illegal Workers Unfair," New York Times, August 11, 2007.
66. 2010 Yearbook of Immigration Statistics (Washington, DC: US Department of Homeland Security, Office of Immigration Statistics, 2011), pp. 99, 102.
67. See Julia Preston, "A Crackdown on Employing Illegal Workers," New York Times, May 30, 2011, p. 1.
68. See Julia Preston and Kirk Semple, "U.S. Hardens Its Stance on an Immigrant Policy," New York Times, February 18, 2011, p. 20. For a critical analysis of the Obama shift from the right, see Alex Nowrasteh, "President Obama's Mixed Legacy on Immigration," the Cato Institute, https://www.cato.org/publications/commentary/president-obamas-mixed-legacy-immigration, January 25, 2017.
69. Hsu and Lydersen, "Illegal Hiring Is Rarely Penalized."
70. Under the H-2/H2A program, which requires farmers to demonstrate that American labor is not available, and to provide housing.
71. Edouardo Porter, "Attack on Illegal Immigration Wilts on America's Farms," International Herald Tribune, March 23, 2006.
72. See Lawrence Downes, "After an Anti-Immigrant Flare-Up, Texas Gets Back to Business," New York Times, April 2, 2007.
73. Jennifer Steinhauer, "Beyond 2012 Field, Nuanced G.O.P. Views on Immigrants," New York Times, October 28, 2011, p. 12.
74. Jesse McKinley and Julia Preston, "Farmers Oppose G.O.P. Bill to Require Verification of Workers' Immigration Status," New York Times, July 31, 2011, p. 12.
75. See Julia Preston, "States Resisting Program Central to Obama's Immigration Strategy," New York Times, May 6, 2011, p. 18; and Julia Preston, "Deportation Program Sows Mistrust, U.S. Is Told," New York Times, September 16, 2011, p. 12.
76. Haeyoun Park, "Which States Make Life Easier or Harder for Illegal Immigrants," New York Times, March 29, 2015.
77. See Oliver Ortega, "Lynn Protesters Denounce Mayor's Immigration Comments," Boston Globe, July 22, 2014.

78. See the National Council of State Legislatures (NCSL) document for a summary: 2012 Immigration-Related Laws and Resolutions in the States (January 1–June 30, 2012), http://www.ncsl.org/documents/statefed/2012ImmigrationReportJuly.pdf. NCSL regularly monitors legislation passed by the states; and "Immigration Law: Nobody Wins," *The Economist*, September 30, 2011.

79. Richard Oppel Jr., "Arizona, Bowing to Business, Softens Its Stand on Immigration," *New York Times*, March 19, 2011; Afonso Serrano, "Tough Immigration Laws in Arizona and Alabama Are Costing the States Billions of Dollars. Business and Agricultural Leaders Have Had Enough," *Time*, June 14, 2012, http://business.time.com/2012/06/14/the-fiscal-fallout-of-state-immigration-laws/.

80. Peter Brownell, *The Declining Enforcement of Employer Sanctions* (Washington, DC: Migration Policy Institute, 2005), pp. 3–5. Also see Hsu and Lydersen, "Illegal Hiring Is Rarely Penalized."

81. See data from USDHS, *The Yearbook of Immigration Statistics 2016*, https://www.dhs.gov/immigration-statistics/yearbook/2016/table39.

82. See The White House, Office of the Press Secretary, Remarks by the President in the State of the Union Address 2013,https://obamawhitehouse.archives.gov/the-press-office/2013/02/12/remarks-president-state-union-address.

83. E. E. Schattschneider, *The Semisovereign People* (New York: Holt, Rinehart and Winston, 1960), chapter 2.

84. Beer, "Federalism, Nationalism and Democracy in America," p. 9.

Chapter 8

1. See Andreas, *Border Games*, chapter 4.

2. Gibney and Hansen, "Deportation and the Liberal State," pp. 1–2.

3. See Andrew Geddes, *Immigration and European Immigration: Beyond Fortress Europe* (Manchester: Manchester University Press, 2008).

4. See Miriam Feldblum, *The Politics of Nationality Reform and Immigration in Contemporary France* (Albany: State University of New York Press, 1999).

5. Ariane Chebel d'Appollonia, *Frontiers of Fear, Immigration and Insecurity in the United States and Europe* (Ithaca, NY: Cornell University Press, 2012), pp. 15–17.

6. See Michel Beine, Justin Gest, Anna Boucher, Eiko Thielemann, Michel Hiscox, Patrick McGovern, Hillel Rapoport, and Brian Bergoon, "Comparing Immigration Policies: An Overview from the IMPALA Database," *International Migration Review* 50, no. 4 (2016), pp. 825–1076, as well as Block and Bonjour, "Fortress Europe or Europe of Rights?," pp. 203–24.

7. On the 7% limit, see Carla N. Argueta, *Numerical Limits on Permanent Employment Based Immigration: Analysis of the Per-country Ceilings* (Washington, DC: Congressional Research Service, July 28, 2016), p. 4, https://fas.org/sgp/crs/homesec/R42048.pdf.

8. See Giovanna Dell'Orto and Vicki L. Birchfield, *Reporting at the Southern Borders: Journalism and Public Debates on Immigration in the U.S. and the E.U.* (New York: Routledge, 2014).

9. Manuela Tobias, "Has There Been a 1,700 Percent Increase in Asylum Claims over the Last 10 Years?" *Politifact*, June 21, 2018, p. 1, https://www.politifact.com/truth-o-meter/statements/2018/jun/21/donald-trump/1700-percent-increase-asylum-claims/. Also see the 2016 survey by the Pew Research Center, *Factank, News in Numbers:* Jacob Poushter, "European Opinions of the Refugee Crisis in 5 Charts," http://www.pewresearch.org/fact-tank/2016/09/16/european-opinions-of-the-refugee-crisis-in-5-charts/,September 16, 2016.

10. Although the level of legal immigration into Italy declined actually between 2011 and 2017, the non-EU foreign population (TCN) of Italy increased, indicating that more migrants were remaining. In 2017, it was 3.5 million, the third largest among the EU countries: See Eurostat, Statistics Explained, "Non-National Population by Group of Citizenship," January 1, 2017, http://ec.europa.eu/eurostat/statistics-explained/index.php?title=File:Non-national_population_by_group_of_citizenship,_1_January_2017_.png.

11. Andreas and Snyder, *The Wall Around the West*.

12. Andreas and Snyder, *The Wall Around the West*, pp. 1 and 219.

13. Zaiotti, *Cultures of Border Control*, pp. 67–69.

14. See Maryline Baumard, "Délai raccourdis, mots-clés de la loi asile immigration," *Le Monde*, February 21, 2018.

15. Scharpf, "Problem-Solving Effectiveness and Democratic Accountability in the EU," p. 14.

16. See the Pew study *Estimated Unauthorized Immigrant Population, by State, 2014*, http://www.pewhispanic.org/interactives/unauthorized-immigrants/.

17. See chapter 6, Table 6.1, *Eurobarometer* (Standard) 84, National Report, Public Opinion in the European Union, United Kingdom, Autumn 2015, as well as *Eurobarometer* (Standard) 85, and *Eurobarometer* (Standard), First Results 87.

    For the United States, see Patrick J. Egan, *Partisan Priorities: How Issue Ownership Drives and Distorts American Politics* (New York: Cambridge University Press, 2013), pp. 26–29; Brenan, "Record High 75% of Americans Say Immigration Is a Good Thing."

18. See Martin A. Schain, *Shifting Tides: Radical-Right Populism and Immigration Policy in Europe and the United States* (Washington, DC: Migration Policy Institute, 2018).

19. Andreas, *Border Games*, p. 85.

BIBLIOGRAPHY

Acosta, Diego, and Andrew Geddes, "The Development, Application and Implementation of an EU Rule of Law in the Area of Immigration Policy," *Journal of Common Market Studies* 51, no. 2 (2013), pp. 179–193.

Alberta, Tim, "Republican Lawmakers Retaliate Against Heritage Foundation," *National Journal*, August 28, 2013.

Anderson, Malcolm, Monica Den Boer, Peter Cullen, William Gilmore, Charles Raab, and Neil Walker, *Policing the European Union* (New York: Oxford University Press, 1996).

Andreas, Peter, *Border Games*, 2nd ed. (Ithaca, NY: Cornell University Press, 2009).

Andreas, Peter, and Timothy Snyder, eds. *The Wall Around the West: State Borders and Immigration Controls in North America and Europe* (Lanham, MD: Rowman & Littlefield, 2000).

Argueta, Carla N., *Numerical Limits on Permanent Employment Based Immigration: Analysis of the Per-Country Ceilings* (Washington, DC: Congressional Research Service, July 28, 2016), https://fas.org/sgp/crs/homesec/R42048.pdf.

Asylum Information Database (AIDA), European Council on Refugees and Exiles, https://www.asylumineurope.org/.

Aussilloux, Vincent, and Boris Le Hir, "The Economic Cost of Rolling Back Schengen," https://www.strategie.gouv.fr/sites/strategie.gouv.fr/files/atoms/files/the_economic_cost_of_rolling_back_schengen.pdf.

Baker, Bryan, and Christopher Williams, *Immigration Enforcement Actions: 2015*, Annual Report, Homeland Security, Office of Immigration Statistics, July 2017.

Ball, Molly, "The Fall of the Heritage Foundation and the Death of Republican Ideas," *The Atlantic*, September 25, 2013, https://www.theatlantic.com/politics/archive/2013/09/the-fall-of-the-heritage-foundation-and-the-death-of-republican-ideas/279955/.

Bastian, Vollmer, "Briefing: Irregular Migration in the UK: Definitions, Pathways and Scale," The Migration Observatory, Oxford University, November 7, 2011.

Bauman, Zygmunt, *Freedom, Concepts in Social Thought* (Minneapolis: University of Minnesota Press, 1988).

Baumard, Maryline, "Délai raccourdis, mots-clés de la loi asile immigration," *Le Monde*, February 21, 2018.

Beer, Samuel H., "Federalism, Nationalism and Democracy in America," *American Political Science Review* 72, no. 1 (1978), pp. 17–19.

Beine, Michel, Justin Gest, Anna Boucher, Eiko Thielemann, Michel Hiscox, Patrick McGovern, Hillel Rapoport, and Brian Bergoon, "Comparing Immigration Policies: An Overview from the IMPALA Database," *International Migration Review* 50, no. 4 (2016), pp. 825–1076. https://journals.sagepub.com/doi/abs/10.1111/imre.12169.

Bellamy, Richard, Joseph Lacey, and Kalypso Nicolaïdes, "European Boundaries in Question," *Journal of European Integration* 39, no. 5 (2017), pp. 484–498.

Berezin, Mable, and Martin Schain, eds., *Europe Without Borders: Remapping Territory, Citizenship, and Identity in a Transnational Age* (Baltimore: Johns Hopkins University Press, 2003).

Bigo, Didier, and Elspeth Guild, eds., *Controlling Frontiers: Free Movement Into and Within Europe* (Burlington, VT: Ashgate, 2005).

Blatter, Joachim K., "Debordering the World of States: Towards a Multi-Level System in Europe and a Multi-Polity System in North America? Insights from Border Regions," *European Journal of International Relations* 7 (2001), pp. 175–209.

Blinder, Scott, "Briefing: Deportations, Removals and Voluntary Departures from the UK," 4th revision, The Migration Observatory, University of Oxford, July 19, 2017.

Block, Laura, and Saskia Bonjour, "Fortress Europe or Europe of Rights? The Europeanization of Family Unification Policies in France, Germany and the Netherlands," *European Journal of Migration and Law* 15, no. 2 (2013), pp. 203–224.

Bonjour, Saskia, "The Transfer of Pre-departure Integration Requirements for Family Migrants Among Member States of the EU," *Comparative Migration Studies* 2, no. 2 (2014), pp. 203–226.

Boucher, Anna, and Justin Gest, *Crossroads: Comparative Immigration Regimes in a World of Demographic Change* (New York: Cambridge University Press, forthcoming).

Bovens, Mark, and Paul t'Hart, "Revisiting the Study of Policy Failures," *Journal of European Public Policy* 23, no. 5 (2016), pp. 656–666.

Bovens, Mark, P. t'Hart, and B. G. Peters, eds., *Success and Failure in Public Governance: A Comparative Analysis* (Cheltenham: Edward Elgar, 2001).

Bowen, John R., "Working Schemas and Normative Models in French Governance of Islam," in *Comparative European Politics*, Special Issue: The Problems with National Models of Integration, A Franco-Dutch Comparison, ed. Christophe Bertossi, Jan Willem Duyvendak, and Martin A. Schain, 10, no. 3 (July 2012), pp. 354–369.

Brenan, Megan, "Record High 75% of Americans Say Immigration Is a Good Thing," Gallup, https://news.gallup.com/poll/235793/record-high-americans-say-immigration-good-thing.aspx, June 21, 2018.

Brian, Tara, and Frank Laczko, *Fatal Journeys: Tracking Lives Lost during Migration* (Geneva: International Organization for Migration, 2014).

Brownell, Peter, *The Declining Enforcement of Employer Sanctions* (Washington, DC: Migration Policy Institute, September 1, 2005).

Bruno, Andorra, *Immigration-Related Worksite Enforcement: Performance Measures*, Congressional Research Service, 7-5700, August 7, 2013, www.crs.gov R40002.

Buxton, Nick, and Fiona Dove, eds., *NeoConOpticon: The EU Security-Industrial Complex* (London: Transnational Institute/Statewatch, 2009).

Buzan, Barry, Ole Wæver, and Jaap De Wilde, *Security: A New Framework for Analysis* (Boulder, CO: Lynn Reinner Publications, 1998).

Caldwell, Christopher, *Reflections on the Revolution in Europe* (New York: Anchor Books, 2010).

Cameron, David, "Free Movement Within Europe Needs to Be Less Free," *Financial Times*, November 26, 2013.

Capps, Randy, Marc Rosenblum, Cristina Rodriguez, and Muzaffar Chisti, *Delegation and Divergence: A Study of 287(g) State and Local Immigration Enforcement* (Washington, DC: Migration Policy Institute, 2011).

Carrera, Sergio, Elspeth Guild, Massimo Merlino, and Joanna Parkin, *A Race Against Solidarity: The Schengen Regime and the Franco-Italian Affair* (Brussels: Center for European Policy Studies, April 2011).

Castan Pinos, Jaume, "Building Fortress Europe? Schengen and the Cases of Ceuta and Melilla," School of Politics, International Studies and Philosophy, Queen's University, Belfast, https://www.qub.ac.uk/research-centres/CentreforInternationalBordersResearch/Publications/WorkingPapers/CIBRWorkingPapers/Filetoupload,174398,en.pdf.

Center for Responsive Politics Open Secrets Database on Lobbyists and Lobbying in the US, 2018, https://www.opensecrets.org/lobby/lobbyist.php?id=Y0000039775L.

Chamie, Joseph, and Luca Dall'Oglio, *International Migration and Development, Continuing the Dialogue: Legal and Policy Perspectives* (Geneva: International Organization for Migration, 2008).

Chebel d'Appollonia, Ariane, *Frontiers of Fear, Immigration and Insecurity in the United States and Europe* (Ithaca, NY: Cornell University Press, 2012).

Clarke, Charles, *The EU and Migration: A Call for Action* (London: The Center for European Reform, 2011).

Clarke, Charles, *"Will Britain Leave the European Union?,"* lecture given by the *Rt. Hon. Charles Clarke at the Munk School of the University of Toronto* on Friday, March 22, 2013.

Claude-Valentin, Marie, "Measures Taken to Combat the Employment of Undocumented Workers in France," in Organization for Economic Cooperation and Development (OECD), *Combating the Illegal Employment of Foreign Workers* (Paris: OECD, 2000).

Clayton, Gena, "The UK and Extraterritorial Immigration Control: Entry Clearance and Juxtaposed Control," in *Extraterritorial Immigration Control: Legal Challenges,* ed. Bernard Ryan and Valsamis Mitsilegas (Leiden: Martin Nijhoff, 2010), pp. 397–431.

Coffe, Hilde, and Job van den Berg, "Understanding Shifts in Voting Behavior Away from and Towards Radical Right Populist Parties: The Case of the PVV between 2007 and 2012," *Comparative European Politics* 15, no. 6 (2016), pp. 872–896.

Cook, Bryan J. "Principal-Agent Models of Political Control of Bureaucracy," *American Political Science Review* 83, no. 3 (September 1989), pp. 965–974.

Cornelius, W. A., T. Tsuda, P. L. Martin, and J. F. Hollifield, eds., *Controlling Immigration: A Global Perspective,* 2nd ed. (Palo Alto, CA: Stanford University Press, 2004).

Cornelius, Wayne, *Evaluating Enhanced US Border Enforcement* (Washington, DC: Migration Policy Institute, 2004).

Courtland Robinson, W. *Terms of Refuge: The Indochinese Exodus and the International Response* (New York: Zed Books, 1998).

Darroch, Gordon, "Geert Wilders Found Guilty of Inciting Discrimination," *The Guardian,* December 9, 2016, https://www.theguardian.com/world/2016/dec/09/geert-wilders-found-guilty-in-hate-speech-trial-but-no-sentence-imposed.

Deardon, Lizzie, "Hungary Planning 'Massive' New Border Fence to Keep Out Refugees as PM Vows to 'Hold Them Back by Force,'" *The Independent,* August 27, 2016, http://www.independent.co.uk/news/world/europe/hungary-massive-new-border-fence-to-keep-out-refugees-prime-minister-orban-turkey-eu-hold-them-back-a7212696.html.

Delany, Erin F., "Justifying Power: Federalism, Immigration and 'Foreign Affairs,'" *Duke Journal of Constitutional Law and Public Policy* 8, no. 1 (2013), pp. 164–165.

Dell'Orto, Giovanna, and Vicki L. Birchfield, *Reporting at the Southern Borders: Journalism and Public Debates on Immigration in the U.S. and the E.U.* (New York: Routledge, 2014).

Desmas, Margot, "Loi asile et immigration: que dit la législation chez nos voisins européens," *Le Monde,* February 23, 2018.

Dixon, David, and Julia Fellat, *Immigration Enforcement Spending Since IRCA* (Washington, DC: Migration Policy Institute, 2005).

Dombrowski, Peter, and Simon Reich, "The EU's Emerging Grand Strategy of Retrenchment: Europe Is Coming Home, American 'Exceptionalism' Isn't," *International Affairs* 93, no. 5 (September 1, 2017), pp. 18–36.

Downes, Lawrence, "After an Anti-Immigrant Flare-Up, Texas Gets Back to Business," *New York Times,* April 2, 2007.

Drutman, Lee, and Alexander Furnas, "Untangling the Webs of Immigration Lobbying," *The Sunlight Foundation,* https://sunlightfoundation.com/2013/03/25/immigration/, March 25, 2013.

Ducourtieux, Cecile, and Julia Pascual, "Les mesures pour lutter contre le terrorisme one du mal à se concrétiser au niveau de l'UE," *Le Monde,* March 24, 2016.

Duyvendak, J. W., and Peter Scholten, "The Invention of the Dutch Multicultural Model and Its Effects on Integration Discourses in the Netherlands," *Perspectives on Europe* 40, no. 2 (2010), pp. 39–49.

Duyvendak, Jan Willem, Tres Pels, and Rally Rujkschroeff, "A Multicultural Paradise? The Cultural Factor in Dutch Integration Policy," in *Bringing Outsiders In: Transatlantic Perspectives on Immigrant Political Incorporation*, ed. Jennifer L. Hochschild and John H. Mollenkopf (Ithaca, NY: Cornell University Press, 2009), pp. 129–139.

Egan, Patrick J., *Partisan Priorities: How Issue Ownership Drives and Distorts American Politics* (New York: Cambridge University Press, 2013).

Ellerman, Antje, *States Against Migrants: Deportation in Germany and the United States* (New York: Cambridge University Press, 2009).

Evans, Goeffrey, and Anand Menon, *Brexit and British Politics* (Cambridge: Polity, 2017).

Favell, Adrian, *Eurostars: Free Movement and Mobility in an Integrated Europe* (Oxford: Blackwell, 2008).

Feldblum, Miriam, *The Politics of Nationality Reform and Immigration in Contemporary France* (Albany: State University of New York Press, 1999).

Fetzer, Joel S., "Why Did House Members Vote for H.R. 4437?," *International Migration Review* 40, no. 3 (Fall 2006), pp. 698–706.

Fifield, Anna, "US Immigration Reform Draws 3000 Lobbyists," *Financial Times*, March 20, 2013.

Follis, Karolina S., *Building Fortress Europe: The Polish-Ukrainian Frontier* (Philadelphia: University of Pennsylvania Press, 2011).

Foot, Paul, *Immigration and Race in British Politics* (Harmondsworth: Penguin, 1965).

Fratzke, Susan, *Not Adding Up: The Fading Promise of Europe's Dublin System* (Brussels: Migration Policy Institute Europe, 2015), https://www.migrationpolicy.org/research/not-adding-fading-promise-europes-dublin-system.

Freeman, Gary, "Modes of Immigration Politics in Liberal Democratic States," *International Migration Review* 29, no. 4 (Winter 1995), pp. 881–902.

Ganzeboom, Harry, and Johanne Søndergaard, "MIPi: A Better Index for Comparing Family Reunification Policies Across Europe," unpublished paper.

Geddes, Andrew, "Europe's Border Relationships and International Migration Relations," *Journal of Common Market Studies* 43, no. 4 (2005), pp. 797–799.

Geddes, Andrew, "Getting the Best of Both Worlds? Britain, the EU and Migration Policy," *International Affairs* 81, no. 4 (2005), pp. 723–740.

Geddes, Andrew, *Immigration and European Immigration: Beyond Fortress Europe* (Manchester: Manchester University Press, 2008).

German Marshall Fund of the United States, *Transatlantic Trends, Immigration* (Washington, DC, 2011), http://trends.gmfus.org/files/2011/12/TTImmigration_final_web1.pdf.

Gibney, Matthew J., "Liberal Democratic States and Responsibilities to Refugees," *American Political Science Review* (March 1999), pp. 169–181.

Gibney, Matthew J., and Randall Hansen, "Deportation and the Liberal State: The Forcible Return of Asylum Seekers and the Unlawful Migrants in Canada, Germany and the United Kingdom," *New Issues in Refugee Research, UNHCR*, Working Paper No. 77, February 2003.

Gittins, Magnus, and Laura Broomfield, *The Organisation of Reception Facilities for Asylum Seekers* (UK Home Office, 2013), https://ec.europa.eu/home-affairs/sites/homeaffairs/files/what-we-do/networks/european_migration_network/reports/docs/emn-studies/27.united_kingdom_national_report_receptionfacilities_en_version_jan2014_final.pdf.

Givens, Terri, and Adam Luedke, "The Politics of European Union Immigration Policy: Institutions, Salience and Harmonization," *Policy Studies Journal* 32, no. 1 (2004), pp. 145–165.

Global Terrorism Database, University of Maryland National Consortium for the Study of Terrorism and Responses to Terrorism's Global Terrorism Database, https://www.start.umd.edu/pubs/START_GTD_Overview2017_July2018.pdf.

Göktürk, Deniz, David Gambling, and Anton Kaes, eds., *Germany in Transit: Nation and Migration: 1955–2005* (Berkeley: University of California Press, 2007).

Gold, Matea, "Immigration Deal Would Boost Defense Manufacturers," *Washington Post*, July 1, 2013.

Gonzales-Barrera, Ana, and Jens Manuel Krogstad, "With Help from Mexico, Number of Child Migrants Crossing U.S. Border Falls," Pew Research Center, April 28, 2015, http://www.pewresearch.org/fact-tank/2015/04/28/child-migrants-border/.

Goodwin, Matthew, "Ukip, the 2015 General Election and Britain's EU Referendum," *Parliamentary Insight* 6, no. 3, (2015), pp. 12–15.

Granados, Samuel, "Why Trump's Wall Contradicts Today's Immigration Trends," *Washington Post*, April 12, 2017.

Groupe d'Information et de Soutien desImmigré(e)s (GISTI), *"Régularisation: la circulaire 'Valls' du 28 novembre 2012 Analyse et mode d'emploi,"* November 2012, http://www.gisti.org/IMG/pdf/np_circ_valls_nov2012.pdf.

Guay, Bertrand, "Une circulaire pour clarifier les critères de régularisation des étrangers sans papiers," *Le Monde*, November 28, 2012.

Guild, Elspeth, "The Europeanisation of Europe's Asylum Policy," *International Journal of Refugee Law* 18, no. 3-4 (September 2006), pp. 630–651.

Guild, Elspeth, "The Legal Framework: Who Is Entitled to Move?," in *Controlling Frontiers*, ed. Didier Bigo and Elspeth Guild (Burlington, VT: Ashgate, 2005), pp. 33–34.

Guild, Elspeth, and Didier Bigo, "The Transformation of European Border Control," *Extraterritorial Immigration Control: Legal Challenges*, ed. Bernard Ryan and Valsamis Mitsilegas (Leiden: Martin Nijhoff, 2010), pp. 257–281.

Guild, Elspeth, Evelien Brouwer, Kees Groenendijk, and Sergio Carrera, *What Is Happening to the Schengen Borders*, CEPS Paper in Liberty and Security, No. 86, December 2015 (Brussels: Center for European Policy Studies).

Guild, Elspeth, and Sergio Carrera, *Rethinking Asylum Distribution in the EU: Shall We Start with the Facts?*, Centre for European Policy Studies, https://www.ceps.eu/system/files/Rethinking%20asylum%20distribution%20in%20the%20EU_0.pdf, June 17, 2016.

Guild, Elspeth, and Paul Minderhoud, eds., *Security of Residence and Expulsion: Protection of Aliens in Europe* (The Hague: Kluwer Law International, 2001).

Guiraudon, Virginie, "Enlisting Third Parties in Border Control: A Comparative Study of Its Causes and Consequences," in *Borders and Security Governance*, ed. Marina Caparini and Otwin Marenin (Geneva: Geneva Center for the Democratic Control of the Armed Forces, 2006).

Guiraudon, Virginie, "Setting the Agenda on Immigration and Asylum in the EU: Experts and the Public," paper presented at the Annual Conference of the American Political Science Association, Boston, August 30, 2002.

Guiraudon, Virginie, and Gallya Lahav, "Comparative Perspective on Border Control: Away from the Border and Outside the State," in *The Wall Around the West: State Borders and Immigration Controls in North America and Europe*, ed. Peter Andreas and Timony Snyder (Lanham, MD: Rowman & Littlefield, 2000), pp. 55–81.

Guiraudon, Virginie, and Gallya Lahav, "The State Sovereignty Debate Revisited: The Case of Immigration Control," *Comparative Political Studies* 33, no. 2 (2000), pp. 163–195.

Hall, Peter, "Policy Paradigms, Social Learning and the State: The Case of Economic Policymaking in Britain," *Comparative Politics* 25, no. 3 (April 1993), pp. 275–296.

Hansen, Randall, *Citizenship and Immigration in Post-War Britain* (Oxford: Oxford University Press, 2000).

Hansen, Randall, "Population Displacement and the Global Refugee System 200 Years after the Congress of Vienna," report prepared for presentation at the Congress of Vienna 2015: In Search of Principles for a Stable World Order, Vienna, October 22–25, 2015.

Hansen, Randall, and Demetrios G. Papademetriou, eds., *Managing Borders in an Increasingly Borderless World* (Washington, DC: Migration Policy Institute, 2013).

Hatton, Timothy J., *Seeking Asylum: Trends and Policies in the OECD* (London: CEPR. Policy Portal), Table 6.1, p. 50, https://voxeu.org/article/seeking-asylum-trends-and-policies-oecd.

Haus, Leah, *Unions, Immigration and Internationalization: New Challenges and Changing Coalitions in the United States and France* (New York: Palgrave Macmillan, 2002).

Hawkins, Oliver, "Asylum Statistics," UK House of Commons Library, briefing paper no. SN01403, September 23, 2018, https://researchbriefings.files.parliament.uk/documents/SN01403/SN01403.pdf.

Heclo, Hugh, *Modern Social Policies in Britain and Sweden* (New Haven, CT: Yale University Press, 1974).

Hentges, Gundrun, "Asylum Policy Influenced by Europeanization," in *Europe's New Racism: Causes, Manifestations and Solutions,* ed. Evans Foundation (New York: Berghahn Books, 2005), pp. 105–131.

Héritier, Adrienne Héritier, *Policy-Making and Diversity in Europe: Escaping Deadlock* (New York: Cambridge University Press, 1999).

Hern, Anne, "Recent Migration Trends: Citizens of EU-27 Member States Become Ever More Mobile While EU Remains Attractive to Non-EU Citizens," *Eurostat, Statistics in Focus,* no. 98 (2008), p. 4.

Hernstein, Richard, and Charles Murray, *The Bell Curve* (New York: Free Press, 1994).

Hirschfeld Davis, Julie, and Frances Robles, "Obama Ends Exemption for Cubans Who Arrive Without Visas," *New York Times,* January 12, 2017.

Hoffmann, Stanley, "Institutional Change in Europe in the 1980s," in *The New European Community: Decision-Making and Institutional Change,* ed. Robert O. Keohane and Stanley Hoffmann (Boulder, CO: Westview Press, 1991), pp. 1–39.

Hooghe, Liesbet, and Gary Marks, "Unraveling the Central State, but How? Types of Multi-Level Governance," *American Political Science Review* 97, no. 2 (May 2003), pp. 233–243.

Hollifield, James, "The Emergence of the Migration State," *International Migration Review* 38, no. 3 (September 2004), pp. 885–912.

Hollifield, James F., *Immigration, Markets and States: The Political Economy of Postwar Europe* (Cambridge, MA: Harvard University Press, 1992).

Hollinger, Peggy, "Council of Europe Warns on Multiculturalism," *Financial Times,* February 16, 2011, https://www.ft.com/content/72c02d9a-39c6-11e0-8dba-00144feabdc0.

Hsu, Spencer, and Kari Lydersen, "Illegal Hiring Is Rarely Penalized," *Washington Post,* June 19, 2006.

Hulse, Carl, "Immigrant Surge Rooted in Law to Curb Child Trafficking," *New York Times,* July 7, 2014.

Itzkoff, Seymour W., *The Decline of Intelligence in America* (Westport, CT: Praeger, 1994).

Jacobson, David, *Rights Across Borders: Immigration and the Decline of Citizenship* (Baltimore: Johns Hopkins University Press, 1997).

Jones, Chris, "Analysis 11 Years of Eurodac," *Statewatch,* January 2014, http://www.statewatch.org/analyses/no-235-eurodac.pdf.

Joppke, Christian, *Challenge to the Nation-State: Immigration in Western Europe and the United States* (Oxford: Oxford University Press, 1998).

Joppke, Christian, *Immigration and the Nation-State: The United States, Germany, and Great Britain* (New York: Oxford University Press, 1999).

Kandel, William A., and Ruth Ellen Wasem, *U.S. Immigration Policy: Chart Book of Key Trends* (Washington, DC: Congressional Research Service, March 14, 2016).

Kasparele, Bernd, "Implementation of Schengen: The Dublin System and the European Border," in *Immigration Policy and Practice: Interventions and Solutions,* ed. Harald Bauder, Christian Matheis, and Nora Crook (New York: Palgrave Macmillan, 2016), pp. 59–79.

Katzenstein, Peter, *Policy and Politics in West Germany* (Philadelphia: Temple University Press, 1987).

Kaunert, Christian, Sarah Leonard, and Adrienne Hériter, *The Development of the EU Asylum Policy: Revisiting the Venueshopping Argument,* European University Institute, Migration Working Group, 2010, https://www.eui.eu/Documents/RSCAS/Research/MWG/201011/10-27-Kaunert.pdf.

Kelly, Lorelei, "DeMint's Departure Is Just the Beginning," *Roll Call*, http://www.rollcall.com/news/kelly_demints_departure_is_just_the_beginning-220056-1.html?pg=1, December 18, 2012.

Kenny, Michael, "The English Question, Identity, Diversity and Nationhood in England," in *Democracy in Britain: Essays in Honor of James Cornford*, ed. Guy Lodge and Glenn Gottfried (London: Institute for Public Policy Research, 2014), pp. 133–144.

Keohane, Robert O., *After Hegemony: Cooperation and Discord in the World Political Economy* (Princeton, NJ: Princeton University Press, 1984).

Keohane, Robert O., and Stanley Hoffmann, "Institutional Change in Europe in the 1980s," in *The New European Community: Decision-Making and Institutional Change*, ed. Robert O. Keohane and Stanley Hoffman (Boulder, CO: Westview Press, 1991), pp. 1–39.

Kim, Christine, and Robert Rector, "The Fiscal Cost of Low-Skill Immigrants to the U.S. Taxpayer," *The Heritage Foundation*, http://www.heritage.org/immigration/report/the-fiscal-cost-low-skill-immigrants-the-us-taxpayer, May 22, 2007.

Kim, Seung Min Kim, "Border Surge Amendment Approved," *Politico-pro*, June 23, 2013.

Kingdon, John W., *Agendas, Alternatives and Public Policies* (London: Longman Classics, 2003).

Kingsley, J. Donald, *Representative Bureaucracy* (Yellow Springs, OH: Antioch Press, 1994).

Koslowski, Rey, "Global Mobility and the Quest for an International Migration Regime," in *International Migration and Development: Continuing the Dialogue: Legal and Political Perspectives*, ed. Joseph Chamie and Luca Dall'Oglio (Geneva: International Organization for Migration, 2008), pp. 103–145.

Kovacheva, Velela, and Dita Vogel, "The Size of the Irregular Foreign Resident Population in the European Union in 2002, 2005 and 2008: Aggregated Estimates," Hamburg Institute of International Economics, Database on Irregular Migration, Working Paper No. 4, 2009, http://irregular-migration.net/index.php?id=162.

Kulish, Nicholas, Caitlin Dickerson, and Ron Nixon, "Immigration Agents Discover New Freedom to Deport Under Trump," *New York Times*, February 25, 2017.

Lavenex, Sandra, *Safe Third Countries: Extending the EU Asylum and Immigration Policies to Central and Eastern Europe* (Budapest: Central University Press, 1999).

Le Carré, John, *The Perfect Spy* (London: Coronet Books, 1986).

Le Monde, information, "Depuis 2012, les effectifs des forces de l'ordre ont diminué," November 18, 2015.

Le Monde, "Nicolas Sarkozy tenté par le discours populiste," June 23, 2005.

Le Monde, "UE: le nombre de migrants arrives par la mer en Grèce a chuté de deux tiers en 2016," January 6, 2017.

Leclaire, Jean-Philippe, and Aziz Mouats, "Khaled Kelkal, premier djihadiste made in France," *Le Monde*, September 18, 2015, http://www.lemonde.fr/m-le-mag/article/2015/09/18/khaled-kelkal-premier-djihadiste-made-in-france_4762322_4500055.html#tDULTgeuZrReF8t0.99.

Léonard, Sarah, "EU Border Security and Migration into the European Union: FRONTEX and Securitisation Through Practices," *European Security* 19, no. 2 (2010), pp. 231–254.

Leparmentier, Arnaud, and Jean-Pierre Stroobants, "Le candidat Sarkozy instrumentalise l'Europe," *Le Monde*, March 13, 2012.

Lind, Dara, "Removals vs. Returns: How to Think About Obama's Deportation Record," *Vox*, April 11, 2014, https://www.vox.com/2014/4/11/5602272/removals-returns- and-deportations-a-very-short-history-of-immigration.

Lobbying Information, *Lobbying Impact Report: Immigration Legislation, 112 Congress*, report available to author in- house only, www.lobbyists.info.

Loch, Dietmar, "Moi, Khalel Kelkal," *Le Monde*, October 7, 1995.

Lowi, Theodore J., *Arenas of Power*, edited and introduced by Norman K. Nicholson (Boulder, CO: Paradigm Publishers, 2009).

Lowi, Theodore J., *The End of Liberalism: The Second Republic of the United States*, 2nd ed. (New York: Norton, 1979).

Market and Opinion Research International (MORI), "MORI Political Monitor, February, 2005," *Financial Times*, February 23, 2005.

Markon, Jerry, Lisa Rein, and Wesley Lowery, "Border Patrol Chief Removed from Post After Clashing with Powerful Union," *Washington Post*, January 26, 2017.

Martin, Philip, "Germany: Managing Migration in the Twenty-first Century," in *Controlling Immigration: A Global Perspective*, ed. James F. Hollifield, Philip L. Martin, and Pia M. Orrenus (Palo Alto, CA: Stanford University Press, 2014), pp. 47–78.

Martin, Philip, and Mark Miller, *Employer Sanction: French, German and US Experiences*, International Migration Papers 36 (Geneva: International Labour Office, 2000).

Martin, Susan F., "Unauthorized Migration: US Policy Responses in Comparative Perspective," presentation at the 2007 annual conference of the International Studies Association, Chicago, Illinois, March 2, 2007.

Martin, Susan F., *A Nation of Immigrants* (New York: Cambridge University Press, 2011).

Massey, Douglas S., Jorge Durand, and Karen A. Pren, "Why Border Enforcement Backfired," *American Journal of Sociology* 121, no. 5 (March 2016), pp. 1557–1600.

Massey, Douglas, Jorge Durand, and Nolan Malone, *Beyond Smoke and Mirrors: Mexican Immigration in an Age of Economic Integration* (New York: Russell Sage, 2002).

McConnell, Grant, *Private Power and American Democracy* (New York: Vintage Books, 1966).

McKinley, Jesse, and Julia Preston, "Farmers Oppose G.O.P. Bill to Require Verification of Workers' Immigration Status," *New York Times*, July 31, 2011.

Medecins Sans Frontieres, *Obstacle Course to Europe: A Policy-made Humanitarian Crisis at EU Borders* (Brussels: Medicins Sans Frontieres, December 2015).

Meissner, Doris, Donald M. Kerwin, Muzaffar Chishti, and Claire Bergeron, *Immigration Enforcement in the United States: The Rise of a Formidable Machinery* (Washington, DC: Migration Policy Institute, 2013).

Menon, Anand, "The Limits of Comparative Politics: International Relations in the European Union," in *Comparative Federalism: The European Union and the United States in Comparative Perspective*, ed. Anand Menon and Martin A. Schain (Oxford: Oxford University Press, 2006), pp. 35–58.

Mermaz, Louis, *Les Geôles de la République* (Paris: Stock, 2001).

Migration Policy Institute, "What Is the Right Policy Toward Unaccompanied Children at U.S. Borders?," https://www.migrationpolicy.org/news/what-right-policy-toward-unaccompanied- children-us-borders, June 2014.

Miroff, Nick, "Deportations Slow under Trump Despite Increase in Arrests by ICE," *Washington Post*, September 28, 2017.

Mitchell, B. R., *International Historical Statistics, Europe, 1750–1993*, 4th ed. (London: Macmillan Reference, 1998).

Mitsilegas, Valsamis, "Immigration Control in an Era of Globalization: Deflecting Foreigners, Weakening Citizens, Strengthening the State," *Indiana Journal of Global Legal Studies* 19, no. 1 (Winter 2012), pp. 42–45.

Moravcsik, Andrew, *The Choice for Europe: Social Purpose and State Power from Messina to Maastricht* (Ithaca, NY: Cornell University Press, 1998).

Moravcsik, Andrew, "Preferences and Power in the European Community: A Liberal Intergovernmentalist Approach," *Journal of Common Market Studies* 31, no. 4 (December 1993), pp. 473–524.

Mostov, Julie, *Soft Borders: Rethinking Sovereignty and Democracy* (New York: Palgrave Macmillan, 2008).

Mudde, Cas, "'Good' Populism Beat 'Bad' in Dutch Election," *The Guardian*, https://www.theguardian.com/world/2017/mar/19/dutch-election-rutte-wilders- good-populism-bad-.

Nail, Thomas, *Theory of the Border* (New York: Oxford University Press, 2016).

Nakamura, David, "On Immigration Legislation, Fissures Emerge within Conservative Ranks," *Washington Post*, May 6, 2013.

Nakamura, David, and Ed O'Keefe, "Timeline: The Rise and Fall of Immigration Reform," *Washington Post*, June 26, 2014.

Nana, Chavi, "With Strict Policies in Place, Dutch Discourse on Integration Becomes More Inclusive," Migration Information Source, https://www.migrationpolicy.org/article/strict-policies-place-dutch-discourse-integration-becomes-more-inclusive, April 19, 2007.

Nelkin, Dorothy, and Mark Michaels, "Biological Categories and Border Controls: The Revival of Eugenics in Anti-immigration Rhetoric," *International Journal of Sociology and Social Policy* 18, no. 5/6 (1998), p. 33.

Neuman, Gerald L., "Anomalous Zones," *Stanford Law Review* 48, no. 5 (May 1996), pp. 1197–1234.

Nevins, Joseph, *Operation Gatekeeper and Beyond: The War on "Illegals" and the Remaking of the U.S.–Mexico Boundary* (New York: Routledge, 2002).

Norland, Rod, and Mujib Mashal, "Europe Makes Deal to Send Afghans Home, Where War Awaits Them," *New York Times*, October 5, 2016.

Nossiter, Adam, "Blocking Migrants Far Away," *New York Times International Edition*, February 27, 2018.

Nowrasteh, Alex, "President Obama's Mixed Legacy on Immigration," the Cato Institute, https://www.cato.org/publications/commentary/president-obamas-mixed-legacy-immigration, January 25, 2017.

Ohmae, Kenichi, *The Borderless World: Power and Strategy in an Interlinked Economy*, rev. ed. (New York: HarperCollins, 1999).

Ohmae, Kenichi, *The End of the Nation State: The Rise of Regional Economies* (New York: The Free Press, 1996).

Oppel Jr., Richard, "Arizona, Bowing to Business, Softens Its Stand on Immigration," *New York Times*, March 19, 2011.

Panizzon, Marion, "Readmission Agreements of EU Member States: A Case for EU Subsidiarity or Dualism?" *Refugee Survey Quarterly* 31, no. 4 (2012), pp. 101–133.

Park, Haeyoun, "Which States Make Life Easier or Harder for Illegal Immigrants," *New York Times*, March 29, 2015.

Parker, George, "David Cameron Launches Attack on EU Migration," *Financial Times*, November 27, 2013.

Parusel, Bernd, and Jan Schneider, *Visa Policy as Migration Channel: The Impact of Visa Policy on Migration Control* (Berlin: German Federal Office for Migration and Refugees, 2012).

Pascouau, Yves, and Henri Labayle, *Conditions for Family Reunification Under Strain: A Comparative Study in Nine EU Member States* (Brussels: European Policy Centre, Odysseus Network, November 2011).

Passel, Jeffrey S., and D'Vera Cohn, *Homeland Security Produces First Estimate of Foreign Visitors to U.S. Who Overstay Deadline to Leave*, Pew Research Center, February 3, 2016, http://www.pewresearch.org/fact-tank/2016/02/03/homeland-security-produces-first-estimate-of-foreign-visitors-to-u-s-who-overstay-deadline-to-leave/.

Passel, Jeffrey, D'Vera Cohn, and Ana Gonzalez-Berrera, "Population Decline of Unauthorized Immigrants Stalls, May Have Reversed," Pew Research Center's Hispanic Trends Project, http://www.pewhispanic.org/2013/09/23/population-decline-of-unauthorized-immigrants-stalls-may-have-reversed/, September 23, 2013.

Pear, Robert, and Carl Hulse, "Immigration Bill Fails to Survive Senate Vote," *New York Times*, June 28, 2007.

Peers, Steve, *Statewatch Analysis, The Revised "Dublin" Rules on Responsibility for Asylum-Seekers: The Council's Failure to Fix a Broken System*, http://www.statewatch.org/analyses/no-173-dublin-III.pdf.

Peters, Margaret E., "Open Tradition, Closed Borders: Immigration in the Era of Globalization," *World Politics* 67, no. 1 (2015), pp. 114–154.

Pellot-Hernandez, Melodie, "Cargo Pre-Inspection Aims to Facilitate Trade Between Mexico, U.S.," *University of North Carolina Journal of International Law* blog, November 8, 2015, http://blogs.law.unc.edu/ncilj/2015/11/08/cargo-preinspection-aims-to-facilitate-trade-between-mexico-us/.

Peterson, John, "Policy Networks," in *European Integration Theory*, ed. Antje Wiener and Thomas Diez (Oxford: Oxford University Press, 2004), pp. 105–125.

Peterson, John, *Policy Networks*, Institute for Advanced Study, Vienna, Political Science Series 90, July 2003.

Pevnick, Ryan, *Immigration and the Constraints of Justice: Between Open Borders and Absolute Sovereignty* (New York: Cambridge University Press, 2014).

Pew Hispanic Center, "Unauthorized Immigrant Population: National and State Trends, 2010," http://www.pewhispanic.org/2011/02/01/unauthorized-immigrant-population-brnational-and-state-trends-2010/, 2011.

Pew Research Center, "Estimated Unauthorized Immigrant Population, by State," http://www.pewhispanic.org/interactives/unauthorized-immigrants/, 2014.

Poushter, Jacob, "European Opinions of the Refugee Crisis in 5 Charts (2016)," Pew Research Center: Factank, September 16, 2016, http://www.pewresearch.org/fact-tank/2016/09/16/european-opinions-of-the-refugee-crisis-in-5-charts/.

Preston, Julia, "270 Illegal Immigrants Sent to Prison in Federal Push," *New York Times*, May 24, 2008.

Preston, Julia, "Farmers Call Crackdown on Illegal Workers Unfair," *New York Times*, August 11, 2007.

Preston, Julia, "Government Set for a Crackdown on Illegal Hiring," *New York Times*, August 8, 2007.

Preston, Julia, "Hoping for Asylum, Migrants Strain U.S. Border," *New York Times*, April 11, 2014.

Preston, Julia, "US Puts Onus on Employers of Immigrants," *New York Times*, July 31, 2006.

Rachman, Gideon, "Refugees or Migrants? What's in a Word?" *The Financial Times*, September 3, 2015.

Radaelli, Claudio, M. "Diffusion without Convergence: How Political Context Shapes the Adoption of Regulatory Impact Assessment," *Journal of European Public Policy* 12, no. 5 (2005), pp. 924–943.

Ramji-Nogales, Jaya, Andrew I. Schoenholtz, and Philip G. Schrag, "Refugee Roulette: Disparities in Asylum Adjudication," *Stanford Law Review* 60 (November 2007), pp. 295–410.

Reimers, David, *Still the Golden Door: The Third World Comes to America* (New York: Columbia University Press, 1985).

Réseau Academique d'Etudes Juridiques sur l'Immigration et l'Asile en Europe, "Study on the Conformity by Member States of 10 EC Directives in The Sector of Asylum and Immigration," Directorate of Justice, Freedom and Security(DG JLS) of the European Commission, 2007, http://odysseus-network.eu/eu-directives/.

Ricard, Philippe, "Migrants: vent de panique européen," *Le Monde*, November 7, 2015.

Riker, William, *Federalism* (Boston: Little Brown, 1964).

Rodier, Claire, *Xénophobie Business: à quoi servent les contrôles migratoires?* (Paris: la Découverte, 2012).

Rosecrance, Richard, "The Rise of the Virtual State: Territory Becomes Passé," *Foreign Affairs*, July–August 1996.

Rosenblum, Marc, *Unaccompanied Child Migration to the United States: The Tension Between Protection and Prevention* (Washington, DC: Migration Policy Institute, 2015).

Rubin, Alissa J., "France Says Deportation of Roma Girl Was Legal but Badly Handled," *New York Times*, October 20, 2013.

Rushton, Philippe, *Race, Evolution and Behavior* (New Brunswick, NJ: Transaction Press, 1994).

Rusin, Sylvia, Jie Zong, and Jeanne Batalova, *Cuban Immigrants in the United States* (Washington, DC: Migration Policy Institute, April 7, 2015).

Russell, Joseph, and Jeanne Batalova, *Refugees and Asylees in the United States* (Washington, DC: Migration Policy Institute, September 27, 2012).

Ruz, Camila Ruz, "What Happens to Failed Asylum Seekers," *BBC News Magazine*, http://www.bbc.com/news/magazine-33849593, August 13, 2015.

Ryan, Benard, and Valsamis Mitsilegas, *Extraterritorial Immigration Control: Legal Challenges* (Leiden: Martin Nijhoff, 2010).

Sandford, Alasdair, "Hungary Completes New Anti-Migrant Border Fence with Serbia," http://www.euronews.com/2017/04/28/hungary-completes-new-anti-migrant-border-fence-with-serbia.

Sassen, Saskia, *Losing Control: Sovereignty in an Age of Globalization* (New York: Columbia University Press, 1996).

Sbragia, Alberta, "Comparing Two Sui Generis Systems," in *Comparative Federalism: The European Union and the United States in Comparative Perspective*, ed. Menon and Schain, pp. 15–35.

Sbragia, Alberta, "Politics in the European Union," in *European Politics Today*, ed. Gabriel Almond, Bingham Powell Jr., Russell J. Dalton, and Kaare Strøm, 3rd ed. (New York: Pearson-Longman, 2006), Chapter 11.

Schain, Martin A., "The Border: Europe, the Immigration Dilemma and the State in France," Straus Institute Working Paper Series (New York: New York University School of Law, February 2011).

Schain, Martin A., "The Extreme-Right and Immigration in Policy-Making: Measuring Direct and Indirect Effects," in *Immigration Policy in Europe: The Politics of Control*, ed. Virginie Guiraudon and Gallya Lahav (New York: Routledge, 2007), pp. 70–93.

Schain, Martin A., "Managing Difference: Immigration Integration in France, Britain and the United States," *Social Research* 77, no. 1 (Spring 2010), pp. 205–237.

Schain, Martin A., *The Politics of Immigration in France, Britain and the United States* (New York: Palgrave Macmillan, 2012).

Schain, Martin A., *Shifting Tides: Radical-Right Populism and Immigration Policy in Europe and the United States* (Washington, DC: Migration Policy Institute, 2018).

Schain, Martin A., "The State Strikes Back: Immigration Policy in the European Union," *European Journal of International Law* 20, no. 1 (February 2009), pp. 93–111.

Scharpf, Fritz W. "Problem-Solving Effectiveness and Democratic Accountability in the EU," MPIfG (Max Plank Institute for the Study of Societies) working paper no. 03/1, 2003, http://www.mpifg.de/pu/workpap/wp03-1/wp03.

Schattschneider, E. E., *The Semisovereign People* (New York: Holt, Rinehart and Winston, 1960).

Scheffer, Paul, *Immigrant Nations* (Cambridge: Polity Press, 2011).

Schmidt, Vivien, "National Patterns of Governance under Siège: The Impact of European Integration," in *The Transformation of Governance in the European Union*, ed. Beate Kohler-Koch and Rainer Eising (London: Routledge, 2005), pp. 155–172.

Schuck, Peter H., *Why Government Fails So Often and How It Can Do Better* (Princeton, NJ: Princeton University Press, 2014).

Schuck Peter, and James Q. Wilson, eds., *Understanding America: The Anatomy of an Exceptional Nation* (New York: Public Affairs Press, 2008).

Schuster, Liza, "Sangatte: A False Crisis," *Global Dialogue* 4, no. 4 (Autumn 2002), pp. 57–68.

Secrétariat Général du Comité interministériel de contrôle de l'immigration, Rapport au Parlement, *Les Orientations de la politique de l'immigration*, troisieme rapport (Paris: La Documentation Française, 2007), https://www.ladocumentationfrancaise.fr/rapports-publics/074000232-les-orientations-de-la-politique-de-l-immigration-troisieme-rapport-etabli-en.

Seghetti, Lisa, "Border Security: Immigration Inspections at Ports of Entry," US Congressional Research Service, January 26, 2015.

Serrano, Alfonso "Tough Immigration Laws in Arizona and Alabama Are Costing the States Billions of Dollars. Business and Agricultural Leaders Have Had Enough," *Time*, http://business.time.com/2012/06/14/the-fiscal-fallout-of-state-immigration-laws/, June 14, 2012.

Sheingate, Adam, "Agricultural Biotechnology: Representative Federalism and Regulatory Capacity in the United States and European Union," in *Comparative Federalism: The European Union and the United States in Comparative Perspective*, ed. Menon and Schain, pp. 311–339.

Shriro, Dora, *Immigration Detention Overview and Recommendations*, Immigration and Customs Enforcement, Department of Homeland Security, https://www.ice.gov/doclib/about/offices/odpp/pdf/ice-detention-rpt.pdf, October 7, 2009.

Simanski, John, and Lesley M. Sapp, "Immigration Enforcement Actions: 2012," *Annual Report 2012*, Department of Homeland Security, https://www.dhs.gov/sites/default/files/publications/ois_enforcement_ar_2012_1.pdf, September 2013.

Siskin, Alison, *Alien Removals and Returns: Overview and Trends, Congressional Research Service Report*, February 3, 2015, https://fas.org/sgp/crs/homesec/R43892.pdf.

Skapinker, Michael, "The Conservatives' Battle over Immigration, Tourists and Students," *The Financial Times*, May 13, 2015.

Soova, Kadri, Liliana Keith, and Michele LeVoy, *Employers' Sanctions: Impacts on Undocumented Migrant Workers' Rights in Four EU Countries* (Brussels: PICUM Platform for International Cooperation in Undocumented Migrants, April 2015), http://picum.org/Documents/Publi/2015/EmployerSanctions.pdf.

Spencer, Ian, *British Immigration Policy Since 1939: The Making of Multi-Racial Britain* (London: Routledge, 1997).

Spire, Alexis, *Accueillir ou Reconduire: Enquête sur les Guichets de l'immigration* (Paris: Editions Raisons d'Agir, 2009).

Stroobants, Jean-Pierre, "Schengen: les vingt-septs crispés sur le contrôl de leurs frontières," *Le Monde*, June 11, 2011, p. 6.

Subramaniam, V., "Representative Bureaucracy: A Reassessment," *American Political Science Review* 61, no. 4 (December 1967), pp. 1010–1019.

Suleiman, Ezra, *Politics, Power, and Bureaucracy in France: The Administrative Elite* (Princeton, NJ: Princeton University Press, 1974).

Sunlight Foundation, Reporting Group, "Goodies for Big Givers in Immigration Bill," https://sunlightfoundation.com/2013/07/02/goodies-big-givers-immigration-bill/, July 2, 2013.

Taylor, Alan, "France Dismantles 'The Jungle' in Calais," *The Atlantic*, October 26, 2016.

Thatcher, Mark, "The Development of Policy Network Analysis, From Modest Origins to Overarching Frameworks," *Journal of Theoretical Politics* 10, no. 4 (1998), pp. 389–416.

The Economist, "Howard's Way," January 27, 2005.

Thielemann, Eiko, and Nadine El-Enamy, "Beyond Fortress Europe? How European Cooperation Strengthens Refugee Protection," paper presented at the 11th Conference of the European Union Studies Association, Los Angeles, California, April 22–25, 2009.

Thorogood, David, and Karin Winqvist, "Women and Men Migrating to and from the European Union," *Statistics in Focus, Population and Social Conditions*, Theme 3 (Eurostat, European Communities, 2003).

Tichenor, Daniel J., *Dividing Lines: The Politics of Immigration Control in America* (Princeton, NJ: Princeton University Press, 2002).

Tobias, Manuela, "Has There Been a 1,700 Percent Increase in Asylum Claims Over the Last 10 Years?" *Politifact*, https://www.politifact.com/truth-o-meter/statements/2018/jun/21/donald-trump/1700-percent-increase-asylum-claims/, June 21, 2018.

Togman, Jeffrey, *The Ramparts of Nations* (Westport, CT: Praeger, 2002).

Torpey, John, *The Invention of the Passport* (Cambridge: Cambridge University Press, 2000).

Torrey, Philip L., "Rethinking Immigration's Mandatory Detention Regime: Politics, Profit and the Meaning of 'Custody,'" *University of Michigan Journal of Law Reform* 48, no. 4 (2015), pp. 879–913.

Toynbee, Polly, "The UK's Stance on the Refugee Crisis Shames Us All," *The Guardian*, https://www.theguardian.com/commentisfree/2015/sep/03/david-cameron-shaming-britain-refugees-europe, September 3, 2015.

Traynor, Ian, "Italy Threatens to Give Schengen Visas to Migrants as EU Ministers Meet," *The Guardian*, June 16, 2015.

Trimikliniotis, Nicos, "Migration and Freedom of Movement of Workers: EU Law, Crisis and the Cypriot States of Exception," *Laws* 2, no. 4 (2013), pp. 440–468.

Trump, Donald, "Make America Great Again," https://www.donaldjtrump.com/positions/immigration-reform, 2016.

UK, Home Office, Immigration Statistics, Entry Clearance of Visa Applications and Resolution, by Country and Nationality, https://www.gov.uk/government/publications/immigration-statistics.

Vaughan, Jessica M. "Deportation Number Unwrapped: Raw Statistics Reveal the Real Story of ICE Enforcement in Decline," Center for Migration Studies, October 2013, https://cis.org/Report/Deportation-Numbers-Unwrapped.

Velicogna, Marco, "Large Scale E-Justice Interoperability: The Case of the Schengen Information System, the Technological Backbone of the European Arrest Warrant and Surrender Procedures," Report prepared for the building interoperability for European civil proceedings online (Bologna: IRSIG-CNR, May 2012).

Viet, Vincent, La France immigrée: Construction d'une politique 1914–1997 (Paris: Fayard, 1998).

Vink, Maarten Peter, and Marc Heibling, "The Use and Misuse of Policy Indices in the Domain of Citizenship and Integration," Special Issue, Comparative European Politics 11, no. 5 (September 2013), pp. 551–554.

Warren, Robert, and Donald Kerwin, "Beyond DAPA and DACA: Revisiting Legislative Reform in Light of Long-Term Trends in Unauthorized Immigration to the United States," Journal on Migration and Human Security 3, no. 1 (2015), pp. 80–108.

Wasem, Ruth Ellen, Cuban Migration to the United States: Policy and Trends, Congressional Research Service, https://fas.org/sgp/crs/row/R40566.pdf, June 2, 2009.

Webber, Douglas, "The Politics of Differentiated Integration in the European Union: Origins, Decision Making and Outcomes," Working Paper Series 2012/1, Monash University European and EU Centre, https://www.yumpu.com/en/document/view/30161058/the-politics-of-differentiated-integration-in-the-european-union-.

Weil, Patrick, La France et ses Etrangers: l'Aventure d'une Politique de l'Immigration de 1938 à nos Jours (Paris: Gallimard, 2004).

Williams, Norman, "Why Congress May Not Overrule the Dormant Commerce Clause," UCLA Law Review 53 (October 2005), pp. 2–3.

Williamson, Hugh, "EU Six Consider Introduction of 'Integration Contracts' for Immigrants," The Financial Times, March 24, 2006.

Wong, Edward, "As Interest Grows in Great Walls, an Ancient Chinese Fortress Beckons," New York Times, December 30, 2016.

Wright, Chris F., "Policy Legacies, Visa Reform and the Resilience of Immigration Politics," West European Politics 35, no. 4 (2012), pp. 726–755.

Yee, Vivian, "Judge Threatens Sessions with Contempt Over Deported Asylum Seekers," New York Times, August 9, 2018.

Zaiotti, Ruben, Cultures of Border Control: Schengen and the Evolution of European Frontiers (Chicago: University of Chicago Press, 2011).

Zapata-Barrero, Ricard, and Nyne De Witte, "The Spanish Governance of EU Borders: Normative Questions," Mediterranean Politics 12, no. 1 (March 2007), pp. 89–90.

Zaun, Natasha, "Why EU Asylum Standards Exceed the Lowest Common Denominator: The Role of Regulatory Expertise in EU Decision-Making," Journal of European Public Policy 3, no. 1 (2016), pp. 136–154.

Zolberg, Aristide, Nation by Design, Immigration Policy in the Fashioning of America (Cambridge: Harvard University Press, 2008).

Zolberg, Aristide, "Matters of State: Theorizing Immigration Policy," in Handbook of International Migration, ed. Charles Hirschman, Philip Kasinitz, and Josh DeWind (New York: Russell Sage Foundation, 1999), pp. 71–93.

Zong, Jie, and Jeanne Batalova, "Refugees and Asylees in the United States, Migration Information Source," Spotlight, June 7, 2017.

Zureik, Elia, and Mark B. Salter, "Global Surveillance and Policing Borders: Borders, Security, Identity," in Global Surveillance and Policing Borders: Borders Security, Identity (Devon: Willan Publishing, 2005), pp. 1–11.

Selected Governmental and Legislative Documents

Calvez, Corentin, "Le Problème de travailleurs étrangers," *Journal Officiel de la Republique Française, Avis et Rapports du Conseil Economique et Social*, March 27, 1969.

Commission of the European Communities, Clandestino Research Project, "Size and Development of Irregular Migration to the EU," October 2009, http://irregular migration.net/typo3_upload/groups/31/4.Background_Information/4.2.Policy_Briefs_EN/ComparativePolicyBrief_SizeOfIrregularMigration_Clandestino_Nov09_2.pdf.

Commission of the European Communities, Communication from the Commission: "Free Movement of Workers—Achieving the Full Benefits and Potential," COM (2002) 694 final, November 12, 2002, http://eurlex.europa.eu/LexUriServ/LexUriServ.do?uri=COM:2002:0694:FIN:EN:PDF.

Commission of the European Communities, "Towards More Accessible, Equitable and Managed Asylum Systems," COM [2003] 315 final, June 2003.

Commission of the European Communities, Communication to the Council and the European Parliament, "Towards Integrated Management of the External Borders of the Member States of the European Union," COM/2002/0233 final, 2002, https://eur-lex.europa.eu/LexUriServ/LexUriServ.do?uri=COM:2002:0233:FIN:EN:PDF.

Commission of the European Communities, "Communication from the Commission to the European Parliament and Council on the Application of Directive 2009/52/EC of June 18, 2009," COM (2014) final, May 22, 2014, Table 3, "Inspections Carried Out in 2012," http://www.europarl.europa.eu/meetdocs/2014_2019/documents/com/com_com%282014%290286_/com_com%282014%290286_en.pdf.

Commission of the European Union, *EU Transport in Figures, Statistical Pocketbook 2014* (Brussels: European Commission 2014), https://ec.europa.eu/transport/sites/transport/files/pocketbook2016.pdf.

Council of the European Union, "Amended Proposal for a Regulation of the European Parliament and of the Council on the Establishment of an Evaluation and Monitoring Mechanism to Verify the Application of the Schengen Acquis 18196/1/11, REV 1, December 9, 2011," http://register.consilium.europa.eu/doc/srv?l=EN&f=ST%2018196%202011%20REV%201.

Council of the European Union, Council Regulation 10597/13 establishing an evaluation and monitoring mechanism to verify the application of the Schengen acquis and repealing the Decision of the Executive Committee of 16 September 1998 setting up a Standing Committee on the evaluation and implementation of Schengen, http://register.consilium.europa.eu/doc/srv?l=EN&f=ST%2010597%202013%20INIT.

Council of the European Union, 13380/10, FRONT 125/COMIX 571, *A Practical Manual for Frontier-Guards*, C(2010) 5559 Final, September 8, 2010, http://register.consilium.europa.eu/doc/srv?l=EN&f=ST%2013380%202010%20INIT.

Council of the European Union, Decision 2015/1601, (EU) of September 22, 2015, "Establishing Provisional Measures in the Area of International Protection for the Benefit of Italy and Greece," https://eur-lex.europa.eu/legal-content/EN/TXT/?uri=celex%3A32015D1601.

Council of the European Union, Directive 2005/85/EC of December 1, 2005 on minimum standards on procedures in Member States for granting and withdrawing refugee status, https://eurlex.europa.eu/LexUriServ/LexUriServ.do?uri=OJ:L:2005:326:0013:0034:EN:PDF.

Council of the European Union, Directive 2004/82/EC of April 29, 2004 on the obligation of carriers to communicate passenger data.

Council of the European Union, Directive 2003/86/EC of September 22, 2003 on the right to family reunification, https://eur-lex.europa.eu/LexUriServ/LexUriServ.do?uri=OJ:L:2003:251:0012:0018:en:PDF.

Council of the European Union, Directive 2003/109/EC of November 25, 2003 concerning the status of third-country nationals who are long-term residents, https://www.easo.europa.eu/sites/default/files/public/Longtermresidency-EN.pdf.

Council of the European Union, "EUNANFOR MED Operation Sophia Authorised to Start Two Additional Supporting Tasks," Press Release 491/16, August 30, 2016, https:// www.consilium.europa.eu/en/press/press-releases/2016/08/30/eunavfor-med-sophia-op-add-supporting-tasks/.

Council of the European Union, Regulation (EC) No. 343/2003, Establishing the Criteria and Mechanisms for Determining the Member State Responsible for Examining an Asylum Application Lodged in One of the Member States by a Third-Country National, https:// eur-lex.europa.eu/legal-content/EN/TXT/?uri=CELEX:32003R0343; https://eur-lex.europa.eu/LexUriServ/LexUriServ.do?uri=OJ:L:2003:050:0001:0010:EN:PDF.

Eurobarometer (Standard) 84, National Report, Public Opinion in the European Union, November 2015, https://ec.europa.eu/commfrontoffice/publicopinion/index.cfm/ResultDoc/download/DocumentKy/72444, 2016.

Eurobarometer (Standard) 85, Public Opinion in the European Union, August 2016, https:// data.europa.eu/euodp/data/dataset/S2130_85_2_STD85_ENG, 2016.

Eurobarometer (Standard) 87, Public Opinion in the European Union, First Results 87, August 2017, http://ec.europa.eu/commfrontoffice/publicopinion/index.cfm/Survey/getSurveyDetail/instruments/STANDARD/surveyKy/2142.

European Commission, "Communication from the Commission to the European Parliament and the Council: On the State of Play of Implementation of the Priority Actions Under the European Agenda on Migration," COM (2016) 85 Final, p. 14, https://eur-lex.europa.eu/legal-content/EN/TXT/?uri=CELEX%3A52016DC0085.

European Commission, "Communication from the Commission to the Council and the European Parliament on EU Return Policy," March 28, 2014, COM (2014) 199 Final, https://eur-lex.europa.eu/procedure/EN/1041853.

European Commission, Eurostat Database for the European Union, http:// appsso. eurostat.ec.europa.eu/nui/; http://epp.eurostat.ec.europa.ey/portal/page/portal/statistics/search_database.

European Commission, Handbook on Integration for Policy-Makers and Practitioners, 2010, 3rd ed., http://euinfo.rs/files/biblioteka-srp/06_Vodic_kroz_inegracije.pdf.

European Commission, "Proposal for a Regulation of the European Parliament and of the Council Establishing an Entry/Exit System (EES) to Register Entry and Exit Data of Third Country Nationals Crossing the External Borders of the Member States of the European Union," COM (2013) 95 final, February 28, 2013, http://www.europarl.europa.eu/RegData/docs_autres_institutions/commission_europeenne/com/2016/0194/COM_COM(2016)0194_EN.pdf.

European Commission, Task Force for the Preparation and Conduct of the Negotiations with the United Kingdom under Article 50 TEU, "Guiding Principles Transmitted to EU27 for the Dialogue on Ireland/Northern Ireland," September 6, 2017, https://ec.europa.eu/commission/sites/beta-political/files/guiding-principles-dialogue-ei-ni_en.pdf.

European Commission, Temporary Reintroduction of Border Control, https://ec.europa.eu/home-affairs/sites/homeaffairs/files/what-we-do/policies/borders-and-visas/schengen/reintroduction-border-control/docs/ms_notifications_-_reintroduction_of_border_control_en.pdf.

European Migration Network (EMN), "Ad-Hoc Query on Safe Countries of Origin and Safe Third Countries," http://www.emn.fi/files/1172/Compilation_BG_EMN_NCP_AHQ_list_of_safe_countries_of_origin_and_safe_third_countries_WIDER.pdf, December 22, 2014.

European Migration Network, "The Use of Detention and Alternatives to Detention in the Context of Immigration Policies Synthesis Report for the EMN Focussed Study 2014" (Brussels: The European Commission, 2015), https://ec.europa.eu/home-affairs/sites/homeaffairs/files/what-we-do/networks/european_migration_network/reports/docs/emn-studies/emn_study_detention_alternatives_to_detention_synthesis_report_en.pdf.

European Migration Network (EMN), "Visa Policy as Migration Channel," Bernd Parusel and Jan Schneider, https://ec.europa.eu/home-affairs/sites/homeaffairs/files/what-we-do/networks/european_migration_network/reports/docs/emn-studies/migration-channel/de_20120510_visapolicy_en_version_final_en.pdf.

European Pact on Immigration and Asylum (13440/08), approved by the JHA Council on September 25 and adopted by the European Council, http://register.consilium.europa.eu/doc/srv?l=EN&f=ST%2013440%202008%20INIT.

European Parliament, Directive 96/71/EC of the European Parliament and of the Council of December 16, 1996, Concerning the Posting of Workers in the Framework of the Provision of Services ("Posted Workers Directive"), https://eur-lex.europa.eu/legal-content/EN/TXT/?uri=CELEX%3A62006CC0319.

European Parliament, Directive 2004/38/EC of the European Parliament and of the Council of April 29, 2004, on the Right of Citizens of the Union and Their Family Members to Move and Reside Freely within the Territory of the Member States, https://eurlex.europa.eu/legalcontent/EN/TXT/?uri=celex%3A32004L0038.

European Parliament, Directive 2008/115/EC of the European Parliament and of the Council of December 16, 2008 on Common Standards and Procedures in Member States for Returning Illegally Staying Third-Country Nationals, https://eur-lex.europa.eu/LexUriServ/LexUriServ.do?uri=OJ:L:2008:348:0098:0107:EN:PDF.

European Parliament, Directive 2009/52/EC of the European Parliament and of the Council of June 18, 2009 Providing for Minimum Standards on Sanctions and Measures Against Employers of Illegally Staying Third-Country Nationals.

European Parliament, Directive 2013/33/EU of the European Parliament and of the Council of June 26, 2013 Laying Down Standards for the Reception of Applicants for International Protection (Recast), https://www.refworld.org/docid/51d29db54.html.

European Parliament, Directorate-General Internal Policies, Policy Department C Citizens' Rights and Constitutional Affairs, The Conditions in Centres for Third Country Nationals, http://www.europarl.europa.eu/RegData/etudes/etudes/join/2007/393275/IPOL-LIBE_ET(2007)393275_EN.pdf, December 2007.

European Parliament Report, The Impact and Consequences of Brexit for Northern Ireland, The European Parliament, Commission on Constitutional Affairs, Policy Department C: Citizens' Rights and Constitutional Affairs, http://www.europarl.europa.eu/RegData/etudes/BRIE/2017/583116/IPOL_BRI(2017)583116_EN.pdf, 2017.

European Union, "Agreement Between the European Union and the Republic of Turkey on the Readmission of Persons Residing Without Authorisation," https://eur-lex.europa.eu/legal-content/EN/TXT/?uri=uriserv:OJ.L_.2014.134.01.0003.01.ENG, December 16, 2013.

Europol, EU Terrorism Situation and Trend Report 2017, https://www.europol.europa.eu/activities-services/main-reports/european-union-terrorism-situation-and-trend-report-2017-tesat-2017.

Eurostat, "Dublin Statistics on Countries Responsible for Asylum Application," http://ec.europa.eu/eurostat/statistics-explained/index.php/Dublin_statistics_on_countries_responsible_for_asylum_application.

Eurostat, Statistics Explained, "Main Countries of Citizenship and Birth of the Foreign, Foreign-Born Population," January 1, 2016, https://ec.europa.eu/eurostat/statistics-explained/index.php?title=File:Main_countries_of_citizenship_and_birth_of_the_foreign_foreign-born_population,_1_January_2016_(%C2%B9)_(in_absolute_numbers_and_as_a_percentage_of_the_total_foreign_foreign-born_population).png&oldid=331054.

Eurostat, Statistics Explained, "Migration and Migrant Population Statistics," October 2010, Table 2, https://ec.europa.eu/eurostat/ statistics- explained/ index.php?title=Special:ListFiles&sort=img_timestamp&limit=50&user=Marcumc&asc=1&desc=.

Eurostat, Statistics Explained, "Non-EU Citizens Subject to the Enforcement of Immigration Legislation in EU Member States," https://ec.europa.eu/eurostat/statistics-explained/

index.php?title=File:Non-EU_citizens_subject_to_the_enforcement_of_immigration_
legislation_in_EU_Member_States,_2008-2017_(number)_1.png&oldid=392384.

Eurostat, Statistics Explained, "Non-National Population by Group of Citizenship," January
1, 2017, http://ec.europa.eu/eurostat/statistics-explained/index.php?title=File:Non-
national_population_by_group_of_citizenship,_1_January_2017_.png.

EU Transparency Register, the European Commission 2019, https://ec.europa.eu/info/about-
european-commission/service-standards-and-principles/transparency/transparency-
register_en.

France, Assemblée Nationale, *Rapport d'Information sur la mise en œuvre des conclusions du rapport
d'information (n° 1879) du 10 avril 2014 sur l'évaluation de la politique d'accueil des demandeurs
d'asile*, http://www.assemblee-nationale.fr/14/pdf/rap-info/i4077.pdf, October 5, 2016.

France, Directeur de la police aux frontières (PAF) de Roissy, *Information Note on the Maintenance
of Immigrants in the Zone d'Attente de Roissy*, internal report obtained by the author, August
5, 2013. This is a follow-up of an earlier report: Controleur Général des Lieux de Privation
de Liberté, *Visite ZA de Roissy-Charles-de-Gaulle 27–28 janvier 2009*, http://www.cglpl.fr/
wp-content/uploads/2010/12/ZA-Roissy-rapport-de-visite-3-07-09.pdf.

France, *Les Chiffres de la Politique de l'Immigration et de l'Intégration, Année 2011* (Paris: la
Documentation Française, 2012), https://www.ladocumentationfrancaise.fr/rapports-
publics/134000159-les-chiffres-de-la-politique-de-l-immigration-et-de-l-integration-
annee-2011.

France, Ministre de l'Intérieur, de l'Outre-mer et des Collectivités territoriales, *Circulaire IOC/
K/1017881/J du 5 août 2010, "Evacuation des campements illicites,"* http://www.errc.org/
uploads/upload_en/file/appendix-2.pdf.

French Senate, *Rapport de commission d'enquête n° 300 (2005–2006) sur l'immigration clandestine*,
de MM. Georges Othily et François-Noël Buffet, fait au nom de la commission d'enquête,
Tomes I et II, déposé le 6 avril 2006, https://www.ladocumentationfrancaise.fr/rapports-
publics/064000340/index.shtml.

Frontex, European Border and Coast Guard Agency, *Annual Risk Analysis*, https://reliefweb.int/
report/world/frontex-annual-risk-analysis-2018.

International Migration Outlook (Paris: Organization for Economic Cooperation and Development
(OECD) Publications, 2013), http://www.obela.org/system/files/International%20
Migration%20Outlook%202013.pdf.

National Audit Office, The Home Office, "Reforming the UK Border and Immigration System,
Report by the Comptroller and Auditor-General," https://www.nao.org.uk/wp-content/
uploads/2014/07/Reforming-the-UK-border-and-immigration-system.pdf, July 22, 2014.

National Council of State Legislatures, NCSL 50-State Searchable Bill Tracking Databases, http://
www.ncsl.org/documents/statefed/omnibus_laws.pdf.

Netherlands State Secretary for Justice, Advisory Commission on Migration Affairs, *External
Processing: Conditions Applying to the Processing of Asylum Applications Outside the European
Union* (The Hague: December 2010), pp. 15–21, https://acvz.org/wp-content/uploads/
2015/09/Advies-ACVZ-NR32-ENG-2010.pdf

OECD, *Trends in International Migration, Annual Report 2003* (Paris: OECD Publications, 2003),
http://www.oecd.org/els/mig/trendsininternationalmigration2003.htm.

UK, A Joint Inquiry by the All Party Parliamentary Group on Refugees and the All Party
Parliamentary Group on Migration. *Report of the Inquiry into the Use of Immigration Detention
in the United Kingdom*, 2015, https://detentioninquiry.files.wordpress.com/2015/03/
immigration-detention-inquiry-executive-summary.pdf.

UK, Home Office, *Managing Migratory Flows in Calais: Joint Ministerial Declaration on UK/French
Cooperation*, https://www.gov.uk/government/uploads/system/uploads/attachment_
data/file/455162/Joint_declaration_20_August_2015.pdf.

UK, Home Office, "A Points-Based System: Making Migration Work for Britain," presented to
Parliament by the Secretary of State for the Home Department, by Command of Her

Majesty, March 2006, Cm 6741, https://assets.publishing.service.gov.uk/government/uploads/system/uploads/attachment_data/file/272243/6741.pdf.

UK, Home Office, National Statistics Office, *Entry Clearance, Visa Applications and Resolution by Category* (London: Home Office, UK Immigration Statistics, 2014), https://www.gov.uk/government/publications/immigration-statistics-july-to-september-2015/visas.

UK, Home Office, National Statistics Office, *Official Statistics: Entry Clearance Visas by Length, 2014* (London: Home Office, UK Immigration Statistics, 2014).

UK, House of Lords/Commons, Joint Committee on Human Rights, Legislative Scrutiny: Borders, Citizenship and Immigration Bill, paper # HL62/HC375, 9th Session, 2008–2009, https://publications.parliament.uk/pa/jt200809/jtselect/jtrights/62/62we04.htm.

UK, Independent Chief Inspector of Borders and Immigration, *An Inspection of How the Home Office Tackles Illegal Working* (London, 2015), https://assets.publishing.service.gov.uk/government/uploads/system/uploads/attachment_data/file/547674/ICIBI-Report-on-illegal-working-December_2015.pdf.

UK, Independent Chief Inspector of Borders and Immigration, *An Inspection of Juxtaposed Controls November 2012—March 2013*, John Vine CBE QPM, Independent Chief Inspector of Borders and Immigration, http://icinspector.independent.gov.uk/wp-content/uploads/2013/08/An-Inspection-of-Juxtaposed-Controls-Final.pdf, 2013.

United States Commission on Immigration Reform (USCIR), Report to Congress, *U.S. Immigration Policy: Restoring Credibility* (Washington, DC: USGPO, 1944).

United Nations High Commissioner for Refugees (UNHCR), *Global Resettlement Statistical Report*, https://www.unhcr.org/protection/resettlement/52693bd09/unhcr-global-resettlement-statistical-report-2014.html 2014.

United Nations High Commissioner for Refugees (UNHCR), *Global Trends: Forced Displacement in 2015*. (Geneva: UNHCR, 2016), https://www.unhcr.org/statistics/unhcrstats/576408cd7/unhcr-global-trends-2015.html.

United Nations High Commissioner for Refugees (UNHCR), *Population Statistics, Data, Asylum Seekers*, http://popstats.unhcr.org/en/asylum_seekers.

US Border Patrol, "Total Illegal Alien Apprehensions by Fiscal Year, 1992–2013," https://www.hsdl.org/?abstract&did=756943.

US Bureau of the Census, Historical Statistics of the United States (Washington, DC: US Government Printing Office, 1975), https://www.census.gov/library/publications/1975/compendia/hist_stats_colonial-1970.html.

US Conference of Catholic Bishops and the Center for Migration Studies, *Unlocking Human Dignity: A Plan to Transform the U.S. Immigration Detention System*, May 2015, http://www.usccb.org/about/migration-and-refugee-services/upload/unlocking-human-dignity.pdf.

US Customs and Border Protection, Apprehensions, Stats and Summaries, https://www.cbp.gov/newsroom/media-resources/stats.

US Customs and Border Protection, Border Security Statistics 2012, http://www.cbp.gov/xp/cgov/border_security/border_patrol/usbp_statistics/.

US Department of Health and Human Services, *Budget in Brief: Strengthening Health and Opportunity for All Americans*, 2015, https://www.hhs.gov/about/budget/fy2015/budget-in-brief/index.html.

US Department of Homeland Security (USDHS), Office of Immigration Statistics, *2010 Yearbook of Immigration Statistics* (Washington, DC: US Government Printing Office, 2011).

US Department of Homeland Security (USDHS), Customs and Border Protection, Immigration Enforcement, *Annual Flow Reports*; Detections of Illegal Border Crossing, https://www.dhs.gov/immigration-statistics/enforcement-actions.

US Department of State, Bureau of Consular Affairs, 2008–2014, Report of the Visa Office, Tables I and XX, http://travel.state.gov/content/visas/english/law-and-policy/statistics/annual-reports/report-of-the-visa-office-2010.html.

US Department of Transportation, Bureau of Transportation Statistics, *2015 North American Freight Numbers*, Washington, DC, 2015.

US Immigration and Customs Enforcement (ICE), *Detention Facility Locator*, http://www.ice.gov/detention-facilities.

US Select Commission on Immigration and Refugee Policy (SCIRP), *U.S. Immigration Policy and the National Interest* (Washington, DC: Government Printing Office, 1981).

US Senate, "Declining Deportations and Increasing Criminal Alien Releases—The Lawless Immigration Policies of the Obama Administration," Judiciary Committee, Subcommittee on Immigration and the National Interest, https://www.judiciary.senate.gov/meetings/declining-deportations-and-increasing-criminal-alien-releases_the-lawless-immigration-policies-of-the-obama-administration, May 19, 2016.

US Senate, "Securing the Border: Fencing Infrastructure and Technology Force Multipliers," Committee on Homeland Security and Governmental Affairs, https://www.hsgac.senate.gov/hearings/securing-the-border-fencing-infrastructure-and-technology-force-multipliers, May 13, 2015.

World Trade Organization Statistics Database, http://stat.wto.org/Home/WSDBHome.aspx.

INDEX

For the benefit of digital users, indexed terms that span two pages (e.g., 52–53) may, on occasion, appear on only one of those pages.

Page numbers followed by f and t indicate figures and tables, respectively. Numbers followed by n indicate notes.

ACF (Administration for Children and Families) (US), 63
Acosta Arcarazo, Diego, 228n25, 245n30
Administration for Children and Families (ACF) (US), 63
administrative detention facilities, 248n85
advocacy groups, 161, 163
Afghanistan, 12–13, 84t, 95, 101, 242n66
AFL-CIO, 257n41
Africa, 12–13, 82–83, 92, 98, 103–4. See also specific countries
Against Mass Migration (Switzerland), 153
AIDA (Asylum Information Database), 244–45n24
airports, 116–17, 119t, 124 See also specific facilities
Alabama, 203–4
Albania, 97–98, 99t
Alberta, Tim, 258n51
Algeria, 83, 85, 98, 130, 149
American Immigration Council, 233n45
Americanism, 2, 189
Americanization, 58
America's Voice, 194–95
amnesty, 190–91, 235n22, 246n52
Amsterdam Agreement, 7
Amsterdam Treaty, 173–74, 241n54
Anderson, Malcolm, 54
Andreas, Peter, 1, 4–5, 9, 18–19, 37, 216–17, 225, 238n5, 243n4, 259n1
anomalous zones, 27
anti-immigrant movements, 189, 204
appeal rights, 2
apprehensions and expulsions, 142

Argueta, Carla N., 259n7
Arizona
    border control, 10, 34, 223
    immigration enforcement, 203–4
Arizona v. United States 567 US, 232–33n29
Asia, 57, 58, 82–83, 85, 103–4, 106
assimilation, 52, 58, 251n12, See also cultural integration
Association of Multiethnic Couples, 161
Asylum Information Database (AIDA), 244–45n24
asylum policy, 59–63, 235n9
Asylum Procedures Directive, 97
asylum processing centres, 154–55
asylum seekers, 2, 12, 19, 70–71, 86–107, 239n25, 241n45, 244–45n24, 253n37, See also refugees
    admissions of, 47
    definition of, 86
    detention of, 139–40
    distribution of, 18, 84t, 100
    Dublin transfers, 95
    Eurodac database, 54, 64–65, 96–97
    in Europe, 54, 88f, 91–101, 154–56
    management of, 27, 84t, 86–87, 154–56, 240n34
    migration routes, 18
    requests for transfer, 96t
    rights of, 2
    from safe countries, 97, 98
    support for, 100
    unaccompanied children, 20
    unauthorized or undocumented, 9–10
    in US, 89f, 102–7

Wæver, Ole, 230n64
waiting zones (*zones d'attente*),
    136, 139
walls and fences, 2, 35–36, 130–35, 155, 212,
    215, 247n62
Warren, Robert, 238n71
Webber, Douglas, 235n24
Weiner, Rachel, 257n41
Wilders, Geert, 168–69
Williams, Christopher, 250n108
Wilson, Pete, 191
women, 12
workers. *See* labor migration
work permits, 52, 66
worksite inspections, 44, 126–27, 127t
work visas, 39, 82
World War I, 56

World War II, 56
Worldwide Refugee Admissions Processing
    System (WRAPS), 242n69
Wright, Chris F., 251n19
Wuthnow, Robert, 234n3

Yugoslavia, 48, 50–51, 93

Zadvydas v. Davis, 250
Zaiotti, Ruben, 16, 160–61, 173, 252n33,
    253n45, 255n89
Zapata-Barrero, Ricard, 247n68
Zaun, Natasha, 238n3, 245n30
zero immigration, 152
Zolberg, Aristide, 26–27, 257n28
zones d'attente (detention and waiting zones)
    (France), 136, 139